THE ROYAL FLEET AUXILIARY

THE ROYAL FLEET AUXILIARY

A CENTURY OF SERVICE

Foreword by

HRH THE DUKE OF YORK

Thomas A Adams

James R Smith

In association with the RFA Association

CHATHAM PUBLISHING

LONDON

Frontispiece: RAS(L): RFA *Blue Rover* refuelling the frigate HMS *Minerva* and the repair ship HMS *Triumph,* January 1972. (RFA Archive)

First published in Great Britain in 2005 by
Chatham Publishing, Lionel Leventhal Ltd, Park House,
1 Russell Gardens, London NW11 9NN
www.chathampublishing.com

and

Stackpole Books, 5067 Ritter Road, Mechanicsburg,
PA 17055, USA

British Library Cataloguing in Publication Data

Adams, Tom
The Royal Fleet Auxiliary: a century of service
1. Great Britain. Royal Navy. Royal Fleeet Auxiliary - History
I. Title II. Smith, James
359.3'1'0941

ISBN-10: 1861762593

Library of Congress Cataloging-in Publication Data
A catalog entry is available from the Library

ISBN 1 86176 259 3

Designed and typeset by Roger Daniels
Printed in China through Printworks Int. Ltd.

Contents

BUCKINGHAM PALACE

3rd August 2005 marks the centenary of the Royal Fleet Auxilary. The original tankers were small and the service provision embryonic. Today the one-stop replenishment ship is a far cry from those early days and the service provision from the RFA has grown out of all proportion. The service is world wide and includes not just fuel and food but also medical facilities, ammunition, distribution of mail and forward repair shops for helicopters. But probably the biggest change is the advent of Amphibious warfare and the part that the RFA has played in the delivery of support from a sea base.

I began my flying at sea from RFA Engadine, the first specialist Aviation Training Ship, and throughout my career in the RN the RFA has always been alongside and indeed the part that the RFA now plays in enhancing the capabilities of the Royal Navy is probably more prominent than ever before with its support to disaster relief operations, provision of humanitarian aid and the vital prevention of the transportation of illegal drugs by sea.

The RFA can be justifiably proud of its 100 years of service not only to the Royal Navy but also to the United Kingdom as it serves and supports the UK's armed services worldwide in a joint defence environment. Congratulations on reaching your 100th year of service and I wish you every continued success in the century to come.

Andrew

Preface

It has been my pleasure to spend most of my seagoing career since 1969 in support of the Royal Navy, and other armed forces, across the globe. I have participated in naval activity from the shores of the five continents to many small and remote islands and dependencies.

I have been fortunate in that most of my experience was gained during peacetime; inevitably there were periods of conflict, bringing some moments of sadness.

Some friendships made during this seafaring life have endured, while others have been enjoyed for perhaps just one voyage, although familiar faces do turn up as we move between ships and this gives rise to much reminiscing. Of course, absence from home is an inevitable part of the seafaring adventure, but it is not always easy for spouses, partners, parents or children, to understand or cope with those long and uncertain periods of separation and it takes a particular type of family to support the seafarer.

What has all of this to do with a book that marks the centenary of the Royal Fleet Auxiliary? Inevitably any book of this type will include the roots, the establishment, the changes that have taken place and where the organisation is today. You will certainly gets lots about the ships, their technical details, dates of service, but what you might not appreciate is the human story, the camaraderie, the seafarer's experience of isolation and adventure of new places, new people and cultures. The story of the Royal Fleet Auxiliary is more than just a series of dates, photographs and descriptions of the ships. It is about the very special people that have come together to serve their nation alongside our armed forces and those of our allies, over the past 100 years. I ask you, the reader, to think of the human story, the people on these hard-worked ships that are not always in the public eye, but are always there when they are needed. Our 'Blue Water' global Navy would have been a 'Brown Water' coastal Navy, without the ships and the people of the Royal Fleet Auxiliary Service, and the world may have become a very different place.

I am proud to be Commodore RFA and privileged to be writing the preface to a book that marks the centenary of the Royal Fleet Auxiliary Service. I believe the past 100 years has demonstrated our position as a world leader in the delivery of valued, versatile and integrated afloat support. I look forward to building on the achievements of all that have sailed, and continue to sail, under the Blue Ensign of the Royal Fleet Auxiliary. It is a Service to be proud of.

R C Thornton MDA RFA
Commodore RFA

Dedication by RFA Association

To deliver world-wide support to customers at consistently high standards including combat support for the Royal Navy and strategic lift for the armed forces. This is the mission statement for the Royal Fleet Auxiliary, which was established 100 years ago. The Service has developed through two World Wars and the Cold War to become the pre-eminent civilian logistic corps at sea, providing a range of combat support services, including substantial platforms for rotary wing operations, forward repair facilities and primary casualty evacuation.

The RFA is simply unique, and the model is much envied, and copied. Over the last 100 years the men and women of the RFA have combined Royal Naval and mercantile custom and practice to deliver a cost-effective service to its customers, and value to the nation – for as the largest single employer of British merchant seafarers, the Service helps sustain and promote our maritime infrastructure. The Service is commanded and managed by its seamen and engineers, providing a splendid example of the UK's seafaring skills in this important maritime year. Today the ships of the RFA are seen world wide, often appearing on our TV screens in both supporting and leading roles in naval operations of all kinds, including disaster and humanitarian relief missions. Little wonder that the RFA has five times received the Wilkinson Royal Navy Sword of Peace, the most recent award being made to RFA *Sir Galahad* for her part in bringing relief to Um Qasr in Iraq.

The story of the RFA over the last 100 years is one of innovation, endeavour, courage and sacrifice, and we in the RFA Association are delighted to have had the opportunity to help bring this book to print in the Centenary year. It is with great pride that we dedicate the book to the men and women of the Royal Fleet Auxiliary, past and present.

Captain Rex Cooper OBE
Chairman RFA Association

About the RFA Association

(Registered Charity No 1093950)

The RFA Association is a charity established to further the efficiency of the RFA by fostering *esprit de corps* and preserving the traditions of the Service; and to relieve Members and former members of the Service, or their dependants, who are in need hardship or distress, or needing support at times of bereavement, injury or conflict. The RFA Association is open to everyone who has served in the RFA or its management, to spouses and widows, and to civilian and military personnel who have served extensively in RFAs. Associate Membership is open to other individuals who qualify by way of special interest or skills and knowledge. Associate Members pay the same subscription and enjoy the same privileges as Full Members, but may not stand for office or vote at the AGM. Each year there is a combined AGM and Reunion, and there is a developing programme of regional and shipboard events. The UK is divided into three regions, and branches are being formed within these, reflecting demand and existing concentrations of RFA personnel. The present membership consists of serving and retired officers and petty officers, retired HQ staff, and early leavers. We are keen to enrol more personnel in all these categories, and other individuals who are interested in advancing the aims of the Association. If you would like to join, or receive further information, please write to me at RFA Association, PO Box 120, Hexham NE48 1XA (Tel 01434 240629 or e-mail lookout @rfa-association.org).

Captain Rex Cooper OBE
Chairman RFA Association

Introduction

The Origins of the Royal Fleet Auxiliary Service

Over the centuries Britain developed and expanded her maritime trading and expeditionary activities, and with such expansion came the need for a positive form of protection for them: a standing navy. In the sixteenth and seventeenth centuries this was gradually achieved, and with it came the creation of ships built and developed for the sole purpose of fighting. However, to make this naval power truly effective required the establishment of a widespread chain of shore bases along the various trading routes – bases that the fighting squadrons could operate from and return to, to receive necessary maintenance and supplies. By the nineteenth century the Royal Navy was supreme, with an unrivalled network of bases around the British Empire, so fighting units could operate freely and effectively in the sure knowledge that shore facilities were readily available.

In parallel with the fighting fleet there had developed a logistics requirement – the need for a seaborne lifeline. This principally was in an ancillary form, as non-commissioned support ships, collectively known as 'fleet auxiliaries', vessels such as store ships, transports and 'victuallers', carrying replenishments of powder and shot, fresh water, victuals, timbers, canvas, cordage and the like, as they plied backward and forward between the fleets and their main bases at home and abroad. Many of these vessels were converted merchantmen or warships no longer fit for service in their original role; these vessels were both naval- and civilian-manned, both Admiralty-owned and taken up on charter. Fleet auxiliaries had become an essential part of the naval support organisation and an Order-in-Council of 9 July 1864 laid down that mercantile-crewed auxiliaries should wear the Blue Ensign defaced by the Admiralty Badge or Seal.

During the nineteenth century there were many technical developments leading to the introduction of steam engines and screw propulsion, thus making the sailing fleet obsolete and necessitating new types of warships. With the abandonment of sail for steam, coal had become the main source of power for the Royal Navy. No change, however, was envisaged in naval policy: the existing bases established coaling facilities, so retaining their fundamental function of maintaining fleet mobility. The establishment and maintenance of the chain of coaling stations placed a new task upon the principal provider – the Naval Stores Department – and as a consequence greater dependence upon the seaborne lifeline. Provision was made for the store ships operated on behalf of the Admiralty Transport Department to be augmented by chartered colliers.

The Admiralty's need to make use of non-commissioned, civilian-manned ships as fleet auxiliaries cannot be disputed. These then fell distinctively into two categories – vessels taken up on charter for use by the Admiralty, and vessels owned and operated by the Admiralty. There was already a distinction between commissioned and non-commissioned ships; however, there arose a further need for positive recognition of the naval auxiliary services and a desire to distinguish between Admiralty-owned vessels and those vessels taken up on charter.

An Admiralty circular letter dated 3 August 1905 directed that a new style – 'Royal Fleet Auxiliary' – be applied to auxiliary vessels manned by mercantile crews and owned by the Admiralty; merchant vessels taken up on transport charter by the Admiralty were to be styled as Mercantile Fleet Auxiliaries. Today these are sometimes known by the acronym STUFT – Ships Taken Up From Trade. The first Admiralty vessels to fall into this new category were the hospital ship *Maine*, the distilling ship *Aquarius*, the collier *Kharki* and the oil tank vessel *Petroleum*.

The registration of these Crown vessels as British registered merchant ships raised an irksome problem. The Admiralty's registration application under the Merchant Shipping Act 1894 for the hospital ship *Maine* could not be legally upheld by the Registrar General of Seamen and Shipping. The Merchant Shipping Act stated that to be registered as a British merchant ship 64/64ths of the ship had to be owned by a British subject or subjects. The Registrar and Crown law officers'

Mercedes, one of the early RFAs, was purchased by the Admiralty in 1908. When built in 1902 by Northumberland Shipbuilding Co for Christie & Co Ltd, Cardiff she was described as the 'finest steam collier afloat'. (J Smith Collection)

reasoning was that the ship was the property of the Sovereign, who at best is not a qualified person under section one of the Merchant Shipping Act. They also reasoned that the Admiralty, in whose name the ship was to be registered, was not a corporate body within the meaning of the Merchant Shipping Act. As a result, Admiralty-owned British merchant ships were required to be registered as the property of The Lord Commissioners of The Admiralty under the name of a named managing owner – the Secretary to the Board of Admiralty. It should be understood that there was no legal requirement to register any Royal Fleet Auxiliary under the Merchant Shipping Act. Not to register, however, would have placed a question mark over their status and subsequent lack of documents that would increase the difficulty of entering foreign ports.

Section 80 of the Merchant Shipping Act 1906 made provision for suitable regulations to be made by Order-in-Council, with regard to the manner by which government ships may be registered as British merchant ships under the Merchant Shipping Acts. As government ships within the meaning of the Acts they were to be eligible for certain 'relaxations'. The 1906 Act came into force on 1 July 1907 and seems to have taxed Whitehall officials. The Director of Transports in an Acquaint expressed a strong view that the Admiralty was anxious to take steps to give effect to Section 80 of the Act. Naval Law officers from the Treasury Solicitors, Admiralty and the Board of Trade arranged an inter-department conference on the subject of Section 80. After some fifteen meetings they issued a report under the title: 'Report of inter-departmental conference on the mode of applying to the Government controlled by the Admiralty the provision of Section 80 of the Merchant Shipping Act 1906'.

There were also interesting remarks made in 1908 by the solicitor for the Board of Trade on what was the proper national colours for registered British ships and it was spelt out that it should be the Red Ensign, except in the case of HM Ships or boats (White Ensign) or the Blue Ensign for those ships with specific approval to wear it.The First Sea Lord concurred that the Admiralty-run RFAs should wear the Admiralty Blue Ensign. The Admiralty also identified the need to formally recognise its own fleet auxiliaries and so the then mainly coal bunkering and freighting service received a 'statutory position' within the framework of the Merchant Shipping Acts in the form of Royal Fleet Auxiliaries. This was achieved by the approval of an Admiralty Order-in-Council, dated 22 March 1911. The Order does not employ the actual term 'Royal Fleet Auxiliary' and it was to be 1913 before it appeared in the Navy List, although the term had been used regularly in Admiralty Transport Department papers from 1906 onwards.

The increasing use of oil fuel brought the need for a new type of auxiliary – the oil-carrying tank vessel. In March 1905 the Admiralty had purchased its first tanker, suitably named *Petroleum*, a vessel primarily intended for the freighting of oil from the Admiralty's various sources in Romania, Mexico and the East Indies. This purchase was followed soon afterwards by the conversion into a tanker of the yard collier *Kharki*, and in March 1907 by the purchase of the *Isla*, a vessel which after a period as a collier was converted to become the Navy's first petrol carrier, carrying fuel for use in submarines.

Oiling at Sea

Meanwhile, arrangements were being

RFA *Serbol*, a 2,000-ton tanker, fitted with an early wireless telegraphy set, evident from the elaborate aerial rig. (World Ship Society)

devised for oiling-at-sea techniques. The Admiralty purchased some 300 feet of 5-inch flexible bronze hose and planned trials with a chartered tanker, the SS *Henri Reith*. In January 1906, however, RFA *Petroleum* was fitted with trial gear with which she was to conduct the world's first oiling-at-sea experiments.

The February 1906 trial, which involved RFA *Petroleum* and the battleship HMS *Victorious*, is reasonably well documented. The method used and the rig devised during the trials are clear: the battleship was 'in line ahead' of the tanker at a distance of some 450 feet and passed between them was a single 5-inch bronze spiral hose, suspended in stirrups from a wire hawser. Water was then pumped through the hose at pressures giving an undulating transfer rate of between 37 and 57 tons per hour.

These trials continued up until June 1906 with the first real oil transfer taking place between *Petroleum* and HMS *Dominion*. After some experience, ships' positions were reversed, with the tanker leading the warship and the hose and suspension rig being fed out from the tanker's stern. The rig, known as the Stirrup Method, was bulky, took hours to set up and suffered from many breakages owing to the high pumping pressures necessary with such hose lengths.

Tanker Construction Planned

Around 1908 the Director of Stores, Sir John Forsey, drew the attention of the Admiralty to the increasing use of oil and the need for providing means of transport for it. Admiralty planners decided to reinforce the few vessels acquired some years earlier, and no doubt working within the parameter of the Merchant Shipping Acts, introduced their first 'RFA' tanker construction programme. The first Admiralty-designed vessel to be built was RFA *Burma*; launched in Greenock in March 1911 as a 'fleet attendant tanker' with a cargo capacity of over 2,000 tons, she was fitted with a capability for oiling vessels when alongside. In 1910 RFAs *Petroleum* and *Kharki* were fitted for oiling-at-sea. In January 1911 *Kharki* carried out trials with the torpedo boat destroyers HMS *Mohawk* and HMS *Amazon*. On 20 November 1911 the new RFA *Burma* carried out oiling-at-sea trials with the battleship HMS *Agamemnon*. Over the following five years, four other 2,000-ton tankers – *Mixol*, *Thermol*, *Trefoil* and *Turmoil*, modifications of the *Burma* design – were built, and although advanced for their day they were somewhat unstable.

In 1913, the first of a group of four smaller tankers was launched. Known as *Attendant*, she was the first of the naval 1,000-tonners; she had a shallow draught and was intended for harbour service. In the following two years three sister-ships were built: *Servitor*, *Carol* and *Ferol*, the latter two being fitted with Bolinder diesel motors, thus earning the distinction of being the Admiralty's first motor tankers. At the same time, a more ambitious tanker design was on the drawing board. Designed with two large eight-cylinder diesel engines, the 8,000-ton overseas tanker RFA *Olympia* was laid down by Vickers of Barrow in July 1913.

In these pre-war years the need for a mobile fuelling force was not seen as necessary – indeed, it was discouraged, as it was liable to be expensive. Consequently, little money was actually spent by Britain on the development of underway replenishment applications, although there appears to have been widespread awareness of its potential in the navies of countries such as Japan, Germany and the United States of America. Fuelling alongside was the British pattern that once established remained the primary fleet attendant function for several decades. It was performed by RFA vessels under the collective term of fleet attendant tankers.

The Director of Transports

The management and manning of RFA vessels was not straightforward. The Director of Stores was responsible to the Admiralty Board for the entire management, financial administration and running of auxiliaries attached to the Fleet Coaling Service and later the Fleet Fuelling Service – overseas tankers (freighters), fleet attendant tankers and colliers. The administration of water tankers, repair ships, salvage vessels and some miscellaneous units was also allowed for. However, from around 1907 the Director of Transports who headed the Admiralty Transport Department had duties that included:

- the provision of hired transports required for the fleet in time of war, whether armed cruiser, collier, stores carrier or tug;
- engagements in peace or war of collier transports, etc; and
- conveyance of naval stores between UK and ports abroad or inter-colonially (but not UK coastwise), including supervision of loading.

In addition, this Director appears to have had responsibilities for appointing Masters and officers in RFAs and undertook duties including sailing orders, provision of crews, and action with the Board of Trade and Lloyd's Register on aspects such as classification and registration. In 1911 the Naval Stores Department laid down that it hoped that a large proportion of crew of registered RFAs would in time be men of the Royal Fleet Reserve (RFR) and Royal Naval Reserve (RNR). One official record shows that by 1913 this scheme was deemed partially successful, service in RFAs being considered continuous and RFR and RNR men serving in them would not be required to serve in HM Ships in wartime. There is little further evidence to show how successful this approach to manning registered RFAs actually was. The inconsistent use of the term 'registered RFAs' in official records was taken to mean RFAs registered under the Merchant Shipping Acts.

Introduction of Radio Communications

There is little evidence to indicate

Replenishment at Sea – a singular skill

Underway replenishment at sea (RAS) is one of the most challenging and demanding activities undertaken by any seafarer. Calling for skill, patience, expert shiphandling and, above, all professional teamwork, its overall demand on both men and ships should not be underestimated. Since its first experiments in oiling at sea with RFA *Petroleum* in early 1906, through very differing requirements of the Arctic and Pacific during the Second World War, NATO standardisation and the extraordinary demands of the South Atlantic in 1982, the RFA has developed, perfected and expanded these techniques to an almost daily routine status.

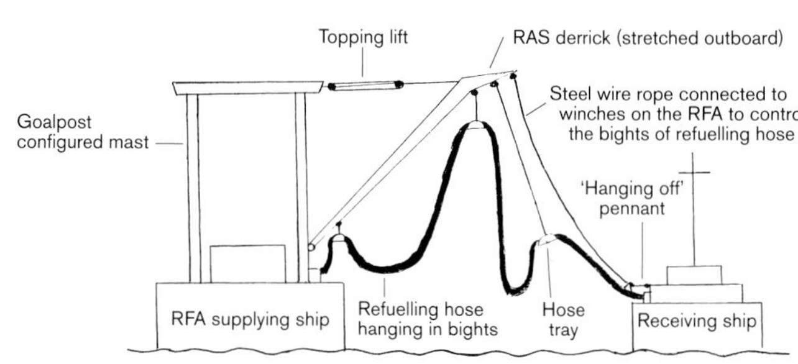

Heavy Jackstay Refuelling Rig. (ANRS)

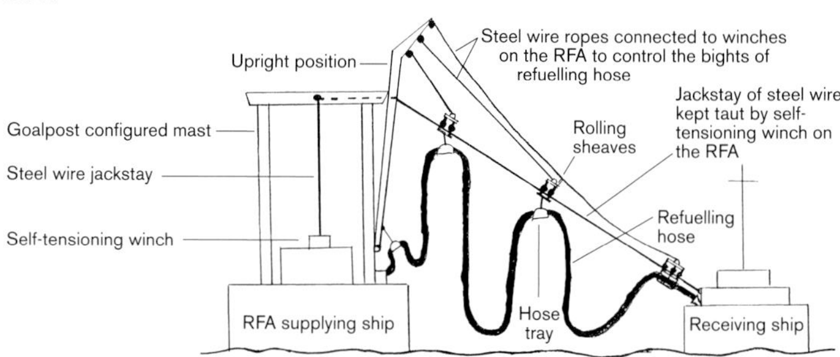

Jackstay Probe Rig. (ANRS)

Above: Known as 'Noddy', the GEC RAS arm is the latest technology. (ANRS)

Left: Another kind of fuel: beer being transferred to a CVL by RAS(L) or RAS(S). (RFA Archive)

Right: RAS(L) RFA *Gold Rover* deploying her starboard derrick rig to refuel HMS *Hardy* and her stern rig to refuel HMS *Exmouth.* (RFA Archive)

RAS(L) hose on the way over. (ANRS)

Operational requirements often mean a RAS has to be conducted in heavy weather. (ANRS)

which was the first Admiralty-owned merchant ship to be fitted with a radio installation. It is assumed that, as merchant ships, their installations were in line with Marconi's rapid developments. Despite the fact that Admiralty-owned merchant ships did not have to be registered under the Merchant Shipping Acts, material dated 1912 shows that the following RFAs were to be fitted with Marconi's 1.5kW standard outfit – spark transmitter, receiver, power supply and aerial system. In RFA *Petroleum* the Marconi installation was Admiralty owned and operated.

RFA *Maine*	hospital ship – ex commercial vessel
RFA *Mercedes*	collier – ex commercial vessel
RFA *Petroleum*	tanker – ex commercial vessel
RFA *Burma*	tanker – Admiralty design, new construction
RFA *Olympia*	tanker – Admiralty design, new construction
RFA *Trefoil*	tanker – Admiralty design, new construction

There is also evidence that the Admiralty-designed *Trinol* class tankers (later known as the 'Fast Leaf' class) and the 2,000-ton *Belgol* class were fitted with the Navy Type 4 wireless telegraphy (W/T) set.

The First World War

On the eve of the First World War the Royal Navy was larger and more powerful than it had ever been, but the inchoate Royal Fleet Auxiliary could claim only seven vessels, including one collier, with a further three completing and four building. Personnel employed in RFA tankers and the collier totalled 152, supported by nine staff employed at the Admiralty on Fleet Fuelling duties. It was, however, about to enter a world war that would see it expand beyond any planner's expectation into a large, effective and indispensable fleet. This fleet comprised a mixture of miscellaneous and specialist vessels, but primarily the Admiralty's tanker fleet. These tankers came into two broad categories: overseas tankers (freighters); and fleet attendant tankers.

During what could be called the '1914 Programme' the Admiralty built or purchased out of Admiralty funds (the Navy Vote) twenty-four overseas tankers. In addition to these there were forty-three tankers designated for fleet attendant use, made up of:

- Twenty-two 1,000-ton fleet attendant tankers of the *Attendant* group (four built by the Admiralty) and *Creosol* class; the eighteen hulls of the *Creosol* class were built by various shipyards between 1916 and 1918, all again carrying names with the established Admiralty suffix 'ol', such as *Birchol* and *Viscol*. Designed for local port and harbour duties, they were unusual ships with their machinery aft and their bridge right forward on the forecastle; between the bridge and the poop there was a long trunk deck, flanked by a low catwalk-like deck known as a 'harbour deck'. Many of this class continued to serve until well after the Second World War. Four of the class – *Oakol*, *Palmol*, *Sprucol* and *Teakol* – were fitted with twin screws and diesel engines that proved to be rather troublesome.
- Fifteen 2,000-ton fleet attendant tankers of the *Burma* group and *Belgol* class, built by the Admiralty for UK offshore and North Sea waters, fitted for fuelling at sea by the Stirrup Method. The ten hulls of the *Belgol* class built between 1917 and 1918 followed the Admiralty naming patterns of using a suffix ending in 'ol', such as *Celerol* and *Rapidol*. Designed for fleet duties they gave worldwide service well into the 1950s.
- Six fast (16-knot) 5,000-ton twin-screw fleet attendant tankers built by the Admiralty as the *Trinol* class but placed on overseas transport of oil fuel duties and transferred to Lane & MacAndrew Ltd, London, for management and renamed.

Intended for operation as Royal Fleet Auxiliaries, there was concern in the Admiralty that the delivery of oil fuel to these Admiralty-owned tankers in neutral ports might be seen as a breach of neutrality. In June 1916 the Director of Stores proposed that the RFAs planning to be used on overseas freighting should be managed during the war like the *Santa Margherita* (ex RFA *Olympia*). She was being managed under the nominal ownership of Mr T Royden and Sons Ltd. This ruse was to conceal their true ownership, thereby avoiding any complications over neutrality laws.

This meant that through the offices of the Admiralty shipping agent the vessels were handed over to the commercial shipping company Lane & MacAndrew Ltd, who ran them in all respects as privately-owned Red Ensign tanker transports. Lane & MacAndrew arranged for registration under the Merchant Shipping Acts and also organised their renaming. As a consequence it appears that Lane & MacAndrew introduced the famous 'leaf' suffix names for these Admiralty vessels. Broadly speaking, this arrangement was to continue until the end of hostilities, but as will be seen later the Admiralty had some difficulty in bringing these arrangements to a close. Furthermore, administration seems to have been even more complicated, judging by an Admiralty document dated 1916. This correspondence from Director of Transports on the subject of RFAs actually details a network of responsibilities spread across various Admiralty departments, such as Director of Naval Construction, Director of Naval Equipment, Director of Dockyards & Dockyard Works and Director of Victualling.

During this war RFA personnel appointed by the Director of Transport were placed under naval discipline under agreement T299, a specific variant of agreement T124. Defensively Equipped Merchant Ship (DEMS) personnel were carried when necessary. Many officers were given temporary RNR/RNVR commissions but all reverted to standard Board of Trade agreements after the Armistice. The following examples are from the October 1917 Navy List:

The collier *Mercedes* and the tanker *Kharki* – Master a Lieutenant RNR, chief officer was a Sub-Lieutenant RNR, chief engineer was an Engineer Lieutenant RNR and 2nd engineer was an Engineer Sub-Lieutenant RNR.

The repair ship *Reliance*'s Master was a Lieutenant Commander RNR, assisted by a Sub-Lieutenant RNR, the chief engineer was an Engineer Lieutenant RNR supported by an Engineer Sub-Lieutenant RNR and an Assistant Paymaster RNR.

Between the Wars

In spite of the size of the Admiralty tanker fleet, by the end of the First World War the RFA hardly existed as a service. The fleet attendant tankers on port and harbour duties were run under the guidance of Coaling Officers and the Naval Store Department was only broadly concerned because The Shipping Controller was managing twenty-eight freighting tankers that were the property of the Crown and had been purchased directly out of the Navy Vote.

In December 1918 a discussion took place on the disposal of surplus tankers. It was approved by the Finance Committee that Admiralty-owned tankers that were no longer required should be disposed of by the Ministry of Shipping in order to centralise the sale of all vessels of commercial value under that Department. It was determined that financial adjustment between the Ministry of Shipping and the Admiralty would be made for vessels paid for by the Navy Vote on the basis of ship-for-ship exchange. In the end sixteen ships were sold and replaced by fifteen other ships out of the Ministry's funds; these were the 'Z tankers', better known in the RFA as the 'War' class. Twelve Admiralty-owned vessels remained with the Ministry of Shipping, on behalf of the Admiralty, despite the end of the war removing the original reasons why the tankers had been placed under commercial management with a number of companies like Davies & Newman, Anglo-Saxon Petroleum Company, Andrew Weir, C T Bowring and Hunting & Sons Ltd.

The Admiralty wanted to regain direct control of its oil-carrying fleet, emphasising that its responsibility to Parliament for the economical cost of fuels supplied for the Royal Navy made this essential. It was also considered more business-like than having to pass all requisitions through another department, and through that department to the ship managers. The Admiralty also believed it was self-evident that commercial managers, whose own interests were naturally paramount and on whom the country had little hold, could not have the same zeal for economy and efficiency as Admiralty officials, who were responsible through the Admiralty Board to Parliament for effective administration. The Admiralty's case for direct control also included the following arguments:

- The Admiralty had its own facilities for docking, refit and repair of these tankers and could therefore save shipbuilder's profits; the work being done in the yards would also guarantee that it has been properly supervised and the repairs efficiently carried out.
- Stores, many of which are common to HM Ships and tankers alike, could be provided much more cheaply owing to the enormous Naval stock purchased.
- As it was frequently necessary to place tankers under Fleet orders, tankers should therefore be manned by officers subject to Admiralty discipline; complaints had been received from the Fleet regarding the present situation.
- It was most desirable that those officers selected should be men in permanent Admiralty employ, preferably holding RNR commissions.

Management

The post-war RFA management philosophy evolved from that of the Ministry of Shipping and was based largely upon commercial tanker practice, since RFA vessels were mainly tankers – functional, simply constructed and operated under Merchant Navy conditions with British-registered and -certified seafarers serving under Board of Trade/National Maritime Board conditions of service.

RFA tankers and stores ships were registered under the terms of the Order-in-Council of 1911. This actually exempted non-commissioned ships in the naval service from the need to comply with certain provisions of the Merchant Shipping Acts, but in practice the Admiralty observed the main provisions of the classification as merchant ships. This enabled the Admiralty to be competitive for seafarers in a difficult labour market; to charter surplus commercial tanker tonnage; and, as will be seen, to earn useful revenue for the Treasury. It also met the obligation of a public employer to conform with recognised and changing safety standards. Board of Trade regulations were applied and ships were subjected to regular inspection to ensure that they were seaworthy and carrying the statutory radio equipment, lifeboats and life saving equipment. Without the necessary safety certificates, a ship was not allowed to sail.

The Director of Stores was responsible to the Board of Admiralty for the entire management, financial administration and running of all auxiliaries attached to the Fleet Fuelling Services, or primarily employed in the transport of naval stores, including the Admiralty-owned freighting tankers that were under commercial management, as well as the fleet supply ship in the Mediterranean. The work involved in administering the fleet of registered RFAs was seen as: control of employment; manning, including victualling of officers and ratings; operating expenses; and the important tasks of docking, running repairs and surveys.

Many Admiralty tankers had cargo

holds for carrying dry stores and careful management of the vessels proceeding from the UK in ballast permitted considerable financial advantage by carrying government stores to Gibraltar, Malta and Bermuda.

Merchant Navy Seafarers

The control of most RFA vessels at the Admiralty made it necessary for civil servants to work with officials of the Shipping Federation, the Officers' Association, the Seaman's Union, the ex-Servicemen's Association, various commercial firms and managers, and the technical departments of the Admiralty, Lloyd's, the Board of Trade (BoT) and the Naval Dockyards. The officers and ratings employed on RFAs possessed Merchant Navy Seaman's Discharge Books and were employed under the conditions of service laid down by the National Maritime Board (NMB). This Board consisted of representatives of shipowners and the recognised societies and unions. The Admiralty, although a shipowner, did not belong to the Shipping Federation; however, a Technical Assistant to the Director of Stores attended meetings of the NMB and it was agreed that the NMB was the authority fixing the minimum rates of pay, leave, conditions of employment, overtime and the like for British seamen.

Despite the practices of the Civil Service and the Royal Navy, the Director of Stores recognised and successfully managed the radically different practices of the Merchant Navy. Some of these are outlined below.

Recruitment

Applications for employment of officers were often received directly at the Admiralty, but mainly through the Shipping Federation for deck officers and from dockyard ports and the Marine Engineers Association for engineering officers. Officers upon first appointment signed an appropriate Board of Trade Agreement and were subject to the rules that generally applied to the Merchant Navy. The one area of difficulty, probably unique to the RFA, was the transfer of officers between ships. Their ships varied between 300 and 10,000 tons in cargo capacity and their nature of duties also varied considerably, from port tankers that hardly every left port, through tankers constantly in attendance on HM Ships, to tankers engaged in worldwide freighting.

The Service appears to have taken a view that junior officers of each grade were employed on the smaller ships but that acquiring experience on other vessels was highly desirable. Because of the nature of the Service transfers were often made at extremely short notice. A vessel might only be in port for 48 hours, and an officer sick or going on leave would have to be replaced urgently. But through experience the Director of Naval Stores adopted a broad policy:

- that officers on tankers stationed abroad should be brought home to the UK on termination of their Agreement;
- that officers on a freighting tanker should be relieved when the amount of leave due to them reached the allowance for two years;
- that the smaller vessels at home were considered suitable employment for new promotions, but often have to be used for temporary employment for senior officers who were awaiting a vacancy after taking leave or having had prolonged employment abroad.

Ratings

In the UK ratings serving in Royal Fleet Auxiliaries were engaged through the Joint Supply Organisation of the National Maritime Board (later to be known as the Merchant Navy Pool). Exceptionally, by friendly arrangements between the Admiralty and the National Union of Seamen, the crews of the fleet attendant tankers attached to the Home Fleet were obtained from the National Association for the Employment of ex Sailors, Soldiers and Airmen. Yard Craft crews manned three port tankers, one each at Portsmouth, Devonport and Sheerness, where the ratings slept ashore.

When freighting tankers were employed in eastern waters for prolonged period, it was more economic and convenient to crew them with Chinese ratings. The fleet attendant tankers based on the Mediterranean, Cape, East Indies and China stations were crewed with local native personnel. All such ratings were obtained through the same channels used by commercial firms and they signed Board of Trade Agreements. Their rates of pay and victualling allowances were determined by the local shipping master.

Agreements

All officers and ratings signed Board of Trade Articles of Agreement at the commencement of a 'voyage', binding them to service for the period of the contract. There were several forms of these Ship's Articles in use in the RFA. Those for the freighting tankers were for a voyage or for six months running, which meant that they terminated on the 30 June and 30 December or the first UK port of call after those dates. There were also Voyage Agreements that were open for up to two years. In order to reduce the expense of relieving officers on tankers allocated permanently to overseas stations, such as Malta, Bermuda, China and the East Indies, officers signed a three-year agreement.

Minimum victualling scales were included in the BoT Agreements but the Admiralty committed itself to a higher standard in order that the Crown should be seen as a good employer; there was also concern that meanness in victualling might result in these Admiralty ships being manned by an inferior type of officer and rating. In a effort to manage victualling costs when the Naval Stores Officers at yards became the RFA agents, increasingly supplies were obtained from Naval sources and an arrangement was made with the NAAFI by which RFAs were supplied on specially reduced terms at all depots at home and overseas, including Singapore.

Radio officers

After the First World War civilian W/T operators gradually replaced the wartime RNVR/RNR telegraphists. It became the practice for the non-RN W/T installations to be supplied from Marconi International Marine Radio Co Ltd, on a hire and maintenance agreement. The Admiralty increasingly began to employ W/T operators directly, but in some ships, like the 'British' group and those still under commercial management, the Marconi Company also provided trained W/T operators. RFA *Olna*, built in 1921, carried RN W/T equipment and the operator was an employee of the management company Davies & Newman. It is understood that directly employed Admiralty staff later replaced him.

The Chartering of Surplus Tankers

Financial stringencies, particularly during the inter-war years, placed restrictions on fleet steaming and on the maintained level of oil fuel reserves. As a result there was a difference between the number of tankers 'owned' by the Admiralty and the number that they continuously employed on Admiralty duties. Consequently a number of vessels were placed in reserve at Rosyth Naval Base. Here they were in the custody of the Naval Stores Department represented by a RFA Chief Engineer and staff responsible for maintaining ships' hulls and machinery in good condition although their Lloyd's surveys were suspended.

The chartering of RFA tankers, whether under commercial management or not, was arranged by the Admiralty, who followed trade practice by putting business through brokers. Between 1921 and 1932 the income from chartering exceeded £1.25 million. This is despite accepting, during the period of the depression in the freight market, rates that did not cover the cost of overheads.

The 1920s and 1930s were decades of great financial stringency. New construction estimates were planned and an increased emphasis was placed upon afloat support. However, the Admiralty generally found it difficult to procure even the minimum numbers of warships it wanted, let alone additional auxiliaries. The Admiralty was aware of the potential of oiling at sea, but at the time naval operations were entirely planned upon the principle that well-stored units operated from established bases and returned to those bases when operations were concluded. As a result the RFAs in service at this time were

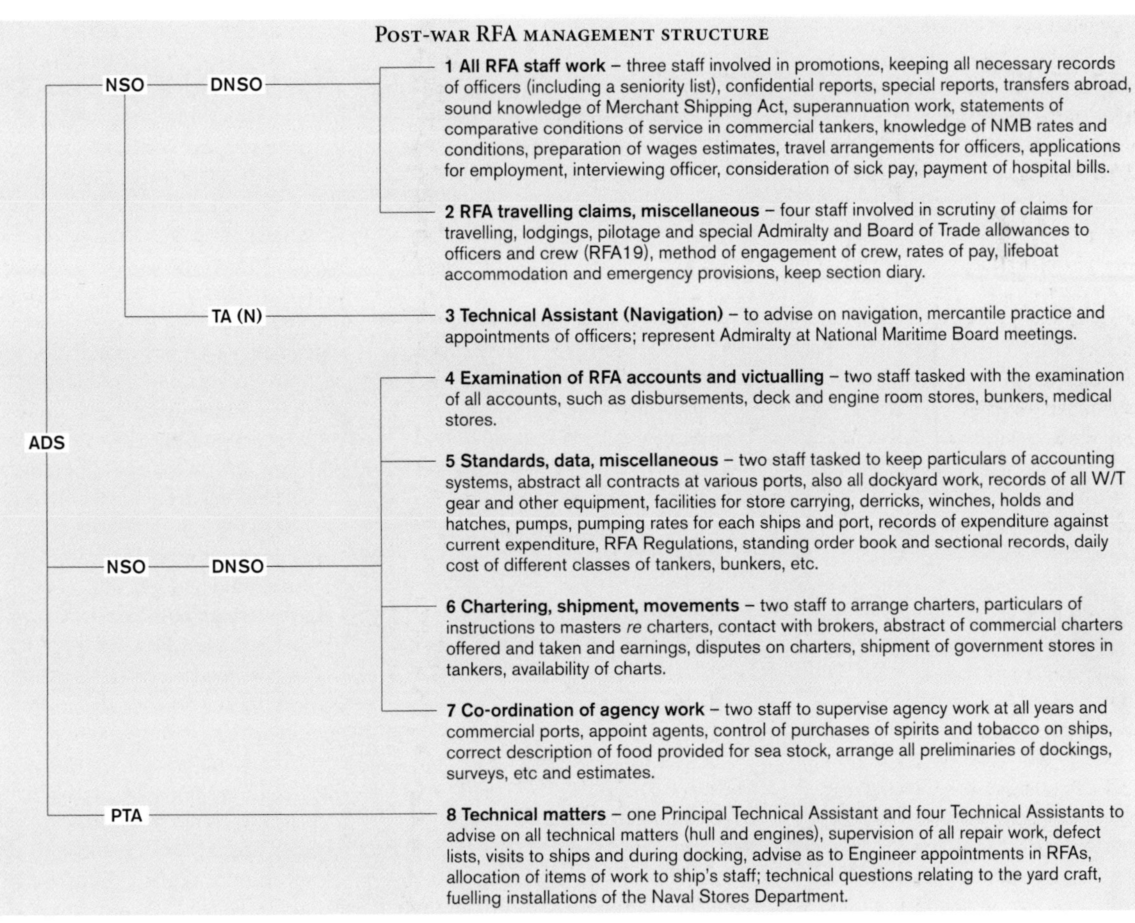

RFA *War Bharata*, one of the Admiralty tankers operated between the wars under the management of British Tanker Co. (RFA Archive)

chiefly employed on the regular freighting of oil and stores between supply and sea bases and in station and harbour duties.

However, this period also saw the rapidly improving capability of aircraft, which meant an increased likelihood of air attacks upon established naval bases. Realisation of this had the result of directing British attention to the greater need for putting the Navy's stores and supplies afloat. In November 1936 the Admiralty convened a 'Supply Ships Committee', to consider the type and numbers of fleet auxiliaries required to sustain stores support to the fleet under 'wartime emergencies'. The Committee recommended, for example, that a number of naval and victualling stores issuing ships of 5,000 tons be taken from trade and converted, and also that a number of armament stores carriers be acquired. The years 1936–8 became a period of reorganisation and improvement, with the tankers under charter and under commercial management being withdrawn and placed under complete RFA manning. Navy Estimates allowed for the modernisation of naval bases and fuelling depots and arrangements were made for stepping up oiling at sea trials. However, it was thanks to the foresight of the Director of Stores, Sir William Gick, that the Admiralty did not enter the Second World War with a worn-out tanker fleet. In 1937 plans were being drawn up for what became the 'Ranger' class fleet attendant tankers and the Admiralty took over from the British Tanker Company six of its 12,500-ton motor tankers that were to become part of the eighteen-hull 'Dale' class.

The Second World War

The work of the Royal Fleet Auxiliary throughout the Second World War parallels both the strategic and tactical operations of the Royal Navy, from the battle of the River Plate in 1939 to the formal signing of the Japanese surrender in Tokyo Bay in 1945, with, amongst others, the hell of the Malta and Russian convoys in between. The war cost the RFA dearly: fourteen ships were lost and two captured, and 115 lives were lost.

The war presented the RFA with many new challenges, including the novel demands of amphibious warfare, which required innovative ship design and new shiphandling skills. The RFA became involved in this through the manning, and to some extent managing, of three 'Dale' class Landing Ship Gantries (LSGs). These vessels were built and intended to be used as RFA tankers, but it is interesting that official records indicate that for the RFA the LSGs were an unforeseen development. When the proposal to adapt them for the transporting of landing craft was first approved, the modifications were on a limited scale and they operated as tankers when not on transport duties. However, the requirements of the Directorate of Combined Operations were rapidly expanded and in order to meet them the later stages of the conversions went far beyond the original proposals.

Another major commitment for the RFA was the British Pacific Fleet Train (BPFT), known as Task Force 112, which was set up in 1944 under the command of a Rear Admiral Fleet Train. The main function of the fleet train was to carry supplies from Sydney, Australia to the intermediate base at Manus in the Admiralty Islands, or to Leyte Gulf in the Philippines where the Royal Navy had begun to use harbour facilities. However, tankers had to go right forward to the operational areas in order to replenish warships at sea. The BPFT was a collection of some sixty ships of many nationalities, assembled not without a good deal of argument with the Ministry of War Transport (MoWT). A similar but much smaller fleet train was built up in the Indian Ocean to serve the East Indies Fleet, as the Eastern Fleet had been renamed after the formation of the British Pacific Fleet.

It was the war in the Pacific that focused minds on a number of important issues, in particular on the need for tankers fitted with the latest equipment for replenishment and fast enough to keep pace with HM Ships during fuelling at sea. To meet this requirement, nine standard design tankers building for the Ministry of War Transport (MoWT) were taken over and renamed as 'Wave' boats. The

Naval Stores Department, subject to certain provision, was also earmarked to crew and manage the escort aircraft carriers *Biter*, *Archer* and *Activity*, although the final reasons why this did not occur are uncertain.

During the war RFA personnel appointed by the Director of Stores (DoS) were engaged under NMB-agreed Ministry of Shipping (later MoWT) agreements identical to the crews of commercial vessels. There were a few additional Admiralty clauses that related only to the periodical relief of offices irrespective of the date of expiry of an agreement. They were subject to the NMB-agreed seafarers' war risk money and VE and VJ allowances as for officers and ratings employed on commercial ships. Some RFAs were on temporary Yard Craft Agreements and a few officers had RNR/RNVR commissions. Defensively Equipped Merchant Ships (DEMS) personnel were carried when necessary. The use of Asiatic crews was significant, but it was increasingly necessary to ship European crews engaged from the Merchant Navy Pool.

During the Second World War a significant number of merchant ships were requisitioned or taken up on government service (MoWT/ Admiralty) by charter, but remained under the management and manning of their parent or third-party companies. Some of these are recorded as being Royal Fleet Auxiliaries, but in the absence of clear official evidence it is the authors' view that this is an error and that such ships on Admiralty service are what the Circular Letter of 1905 clearly calls Mercantile Fleet Auxiliaries.

Experience and Change

The post-war history of the Royal Fleet Auxiliary runs very closely alongside that of the Royal Navy. Worldwide operations included UN support in Korea (1950), Suez (1956), Operation Grapple supporting Atomic Bomb tests in the Pacific (1957), Kuwait (1961), Indonesian confrontation (1965), the three 'Cod Wars' (1958–61, 1972–3, 1975–6), Beira patrol supporting UN sanctions against Rhodesia (1966), Aden withdrawal (1967), Gulf (1978), South Atlantic (1982), Lebanon (1983), Kuwait (1990), Bosnia (1991), withdrawal from Hong Kong (1997), Kosovo (1999), Sierra Leone (2000), Gulf War (2003), not to mention numerous NATO exercises and trials, the shadowing of Soviet naval units, and humanitarian deployments.

The immediate post-war period brought demobilisation. The wartime demands on RFAs, and in particular those of the Pacific Fleet Train, not only highlighted the structural shortcoming of the ships but also focused on the strengths and weaknesses of how RFAs were crewed. For operational reasons there was an increasing need to engage UK ratings from the Merchant Navy Pool wherever a vessel happened to be, even though records show that ratings from the Pool were sometimes difficult to handle and often so troublesome that some had to be landed. Some were even charged and imprisoned during voyages at intermediate ports. Crews were recruited through the Pool, which forbade any selection, so that a good crew was only obtained by chance and of course the Admiralty had no special inducements to offer to make its service attractive; indeed, RFA conditions of service and rates of pay were lagging behind those of commercial tanker companies. Such companies therefore commanded and retained the services of the best seaman obtainable, leaving the rest for the lesser attractive companies.

In the year November 1947 to October 1948, 128 second officers, third engineers and electricians left the RFA. With thirty of the thirty-three RFA freighting tankers manned by Asiatic crews and sixteen fleet attendant tankers with local UK crews, the Director of Stores (DoS) reviewed the manning of RFAs. There was an increasing need to familiarise Admiralty crews with the method and equipment for replenishment at sea, in peace, since they would be called upon to use the systems in war. At this point it is interesting to note that the ship that gained the greatest commendation for excellence in oiling at sea in the Pacific in 1945 was RFA *Wave King*, crewed by Shetland Islanders. The DoS recognised the need to select and retain in service a corps of permanent petty officers (POs) – men who hold positions in all departments of a ship – so the RFA took a major step in improving the conditions of petty officers, based on those of the commercial tanker companies, over and above the National Maritime Board rates and conditions. In July 1947 the main features were:

- introduction of contracts allowing continuous pay and employment after one year's satisfactory service in an RFA freighter;
- higher rates of monthly pay;
- pay when standing by the ship in port;
- when applicable, an Eastern Bonus of 25 per cent on basic pay; and
- additional leave.

The situation slowly began to improve with the forthcoming years seeing the introduction of sick pay, seniority increments for contract petty officers and chief cooks, extension of contracts to ABs (Able Seamen) and AB signalmen, a superannuation scheme for POs and AB signalmen, introduction of Replenishment at Sea (RAS) allowance for all POs and ratings on UK-manned replenishment ships, and the introduction of the post of Commodore RFA.

At the end of the Second World War the Admiralty was allocated eleven 'Wave' class tankers that had been built for the Ministry of War Transport, to add to the fleet of nine already in Admiralty hands. These MoWT vessels were under commercial management when taken over by the DoS during 1947–8. Comments by an RFA Technical Assistant on the conditions of Admiralty tankers under commercial management both before and after the war make interesting reading: for example, *Wave Liberator* had been commercially managed for three years and the DoS report on handing over indicated that mechanical defects accrued from inefficient handling, while the accommodation and ship generally was a floating slum; and, on taking over, the RFA found *Wave Master* (commercially managed for four years) to be running with a stripped and cracked HP turbine, but there was a lack of interest shown by the ship's engineers and apart from excessive fuel consumption ultimately the turbine had to be replaced at significant public cost.

The first important post-war addition to the RFA has to be seen as the three 'Tide' class fleet replenishment tankers; at 18,000 deadweight tons, *Tiderace*, *Tiderange* and *Tidereach* were far removed from the commercial concept of a tanker. Of naval design, large, fast and built to high standards, they redefined the uniqueness of the role and equipment of the fleet tanker. They carried three different grades of cargo with separate pumps and sufficient power to be available to enable all these pumps to be used whilst steaming at 15 knots. There was a lot of top-weight in the form of replenishment at sea derricks, automatic tensioning winches, many conventional type winches and pipe work. All of these were carried on a RAS deck above the traditional tank tops.

In June 1956 the London Commonwealth Prime Ministers' Conference discussed Britain's future naval strategy and the vulnerability of static bases in the face of worldwide change. Consideration was given to the provision of 'Fleet Trains' to supply warships at sea, while the annual Navy Estimates for the first time listed repair, supply vessels and so forth under the heading 'Fleet Support and Auxiliaries'. The Admiralty then announced plans to build up a force of such ships, so a change of course was being executed towards direct fleet support with a major renewal programme for hulls and equipment.

So began a period of major fleet modernisation, with the bareboat chartering of motor tankers for freighting duties that reintroduced the 'Leaf' name to the fleet, and the introduction of specially designed and purpose-built new tonnage for front-line duties with the fleet – ships with the latest RAS technology and with aviation facilities that were permanently manned with a full RAS complement even if temporarily on freighting duties. This meant reorganisation and greater operational effectiveness. The training of RFA officers and ratings always followed the traditional pattern of the British Merchant Navy with Merchant Navy Training Board, Shipping Federation course and Nautical College courses. Deck officers (traditionally known as 'mates') and engineer officers (traditionally known as 'clankies') requiring Board of Trade (later MoT) certificates of competency (known as 'tickets'). With this increased fleet work, including the unique work of replenishing at sea with specialised equipment including helicopters, specific training for RFA personnel had to be made available. For example, fire-fighting and damage control, use of gyros, tanker safety, fuel quality control, blind pilotage, the use of command systems, cryptographic equipment, and naval communications were all outside the traditional merchant shipping sphere of competence.

Today the complement of RFAs is essentially structured in a similar way to the conventional Merchant Navy, although changes regarding rank structure have occurred. Officers and ratings undergo specialist courses at Royal Navy establishments and obtain additional military qualifications in order to work efficiently with naval vessels. Therefore trained crewing levels have to be maintained to operate a ship effectively under exercise and warfare conditions. This means high-grade damage control and fire-fighting capabilities, and the maintenance and manning of self-defence weapons; it means running ships at 'defence watches' and at 'action stations'. This results in each department on board an RFA being larger than a commercial ship of similar size. Discipline in the RFA is governed by the RFA Code of Conduct, which is very similar to the Merchant Navy Code of Conduct, but reflecting the predominantly military nature of RFA duties.

Change of Status and Change of Management

It is not this book's purpose to cover in detail the Falklands War, but it is for us to record the exceptional effort undertaken by the twenty-two of the RFA's twenty-seven ships and all the personnel that were engaged directly and indirectly in Operation Corporate and its supporting actions. This was not without loss, and it was the awful televised scenes from Bluff Cove with the burning hulls of RFAs *Sir Galahad* and *Sir Tristram* that first brought the RFA into many people's homes. Those intrigued enough to enquire about the RFA were to discover the longevity and uniqueness of this very British organisation. The war also brought the first formal award of Battle Honours to RFAs, as well as the practical realisation that the Navy cannot operate in a war or be sustained away from home without the direct close support and force-multipliers provided by the RFA. Furthermore, the Falklands War generated official concern about the nature of the RFA's role in support of the Britain's armed forces, and proved the catalyst for future changes.

It had long been said that the RFA was answerable to two masters: its 'owner' the Ministry of Defence (Navy), and the 'regulator', the Ministry of Transport. Such a relationship was now seen as restricting the RFA in reaching its full potential. With the construction and operation of a new concept in fleet support – the Auxiliary Oiler Replenishment (AOR) – a combined fuel oil, stores and ammunition-issuing ship fitted with defensive armament and extensive aviation facilities, there would undoubtedly be legal difficulties for these 'merchant ships'.

In April 1985 it was announced in Parliament that it was the Government's intention to remove all RFAs from the Register of British Shipping. The Merchant Shipping Acts would cease to apply and this was to be done without changes to the conditions of service of the British Registered Seafarers who manned the RFA. This was a complex issue that seemed to overlook related issues behind the original Admiralty Order-in-Council of 1911. Nonetheless, that long-established RFA strength – compromise – came into play, and rather than deregistration it became 'change of status', ultimately moving the 'regulator' responsibilities from the Department of Transport to the Ministry of Defence.

In 1989 this 'change of status' was formalised by The Merchant Shipping (Ministry of Defence) Order-in-Council 1989 No 1991. This was augmented by a 'letter of understanding' between MoD (Navy) and the Department of Transport indicating that RFAs would continue to conform to the requirements of most of the Merchant Shipping Acts of 1894, 1970, 1979 and 1988 and remain British-registered merchant ships. Surveys and inspections would continue to be undertaken by the Department of Transport and Lloyd's Register on an agency basis. They continue to conform with the International Conventions for Safety of Life at Sea (SOLAS). Documents on passenger safety, marine pollution and radio safety are issued, as is the paperwork on tonnage measurement, cargo ship construction and load lines. Overall this permits the RFA to work operationally unrestricted by legal constraints imposed by the Merchant Shipping Acts. The Registrar General of Shipping and Seamen verified that service in RFAs continues to be recognised as merchant service.

New Management

In 1989, with the imminent introduction of the AORs, the Chief of Fleet Support directed that a study should be carried out into the command and control arrangements of the RFA. In December 1991 the Navy Board approved the transfer of full command of the RFA from the Chief of Fleet Support to Commander in Chief Fleet and the setting up of a Type Commander organisation. The Commodore RFA (COMRFA) became the type commander of the RFA Flotilla (RFAFLOT), so taking day-to-day responsibility away from the civil servants of the RNSTS. The new COMRFA headquarters formed in Empress State Building, London before relocation to Portsmouth Naval Base. This new organisation dropped the traditional language of 'Superintendent' as COMRFA was to be assisted by Chief Staff Officers who headed three divisions – Operations and Warfare (X), Engineering and Systems (E) and Policy and Finance (S).

The Director General Fleet Support (Ships) became responsible for managing the engineering support for the RN, RFA and other MoD-owned vessels and is home of the Commodore Chief Engineer (RFA). In 1999 a Fleet First study was commissioned by Commander-in-Chief Fleet to review the management structure of his headquarters. One of the consequences of this was that the Type Command structure was disbanded and during 2001/02 a new Fleet Headquarters organisation was shaped with 'current and future fleet' capability delivered by the three-star level Deputy Commander-in-Chief through, at two-star level, a Chief of Staff (Warfare) and a Chief of Staff (Support).

The Chief of Staff (Support) is supported by four one-star level Assistant Chiefs of Staff, one of whom – Assistant Chief of Staff (Sustainability) – is Commodore RFA. Initially established as a Merchant Navy courtesy sea-going appointment in 1951, he is now responsible for the planning, exercise and management of all matters relating to logistics and sustainability of British maritime forces. As head of the Royal Fleet Auxiliary Service he is now directly accountable to the Commander-in-Chief Fleet and is the largest single employer of British Registered Seafarers.

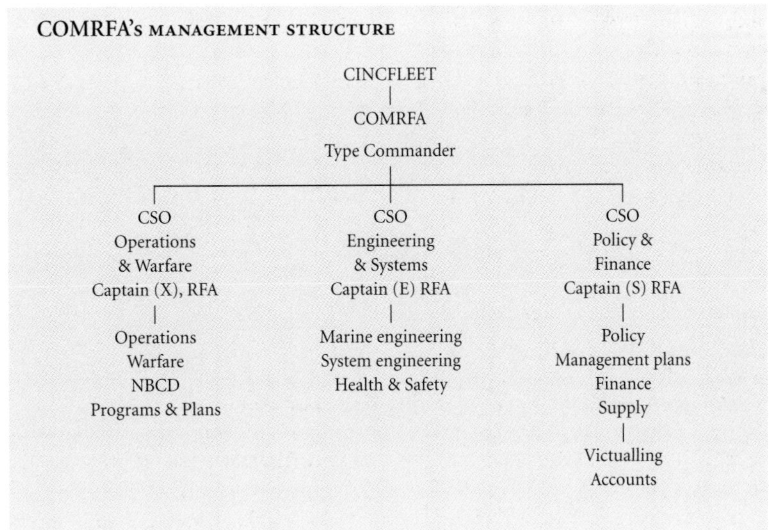

Current top-level command structure

CINCFLEET
|
DCINC
|
Chief of Staff (Support)
|
Assistant Chief of Staff (Sustainability) – Commodore of the RFA and Head of the Fighting Arm - RFA

VERTREP: the busy flight deck of RFA *Stromness.* (RFA Archive)

Evolution of Roles

Modern warships use an enormous range of stores, fuel, food, munitions and aviation spares, and today the core task of the Royal Fleet Auxiliary is to supply RN and NATO ships at sea with those requirements. In 1939 the RN did not take on fuel when underway at sea; today more than 90 per cent of all fuel used by the RN is received underway. In addition, the RFA provides front line support to amphibious and aviation operations, primary casualty reception, battle damage repair and secure sealift for the Royal Marines and the Army.

Stores issuing ships

Prior to the Second World War the RFA operated one fleet supply ship – *Perthshire*, later replaced by *Reliant* (1) – and one ocean-going freighter – *Bacchus*. During the war a number of Canadian-built standard ships ('Fort' class) were allocated to the Admiralty but were operated initially under commercial manning and management by companies such as Ellerman & Bucknall, Alfred Holt, Eastern and Australian Steam Ship Co. Fitted out for stores issuing, their operational loading included naval stores, victualling stores, air stores, armament stores or a combination of these. Embarked Admiralty stores personnel performed the stores management task. They were later taken over under DoS manning and management as armament and naval/victualling stores issuing ships, tasked by the Department of Armament Supply and the Director of Victualling. Additional 'Fort' class dry cargo freighters joined *Bacchus* to form the Naval Freighting Service, manned and managed by DoS but tasked by the Director of Movements. The stores issuing ships played an important role in developing the concept of afloat support that led directly to techniques of underway replenishment of stores and VERTREP, experience that was later applied to new stores support ships and the fast fleet replenishment ships, such as *Resurgent*, *Reliant* (2) and the highly successful 'Ness' class. These were the forerunners of the 'Fort' class of today.

Amphibious operations

As noted earlier, the RFA's relationship with landing ships began during the Second World War with three LSGs, ships that securely transported troops and their pre-loaded equipment to many theatres of operations. In 1970 a number of 'Sir' class landing ships (logistics) (LSLs), which were then classified as passenger ships) and the old LST3 *Empire Gull* were transferred from commercial management by British India to the MoD(Navy) for RFA manning and management. After the Falklands War in 1982, with the operational loss of the two LSLs *Sir Galahad* and *Sir Tristram*, two commercial roll-on-roll off ships were bareboat-chartered as *Sir Caradoc* and *Sir Lamorak*. The badly damaged *Sir Tristram* was recovered and rebuilt, a new *Sir Galahad* (2) was constructed, and *Sir Bedivere* has virtually been rebuilt. The elderly LSLs are now being replaced by the latest in amphibious ship design – the 'Bay' class landing ships dock (auxiliary). The first of class is due to commence trials in 2005.

Aviation operations

The kite balloon ship *City of Oxford* of 1916 could be interpreted as the RFA's first move into naval aviation, or when in 1944 the Admiralty looked at the possibility of the RFA manning a number of trade-protection aircraft carriers. The 'R' class fleet replenishment ships of 1967 did carry a permanent helicopter detachment, but it was not until the commissioning of the 8,000-ton *Engadine* in the same year, that the RFA and the Fleet Air Arm really got together. Reviving a name with naval aviation connotations, she was the Navy's first purpose-built helicopter training ship. Commanded and manned by the RFA and with permanently deployed RN personnel responsible for all helicopter operations and maintenance, she was followed by the *Reliant* (3) with its containerised ARAPAHO system, and then the versatile *Argus* of today.

Primary casualty reception

At the Hague Conference of July 1899 agreement was reached for the adaptation to maritime warfare of the principles of the Geneva Convention of 1864. This created the concept of the hospital ship as a protected Red Cross vessel. Since 1905 the responsibility for the crewing and running of the Royal Navy's permanent hospital ships has been trusted to the RFA. Until 1954 these ships, the various *Maines* and the *Berbice*, were equipped and registered for protection under the Geneva Convention. As a modern-day successor, the RFA *Argus* is fitted as a primary casualty receiving ship with a ninety-bed hospital and facilities that staff on the previous RFA-run hospital ships could not have foreseen.

Battle damage repair

In 1983 RFA *Diligence* added another, not exactly original dimension to the work of the RFA. *Diligence* is a forward repair ship specially equipped to provide a wide range of repairs and maintenance facilities for surface vessels and submarines in the South Atlantic. She also provided essential services during both Gulf wars and has undertaken worldwide service, including Operation Garron in the aftermath of the Asian tsunami. A sophisticated and extremely versatile ship, she is crewed by the RFA and worked by a specialist Royal Navy technical team. The RFA first manned repair ships during the First World War: RFA *Reliance* was crewed by the RFA and worked by skilled dockyard staff; it also crewed two submarine depot ships, *Sobo* and *Sokoto*.

The future is based on MARS

Looking at our fleet list one can see that RFA tonnage is ageing. New tonnage is entering service – the 'Wave' (2) class fleet tankers and the 'Bay' class landing ships – but the workhorses of the fleet, the single-hull 'Rover' and 'Leaf' tankers, need replacing, if only to meet new international environmental regulations. The 'Fort' (2) class stores support ships are getting older, while *Diligence* is due to decommission next year and *Argus* in 2008.

There are new concepts of sea basing and a joint casualty treatment ship, all part of the requirements driving the Military Afloat Reach and Sustainability (MARS) programme being run by the Defence Procurement Agency. There are assumptions that there will be eight to twelve ships in a number of different classes and during the first decade of its second century these new Royal Fleet Auxiliaries will replace the ageing tankers and stores support ships.

Over the past 100 years the Royal Fleet Auxiliary Service has been adaptable, as it has developed to meet the changing needs of naval warfare and developed an *esprit de corps* and unique sense of identity.

A farewell flypast over the aviation support ship RFA *Engadine*, the first purpose designed helicopter training vessel. (RFA Archive)

CHAPTER 1

The Early Years, 1905–1913

1905

1905: The collier ss *Kharki*, 675 grt, (purchased in 1902) is converted to an oil tank vessel and later classed as a RFA. *Aquarius* (ex *Hampstead*), 3,660 tons, purchased by the Admiralty in 1902; she is described as a RFA water tanker; 1907 converted into a depot ship; sold 14 May 1920. *Aquarius*, distilling ship grounded on Kimmeridge Ledge, off Portland in thick fog when travelling at 9 knots; the Master was held to blame; however, records show that he had a good record having previously spent two years in command of the yard craft collier *Kharki*.

6 March: Oil tank vessel (tanker) ss *Petroleum*, 4,686 grt, built by Swan Hunter, Wallsend (yard no 280) for Petroleum United Agencies, London, launched 18 November 1902 and was the biggest tanker in the world; purchased by the Admiralty on 6 March 1905 for £61,122 plus a conversion cost of £8,340 for service as an Admiralty (RFA) tanker; first oil-burner the Admiralty had, but was found to be too dangerous and was converted into a coal burner; primarily intended for freighting oil; initially manned on Yard Craft agreement.

3 August: Circular letter issued that granted the term Royal Fleet Auxiliary to Admiralty-owned fleet auxiliaries.
First named Royal Fleet Auxiliary is RFA *Maine*, Hospital Ship in Admiralty Circular Letter No 9.

8 August: RFA *Petroleum* left Wallsend for Gibraltar, attached to Atlantic Fleet; at Gibraltar crew were initially on yard craft agreement.

11 August: British Admiralty Instructions issued by Naval Stores Circular for experiments and durability trials for oiling-at-sea.

16 November: Conference on the battleship HMS *Hindustan* agreed arrangements for modifying RFA *Petroleum* for oiling-at-sea trials.

November: RFA *Petroleum* taken in hand for modification for being taken in tow and passing hoses for supply of oil over her bow.

1 December: *Heliopolis* launched by D & W Henderson, Glasgow for Alliance Steamship Co, London (Harris & Dixon Ltd, managers) – 1913 purchased by Admiralty for conversion into a hospital ship.

Colliers
Colliers employed by the Admiralty were engaged under two different forms of charter. Collier Transports were engaged under Transport Regulations and were seen as Mercantile Fleet Auxiliaries, not Royal Fleet Auxiliaries. Short-term Coastwise Time Charters were frequently used when vessels were required for a week or a month, such as during fleet manoeuvres. Colliers that were required for continuous service at home ports, such as Chatham, were Collier Transports.

ADMIRALTY SW

3rd August 1905

Circular Letter No 9 T 3487 of 1905

My Lord Commissioners of the Admiralty have decided that the title 'HMS' shall in future be strictly confined to commissioned ships flying the White Ensign and shall never be applied to fleet auxiliaries which are manned by mercantile crews, whether they are owned by the Admiralty or taken up on Transport Charter.

My Lords are pleased to direct that auxiliaries which belong to the Admiralty shall in future be styled as 'ROYAL FLEET AUXILIARIES' and that those which are taken up on Transport charter shall be styled 'MERCANTILE FLEET AUXILIARIES'.

The special character of any of these ships should be denoted after the name and whenever brevity is desired the initials RFA or MFA should be used. Thus the Maine should be styled RFA Maine, Hospital Ship, and the Sirdar, MFA Sirdar, Collier Transport.

By Command of their Lordships,

Evan Macgregor

All Commanders-in-Chief, Captains, Commanders, Commanding Officers of HM Ships & Vessels

This is a verbatim reproduction of the letter

RFA *Maine* (1)

HOSPITAL SHIP

Pennant: – **Official number:** 94303
Port of registry: London **Callsign:** –
Builder: Wm Gray & Co, West Hartlepool
Machinery: Steam 3-cyl triple expansion by Central Marine Engineering Works, West Hartlepool; 310 nhp; single shaft; 11 knots
Dimensions (loa/bp x beam): 315.2/–ft x 40.2ft
Tonnage measurements: 2,780 grt, 1,690 nrt
Displacement: – **Complement:** RFA + medical
Remarks: +100A1 +LMC commercial design converted for Admiralty use. Regarded as the first RFA, the hospital ship *Maine* (1901–14) completed as *Swansea* in 1887 for Baltimore Storage & Lighterage Co, London; 1888 renamed *Maine*; 1892 registered owners Atlantic Transport Co Ltd, London; 29 June 1901 formally presented to the Admiralty, renamed HMHS *Maine*. She is mentioned in the circular letter of 1905.

The hospital ship *Maine* (1), the first ship formally described as an RFA. (ANRS)

1906

1906: The collier *Mercedes*, completed on 11 February 1902 by Northumberland Shipbuilding Co, Newcastle for Christie & Co, Cardiff, is chartered by the Admiralty at a cost of £23,336 for service as a collier. *Kharki*, completed by Irvine Shipbuilding & Engineering Co as a collier on 1 March 1900 for commercial owners, and purchased by the Admiralty eighteen days later, is converted into a tanker. *Aquarius*, launched at Sunderland as *Hampstead* 25 September 1900, purchased and renamed by the Admiralty in 1902 for service as a stores and distilling ship, is commissioned for service under the White Ensign as a repair and distilling ship.

27 January: A Naval Stores Coal memo was issued ordering arrangements to be made for experiment and durability trials to be carried out by HMS *Victorious* and RFA *Petroleum* with a view to testing, as far as possible, the new arrangements for towing the RFA and embarking oil fuel from her when at sea.

February: Oiling-at-Sea trials between tanker RFA *Petroleum* and the RN Atlantic Fleet's 14,900-ton *Majestic*

One of the first experiments with oiling at sea: RAS(L) stirrup method. (ANRS)

First oiling-at-sea trial

Separation 450 feet with a single 5-inch Admiralty-pattern flexible bronze hose was passed, suspended in stirrups from a wire hawser – Stirrup Rig. Transfer rate was variable at 37 to 57 tons per hour. The outfit was that originally purchased for trial in *Henri Reith*.

Coaling at sea, an early and unsuccessful experiment.

class battleship HMS *Victorious*. Only water was pumped through the hose, as the battleship was not fitted to burn oil fuel. The battleship was in 'line ahead' and towed the tanker.

These trials continued up until June 1906:

- HMS *Hindustan*: 202 tons of fuel transferred alongside in harbour.
- HMS *King Edward VII*: 184 tons of fuel transferred when in dock.
- HMS *Dominion*: some 50 tons of fuel transferred when underway at sea – the first oil fuel transfer at sea.
- HMS *Commonwealth*: 204 tons of fuel transferred when underway at sea.

Engineer-Commander Henry Wray Metcalfe RN designed a coaling-at-sea system known as the Metcalfe Apparatus.

The steam collier *Torridge* was chartered from Torridge Steamship Co Ltd (W J Tatem & Co), Cardiff and operated under Admiralty orders as a Mercantile Fleet Auxiliary; she was fitted out with coaling-at-sea apparatus for trials with the Channel Fleet.

11 April: Director of Transports informed the Master of RFA *Maine* that in future, appointments of Masters in RFAs would terminate like those of officers with six-month agreements.

1 July: Merchant Shipping Act 1906 comes into force.

24 July: *Hermione* (later to become RFA *Nucula*) launched.

September: *Hermione*, 4,614 grt tanker completed by Armstrong Whitworth & Co at Newcastle for C T Bowring, London.

5 October: *Argo* launched.

November: *Argo* completed at Kelvinhaugh for commercial owners.

5 December: Coaling-at-Sea Conference at the Admiralty agreed oiling-at-sea practice with destroyers. As a result the Admiralty ordered more 3.5-inch flexible bronze hose in lengths of 40 and 20 feet.

29 December: HM Treasury approved expenditure by the Admiralty for the provision of a petrol carrier.

Merchant Shipping Act 1906
Section 80 of this Act is the statutory instrument permitting future regulations to be made by Order-in-Council for the registration of Government Ships, not of the Royal Navy, as Crown-owned British Merchant Ships under the Merchant Shipping Acts. See Order-in-Council No 121 of 1911. Section 80 was originally known as the Government Ships Bill.

RFA *Petroleum*

COMMERCIALLY-DESIGNED TANKER

Pennant: X51 **Official number:** 118493
Port of registry: London **Callsign:** GSDV
Builder: Swan Hunter and Wigham Richardson
Machinery: Steam 3-cyl triple expansion by North Eastern Marine Engineering. 2,000ihp; single shaft; coal bunkers; 10.5 knots (machinery was also able to burn oil on Ruspen & Ecles system)
Dimensions (loa/bp x beam): 381.5/370ft x 48.8ft
Tonnage measurements: 4,685 grt, 6,670 dwt
Displacement: 9,900 tons full load **Complement:** 45
Remarks: +100A1 +LMC commercial design converted for Admiralty use. RFA *Petroleum*, tanker – sometimes regarded as the first RFA, but was actually the first operational tanker. Cargo capacity 6,200 tons in six cargo tanks plus 668 tons oil fuel, 632 tons coal and 210-ton reserve bunkers. Her deck fitting pipes extensively modified for Admiralty 5-inch hose connections and a 6-inch pipe line to the forecastle with 5-inch hose connections; 600 feet of Admiralty-Pattern metallic hose fitted with Admiralty-Pattern 5-inch connections were supplied.

RFA *Petroleum*, the Admiralty's first ocean-going tanker. (World Ship Society)

1907

1907: Admiralty Transport Department, a Ministry of Transport department headed by the Director of Transports, was responsible for appointing Masters and Officers for RFAs. In 1917 his duties transferred to Ministry of Shipping.

Kharki, recently converted into a tanker, is not required for oiling at sea but reportedly fitted with 300 feet of 5-inch flexible hose for oiling HM Ships.

6 March: SS *Thistle*, collier, 510 grt (later to become RFA *Isla*), completed in 1903 by Garston Graving Dock Co for J Brewster & Sons at Whitehaven, purchased from the trade through the Admiralty Shipping Agent (C W Kellock & Co, London) for £8,925; over the next three years £16,277 was spent on conversion to petrol carrier for conveyance of petrol to submarines.

June: *Aquarius* becomes a depot ship.

RFA *Kharki*

COMMERCIALLY-DESIGNED COLLIER CONVERTED TO ADMIRALTY TANKER

Pennant: X31/X34 **Official number:** 112680
Port of registry: London **Callsign:** GRMO
Builder: Irvine Shipbuilding and Engineering Co Ltd
Machinery: Steam 3 cyl triple-expansion by McKie & Baxter, Glasgow; single shaft; 9 knots
Dimensions (loa/bp x beam): 185.2/–ft x 29.1ft
Tonnage measurements: 681 grt, 764 dwt (as built)
Displacement: 1,430 tons **Complement:** 17
Remarks: +100A1 +LMC. March 1900 purchased for £14,650 and delivered to HM Pembroke Dock. Converted at a cost of £7,324 for the conveyance of lubricating oil from contractor's works to home dockyards and depots. 27,000 gallon capacity; fitted with two Worthington pumps (ex HMS *Mars*) for a delivery of 12,000 gallons per hour.

RFA *Kharki* – built as a collier she was acquired by the Admiralty in 1902; in 1905 the ship was converted for service as an early RFA tanker. (RFA Archive)

6 June: RFA *Petroleum* readied for further oiling-at-sea trials after modifications based on 1906 trials.
July/August: *Isla* to Sheerness for conversion.
19 December: *Buyo Maru* launched.

1908

7 January: *Petroleum* on passage from Port Arthur was damaged in a hurricane.
19 January: *Mercedes*, collier, 4,487 grt, purchased by the Admiralty for RFA Service at a cost of £37,250; based at Devonport on coal freighting duties. Fitted with the Temperley Transporter gear – coaling-at-sea trials with *Mercedes* not successful and appear not to have gone past the experimental stage.
February: *Buyo Maru* (later to become RFA *Delphinula*), 5,238 grt, completed by Armstrong Whitworth & Co at Newcastle for H E Moss & Co, London and sold to Toyo K K, Tokyo.
9 April: *Isla*, approved for temporary use as a collier.
9 November: *Tay and Tyne* (later to become *Industry* (2)) launched:

RFA *Mercedes*

COMMERCIALLY-DESIGNED COLLIER

Pennant: X28/Y3 (1928)
Official number: 114846
Port of registry: London
Callsign: TGLR
Builder: Northumberland Shipbuilding Co, Newcastle for Christie & Co, Cardiff
Machinery: Steam 3-cyl triple-expansion by North Eastern Marine Engineering; single shaft; 753 ton bunkers; 10.5 knots
Dimensions (loa/bp x beam): 351.5/–ft x 51ft
Tonnage measurements: 4,487 grt, 7,100 dwt
Displacement: 9,930 tons
Complement: 43
Remarks: +100A1; +LMC commercial design converted for Admiralty use; built for trading between Australasia and the west coast of America; fitted with Temperley Transporters for coaling ships at sea; duties home trade carrying coal from Bristol Channel ports to Plymouth, Portland and Portsmouth; at Portsmouth coal was discharged into Collier *C1*; coaling HM Ships and vessels in home waters and home dockyards.

1909

January: *Tay and Tyne* completed by at Dundee for commercial owners.
6 May: TSS *Berbice* launched (later to become RFA *Berbice*, hospital ship) by Harland & Wolff, Belfast.

The Royal Mail steamship *Berbice* before conversion into a hospital ship. (ANRS)

1910

1910: Oiling-at-sea experiments with tanker ahead 'towing' the receiving ship; pumps were improved with resulting increase in flow rates. *Petroleum* and the tanker *Kharki* were fitted for towing and being towed and *Kharki* fitted out for oiling-at-sea experiments.

22 June: *Knight Companion* launched.

August: *Knight Companion*, 7,443 grt (later to become RFA *Reliance*) completed by O'Connell & Co at Glasgow for Greenshields, Cowie & Co.

September: *Mercedes* fitted with a modified Metcalfe Rig for coaling-at-sea trials.

31 October: *Isla* inclination tests at Sheerness.

RFA *Isla*

PETROL CARRIER

Pennant: X93/X29/X33 **Official number:** 113134

Port of registry: London **Callsign:** –

Builder: Gartston Graving Dock & Shipbuilding Co as *Thistle* for J Brewster & Sons, Whitehaven

Machinery: Steam 2-cyl compound engine by Hutson & Sons Ltd; coal bunkers; single shaft; 10 knots

Dimensions (loa/bp x beam): 176/169ft x 26ft

Tonnage measurements: 518 grt, 348 dwt

Displacement: – **Complement:** 15

Remarks: +100A; commercially-designed collier converted for Admiralty use as a petrol carrier; twenty-two rectangular tanks, varying in capacity from 6,400 to 2,250 gallons, fitted; 2.5-inch flexible hoses; four rotary pumps.

1911

1911: A design for a new 4,590-ton displacement naval hospital ship was prepared and tenders invited. *Mercedes* fitted with Metcalf coaling gear (ex *Torridge*); practice carried out off Portland at getting the gear from collier to a battleship but no actual coaling took place. *Kharki*, tanker, carried out oiling at sea trials with the destroyers HMS *Mohawk* and HMS *Amazon* – using stirrup method up to 80 tons of fuel transferred.

21 March: *Burma* launched.

June: *Burma*, 1,832 grt, completed as the first Admiralty-constructed oil tanker – by Greenock & Grangemouth Dockyard Co at Greenock.

August: *Burma*, Admiralty-designed 2,000-ton oil tank vessel (tanker) is fitted for oiling destroyers at sea by 'towing' and oiling battleships or cruisers by being 'towed'.

August–September: *Burma* carried out oiling-at-sea trials at Portland with torpedo boat destroyers: HMS *Mohawk* – 117 tons transferred; HMS *Swift*, using stirrup method on one hose with one tow wire and two hoses – one from each quarter – 270 tons transferred – towing wire broke damaging the hoses; a second trial with stirrup method transferred 212 tons; and HMS *Amazon* received 105 tons and later 79 tons using no stirrups on both evolutions. CinC Home Fleet reported that 'use of tanker vessels for oiling destroyers at sea was unlikely to be of service and that further trials were unnecessary'.

10 November: *Burma* carried out oiling-at-sea trials with battleship HMS *Agamemnon*.

Admiralty Committee on the use of Oil Fuel in the Navy (1911–12)

The Admiralty, increasingly disturbed by the oil supply problem, set up this Committee under the chairmanship of the Fourth Sea Lord, Captain W C Pakenham RN. Its terms of reference:

1. How can a sufficient supply of oil be obtained and a sufficient reserve stored in the UK to enable use of oil fuel only in all new construction?
2. What steps should be taken to establish the reserve of oil? From what sources, in what ships, and along what routes can it be obtained?
3. Generally to report on advantages or otherwise of relaying upon oil for the Naval Service, including effects on personnel and cost.

The Committee issued a range of Departmental and other reports and minutes and an interim report dated 19 January 1912. This suggested the need to set up a more thorough enquiry. This led to the setting up of the Royal Commission on Fuel and Engines under the chairmanship of Admiral of the Fleet Lord Fisher.

The Admiralty Committee studied financial aspects of freighting oil, based on the Admiralty's operation of RFA *Petroleum* and in its report stated 'although at the time there was little difference in cost per ton of oil freighted commercially for them – it would ultimately be more economical for the Admiralty to freight its own oil'.

1912

1912: The term Royal Fleet Auxiliary appears in the Navy List for the first time. The Navy Estimates make provision for an additional naval hospital ship, to be registered under the Merchant Ship Act 1906, Section 80 – estimated cost £68,838.

Petroleum released from oiling-at-sea trials owing to freighting urgency UK – Romania. *Mercedes* fitted with a Marconi W/T installation, before sailing to Gibraltar for a refit that included fitting of her wireless masts. *Mercedes* conducted inconclusive coaling-at-sea trial with HMS *Dominion*. Admiralty Acquaint indicated that the naval

Radio on RFAs

There is little evidence to indicate which was the first Admiralty-owned merchant ship to be fitted with a radio installation. It is assumed that, as merchant ships, installations were in line with Marconi's developments. Despite the fact that Admiralty-owned merchant ships did not have to be registered under the Merchant Shipping Acts, material dated 1912 shows that the following RFAs were to be fitted with Marconi's 1.5kW standard outfit – spark transmitter, receiver, power supply and aerial system. In RFA *Petroleum* the Marconi installation was Admiralty-owned and operated.

RFA *Maine*	hospital ship – ex commercial vessel
RFA *Mercedes*	collier – ex commercial vessel
RFA *Petroleum*	oiler – ex commercial vessel
RFA *Burma*	tanker – Admiralty design, new construction
RFA *Olympia*	tanker – Admiralty design, new construction
RFA *Trefoil*	tanker – Admiralty design, new construction

There is also evidence that the Admiralty-designed *Trinol* class tankers (later known as the 'Fast Leaf' class) and the 2,000-ton class were fitted with the Navy Type 4 W/T set.

Admiralty Order-in-Council for the regulation of the Naval Service No 121 (Statutory Rules and Order 1911 No 338)

Registration as British Ships, under the Merchant Shipping Acts of Government vessels in the service of the Admiralty not forming part of the Royal Navy – 22 March. This is the backbone legislation under which the RFA worked and its ships were registered or not registered.

Royal Commission on Fuel and Engines

Chairman Admiral of the Fleet Lord Fisher of Kilverstone. Initial report published on 27 November 1912 was secret. Indicated 'oil-firing over coal produces higher speed, increased radius of action, speedier and easier refuelling, reduction of stokehold personnel by 50%, quicker initial production of steam, saving in cost of construction'. This was backed by further secret reports on 27 February 1913 and 10 February 1914.

hospital ship provided for in the 1911/1912 Estimates was to be named *Mediator*.

21 May: *Isla* registered under the Merchant Shipping Act.

7 October: *Attendant* laid down.

14 November: *Carol* laid down. *Knight Companion* purchased by the Admiralty for £120,000 and converted at Devonport into a repair ship – commissioned as HMS *Reliance* under the White Ensign.

1913

15 January: *Trefoil* laid down.

18–19 February: *Heliopolis*, berthed at Antwerp, inspected by RN Fleet Surgeon and naval construction and engineering staff for her suitability for conversion into a hospital ship.

17 February: The cargo ship *Heliopolis* purchased by the Admiralty for conversion into a naval hospital ship.

27 February: Second secret report from the Royal Commission on Fuel and Engines.

7 March: *Lake Champlain* renamed *Ruthenia* for commercial owners.

April: *Mercedes* fitted with W/T outfit.

15 May: Admiralty records indicate that it was agreed that the *Heliopolis*, purchased for conversion, should be renamed *Mediator*.

5 July: *Attendant* launched. *Carol* launched by HM Dockyard, Devonport; she had been built on a covered slip as one of the first oil carriers to have her engines and boilers situated almost right aft; her Swedish diesel engine gave endless trouble and her maiden voyage from Devonport to Liverpool took three months because of breakdowns.

10 July: *Olympia* laid down at Vickers, Barrow, later to be renamed *Santa Margherita*.

21 July: *Servitor* laid down.

27 October: *Trefoil* launched at Pembroke Dock but was considerably delayed during completion as warships had priority. She was an experimental ship, which proved to be mechanically unsatisfactory, and she was little used.

3 November: *Turmoil* (1) laid down.

14 November: *Ferol* laid down.

Burma group

ADMIRALTY-DESIGNED HARBOUR TANKERS

RFA *Burma*, RFA *Trefoil*, RFA *Mixol*, RFA *Turmoil*, RFA *Thermol*

Machinery: 3-cyl triple-expansion by Kincaid, Greenock; 8 knots

Dimensions (loa/bp x beam): 279/270ft x 39ft

Tonnage measurements: 1,832 grt, 2,500 dwt

Displacement: 3,945 tons full load **Complement:** 30–36

Remarks: +100A; +LMC, first 2,000-ton medium size class of tankers ordered by the Admiralty; generally of similar dimensions but they were not actually sister-ships – *Burma*, *Mixol*, *Thermol* and *Turmoil* fitted with steam engines and *Trefoil* with Vickers internal combustion engines. Records show that *Burma* was estimated to cost £40,107. Fitted with two pumps, rate 100 tons per hour, limited oiling-at-sea arrangements.

The basic details are based on RFA Burma *as built*

CHAPTER 2

THE FIRST WORLD WAR, 1914–1918

1914

1914: *Industry* (1) transfers to RFA manning. *Isla* is re-rated as a tanker to become the Admiralty's first spirit carrier. Auxiliaries allocated pennant numbers with various flag superiors – D, N (ceased in 1916) and P and those allocated for operation under commercial management Y3 for colliers and Y7 for tankers/transports.

21 January: *Petroleum* collided with and sank a small Turkish schooner in the Bosphorous.

10 February: Final secret report from the Royal Commission on Fuel and Engines, chaired by Admiralty of the Fleet Lord Fisher.

1 April: Humanitarian aid – *Petroleum* rescued the crew of the wrecked Norwegian barque *Chaka*.

26 May: *Servitor* launched.

June: *Mercedes* sailed to Biorka Sound in the Baltic with part of the Grand Fleet; crew entertained by Russians at Kronstadt; returned to UK for a naval review.

17 June: Marine loss – RFA *Maine* – south coast of Isle of Mull, Firth of Lorne, west coast of Scotland; this hospital ship was lost by a navigation error when she grounded during fog, no casualties reported; 20 June 1914 Admiralty statement said that it was decided, due to economic reasons, to abandon any salvage attempts; naval ratings then removed all personal effects, medical stores and portable equipment; and on 6 July the hull sold for scrap.

6 July: Admiralty decided that *Mediator* should be renamed RFA *Maine*.

14 July: *Heliopolis* renamed *Maine* – Pembroke Dock for conversion into naval hospital ship.

August: *Attendant* completed by HM Dockyard at Chatham; first of the first 1,000-ton group Admiralty tankers. *Ruthenia* requisitioned by the Admiralty as a British Expeditionary Force (BEF) transport. The tanker *Attendant*, 1,016 grt, completed by Chatham Dockyard; 3 cyl. triple expansion by builder; Director of Transport manning and Director of Stores registration under the Order-in-Council 1911.

RFA fleet list and disposition, June 1914

	Status	Disposition
RFA *Burma*	tanker	Sheerness
RFA *Industry*	store ship	Portsmouth
RFA *Isla*	petrol carrier	–
RFA *Kharki*	tanker	Portland
RFA *Maine*	hospital ship	–
RFA *Mercedes*	collier	Portsmouth
RFA *Petroleum*	overseas tanker	Portland
RFA *Attendant*	tanker	completing at Chatham
RFA *Carol*	tanker	completing at Devonport
RFA *Trefoil*	tanker	completing at Pembroke
RFA *Ferol*	tanker	building at Devonport
RFA *Olympia*	overseas tanker	building at Vickers, Barrow-in-Furness
RFA *Servitor*	tanker	building at Chatham
RFA *Turmoil*	tanker	building at Pembroke

4 August: Declaration of war against Germany – First World War (also known as The Great War) commences.

3 October: *Ferol* launched at Devonport; like her sister-ship *Carol*, she was built on a covered slip and suffered similar problems with her Swedish internal combustion engines.

19 October: *Aro* purchased by the Admiralty from the African Steamship Co, Liverpool (Elder Dempster & Co, managers) for £55,000 for conversion into a submarine depot ship to be based at Rosyth.

28 October: *Perthshire* purchased by the Admiralty for service as the dummy battleship HMS *Vanguard*.

4 November: *Ruthenia* arrived Belfast under strict secrecy for conversion into the dummy battleship HMS *King George V*.

1915

1915: *Mercedes* was refitted at Cardiff, ballast tanker fitted for carrying oil fuel, then to Loch Ewe where she acted as W/T ship; records also indicate her complement had RN and RNR ratings for working cargo and mercantile ratings worked the winches. *Soyo Maru* (ex *Hermione*) purchased by Shipping Controller and renamed *Nucula* under commercial managers. *Buyo Maru* purchased by the Admiralty and renamed *Delphinula*, 5,238 grt, under commercial management. *Aquarius* served Mediterranean submarines, then as a water carrier and depot ship.

January: *Ferol*, 850 grt, motor tanker completed by Devonport Dockyard. *Ruthenia* purchased by the Admiralty for conversion.

17 April: Oiling-at-sea trials using stirrup method involving destroyer HMS *Beaver* and chartered Anglo American Oil Company's steam tanker *Ottawa* – 9 tons transferred; these trials were as suggested in NS Coal 3704/15 pamphlet.

May: *Servitor*, 1,020 grt, completed by Chatham Dockyard as a harbour tanker at a cost of £57, 867, in service at Sheerness.

10 May: *Bacchus* (1), 2,343 grt, is launched by William Hamilton at Port Glasgow and completed for the Admiralty as a water carrier.

28 May: Oiling at sea – trials in Firth of Forth using stirrup method involving destroyer HMS *Hind* and the chartered tanker *Ottawa* – 13 tons transferred.

31 May: Oiling at sea – trials undertaken using stirrup method involving destroyer HMS *Hydra* and the chartered tanker *Ottawa* – 8 tons transferred.

June: Order-in-Council approved a scheme of pensions, grants, allowances for men and dependants injured or disabled, officer and ratings serving in fleet auxiliaries. *Patrician* (ex dummy battleship HMS *Invincible*) converted into a tanker and renamed RFA *Tarakol*.

19 June: *Canning* purchased from the Liverpool, Brazil & River Plate Steam Navigation Co Ltd, Liverpool for conversion and service as a kite balloon ship and later a depot ship at Scapa Flow.

July: *Ruthenia*, 7,392 grt, converted into a stores ship and water carrier. *Mount Royal* (ex dummy battleship HMS *Marlborough*) converted into a tanker and renamed RFA *Rangol*.

7 July: SS *Montezuma* (ex dummy battleship HMS *Iron Duke*) purchased by the Admiralty and converted into a tanker; renamed RFA *Abadol*.

22 July: *Viscol* ordered from Craig, Taylor & Co at Stockton. *Plumleaf* ordered.

14 August: *Innisinver*, 127 grt, launched 25 May 1913 by A Jeffrey & Co, Alloa for Coastal Motor Shipping Co (J M Paton, manager), Glasgow; one 2 cyl. internal combustion engine by Tuxham engine Co, Valby, Copenhagen; purchased by the Admiralty for service as an RFA-manned 'Innis' class water carrier, named unchanged; the 'Innis' class with their internal combustion engineers were probably regarded by the Admiralty as experimental.

17 August: *Orangeleaf* ordered.

18 August: *Appleleaf, Brambleleaf, Cherryleaf, Pearleaf* ordered. *Plumleaf* order confirmed.

19 August: *Orangeleaf* order confirmed.

September: *Perthshire*, 5,881 grt, paid off from service as the dummy battleship HMS *Vanguard*, then used as Coaling Officer's Ship at Scapa Flow carrying canteen stores and a reserve stock of up to 1,600 tons of oil fuel; then converted to a water tanker.

7 September: *Innisfree*, 95 grt, launched 3 March 1913 by Peter McGregor & Sons, Kirkintilloch for Coastal Motor Shipping Co (J M Paton, manager), Glasgow; purchased by the Admiralty for

RFA *Bacchus* (1)

ADMIRALTY-DESIGNED STORE SHIP AND WATER CARRIER

Pennant: X22/X03 **Official number:** 139059
Port of registry: London **Callsign:** –
Builder: William Hamilton, Port Glasgow as TSS 229
Machinery: 3 cyl. triple expansion; twin shaft; 10 knots
Dimensions (loa/bp x beam): –/295ft x 44ft
Tonnage measurements: 2,343 grt, 2,000 dwt
Displacement: – **Complement:** 52
Remarks: +100A1; +LMC; commercial design converted for Admiralty use, had limited passenger accommodation; originally planned for the Indo-China Steam Navigation Co, purchased by the Admiralty when on the stocks. Fitted out as a distilling ship, served in the Mediterranean (Dardanelles) and in the North Russian expedition.

The first RFA *Bacchus* acquired by the Admiralty during the First World War. (World Ship Society)

Attendant group

ADMIRALTY-DESIGNED 1,000-TON HARBOUR TANKERS

RFA *Attendant*, RFA *Ferol*, RFA *Carol*, RFA *Servitor*
Machinery: 3 cyl triple expansion by Chatham Dockyard; single shaft; 7 knots
Dimensions (loa/bp x beam): 210/200ft x 34ft
Tonnage measurements: 1,020 grt, 1,200 dwt
Displacement: 2,170 tons full load **Complement:** 17
Remarks: +100A1; +LMC1; first 1,000-ton class of Admiralty tankers, these four coastal tankers were of similar dimensions. *Attendant* and *Servitor* were fitted with 3 cyl. triple expansion engines and *Carol* and *Ferol* with two 2 cyl. Bolinder/Fairfield internal combustion engines.
The details are based on RFA Attendant *as built.*

service as an RFA-manned 'Innis' class water carrier, name unchanged.

8 September: *Cevic* (ex dummy battleship HMS *Queen Mary*) purchased by the Admiralty for conversion into a fleet tanker.

16 September: *Innisshannon*, 238 grt, launched 2 April 1913 by William Chalmers & Co, Rutherglen for Coastal Motor Shipping Co, Glasgow; purchased by the Admiralty for service as an RFA-manned 'Innis' class water carrier, name unchanged.

20 September: *Innissulva*, 235 grt, launched 16 April 1914 by William Chalmers & Co, Rutherglen for Coastal Motor Shipping Co, Glasgow; purchased by the Admiralty for service as an RFA-manned 'Innis' class water carrier, name unchanged.

October: *Oliphant* purchased on the stocks by the Admiralty.

2 October: *Innisjura*, 127 grt, launched 19 June 1913 by A Jeffrey & Co, Alloa for Coastal Motor Shipping Co, Glasgow; purchased by the Admiralty for service as an RFA-manned 'Innis' class water carrier, name unchanged.

23 October: *Santa Margherita* (formerly *Olympia*) launched.

Olympia class

ADMIRALTY-DESIGNED OCEAN TANKERS

RFA *Olympia*, RFA *Olaf* (cancelled), RFA *Olivia* (cancelled), RFA *Olna* (cancelled)

Builder: Vickers Ltd, Barrow in Furness

Machinery: Two 8 cyl four-stroke, single acting internal combustion engines by Vickers Ltd, Barrow; 2,500 bhp; twin shaft; 450-ton bunkers; 11 knots

Dimensions (loa/bp x beam): 460/440ft x 54.3ft

Tonnage measurements: 7,499 grt, 11,500 dwt

Displacement: 13,450 tons full load **Complement:** 43

Remarks: +100A1; +LMC; three of this class of large tankers were cancelled; Admiralty-owned tanker *Olympia* was renamed *Santa Margherita*; construction was delayed by war priorities; placed under the commercial management of T Royden & Sons, Liverpool and later with the Anglo-Saxon Petroleum Co, London. This design of ship, using the then largest diesel engine available was notable for its all-electric auxiliaries.

Nucula, a tanker purchased in 1915 and eventually loaned to the RNZN. (World Ship Society)

1916

1916: Pennant numbers – the flag superior X was allocated to RFA vessels and remained in place until replaced by flag superior A of the 1947 system. *Santa Margherita*, 7,499 grt, completed by Vickers Ltd at Barrow and placed under commercial management of T Royden & Sons, Liverpool. Admiralty-owned *Cevic* being converted into a tanker renamed RFA *Bayol*. Ministry of Shipping (The Shipping Controller) is formed. *Oletta*, 5,882 grt, launched by J Redhead & Sons, South Shields as *Briarleaf*. *Olivet*, 5,948 grt, launched by Earles Shipbuilding Co, Hull as *Elmleaf*. *Oleander*, 5,838 grt, launched by Napier & Miller Ltd, Old Kilpatrick, Glasgow as *Fernleaf*. *Oleaster*, 5,162 grt, launched by William Hamilton & Co, Port Glasgow as *Hollyleaf*. Oiling at sea – arrangements on Royal Fleet Auxiliaries – tanker towed the receiving ship; special arrangements for purpose: (1) oil pumps capable of working against high delivery, and (2) special towing fittings.

January: *Reliance*, 9,220 grt, repair and store ship, is transferred to RFA for service off Dardanelles; ship's complement was a mix of RFA crew, RNR and Dockyard staff.

5 February: *Creosol* first of the second 1,000-ton group of Admiralty tankers is launched by Short Brothers at Sunderland.

21 February: *Viscol* launched at Stockton.

March: *Maine* (ex *Heliopolis*) – conversion into hospital ship not completed and hull sold.

4 March: *Distol* launched by William Dobson & Co, Newcastle.

7 March: *Maine*, conversion to a hospital ship – this vessel was considered by some as totally unsuitable for this conversion and for service as a hospital ship; Admiralty auctioneers Fuller, Horsey, Sons and Casell were to offer her for sale by auction at Baltic & Shipping Exchange, London on Wednesday 1 March – as lies at HM

Dockyard Pembroke Dock; purchased Harris & Dixon Ltd, London and reverted to her original name *Heliopolis*; estimated that total public expenditure on this ship exceeded £120,000.

14 March: *Innistrahull*, 238 grt, launched 2 April 1913 by William Chalmers & Co, Rutherglen for Coastal Motor Shipping Co, Glasgow; purchased by the Admiralty for service as an RFA-manned 'Innis' class water carrier, name unchanged. War loss – RFA *Innistrahull* – recorded in the Ministry of Shipping Service List as lost on Admiralty Service but precise details of when and how are unavailable.

4 April: *Kimmerol* launched by Craig, Taylor & Co at Stockton.

5 April: *Philol* launched by Tyne Iron Shipbuilding Co, Newcastle.

19 April: *Bacchus* (1) commissioned as a tender to HMS *Blenheim*.

29 April: *Thermol* launched by the Greenock and Grangemouth Dockyard Co, Greenock.

2 May: *Califol*, 6,572 grt, launched by Sir Raylton Dixon & Co, Middlesborough as *Roseleaf*.

9 June: *Saxol*, 6,124 grt, converted from a store carrier to a tanker with the fitting of cylindrical tanks in her holds.

17 June: *Mixol* launched by Caledon Shipbuilding and Engineering Co, Dundee.

23 June: *Scotol* launched by Tyne Iron Shipbuilding Co, Newcastle.

27 June: *Saxol* purchased by the Admiralty for service as a fleet tanker.

July: *Distol*, 1,173 grt, completed by William Dobson & Co at Newcastle.

10 July: *Rangol* purchased by the Admiralty for service as a fleet tanker; Director of Transport manning and Director of Stores registration.

21 July: *Santa Margherita* (formerly RFA *Olympia*), oiler transport 121, completed; awaiting trials in Firth of Forth.

28 July: *Santa Margherita* sailed on maiden voyage Rosyth to the Persian Gulf for a cargo of 8,048 tons; reportedly suffered many defects.

31 July: *Viscol*, 1,163 grt, completed by Craig, Taylor & Co at Stockton at a cost of £68,523.

August: *Thermol*, 1,901 grt, completed by Greenock & Grangemouth Drydock Co at Greenock for £103,535. *Philol*, 1,178 grt, completed by Tyne Iron Shipbuilding at Newcastle. *Roseleaf* completed and under management of Lane & MacAndrew Ltd, London.

4 August: *Trinol* (later *Plumleaf* (1)) launched by Swan Hunter & Wigham Richardson at Wallsend, cost £261,901.

15 August: *Oliphant*, 5,489 grt, launched by Irvines Shipbuilding and Drydock Co, Wet Hartlepool as *Palmleaf*.

19 August: *Oldbury*, 5,873 grt, launched by Short Brothers Ltd, Sunderland as *Birchleaf*.

22 August: *Creosol*, 1,179 grt, completed by Short Brothers Ltd at Sunderland.

30 August: *Olalla*, 5,631 grt, launched by Craig Taylor & Co, Stockton as *Laureleaf*.

September: PLA *Hopper No 5* chartered by the Admiralty, converted into a tanker and renamed RFA *Blackol*.

9 September: PLA *Hopper No 7* chartered by the Admiralty, converted into a tanker and renamed RFA *Purfol*.

12 September: *Gypol* (later *Pearleaf* (1)) launched by William Gray & Co at West Hartlepool; cost £267,540. *Olga*, 5,768 grt, launched by Ropner & Sons, Stockton-on-Tees as *Ashleaf*.

14 September: *Kurumba* launched.

October: *Kimmerol*, 1,168 grt, completed by Craig, Taylor & Co at Stockton. PLA *Hopper No 6* chartered by the Admiralty, converted into a tanker and renamed RFA *Greenol*. PLA *Hopper No 8* chartered by the Admiralty, converted into a tanker and renamed RFA *Silverol*.

2 October: *Tarakol* (ex *Patrician*),

Creosol class

ADMIRALTY-DESIGNED 1,000-TON CLASS HARBOUR TANKERS

RFA *Birchol* (1), RFA *Boxol*, RFA *Creosol*, RFA *Distol*, RFA *Ebonol* (1), RFA *Elderol*, RFA *Elmol*, RFA *Hickorol*, RFA *Kimmerol*, RFA *Larchol*, RFA *Limol*, RFA *Oakol* (1), RFA *Palmol*, RFA *Philol*, RFA *Scotol*, RFA *Sprucol*, RFA *Teakol* (1), RFA *Viscol*

Machinery: Steam 3 cyl. triple expansion by J Dickson, Sunderland; single shaft; bunkers 103 tons; 9.5 knots; consumption 13.5 tpd

Dimensions (loa/bp x beam): 221/210ft x 34.7ft

Tonnage measurements: 1,178 grt, 1,863 dwt

Displacement: 2,368 tons **Complement:** 19

Remarks: +100A1; +LMC, 1.5ft summer freeboard, built for £66,400; a number of ships in this class were fitted with diesel engines.

The details are based on RFA Scotol *as built*

Larchol:1,000-ton tanker. (World Ship Society)

being converted for the carriage of oil, ceases to be treated as an RFA vessel.

7 October: *Saxol* management transferred to Lane & MacAndrew Ltd, London and renamed *Aspenleaf.*

26 October: *Bornol* (later *Orangeleaf* (1)) launched by J Thomson & Sons, Sunderland cost £265,000. *Olmos*, 5,861 grt, launched by Richardson, Duck & Co, Stockton as *Beechleaf.*

28 October: *Oligarch*, 7,339 grt, launched by Barclay, Curle & Co at Whiteinch as *Limeleaf.* Originally laid down as a cargo ship for British India Line.

November: *Beechleaf* management transferred to Lane & MacAndrew, London.

9 November: RFA *Persol* (later *Cherryleaf* (1)) launched by Sir Raylton Dixon & Co, Middlesborough; cost £266,000.

10 November: *Scotol*, 1,177 grt, completed by Tyne Iron Shipbuilding Co at Newcastle at a cost of £63,967.

11 November: *Oleary*, 5,311 grt, launched by Bartram & Sons, Sunderland as *Dockleaf.*

16 November: PLA *Hopper No 4* chartered by the Admiralty, converted into a tanker and renamed RFA *Battersol.*

17 November: *Rangol* management transferred to Lane & MacAndrew, London and renamed *Mapleleaf.*

25 November: *Palmleaf* completed by Irvine Shipbuilding at West Hartlepool under management of Lane & MacAndrew, London.

28 November: *Texol* (later *Appleleaf* (1)) launched by Workman Clark & Co, Belfast; cost £265,000.

30 November: *Bacchus* (1) deployed to Razegh for service as a distilling ship on army support.

December: *Oligarch* completed as *Limeleaf* and under management of Lane & MacAndrew Ltd, London; her conversion to a tanker was considered unsatisfactory. *Birchleaf* management transferred to Lane & MacAndrew, London. *Briarleaf* completed and under management of Lane & MacAndrew, London.

Brambleleaf (1). This is a splendid example of the 5,000-ton 'Fast Leaf' class tankers that entered service during the First World War. (World Ship Society)

8 December: *Olalla* (now *Laureleaf*) ceased to be consider as an RFA, completed and under management of Lane & MacAndrew Ltd, London.

9 December: *Olinda*, 7,338 grt, launched by Barclay, Curle & Co, Whiteinch as *Boxleaf.* Originally laid down as a cargo ship for British India Line.

28 December: *Rumol* (later *Brambleleaf* (1)) launched by Russell & Co, Port Glasgow; cost £279,850.

30 December: Damaged by enemy action – the Admiralty-tasked oiler transport *Aspenleaf* on passage Sabine, Texas to the UK damaged by mine in English Channel; lost cargo valued at £19,284; ship out of service until June 1917.

1917

1917: The Director of Transports was transferred into the newly-formed Ministry of Shipping (Shipping Controller). *Bacchus* serves as a stores ship. *Trefoil* transferred from HM Dockyard Pembroke and completed by Vickers Ltd, Barrow-in-Furness for the Admiralty. *Belgol*, first of the second group of 2,000-ton Admiralty tankers, enters service. The converted tanker RFA *Bayol* transferred to the Shipping Controller under management of Lane and MacAndrew and renamed *Bayleaf. Canning* becomes a depot ship at Scapa Flow. *Tarakol* management transferred to Lane & MacAndrew Ltd, London and ship renamed *Vineleaf.*

January: PLA *Hopper No 3* chartered by the Admiralty, converted into a tanker and renamed RFA *Barkol. Fernleaf* completed and under the management of Lane & MacAndrew Ltd, London.

10 January: *Kurumba*, 3,978 grt, completed by Swan Hunter & Wigham Richardson at Newcastle; ordered for Australian naval service; cost £141,000.

February: *Texol* completed at a cost of £287,234; renamed *Appleleaf* (1) and management transferred to Lane & MacAndrew, London. *Boxleaf* completed by Barclay Curle at Glasgow; under the management of Lane & MacAndrew Ltd, London.

7 February: *Abadol* transferred to the management of Lane & MacAndrew Ltd, London.

16 February: *Appleleaf* (ex *Texol*) first of the Admiralty design 'Fast Leaf' (ex *Trinol*) class of 5,000-ton tankers enters service. Six of these ocean tankers were built for escort tanker duty on North Atlantic convoys.

26 February: *Abadol* renamed *Oakleaf.*

March: *Elmleaf* and *Hollyleaf* completed and under the management of Lane & MacAndrew Ltd, London.

7 March: *Turmoil* launched at Pembroke Dock – she was an experimental ship that proved to be mechanically unsatisfactory and was little used.

Emergency wartime construction, purchases and charters

Eighteen vessels of varying types were acquired second-hand and converted, or purchased and converted while on the stocks, or, in a few cases building as tankers. Some were also converted after service with the Dummy Battleship Squadron. Originally intended to operate as Royal Fleet Auxiliaries, however, owing to reasons of international law and the operation of the US Neutrality Act these overseas oilers became Mercantile Fleet Auxiliaries being renamed, placed under civilian management of Lane and MacAndrew Ltd, London and operated as Red Ensign. Official Lists of RFAs show that the Director of Stores was involved with their manning and they carried some stores paid for from the Admiralty account. Operationally they remained under Admiralty control. This particular group are accurately known as the 'Leaf' Group.

Ashleaf: 1916 acquired on completion as RFA *Olga*; renamed *Ashleaf*; oiler transport no 153, base port Devonport; 29 May 1916 war loss.
Aspenleaf: 1900 completed as Elder Dempster's *Lake Erie*; 1914 acquired by the Admiralty for service as dummy battleship HMS *Centurion*; converted to a tanker to be named RFA *Saxol*, entered service as *Aspenleaf*; oiler transport no 170, base port Portsmouth.
Bayleaf: 1894 completed as White Start Line's *Cevic*; 1914 acquired by the Admiralty for service as dummy battleship HMS *Queen Mary*; converted to tanker to be renamed RFA *Bayol*, entered service as *Bayleaf*; oiler transport no 173.
Beechleaf: 1917 acquired by Admiralty upon completion as a tanker as RFA *Olmos*; renamed and entered service as *Beechleaf*; oiler transport no 154, base port Devonport.
Birchleaf: 1916 acquired by Admiralty on completion as the tanker RFA *Oldbury*; renamed and entered service as *Birchleaf*; oiler transport no 153, base port Devonport.
Boxleaf: 1916 acquired by Admiralty on completion as the tanker RFA *Olinda*; renamed and entered service as *Boxleaf*; oiler transport no 159, base port Devonport.
Briarleaf: 1916 acquired by the Admiralty on completion as the tanker RFA *Oletta*; renamed and entered service as *Briarleaf*; oiler transport no 151, base port Devonport.
Dockleaf: 1917 completed for the Admiralty as the tanker RFA *O'Leary*, renamed and entered service as *Dockleaf*; oiler transport no 161, base port Devonport.
Elmleaf: 1917 completed for the Admiralty as the tanker RFA *Olivet*; renamed and served *Elmleaf*; oiler transport no 157, base port Devonport.
Fernleaf: 1917 completed for the Admiralty as the tanker RFA *Oleander*, renamed and entered service as *Fernleaf*; oiler transport no 162, base port Devonport.
Hollyleaf: 1917 completed for the Admiralty as the tanker RFA *Oleaster*; renamed and entered service as *Hollyleaf*; oiler transport no 160, base port Devonport.
Laurelleaf: 1916 acquired by the Admiralty on completion as the tanker RFA *Olalla*; renamed and served as *Laurelleaf*; oiler transport no 153, base port Devonport.
Limeleaf: 1916 acquired by the Admiralty on completion as the tanker RFA *Oligarch*; renamed and served as the tanker *Limeleaf*; oiler transport no 158, base port Devonport.
Mapleleaf: 1898 completed as Elder Dempster's *Mount Royal*; 1914 acquired by the Admiralty for service as dummy battleship HMS *Marlborough*; converted to tanker RFA *Rangol*, renamed and served as *Mapleleaf*; oiler transport no 174.
Oakleaf: 1898 completed as Elder Dempster's *Montezuma*; 1914 acquired by the Admiralty for service as dummy battleship HMS *Iron Duke*; converted to tanker RFA *Abadol*, renamed and served as *Oakleaf*; oiler transport no 172; 27 July 1917 war loss.
Palmleaf: 1916 completed for the Admiralty as the tanker RFA *Oliphant*, before entering service she was renamed *Palmleaf*; oiler transport no 152, base port Devonport; 1917 war loss.
Roseleaf: 1916 completed for the Admiralty as the tanker RFA *Califol*, before entering service she was renamed *Roseleaf*; oiler transport no 171, base port Portsmouth.
Vineleaf: 1901 completed as T & J Harrison's *Patrician*; 1914 acquired by Admiralty for service as dummy battleship HMS *Invincible*; converted into tanker RFA *Tarakol*, renamed and entered service as *Vineleaf**; oiler transport no 175, base port Portsmouth.
None of the survivors entered the post-war Admiralty fleet – seven sold to Anglo Saxon Petroleum Co Ltd (Shell Tankers), six were sold to British Tanker Co and two sold to Dutch owners.
In 1917 the Admiralty also ordered a further four tankers from the Merchant Shipbuilding Corporation, Chester, Pa, USA. These were to have been named *Autumnleaf*, *Springleaf*, *Summerleaf* and *Winterleaf*. All four were taken over while building and completed for the US Navy.
*Source PRO document MT23/658 Admiralty Transport Department.

Ex Port of London Authority hopper barges chartered
Between 1916 and 1917 the Admiralty chartered six Port of London Authority (PLA) hoppers used for working with the dredgers in London as the demand for tankers became more acute. These 204-foot single-shaft barges were powered by 3-cyl triple expansion machinery and were suitable for rapid conversion by plating over their bottom sludge door joints and by installing a pipeline and pump system. All six of the class were coal burners and upon requisition there were renamed to reflect leading parts of London on the River Thames. Between 1919–20 they were returned to the PLA and resumed their previous duties. They are recorded in official records as Royal Fleet Auxiliaries.
RFA *Battersol* (ex PLA *Hopper No 4*)
RFA *Blackol* (ex PLA *Hopper No 5*)
RFA *Greenol* (ex PLA *Hopper No 6*)
RFA *Barkol* (ex PLA *Hopper No 3*)
RFA *Purfol* (ex PLA *Hopper No 7*)
RFA *Silverol* (ex PLA *Hopper No 8*)

11 March: *Trinol* completed; renamed *Plumleaf* (1) and management transferred to Lane & MacAndrew, London.
20 March: *Gypol* completed; renamed *Pearleaf* (1) and management transferred to Lane & MacAndrew, London.
23 March: *Celerol* launched by Short Brothers Ltd, Sunderland.
24 March: *Pearleaf* ran trials.
3 April: *Dockleaf* completed and under the management of Lane & MacAndrew Ltd, London.
19 April: Damaged by enemy action – the Admiralty-tasked tanker transport *Limeleaf*, ship out of service until December 1918.
18 April: *Persol* (later to become *Cherryleaf*) runs trials.
23 April: *Belgol* launched by Irvine at West Hartlepool. *Rapidol* launched by William Gray at West Hartlepool. *Persol*, 5,900 grt, completed by Sir Raylton Dixon at Middlesborough; renamed *Cherryleaf* (1) and management transferred to Lane & MacAndrew, London. *Rumol* runs trials.
1 May: *Rumol* 5,900 grt, completed by Russell & Co at Port Glasgow; renamed *Brambleleaf* (1) and management transferred to Lane & MacAndrew, London.
10 May: *Elderol* launched by Swan Hunter & Wigham Richardson, Wallsend.
21 May: *Fortol* launched by A Macmillan & Sons, Dumbarton.

Fernleaf. Built as the Admiralty tanker *Oleander*, she was renamed and entered service under the management of Lane & MacAndrew, then sold to the British Tanker Company in 1920 and renamed *British Fern*. (World Ship Society)

Belgol class

ADMIRALTY-DESIGNED 2,000-TON CLASS TANKERS

RFA *Belgol*, RFA *Celerol*, RFA *Fortol*, RFA *Francol*, RFA *Montenol*, RFA *Prestol*, RFA *Rapidol*, RFA *Serbol*, RFA *Slavol*, RFA *Vitol*

Machinery: Steam 3 cyl triple expansion; 3,650 hp; single shaft; bunkers 320 tons; 14.5 knots; consumption 38 tpd

Dimensions (loa/bp x beam): 335/320ft x 41.5ft

Tonnage measurements: 2,647 grt, 2,226 dwt

Displacement: 5,578 tons full load **Complement:** 39

Remarks: +100A1; +LMC; heavy fuel consumption; RFA *Belgol* cost £183,757

The details are based on RFA Belgol *as built*

Celerol, launched 23 March 1917, had a long RFA career, until sold for scrap in 1958. (World Ship Society)

24 May: *Vitol* and *Slavol* launched by Greenock & Grangemouth Dockyard Co at Greenock.
30 May: War loss – the Admiralty-tasked oiler transport *Ashleaf* on passage Trinidad to the UK torpedoed and lost; cargo valued at £92,000.
31 May: *Bornol* runs trials.
1 June: *Bornol*, 5,927 grt completed by J Thomson & Sons at Sunderland; renamed *Orangeleaf* (1) and management transferred to Lane & MacAndrew, London.
3 June: Damaged by enemy action – the Admiralty-tasked oiler transport *Dockleaf* damaged by mine; ship out of service until June 1918.
9 June: *Argo* chartered by the Admiralty for service as a Q ship.
16 June: *Birchol* (1) launched by Barclay Curle & Co Ltd at Whiteinch.
19 June: *Larchol* launched by Lobnitz & Co at Renfrew.
20 June: *Olynthus* (1) laid down as *British Star*.
23 June: *Elderol*, 1,169 grt, completed by Swan Hunter & Wigham Richardson.
28 June: *Tay and Tyne* chartered by the Admiralty at a cost of £22,000 for service as a Q ship and served under the names *Cheriton* and *Dundreary*.
4 July: *Sprucol* launched by Short Brothers Ltd at Sunderland.
5 July: *Montenol* launched by William Gray & Co at West Hartlepool.
7 July: *Serbol* launched by Caledon Shipbuilding and Engineering Co, Dundee.

23 July: *Elmol* launched by Swan Hunter & Wigham Richardson at Wallsend.
17 August: *Teakol* (1) launched by Short Brothers Ltd, Sunderland.
19 August: *Larchol*, 1,162 grt, completed by Lobnitz & Co, Renfrew.
25 August: *Cherryleaf* (1) missed by torpedo in the English Channel.
27 August: *Elmol*, 1,170 grt, completed by Swan Hunter & Wigham Richardson at Newcastle.
28 August: *Rapidol*, 2,648 grt, completed by William Gray & Co, West Hartlepool.
31 August: *Fortol*, 2,629 grt, completed by A Macmillan & Son at Dumbarton.
4 September: *Prestol* launched by Napier & Miller at Old Kilpatrick.
6 September: *Pearleaf* (1) chased by a submarine off the NW coast of Scotland but managed to escape.

Hickorol, launched 30 November 1917; this hardy little tanker served the RFA until 1947 then she took on a second career as the commercial tanker *Hemsley II*. In1950 she became the Greek *Grammos* and in 1956 was renamed *Ardenza*. (World Ship Society)

10 September: *Celerol*, 2,649 grt, completed by Short Brothers Ltd at Sunderland.
12 September: *Birchol* (1), 1,115 grt, completed by Barclay, Curle at Glasgow.
22 September: *Oakol* (1) launched by William Gray & Co at West Hartlepool.
26 September: *Tay and Tyne* purchased by the Admiralty for £33,750 for service as a store ship.
27 September: *Boxol*, 1,115 grt, completed by Barclay, Curle & Co at Glasgow.
October: *Mercedes* docked at Birkenhead to discharge mercantile ratings, then to Cardiff to hand over to Messrs Rees Jones who as ship managers were to run her for the Admiralty.
4 October: *Vitol*, 2,369 grt, completed by Greenock & Grangemouth Dockyard Co at Greenock.
16 October: *Ebonol* (1) launched by Clyde Shipbuilding Co at Port Glasgow.
18 October: *Limol* launched by Lobnitz & Co, Renfrew. *Francol* launched by Earle's Shipbuilding & Engineering Co at Hull.
19 October: *Belgol*, 2,647 grt, completed by Irvine Shipbuilding at West Hartlepool.
22 October: *Olwen* (1) launched at Palmers Shipbuilding & Iron Co at Jarrow as *British Light* for the Shipping Controller.
1 November: *Slavol*, 2,622 grt, completed by Greenock & Grangemouth Dockyard Co, Greenock, for £188,714.
8 November: *Petrobus* launched by Dunlop Bremner at Port Glasgow.
10 November: *Appleleaf* (1) mined in the North Sea, but was towed into port for repairs; out of service until

'Fast Leaf' (ex *Trinol*) class

ADMIRALTY-DESIGNED 5,000 TON CLASS FLEET ATTENDANT TANKERS

RFA *Appleleaf* (1) (ex RFA *Texol*)
RFA *Brambleleaf* (1) (ex RFA *Rumol*)
RFA *Cherryleaf* (1) (ex RFA *Persol*)
RFA *Orangeleaf* (1) (ex RFA *Bornol*)
RFA *Pearleaf* (1) (ex RFA *Gysol*)
RFA *Plumleaf* (1) (ex RFA *Trinol*)

Machinery: Steam 6 cyl triple expansion, 3,650 hp; twin screw; bunkers 320 tons; 15 knots; consumption 57 tpd
Dimensions (loa/bp x beam): 426.7/405ft x 54.5ft
Tonnage measurements: 5,900 grt, 7,300 dwt
Displacement: 12,300 tons full load
Complement: 66 European/90 Lascar
Remarks: +100A1 +LMC; known in the DNC files as *Texol* class; all were designed to be fitted with stirrup method oiling-at-sea outfits; heavy fuel consumption
The details are based on RFA Appleleaf *(1) as built*

RFA *Pearleaf* (1) and her five sisters were powerful twin-screw tankers fitted with six boilers and four cargo pumps. With a pumping power of 2,000 tons per hour, for many years this was too high to be used by HM Ships. (World Ship Society)

8 April 1918.

14 November: *Palmol* launched by William Gray & Co at West Hartlepool.

20 November: *Montenol*, 2,646 grt, completed by William Gray & Co, West Hartlepool.

30 November: *Hickorol* launched by A Macmillan at Dumbarton.

12 December: *Ebonol* (1), 1,158 grt, completed by Clyde Shipbuilding Co at Port Glasgow. *Appleleaf* (ex *Texol*) undergoes trials in Belfast Lough.

14 December: *Prestol*, 2,629 grt, completed by Napier & Miller at Glasgow.

18 December: *Limol*, 1,159 grt, completed by Lobnitz & Co, Renfrew. *Francol*, 2,607 grt, completed by Earle's Shipbuilding & Engineering at Hull.

19 December: *Argo* purchased by the Admiralty.

23 December: *British Light*, 6,470 grt, (later to become *Olwen* (1) completed by Palmers Shipbuilding & Iron Co at Jarrow; main machinery 3 cyl. triple expansion by the builder, for the Shipping Controller and placed under commercial management with British Tanker Co.

24 December: Damaged by enemy action – the Admiralty-tasked oiler transport *Elmleaf* on passage Port Arthur, Texas to the UK damaged by torpedo; lost cargo valued at £24,549; ship out of service for many weeks.

1918

1918: *Sprucol*, 1,100 grt, completed by Short Brothers Ltd at Sunderland; main machinery 2 x 4 cyl internal combustion engines by Bolinder. Auxiliaries allocated pennant numbers with flag superior X.

January: *Serbol*, 2,669 grt, completed by Caledon Shipbuilding & Engineering at Dundee.

10 January: Damaged by collision at Invergordon – the Admiralty-tasked oiler transport *Fernleaf* was out of service until 25 March 1918.

24 January: *Teakol* (2), 1,137 grt, completed by Short Brothers Ltd, Sunderland.

February: *Petrobus*, 'Pet' class spirit carrier, 480 grt, completed by Dunlop, Bremner at Port Glasgow; cost £48,613.

7 February: War loss – RFA *Creosol* – 54.52N 1.11.30W (off east coast of UK) – on passage Humber to Sunderland when torpedoed by *UC17*; her cargo had been taken from double bottoms of ss *Largo Law* which had loaded at New York; value of lost cargo £3,225.

9 February: Admiralty ships, *eg* tankers, placed under commercial management were to be controlled by Director of Transports, but this department was in the event incorporated into the Ministry of Shipping.

14 February: *Olynthus* (1) launched by Swan Hunter & Wigham Richardson, Wallsend as *British Star* for the Shipping Controller.

16 February: *Petrella* launched by Dunlop Bremner at Port Glasgow.

18 February: Damaged by bad weather off Oban – the Admiralty-tasked oiler transport *Bayleaf* was out of service until 11 May 1918.

23 February: Damaged by enemy action – the Admiralty-tasked oiler transport *Birchleaf* torpedoed when on passage in the Irish Sea; ship out of service until 11 May 1918.

7 March: War loss – RFA *Vitol* – 52.37.55N 05.4.07W (Irish Sea) this tanker was on passage Liverpool to Queenstown when a U-boat, off Holyhead, torpedoed her; cargo loss valued at £17,919.

9 March: *Oakol* (1) 1,144 grt, completed by William Gray & Co at West Hartlepool.

23 March: *British Star* completed for the Shipping Controller and placed under commercial management with British Tanker Co.

26 March: Damaged by enemy action – the new Admiralty-tasked oiler transport *British Star* torpedoed off the Tyne; ship out of service until 7 September 1918.

April: *Petrella*, 'Pet' class spirit carrier, 475 grt, completed by Dunlop, Bremner at Port Glasgow; cost £48,613.

The War of Intervention

During March 1918 the Allies poured large quantities of munitions into Russia via the ports of Archangel and Vladivostok and then allied troops landed at Murmansk and Vladivostok; by November 1918 the Baltic Force conducting Royal Naval operations was having some disciplinary troubles both in its warships and amongst the civilian crews of fleet auxiliaries.

In the Mediterranean the Allies landed in the Black Sea area and the Royal Navy maintained a battle squadron supported by fleet auxiliaries in Black Sea ports and at Constantinople and other Turkish ports.

Palmol, a 1,000-ton tanker painted in dazzle camouflage; this paint scheme was first trialled on RFA *Industry*. (World Ship Society)

Petrobus, a fine example of the 500-ton 'Pet' Class of spirit carrier. (World Ship Society)

27 April: *Petronel* launched by Dunlop, Bremner at Port Glasgow.
9 May: Damaged by fire on the Clyde – the Admiralty-tasked oiler transport *Appleleaf*; 150 ton of cargo lost, ship out of service until 7 September 1918.
25 May: *Dredgol* launched to order of the Calcutta Port Commission.
28 May: *Palmol* 1,144 grt, completed by William Gray & Co at West Hartlepool.
June: *Petronel*, 'Pet' class spirit carrier, 475 grt, completed by Dunlop, Bremner at Port Glasgow; cost £48,146. *Dredgol*, 4,614 grt, completed by William Simons & Co at Renfrew; acquired by the Admiralty and

Miscellaneous RFA vessels

Official Lists of RFAs, such as the Ministry of Shipping's Service Lists of April 1919 and January 1921 show that the Royal Fleet Auxiliary was involved with the following vessels. However, little to no information is actually available on what they are or what they did. The following examples are listed in alphabetical order and where known their pennant number (flag superior X) is shown.

Bison: shown in the Service List as having served as a RFA store vessel.
Blackstone: 15 October 1915–1921 hired by the Admiralty for service as a 148 grt oil carrier; pennant no X01, served as RFA.
Buffalo: built 1916, Admiralty service as a mooring vessel; pennant no X42, served as RFA.
Bullfrog: 1915–23 purchased by the Admiralty for service as a salvage vessel; pennant no X03, served as RFA.
Dapper: 1915–23 Admiralty service as a salvage vessel; pennant no X30, service as RFA.
Fidget: purchased by Admiralty, shown in Service List as having served as RFA.
Limpet: 1912 launched; 298 grt, 112ft length x 31.5ft beam; 1915 purchased by the Admiralty for service as a mooring vessel; pennant no X18, served as RFA; May 1922 sold and renamed *T I C Limpet*.
Victorious: 4,000-ton vessel shown in the Service List as having served as RFA 22 February 1916.
Waterwitch: built 1915, 584 grt shown in Service List as having served as RFA.
Wave: built 1915, purchased by Admiralty, 582 grt shown in Service List as having served as RFA.

Miscellaneous salvage vessels

The acute shortage of salvage vessels during the First World War caused the Admiralty to convert a number of old composite sloops and gunboats for this purpose. Being of composite construction, their hulls were sturdy and it was a relatively straightforward matter to replace their elderly machinery. The Liverpool Salvage Association had used two ex-naval gunboats *Ranger* and *Limpet* for some years; the success of these conversions provided the inspiration. Three *Mariner* class sloops – *Mariner*, *Racer* and *Reindeer* – were taken in hand for conversion in November 1915. At the same time, the two smaller gunboats, *Thrush* and *Melita,* were also taken in hand. Official Lists of RFAs show that the Royal Fleet Auxiliary was involved with their manning when operationally under Admiralty control, for example:

Racer: 6 August 1884 launched by HM Dockyard, Devonport as HMS *Racer*; 633 grt, steam 3 cyl triple expansion by Hawthorn Leslie, single shaft, 12 knots; June 1917 taken in hand for conversion into a salvage vessel; 1920–5 participated in the successful salvaging of gold from the White Star liner *Laurentic* (14,892grt/1908) which had been sunk in 1917; only 25 bars out of a total of 3,211 were not recovered; during this operation she was an RFA; 1925 placed on the sale list; 6 November 1928 sold to Hughes Bolckow & co, for breaking-up at Blyth.

Melita: 30 April 1888 launched by HM Dockyard, Devonport as HMS *Ringdove*; 421 grt, steam 3 cyl triple expansion by builders, single shaft, 13 knots; November 1915 taken in hand for conversion into a salvage vessel; 7 December 1915 renamed *Melita*; 22 January 1920 sold to Ship Salvage Corporation, Plymouth (J R Delaney, manager), renamed *Telima*.

converted into a tanker.

30 June: *Oligarch* launched by Workman, Clark & Co at Belfast as *British Lantern* for the Shipping Controller.

10 July: Damaged by enemy action – RFA *Sprucol* torpedoed at 54.24N 0.25E; 950 tons cargo lost, docked at Hull and out of action for over four months.

1 August: *British Lantern* completed for the Shipping Controller and placed under commercial management with British Tanker Co.

14 August: *Aro* becomes a troopship.

15 August: *Mercedes* serves as an Expeditionary Force Transport.

9 September: *Olcades* launched by Workman, Clark & Co, Belfast as *British Beacon* for the Shipping Controller.

Miscellaneous requisitions and purchases

Some official lists marked as 'List of RFAs' show a number of vessels as having spent some time rated as Royal Fleet Auxiliaries during the First World War. These records are extremely sketchy and some of these vessels were 'Yard Craft', partially or wholly Dockyard-manned, partly by RNR or Reserve Fleet personnel. Some of the depot ships staffed by skilled civilian Dockyard workers were for a time White Ensign. The Director of Stores was understood to have been concerned with their manning and operationally they remained under Admiralty control. Examples:

Aro: 9 May 1898 launched by Sir Raylon Dixon & Co, Middlesborough as *Eboe* for Elder Dempster & Co, Liverpool; completed as passenger ship *Albertville*; 1904 renamed *Aro*; 3,794 grt, steam 3 cyl triple expansion by T Richardson & Sons Ltd, Hartlepool, single screw, 13 knots; October 1914 purchased by Admiralty for conversion into a submarine depot ship retaining the name *Aro*; 1915–18 based at Rosyth.

City of Oxford: 15 June 1882 launched by Barclay, Curle, Whiteinch as *City of Oxford* for City Line, Glasgow; 4,019 grt, steam 3 cyl triple expansion by the builders, single screw; 1901 acquired by Ellerman Lines, London; October 1914 purchased by Admiralty for service as the dummy battleship HMS *St Vincent*; 1915 based at Scapa Flow before conversion Harland & Wolff into a kite balloon ship; 1919 resold to Ellerman & Bucknall Steamship Co, London.

Delphinula: 1908 completed by Armstrong, Whitworth, Newcastle for H E Moss & Co, London, but sold on completion to Toyo KK, Tokyo and renamed *Buyo Maru*; 5,238 grt; steam 3 cyl triple expansion by North Eastern Marine Engineering; the tanker was acquired by Anglo-Saxon Petroleum Co on behalf of the Admiralty, renamed *Delphinula*; 1936 reduced to fuel hulk at Alexandria, later Gibraltar; October 1946 sold for breaking up in Spain.

Crenella: 17 May 1897 launched by Palmers Shipbuilding & Iron Co, Jarrow as *Montcalm* for African Steamship Co, Liverpool; 5,508 grt, steam 3 cyl triple expansion by builders, single screw, 13 knots; August 1914 requisitioned for government service; converted into dummy battleship HMS *Audacious*; 19 January 1916 purchased by Admiralty and management allocated to Frederick Leyland, Liverpool for service as a store ship; 12 August 1916 ordered to Graysons Dock, Liverpool for conversion into a tanker; 26 October 1916 conversion completed, management transferred to Anglo Saxon Petroleum Co, London; 18 November 1916 renamed *Crenella*; 11 October 1917 ownership transferred to the Shipping Controller; 26 November 1919 sold to Anglo Saxon Petroleum Co, London.

Sobo: 29 September 1898 launched by Barclay, Curle & Co, Whiteinch as the passenger ship *Sobo* for African Steamship Co, Liverpool (Elder Dempster & Co, managers); 3,652 grt, steam 3 cyl. triple expansion, single screw, 12.5 knots; 1915 purchased by the Admiralty for £55,000 for conversion into a spare torpedo depot ship for the Grand Fleet at Crombie; 12 February 1920 sold to Soc Anon Les Affreteurs Reunis, Paris and renamed *Jupiter*.

RFA *Delphinula*: this unconventional-looking tanker was operated by Toyo Kisen Kaisha of Tokyo as the *Buyo Maru* before being acquired for the Admiralty in 1918. (ANRS)

Sokoto: 25 February 1899 launched by Vickers Sons & Maxim, Barrow as the passenger ship *Sokoto* for British and African Steamship Co, Liverpool (Elder Dempster & Co, managers); 2,092 grt, steam 3 cyl triple expansion by builder, single shaft, 12 knots; 26 October 1915 purchased by the Admiralty for conversion into a submarine depot ship for service at Scapa Flow; 29 July 1919 sold to Cia Naviera Sevillana SA, Seville for £95,000, renamed *Tableda*.

11 September: *Pearleaf* (1) missed by torpedo in the North Sea.
9 October: *British Beacon* completed for the Shipping Controller and placed under commercial management with British Tanker Co.
11 October: *War Afridi* launched by R Duncan & Co, Port Glasgow for the Shipping Controller.
18 October: *Industry* (1) torpedoed while under escort by the armed trawler *Persian Empire* but made it back to port.
4 November: *War Bahadur* launched.
11 November: Armistice – hostilities cease at 11.00am.
December: *War Bahadur*, 5,559 grt, completed by Armstrong, Whitworth at Newcastle for the Shipping Controller.
5 December: *War Sepoy* launched by William Gray & Co at West Hartlepool for the Shipping Controller.

Prizes (allocated under The Naval Prize Acts 1864 to 1916)

Some official lists show a number of vessels as having spent some time rated as Royal Fleet Auxiliaries during the First World War. These records are extremely sketchy and some of these vessels were 'Yard Craft', partially or wholly Dockyard-manned, partly by RNR or Reserve Fleet personnel. The Director of Stores was understood to have been concerned with their manning and operationally after being allocated to the Admiralty they remained under Admiralty control.

Hungerford: 15 February 1913 launched by Weser Actien Gesellschaft 'Weser', Bremen as *Lauterfels* for Deutsche Dampschiffahrts-Gesellschaft Hansa, Bremen; 5,811 grt, steam 3 cyl triple expansion by builders, single shaft, 11 knots; August 1914 detained at Port Said; 22 January 1915 detention confirmed by the Prize Court; allocated to the Admiralty and renamed *Hungerford*, under management of Grahams, London; 28 July 1915 became RFA distilling ship; 22 June 1917 became collier *Y3.1687*; 1918 management transferred to George Heyn & Sons, Belfast; 16 April 1918 war loss.

Polavon: 18 November 1905 launched by Flensburger Schiffsbau Gesellschaft, Flensburg as *Gutenfels* for Deutsche Dampschiffahrts-Gesellschaft Hansa, Bremen; 5,576 grt, steam 4 cyl quadruple expansion by the builders, single screw, 10 knots; August 1914 captured by the Royal Navy, taken to Port Said, allocated to the Admiralty by the Prize Court, renamed *Polavon* for service as a distilling ship under management of Grahams & Co, London; 1915 management transferred to Anglo Saxon Petroleum Co, London; September 1916 allocated for conversion to a tanker, send to Hong Kong for conversion; 15 December 1916 damaged by fire prior to running trials; renamed *Turritella*; 27 February 1917 when on passage Tarakan, Borneo to Port Said with a cargo of fuel she was captured by the German auxiliary cruiser *Wolf*, prize crew placed aboard and renamed *Iltis*; 5 March 1917 intercepted by HMS *Odin* in the Red Sea and scuttled by her crew.

Polgowan: 15 June 1900 launched by Swan & Hunter Ltd, Wallsend as *Macedonia* for A C de Freitas & Co, Hamburg; taken over by Hamburg Amerika Line as one of the 14 ships in the de Freitas Fleet; 4,358 grt, steam 3 cyl triple expansion by North Eastern Marine Engineering, Wallsend, single shaft, 12 knots; 28 March 1915 captured off Las Palmas by the Royal Navy; allocated to the Admiralty by the Prize Court, renamed *Polgowan* for service as a fleet messenger; 23 February 1917 became a mercantile collier (*Y3.1499*) under management of A W Pickard, London; 1919 ceded to Great Britain (Shipping Controller) and placed under management of Union Castle Mail Steamship Co, London; 1920 sold to A Rappoport, London.

Polmont: 29 August 1912 launched by W Dobson & Co, Newcastle as *Karpat* for Hungarian Levant Steamship Co, Budapest; 4,478 grt, steam 3 cyl triple expansion by North Eastern Marine Engineering, Wallsend, single shaft; August 1914 seized at South Shields, 1915 allocated to the Admiralty, renamed *Polmont* and placed under management of Everett & Newbiggin, Newcastle; 13 March 1916 serving as a water carrier; 30 April 1916 became a collier; 1916 management transferred to Raeburn & Verel, Glasgow, renamed *Polish Monarch*; 1921 sold to Soc di Nav Marittima 'Levante', Fiume.

Polshannon: 7 June 1910 launched by J C Tecklenborg A G, Geestemunde as *Birkenfels* for Deutsche Dampschiffahrts-Gesellschafft Hansa, Bremen; 6,126 grt, steam 4 cyl quadruple expansion, single shaft, 10 knots; 20 August 1915 taken at Cape Town, renamed *Tandem* under management of Federal Steam Navigation Co, London; 3 September 1915 renamed *Polshannon* by the Shipping Controller and used as an tanker; 1919 management transferred to Anglo Saxon Petroleum Co, London 1920 sold to Anglo Saxon Petroleum Co, London.

Princetown: 21 August 1902 launched by Bremer Vulkan Schiffbau & Maschinenfabrik, Vegesack as *Prins Adalbert*, a passenger ship for Hamburg-Amerikanische Packetfahrt A G, Hamburg; 6,060 grt, steam 2 x 4 cyl quadruple expansion by builders, twin shaft, 12.5 knots; 4 August 1914 seized at Falmouth and placed under the management of Gillatly, Hankey & Co, London; 17 December 1914 brought into service as an accommodation ship at Invergordon and then converted for use as a repair ship; January 1916 renamed *Princetown*; 17 January 1917 purchased by H Clarkson & Co, London for £152,00, on behalf of Cie Nav Sud Atlantique, Paris, renamed *Alesia*; 6 September 1917 war loss.

The prefixes 'Hun' *and* 'Pol' *were allocated to enemy ships taken as prizes or condemned by the Prize Court.*

CHAPTER 3

Between the Wars, 1919–1938

1919

1919: Official end of the First World War with the Treaty of Versailles. *Industry* (1) disposed of. *Perthshire* converted into an oiler and proceeded to Malta for service as a mobile fuel hulk. *Santa Margherita* sold commercially, renamed *Marinula*. *Ruthenia* converted into an oiler. *Kurumba* handed over to the Australian Navy.

6 February: *War Sepoy*, 5,557 grt, completed by William Gray & Co at West Hartlepool for the Shipping Controller; placed under commercial management with Hunting and Sons, London.

March: Archangel River Expedition – RFA *Bacchus* (1) allocated as a tender to repair ship HMS *Cyclops*.

2 March: The repair ship *Reliance* pays off at Devonport, sold by Ministry of Shipping for £305,000.

19 March: *War Pathan* launched.

16 April: *Argo* re-enters service as a coastal store carrier.

May: *War Pathan*, 5,800 grt, completed by Sir James Laing & Sons at Sunderland for the Shipping Controller; placed under commercial management with Andrew Weir & Co, London.

13 June: *War Nawab* launched.

28 June: *War Diwan* launched.

August: *War Nawab*, 5,800 grt, completed by Palmers Co Ltd at Jarrow for the Shipping Controller; placed under commercial management with British Tanker Co. *War Nizam* launched.

21 August: *War Diwan*, 5,800 grt, completed by Lithgow's Ltd at Port Glasgow for the Shipping Controller; placed under commercial management with C T Bowring & Co, London.

30 September: *War Hindoo* launched.

October: *War Hindoo*, 5,800 grt, completed by W Hamilton & Co Ltd at Port Glasgow for the Shipping Controller; placed under commercial management with Gow Harrison & Co, Glasgow. *War Nizam*, 5,800 grt, completed by Palmers Co Ltd, at Jarrow for the Shipping Controller; placed under commercial management with British Tanker Co.

9 October: *War Methar* launched.

24 October: *War Krishna* launched.

11 November: *War Afridi* launched.

24 November: *War Bharata* launched.

26 November: *War Krishna*, 5,800 grt, completed by Swan Hunter & Wigham Richardson at Wallsend for the Shipping Controller; only ship

Radio on RFAs

Wireless telegraphers (also known as 'Sparks') from the RNVR/RNR served on RFA vessels during the First World War. They generally operated installations formed from RN W/T equipment. It is known that prior to the First World War the oiler RFA *Petroleum* was fitted with Admiralty-owned and operated equipment. The operator, W J Leighton, is believed to have served on this one ship for around 16 years. Following the First World War civilian W/T operators gradually replaced the wartime RNVR/RNR telegraphists. It became the practice for the non-RN W/T installations to be supplied from Marconi International Marine Radio Co, on a hire and maintenance agreement. While some RFAs carried Marconi operators, the Admiralty increased direct recruitment. These Wireless Telegraphic operators (W/T operators) were responsible for operating and maintained all of a ship's radio equipment and associated power supply units and aerial systems. However, in some ships, *eg* 'British' group and those still under commercial management, the Marconi Company provided trained W/T operators. RFA *Olna*, built in 1921, carried RN W/T equipment and the operator was an employee of the management company Davies & Newman. It is understood RFA staff later replaced him.

Operators served under National Maritime Board (NMB) conditions. Admiralty Fleet Order P162/1940 instructed modifications to the RFA Handbook (BR 875) including replacing the term W/T operator with 'Radio Officer'. They were represented by the Radio Officers Union (formerly the Association of Wireless Telegraphists) and later the Radio and Electrical Officers Union.

War Nawab: one of a new class of tankers that were laid down towards the end of the Great War, they formed the backbone of the RFA's inter-war freighting services. (World Ship Society)

RFA *War Brahmin*, the only one of her class to be built with patent davits. (World Ship Society)

Tanker Company. *Tay and Tyne* renamed *Industry* (2). *Barkol, Battersol, Blackol, Greenol, Purfol, Silverol* – charters ended, all returned to Port of London Authority and reverted to their original names.

January: *Nucula* stated to be in poor condition, recommended for disposal by the Director of Transport; Admiralty approved expenditure of £50,000 to refit her for retention, and she was purchased on their behalf by Anglo Saxon Petroleum Co Ltd and placed under their management.

Articles of Agreement
The National Maritime Board agreement entered into by the Master of a merchant ship, hence RFA, with his officers and crew. Approved by the Board of Trade and its successors, these contain conditions of employment, wages, period of time, limits of voyages at sea etc. The contracting parties sign in front of a Superintendent of Merchant Marine, for example:

Eng1 – foreign-going ships single voyage not exceeding two years or running agreements for two months.

Eng4 – home trade and coasting vessels of 200 grt and over, harbour and coastal vessels.

Eng6 – home trade and coasting vessels under 200 grt.

Chinese Hong Kong Eng1 – approved by Hong Kong Government, single voyage not exceed two years.

National Maritime Board (NMB)
Set up by the Ministry of Shipping during the First World War to look at and monitor the conditions of employment in Merchant Shipping, it proved to be such a success that in 1919 it was decided to continue it. Administered by a permanent independent staff, it was financed by a levy on shipowners and seafarers representatives including masters, merchant officers and seamen including RFA.

The Merchant Navy Establishment was set up as a result of the NMB and comprised a series of officers around the UK that were tasked with providing employment to registered British seafarers. The NMB's objective was to provide a form of machinery for joint negotiations between owners and seafarers, regarding pay, leave and travelling expenses of British seafarers. However, with the contraction of the British Merchant Navy the Board was run down and ceased in September 1990. By this time 90 per cent of RFA personnel were serving under company service contracts and RFA pay and conditions were determined by MoD in conjunction with HM Treasury.

of her class to have her machinery and funnel aft; placed under commercial management with Davies and Newman, London.

28 November: *War Brahmin* launched.

3 December: Admiralty-tasked tanker *Appleleaf* grounded on passage Libau to Copenhagen.

6 December: *War Sirdar* launched.

17 December: *Reliance* handed over to purchaser Salvatore ea Emanuele Fratelli Accami, Genoa, renamed *Emmanuelle Accame*.

29 December: *War Pindari* launched.

1920

1920: First Technical Adviser to the Director of Stores (later this post was to become known as Marine Superintendent), Commander W Gregory RNR appointed. Navy Estimates make provision in Vote 3 for two naval hospital ships. *British Beacon, British Lantern, British Light* and *British Star* transferred to Admiralty ownership, all remained under management of British

4 January: *Aro* sold to W R Davies, Liverpool for £40,000.

10 January: *Canning* sold to J Vassilou, Piraeus for £100,000 for further commercial service.

24 January: *Teakol* (1) sold commercially and renamed *San Dario*.

27 January: *War Bahadur* in collision with Greek ss *Athena* at Port Said.

29 January: *War Afridi*, 5,800 grt, completed by R Duncan & Co at Port Glasgow for the Shipping Controller; placed under commercial management with C T Bowring, Liverpool. *Ferol* sold commercially and renamed *Osage*. *Oakol* (1) sold commercially and renamed *Orthis*. *Palmol* sold commercially and renamed *Invercorrie*.

British Light, later RFA *Olwen* (1). (World Ship Society)

February: *War Brahmin*, 5,800 grt, completed by Lithgow's Ltd at Port Glasgow for the Shipping Controller; placed under commercial management with C T Bowring, Liverpool. *War Sirdar*, 5,800 grt, completed by Sir James Laing & Sons Ltd at Sunderland for the Shipping Controller; placed under commercial management with Hunting & Sons, London.

March: *War Pindari*, 5,800 grt, completed by Lithgow's Ltd at Port Glasgow for the Shipping Controller; placed under commercial management with C T Bowring, London.

2 March: *War Methar*, 5,800 grt, completed by Armstrong Whitworth & Co at Newcastle for the Shipping Controller; placed under commercial management with Hunting & Sons Ltd, London.

18 March: *War Sudra* launched. *Innisjura*, water carrier, sold to Renhold J Frisk, Cardiff, name unchanged.

20 March: *War Bharata*, 5,800 grt, completed by Palmers Co Ltd, at Jarrow for the Shipping Controller; placed under commercial management with C T Bowring, Liverpool; transferred to Admiralty ownership, placed under commercial management.

31 March: *Sprucol* sold commercially and renamed *Juniata*.

21 April: *Innisulva*, water carrier, sold to Renhold J Frisk, Cardiff, name unchanged.

May: *War Sudra*, 5,800 grt, completed by Palmers Co Ltd, at Jarrow for the Shipping Controller; placed under commercial management with British Tanker Co, London.

14 May: *Aquarius* sold commercially for £60,000 and renamed *Santi*.

14 June: *Olna* (1) laid down.

19 July: *Innisinver*, water carrier, sold to Stick-Diesel Oil Engines Ltd on behalf of Alexander Ferguson, London for £3,800, name unchanged.

28 July: *Mercedes* sold commercially for £27,500, name unchanged.

RFA *Berbice*

NAVAL HOSPITAL SHIP

Pennant: –
Official number: 124676
Port of registry: London
Callsign: –
Builder: Harland & Wolff, Belfast (yard no 405)
Machinery: Steam quadruple expansion by builder, 1,450 ihp; twin screw; 13 knots
Dimensions (loa/bp x beam): 300.7/–ft x 38.2ft
Tonnage measurements: 2,379 grt, 1,225 dwt
Displacement: –
Complement: RFA + medical

The naval hospital ship RFA *Berbice*. (ANRS)

Remarks: +100A1 +LMC; commercial design luxury liner; 6 May 1909 launched; July 1909 completed for the Royal Mail Steam Packet Co; 4 December 1915 requisitioned for service as a military hospital ship on T97 charter to 20 August 1920; August 1920 recognised by the International Committee of the Red Cross as a naval hospital ship ICRC No 18; 1920 purchased by Admiralty for service as a hospital ship; 1922 sold as part of defence cuts.

August: ss *Berbice* purchased by the Admiralty for service as RFA *Berbice*, hospital ship.

October: Admiralty purchases ss *Panama*, renames her *Maine* (3) for service as an RFA-crewed naval hospital ship; estimated cost of purchase and conversion £225,435, actual expenditure up to 31 March 1922 £276,453.

14 October: *Innisshannon*, water carrier, handed over to the Disposal Board.

24 November: *Innisfree*, water carrier, sold to A/S Trafikant (P Einarsen and M Anderson, managers), Bergen for £1,213, renamed *Nutta*.

1 December: *Oleander* (2) laid down.

RFA *Perthshire*

SUPPLY SHIP

Pennant: X05/X48 — **Official number:** 102638

Port of registry: London — **Callsign:** GSDM

Builder: Hawthorn Leslie, Hebbum

Machinery: Steam 3 cyl triple expansion by builder; 2 Scotch boilers; 1,450 ihp; 1,600 ton bunkers; 10 knots

Dimensions (loa/bp x beam): 430/–ft x 54ft

Tonnage measurements: 5,851 grt, 7,225 dwt

Displacement: – — **Complement:** 69

Remarks: +100A1 +LMC commercial design liner; 28 October 1914 requisitioned by the Admiralty; 3 September 1915 purchased by the Admiralty and converted into a water tanker; June 1920 Malta tanker and stores carrier to the Bosphorus with RFA crew; 1923 hulked at Malta as an oil store with 3,607 tons and 800 tons coal; 1924/25 reconditioned and fitted out at Malta Dockyard as a fleet stores for naval/victualling stores with distilling capacity; 26 February 1934 sold Soc Anon Cantiere di Portovenera, Spezia for breaking up.

1921

1921: First Technical Assistant (later known as Engineer Superintendent), Mr J Brown appointed. Centralised storekeeping introduced and remained the standard type of ship racking, *ie* pigeonholes, until replaced by in the 1960s by Moore's Adjustable Storage Cabinets, system evolved over a number of years by Naval Store Department Staff. *War Afridi*, *War Bahadur*, *War Bharata*, *War Diwan*, *War Krishna*, *War Hindoo*, *War Nawab*, *War Nizam*, *War Pathan*, *War Pindari*, *War Sepoy*, *War Sirdar* and *War Sudra* transferred to Admiralty ownership, all remaining under commercial management. *Perthshire* converted into a stores ship at Malta; used to carry naval stores to the Bosphorus

Management of the RFA

In October 1921 all duties in connection with RFA oilers, RFAS *Bacchus*, *Berbice* and *Maine* were transferred to the Director of Stores at the Admiralty. The general system of management, pay rates and conditions evolved by the Ministry of Shipping and taken over from them by the Admiralty.

RFA *Maine* (3)

NAVAL HOSPITAL SHIP

Pennant: – — **Official number:** 115276

Port of registry: London — **Callsign:** GRQM

Builder: Fairfield Shipbuilding & Engineering Co, Govan (yard no 419)

Machinery: Steam 3 cyl triple expansion by builders; single shaft; 13 knots

Dimensions (loa/bp x beam): 401.2/–ft x 52.3ft

Tonnage measurements: 6,599 grt, – dwt

Displacement: – — **Complement:** RFA + medical

The elegant hospital ship RFA *Maine* (3), formerly the Pacific Steam Navigation Company's passenger ship *Panama*. (ANRS)

Remarks: +100A1; +LMC commercial designed passenger ship *Panama* for Pacific Steam Navigation Co, Liverpool; May 1902 completed, maiden voyage Liverpool – Valparaiso; 1915 chartered by the Admiralty for service as a naval hospital ship; October 1920 purchased by the Admiralty and renamed *Maine* (3); July 1935 had her hospital ship colours removed (with ICRC permission) to take part in the Silver Jubilee Fleet Review at Spithead; 22 October damaged by mines in Corfu channel; 21 February 1947 paid off; 8 July 1948 arrived Bo'ness for scrapping by McClellan & Sons.

(Constantinople) during the Allied occupation. Oiling at sea – trials by RFA *Francol* with cruiser HMS *Cairo*.

January: *Servitor* for disposal at Sheerness.

23 February: *Innisshannon* sold to Max S Hilton, London for £5,250, name unchanged.

9 March: Hospital ship *Maine* underwent inclining experiments at Portsmouth Dockyard.

21 June: *Olna* (1) launched.

16 July: Disabled by grounding – the Admiralty-tasked tanker *Pearleaf*, grounded off Borneo; 1,333 tons of oil jettisoned; docked Singapore; no damage.

Merchant Navy uniforms

The standard Merchant Navy Uniform – Order in Council of 13 December 1921 authorised the standard uniform for the British Mercantile Marine. Based on the Mercantile Marine (Uniforms) Order 1918 and the British Mercantile marine Uniform Act 1919 – this order introduced distinctive lace and specialisation colours, for example – purple for engineers, pale green for electricians, scarlet for ship's surgeons and white for pursers. There is no firm record of when the RFA adopted the 'diamond'.

'War' class

STANDARD DESIGN TANKERS

RFA *War Afridi*	RFA *War Bahadur*	RFA *War Bharata*
RFA *War Brahmin*	RFA *War Diwan*	RFA *War Hindoo*
RFA *War Krishna*	RFA *War Mehtar*	RFA *War Nawab*
RFA *War Nizam*	RFA *War Pathan*	RFA *War Pindari*
RFA *War Sepoy*	RFA *War Sirdar*	RFA *War Sudra*

Machinery: One 3 cyl triple expansion by Rankin & Blackmore, Greenock; 3 Scotch boilers; single screw; 3,000 bhp; bunkers 700 tons; 11.5 knots; consumption 24 tpd

Dimensions (loa/bp x beam): 410/400.3ft x 52.2ft

Tonnage measurements: 5,574 grt, 8,320 dwt

Displacement: 11,680 tons full load **Complement:** 44

RFA *War Pathan* was operated under the management of Andrew Weir & Co and for a time was painted in their colours; 1947 sold to P Bauer and renamed *Basingbank*. (World Ship Society)

Remarks: +100A1 +LMC +RMC, cost £218,725 for Ministry of Shipping, and placed under the management of C T Bowring & Co, Liverpool as oiler transport 337 under Admiralty ownership; 22 April 1937 management transferred to the Admiralty (Director of Stores); July 1943 fitted with tanks in forward hold for pumps for diesel oil – 120 tons; 1946 at Hong Kong as a floating depot; October 1947 for service as harbour tanker on Yard Craft status' 1958 broken up.

The 'War' class were not identical; details are based on RFA War Afridi *as built.*

RFA *Olna* (1), built and engined at Devonport Dockyard in 1921 and placed under the management of Davies & Newman until 1936. (World Ship Society)

9 September: *Isla* sold commercially and renamed *Pass of Brander*.

27 October: *Olna* (1), 7,023 grt, completed by HM Naval Dockyard, Devonport for the Admiralty; placed under commercial management with Davies and Newman Ltd.

7 November: *Olcades* damaged HMS *Renown* when fuelling her at Suez.

10 December: Admiralty-tasked tanker *War Afridi* in collision with SS *Bogota* at Old Kilpatrick.

1922

1922: British ships based in Istanbul – Mediterranean Fleet held authority

Oleander (1) was built by HM Dockyard Pembroke and engined by HM Dockyard Chatham as part of the Government's post-war policy to retain employment in the dockyards. (World Ship Society)

'Ol' class

ADMIRALTY-DESIGNED 10,000-TON TANKERS

[ex 'British' group]

RFA *Olcades* (ex *British Beacon*)
RFA *Oligarch* (2) (ex *British Lantern*)
RFA *Olynthus* (1) (ex *British Star*)
RFA *Oleander* (1)
RFA *Olna* (1)
RFA *Olwen* (1) (ex *British Light*)

Machinery: Steam 3 cyl triple expansion by builders; 3 Scotch boilers; 3,100 bhp; single shaft; 11 knots
Dimensions (loa/bp x beam): –/419.7ft x 54.3ft
Tonnage measurements: 6,470 grt, 9,220 dwt
Displacement: 13,690 tons full load **Complement:** 43

British Lantern, later RFA *Oligarch.* (World Ship Society)

Remarks: +100A1; +LMC, these six large ocean-going tankers were approximately of the same dimensions, although not sister-ships; *Olwen* was ordered as *British Light* for the British Tanker Co (BTC); completed for the Shipping Controller for £191,789 under BTC management; 1922 acquired by the Admiralty and remained under BTC management; 17 April 1937 management transferred to the Admiralty, renamed RFA *Olwen*; 1948 sold to Esmalilji Abdulhusein Co, Karachi and renamed *Mushtari*; 1961 broken up.
Details are based on RFA Olwen *as built*

in the straits from the Black Sea to Gallipoli and in particular at Istanbul and Chanak (Bosphorus). *Thermol* and *Mixol* had unsatisfactory stability and both were laid up in drydock at Gibraltar until 1935. *War Sepoy* carried the first cargo of oil to the new storage tanks at Singapore. *Nucula* transferred from Anglo Saxon Petroleum Co Ltd to Admiralty management, service at Hong Kong. *Appleleaf* (1), *Cherryleaf* (1), *Orangeleaf* (1), *Pearleaf* (1) and *Plumleaf* (1) laid up in reserve at Rosyth until 1926. *Brambleleaf* (1) in reserve at Gibraltar until 1925. *Servitor* sold commercially for £5,000, and renamed *Puloe Brani.*

February: *Berbice* to be relieved in Mediterranean Station by *Maine* on completion of latter; *Berbice* to be paid off for disposal.

26 April: *Oleander* (2) launched.

June: *Nucula* acquired by the Admiralty for service as an oiler on the China Station.

20 October: *Oleander* (2), 7,048 grt, completed by HM Naval Dockyard, Pembroke for the Admiralty; placed under commercial management with Davies and Newman Ltd; she had been built with 'odds and ends' of cheap fittings and second-hand machinery; her main engine bed plate was permanently cracked; one of the most unpopular ships in the RFA.

25 November: *London Importer* (later to become RFA *Reliant* (1)) launched.

1923

1923: RFA *Petroleum* freighting and fleet attendant duties Gibraltar and Malta. RFAs *Trefoil* and *Turmoil* (1) were mechanically unsatisfactory and laid up in reserve at Rosyth until 1935. Oiling at sea – trials RFA *Prestol* towing RFA *Carol.*

6 February: *War Methar* fouled with the Italian *Presidente Wilson* at Gibraltar and was badly damaged.

April: *Perthshire* finally leaves the Bosphorus (Constantinople), returns to Malta.

1 September: Humanitarian relief – RFA *Nucula* ordered to Nagasaki to act as base oiler during the Yokohama earthquake relief operations.

October: *Kharki* badly damaged in a typhoon at Hong Kong.

December: *London Importer* completed by Furness Shipbuilding at Haverton Hill on Tees for Furness Line for employment on the 'banana trade'.

11 December: *War Brahmin* slightly damaged in a collision with HM Ships *Delhi* and *Danae* when fuelling the Special Service Squadron off Sierra Leone; she then proceeded Trinidad for a cargo and then Devonport for discharge and repair.

27 December: The Admiralty tanker *British Lantern* damaged when fuelling HMS *Hood* at Capetown.

1924

1924: *Petroleum* towed an oil barge built at Chatham Naval Dockyard and carried the first cargo of oil fuel to the tanks at Port Stanley, Falkland Islands; prior to this the Falklands had been a coaling station. *Perthshire* commences reconditioning as the Mediterranean Fleet's supply ship for refrigerated and general stores. *Nucula* fuelled ships of the Special Service Squadron led by HMS *Hood* on world tour and accompanied them to Australia and New Zealand

27 May: *Nucula* was converted at a cost of £2,500 for European crewing and transferred to New Zealand government for service as a naval oiler at a rate of £6,500 per annum.

16 September: *Industry* (2) (ex *Tay and Tyne*) for sale as lies at Chatham.

30 September: Admiralty Conference on Armament of Oilers, held by Trade Division of the Naval Staff.

30 October: *Industry* (2) sold commercially to C A Bland & Son, London SW1 on behalf of Mr James Kell, Sunderland for £2,610, and renamed *Morejarl 1*.

Oil Board (1925–1939)

A sub-committee of the Committee of Imperial Defence (CID), the Oil Fuel Board (or Oil Board as it was known) was set up in March 1925 on the advice of the Principal Supply Officers of the Armed Forces. Under the chairmanship of Admiralty's Civil Lord, it comprised representatives of the armed services, Foreign Office, Board of Trade, HM Treasury and Scientific and Industrial Research Department. Its task was to keep the question of oil and tanker requirements under review – the control and allocation of oil supplies.

Once a year the Board reported to the CID on political, economic and technological developments in the oil industry. For example in November 1934 it was asked to prepare supply plans for a European war, with target date of 1 January 1940; March 1935 it set up a sub-committee called the Tanker Tonnage Committee. For most of its information the Oil Board looked to the Board of Trade (BoT) Sea Transport Department.

1925

1925: *Francol* has the lower portion of her fore hold fitted as a temporary magazine.

1926

1926: *William Scoresby*, research ship, launched by Cook, Welton & Gemmel Ltd, Beverly (yard no 477) for the government of the Falklands Islands. *Appleleaf* (1), *Cherryleaf* (1), *Pearleaf* (1) and *Plumleaf* (1) on commercial charter until 1930. *Orangeleaf* (1) on commercial charter until 1935. *Attendant* in reserve at Rosyth until 1935. *Burma* placed in reserve at Rosyth. *Celerol* in reserve at Rosyth until 1935. Oiling at sea – trials conducted between HMS *Ramillies* and RFA *Brambleaf* with the hose-hawser method; trials conducted with *Belgol* with the trough method.

January: *War Pathan* struck submerged wreckage *en route* to Trinidad; top of propeller knocked off.

April: *War Methar* comes under in-house Admiralty (Director of Stores) management as an RFA.

1927

1927: *Ruthenia* is laid up at Singapore with worn-out boilers; converted for service as an oil fuel jetty and pumping station at Woodlands Naval Oil Fuel Jetty. *Prestol* at Portland received a ship's library from the British Sailors' Society and arrangements were made for other RFAs to receive one.

30 June: The tanker *Berta* launched.

14 July: *Berta* completed by Harland & Wolff, Belfast (yard no 798) for Anglo Saxon Petroleum Co Ltd, London transferred upon completion to N V Curacaosche Scheepvaart Maatschappij, Willemstad.

1928

6 January: *Carol* placed in reserve at Rosyth until 1935. *Racer*, salvage vessel, sold by competitive tender as lies Portsmouth, to Hughs Bolckow Shipbreakers, Blyth for £5,955.

April: Humanitarian relief – *Perthshire* despatched from the UK with relief supplies for the victims of the Corinth earthquake.

4 May: *Bacchus* (1) in collision in fog in the English Channel with the Greek vessel *Joannis Fafalos* (3,122 tons/1900) which sank with the loss of 12 lives; *Bacchus* damaged, making water, temporarily abandoned, re-boarded and the engines started and made for Portland; later towed to Portsmouth for repair; *Bacchus* was blamed for this incident for proceeding too fast in the prevailing conditions.

June: The liner *Jervis Bay* on passage Brisbane to London radioed through with a report of stowaways followed by 'mutiny threatened to set fire to the ship'; an armed Royal Navy party from Colombo was sent in RFA *Slavol* and boarded the ship.

Tower Hill Memorial, London (known as the Merchant Navy Memorial)
This monument, designed for the Commonwealth War Graves Commission by Sir Edwin Lutyens, was begun in 1927 and HM The Queen unveiled it on 12 December 1928. It commemorated 11,919 men from the Merchant Navy and fishing fleets lost during the First World War who have no grave but the sea. The memorial was extended to commemorate nearly 24,000 names from the Merchant Navy who lost their lives during the Second World War and have no known grave. Designed by Sir Edward Maufe this was unveiled by HM Queen Elizabeth II on 5 November 1955. The RFA was represented at the unveiling by two Captains, a Chief Engineer and a Boatswain as wreath bearer.

This memorial does not carry the names of Lascar seamen known to have been domiciled in India (and Pakistan) – they are commemorated at Bombay and Chittagong; Chinese seamen known to have been domiciled in Hong Kong or China were commemorated when their names were added to the 1914–18 memorial at Hong Kong.

The RN, Royal Marines, RNR, DEMS and Royal Maritime Artillery Regiment personnel lost when serving aboard RFAs are not recorded. They are commemorated on appropriate Naval and Army memorials.

1929

1929: *Ruthenia* – ship's registry cancelled.

April: *War Pathan* comes under in-house Admiralty (Director of Stores) management and manning as an RFA.

May: The self-propelled Temperley coaling craft *C65* is renamed RFA *Nora* to improve signalling to shore stations when on coastwise store carrying duties.

November: RFA Pensions – regulations made for a scheme of retiring allowances and gratuities for RFA officers (Masters, Chief Officers, Second Officers, Chief Engineers, Second Engineers and Third Engineers) holding Board of Trade 'tickets' and serving under BoT agreements.

2 November: *Discovery II*, research ship, launched by Ferguson Bros, Port Glasgow for the National Oceanographic Council.

1930

1930: *Pearleaf* fitted to carry aviation spirit and explosives; *Brambleleaf* had four cylindrical tanks installed to carry aviation spirit. Admiralty approval given for the New Zealand Government to sub-charter *Nucula* to commercial firms for time or

RFA *Reliant* (1)

FLEET SUPPLY SHIP

Pennant: X25
Official number: 147557
Port of registry: London
Callsign: GUND
Builder: Furness Shipbuilding, Haverton Hill
Machinery: Two Brown Curtis single reduction geared turbines; 5,000 shp; single shaft by Richardsons, Westgarth, Middlesborough; 14 knots
Dimensions (loa/bp x beam): 471.6/450ft x 58ft
Tonnage measurements: 7,928 grt, 11,340 dwt
Displacement: –
Complement: 143

The stores ship RFA *Reliant* (1); formerly Furness Withy's *London Importer*, her large refrigerated capacity made her a valuable acquisition. (ANRS)

Remarks: +100A1 +LMC; commercial design ordered for Furness Withy, London; December 1923 completed as *London Importer*; 23 March 1933 purchased by the Admiralty for £46,000 for conversion into a fleet store ship primarily for the Mediterranean supply service with naval and victualling and some NAAFI stores; renamed RFA *Reliant*; 1937 fitted for defensive armament, W/T outfit replaced; 1938 alterations and additions to provide addition 'tween decks; 1942 transferred for East of Suez service; 12 March 1948 to Ministry of Transport for disposal at Garloch, sold to East & West Steamship Co, Pakistan.

voyage charters

September: *Petroleum* reduced to care and maintenance status.

December: *Oligarch* laid up at Portsmouth until June 1931.

1931

1931: Admiralty undertook an exhaustive look at the question of manning RFAs with naval personnel, or, at any rate, men on a permanent form of engagement. *War Bahadur* in reserve at Rosyth until 1935. *War Bharata* in reserve at Rosyth until 1934.

January: *Olcades* laid up at Devonport until April.

1 January: *Nucula*'s rate of hire to New Zealand Government reduced to £3,250 per annum.

May: *Petroleum* crew on a monthly agreement.

26 June: *Kharki* sold commercially on competitive tender to Twong Tai at Hong Kong, for £2,046.9.3, name unchanged.

July: *Olcades* laid up at Portsmouth until June 1932.

21 December: *Fortol* laid up at Rosyth until 1935. *Dredgol* laid up at Rosyth.

1932

1932: Oiling at sea – over an extended period a series of trials was carried out in all Fleets and as a result:

- The stirrup method became regarded as the standard system of oiling HM Ships at sea and in exposed anchorages.
- The hose-hawser system was abandoned.
- The trough (abeam) system was suitable for oiling destroyers in fair weather from larger ships.
- The possibility of fuelling more than one vessel at the same time and the use of two hoses for each vessel was noted.

Station allowances first paid to RFA crew serving in vessels allocated to a station abroad, specifically on fleet attendance, *eg* Mediterranean and Far East. *Olna* (under Davies & Newman management) is first British vessel fitted with Oertz rudder. *Montenol* and *Rapidol* in reserve at Rosyth until 1935.

June: Oiling at sea – instruction were issued for existing hose-hawsers on tanker to be dismantled with the hoses and hawsers to be utilised for ordinary requirements.

July: *Olwen* laid up at Sheerness until August.

August: *Petroleum* towed the tug *C307* from Portsmouth to Malta.

1933

1933: *War Bharata* comes under in-house Admiralty (Director of Stores) management and manning as an RFA.

24 March: *London Importer* purchased by the Admiralty for £46,000; converted into a fleet supply ship, renamed RFA *Reliant* (1); replaces *Perthshire* as the Mediterranean Fleet's supply ship.

1934

26 February: *Perthshire* is relieved by RFA *Reliant* (1) and is sold, by competitive tender as lies at Malta, to Soc Anon Cantiere Di Portovenera, Spezia for £6,602 for scrap.

20 March: *Perthshire* left Malta for demolition in Italy.

1935

1935: Tanker Tonnage Committee as a sub-committee of the Oil Board was set up to consider supply of tankers for services need in wartime; exercise strict control on use of British and neutral tanker tonnage; executive duties carried out by Director of Sea Transport in co-operation with Director of Stores to deal with Admiralty requirements. During the late 1930s there was a considerable world surplus of tanker tonnage with over 100 tankers laid up from March 1935 to 1939. *Mixol* was reactivated for the Italo-Abyssinian conflict, but was found to be unsuitable so she returned to the UK; placed in reserve. *Bacchus* (1) sent to Mersa Matruh to serve as a distilling ship for the Army on the outbreak of the Italo-Abyssinian war. *Rapidol* re-entered service for duties during the Italo-Abyssinian war. Armament – RFA *Prestol* conducted paravane experiments for HMS *Vernon*, cutting dummy mines at Spithead.

1 March: Navy Estimates allow for new

The first RFA *Bacchus* laid up for disposal prior to the Second World War. (World Ship Society)

Fortol, a 2,000-ton tanker converted to a white oil carrier in 1935. (World Ship Society)

store freighter (to become RFA *Bacchus* (2)).

7–15 March: Oiling at sea – Exercise ZL was a combined fleet exercise of attack and defence of trade and involved RFAs *Belgol*, *Brambleleaf* and *Cherryleaf*; none of the RFAs were fitted for RAS, but this exercise is the first recorded successful use of the trough method of oiling at sea.

28 March: Oiling at sea – Admiralty ordered further trials with the stirrup and trough methods.

28 June: *Burma* sold as lies at Rosyth, by competitive tender, to P & W McLellan, Glasgow for £3,715 for breaking up. *Turmoil* (1) sold as lies at Rosyth, by competitive tender, to P & W McLellan, Glasgow for £4,905 for breaking up. *Carol* sold as lies at Rosyth, by competitive tender, to P & W McLellan, Glasgow for £2,722 for breaking up. *Trefoil* sold as lies at Rosyth, by competitive tender, to P & W McLellan, Glasgow for £5,865 for breaking up. *Attendant* sold as lies at Rosyth, by competitive tender, to P & W McLellan, Glasgow for £2,722.

16 July: Silver Jubilee Fleet Review at Spithead – RFA *Maine*.

23 July: Report on Radio Direction-Finding – later to be known as Radar.

1 August: *Attendant* removed from Rosyth, resold to Hemsley Bell Ltd, Southampton, Admiralty share £464, name remained unchanged.

3 August: *Dredgol* sold as lies Rosyth to Arnott Young & Co (Shipbreakers), Glasgow for £5,514, removed from Rosyth.

26 August: Oiling at sea – a report from Commander-in-Chief Mediterranean indicated the tendency to favour the trough method when oiling from battleships.

October: *Fortol* re-entered service as a white oil carrier until RFA *Green Ranger* took over during the Second World War.

16 October: *Fort Amherst* launched.

17 December: *Bacchus* (2) ordered.

1936

1936: Humanitarian aid – Spanish Civil War – hospital support by RFA *Maine* based in Malta until 1938. *Delphinula* becomes a fuel hulk at Alexandria then Gibraltar as a fuel hulk. *War Afridi*, *War Nawab*, *War Nizam* and *War Pindari* come under in-house Admiralty (Director of Stores) management and manning as RFAs. *Hickorol* placed in reserved as her tanks were judged to be in poor condition. *Abbeydale* ordered from Swan Hunter & Wigham Richardson, Newcastle for British Tanker Company – this BTC three-twelve design motor tanker taken over by the Admiralty as on the stocks. *Aldersdale*, *Arndale*, *Bishopdale*, *Boardale* and *Broomdale* ordered by British Tanker Company, all taken over by the Admiralty. RFA introduces Company Service Contracts for officers.

January: SS *Fort Amherst* (later to become RFA *Amherst*) completed for Furness Withy & Co (Furness Line) as a passenger cargo liner by Blythswood Shipbuilding, Glasgow.

14 February: *Bacchus* (1) is laid down.

20 February: RFA *Petroleum* paid off and laid up for disposal.

May: *Bacchus* (1) is renamed *Bacchus II* to free the name for the new ship; laid up for disposal.

13 June: Breaking-up of *Burma*, *Carol*, *Trefoil* and *Turmoil* at Bo'ness completed.

July: Oiling at sea – the trials and report had been about oiling at sea between HM Ships and the question

During the Spanish Civil War a serious situation arose involving attacks on neutral ships, particularly in the Mediterranean, resulting in the sinking of a number of British and other merchant vessels and the loss of seafarers' lives. This resulted in the Nyon Agreement and ships protected under this accord were painted with identifying stripes – this photo shows the new RFA *Bacchus* (2) with Nyon Agreement identification markings amidships. (World ship Society.

Based on the British Tanker Company's 'three Twelves' standard the RFA *Abbeydale* was the first of a significant class of ocean-going motor tankers acquired for the RFA. (World Ship Society)

was raised whether a standard method cold be adopted for RFA oilers – 2,000 and 5,000 tonners.

15 July: *Bacchus* (2) is launched.

2 August: *Fortol* placed in reserve at Devonport.

13 August: *Petroleum* – approval given for this ship to be disposed of as part of a transfer of ships agreement in exchange for *Majestic*.

September: *Aldersdale* and *Boardale* laid down.

September: Oiling at sea – Admiralty approved to adopt the trough method (abeam) as the standard system of oiling destroyers at sea from capital ships.

20 September: *Bacchus* (2), naval store carrier, 2,343 grt, completed by Caledon Shipbuilding & Engineering at Dundee for the Admiralty.

28 September: *Bacchus* (2) registered in London.

5 November: Supply Ships Committee – set up to consider number and types of auxiliaries (except oilers) required for maintaining supplies to the Fleet in certain emergencies and arrangements for manning and fitting out. Representatives from various Admiralty departments were on this Committee including Director of Stores, Director of Victualling, Director of Plans, Director of Armament Supply and Military Branch; Committee reported in Spring of 1937.

28 December: *Abbeydale*, freighting tanker, launched.

> **Spanish Civil War (1936–1939)**
> Submarines of the Fascist powers were attacking ships supplying the Spanish Government forces. By international agreement (the Nyon Agreement), international naval patrols to enforce maritime law and prevent acts of piracy were established. RFA tankers undertook station duties:
>
> | | |
> |---|---|
> | RFA *Cherryleaf* | Barcelona |
> | RFA *Brambleleaf* | Oran |
> | RFA *Plumleaf* | Gibraltar |
> | RFA *Montenol* | La Rochelle, |
>
> the oiler having been taken out of reserve for this duty

1937

1937: Merchant Navy Training Board formed. Uniform colour scheme adopted for RFA freighting oilers, fleet attendant oilers, fleet supply ships, store-carrying vessels in Home waters and in the Mediterranean. Priority decision to standardise the W/T equipment in all RFAs over 1,000 tons. *War Sepoy* and *War Sirdar* come under in-house Admiralty (Director of Stores) management and manning as RFAs.

January: *Arndale* and *Broomdale* laid down.

11 January: Master appointed to RFA *Abbeydale*.

12 January: *British Beacon* comes under in-house Admiralty (Director of Stores) management and manning as an RFA and renamed *Olcades*.

21 January: *Oleander* under Davies & Newman management comes under in-house Admiralty (Director of Stores) management and manning as an RFA.

February: *Plumleaf* at Barcelona and Malta.

18 February: *Cherryleaf* sailing to Gibraltar on passage to Barcelona.

March: *Abbeydale*, 8,299 grt, completed by Swan Hunter and Wigham Richardson at Neptune Yard for the Admiralty. *Prestol* and *Montenol* at Gibraltar and La Pallice.

5 March: *Abbeydale* on passage Tyne to Trinidad on maiden voyage.

8 March: HM Ships in Spanish waters painted up in red and blue distinguishing funnel bands; RFAs

in Spanish waters were not expected to follow this but it seems that some did.

26 March: *Petroleum* sold to T W Ward Ltd for £6,250 and removed from Sheerness for breaking up.

17 April: *British Light* comes under in-house Admiralty (Director of Stores) management and manning as an RFA and renamed *Olwen*.

22 April: *Boardale* launched

20 May: *Slavol* represented the Royal Navy at the King George VI Coronation Review celebration at Mahe, Seychelles. *Brambleleaf* (1) participated in the King George VI Coronation Fleet Review at Spithead.

21 May: *Bishopdale* – RFA Master appointed.

26 May: Circular Letters – decision made to adopt a form of 'Circular Letter' as a means of communicating instructions to the various class of RFAs. The instructions to be communicated were to be of 'more or less' permanent character but insufficiently general to be embodied in RFA Regulations.

June: *War Krishna* opened a new Chinese crew agreement at Sunderland until 15 June 1939.

6 June: *Bishopdale*, 8,402 grt, completed by Lithgows at Port

RFA *Bacchus* (2)

ADMIRALTY-DESIGNED STORE FREIGHTER

Pennant: X03 **Official number:** 164723
Port of registry: London **Callsign:** GXYB
Builder: Caledon Shipbuilding & Engineering Co, Dundee
Machinery: Steam 3 cyl triple expansion by North East Marine Engineering; 3 Scotch boilers, 2,000ihp; 643 ton bunkers; 12 knots
Dimensions (loa/bp x beam): 338.5/327ft x 49.4ft
Tonnage measurements: 3,249 grt, 2,856 dwt
Displacement: 6,325 tons **Complement:** 49

RFA *Bacchus* (2) at Capetown. (RFA Archive)

Remarks: +100A1 +LMC, Admiralty design, completed in September 1936 as a naval store freighter for mixed cargo – naval, victualling, armament and general stores plus limited passenger accommodation; reported fitted with the distilling plant from HMS *Resolution*; 1942 fitted as a naval stores issuing ship; 1946 converted back to a store freighter in Hong Kong; 1964 sold to Singapore shipbreakers.

RFA *Bishopdale*, one of four freighting tankers ordered by the British Tanker Co in 1936 and taken over by the Admiralty. (World Ship Society)

Radio on RFAs

In 1937, it was decided to standardise W/T transmitter and receiver equipment in all RFAs, over 1,000 tons, with a 2kW installation and to have this completed by 1940, in accordance with the 1932 International Radio Conference at Madrid. Equipment to facilitate commercial and fleet work was hired from and maintained by the Marconi International Marine Co. First fitted in the new motor tankers – *Abbeydale, Arndale, Aldersdale, Bishopdale, Boardale* and *Broomdale* – the new outfit included:

Marconi type 387 Marconi type 388 Marconi type 389 and Marconi type 550	transmitters, 2kW, with emission modes CW and ICW covering frequencies 115-500 kc/s (kMz) and 4.9-17.8m/cs (mHz)
Marconi type 352A/272	receivers covering 15 kc/s to 20 mc/s
Marconi type 579 D/F	fitted in some ships
Emergency transmitter	'spark' transmitter of 500 kc/s wave

Glasgow for the Admiralty.

25 June: *Celerol* arrives at La Pallice.

4 July: *British Lantern* comes under in-house Admiralty (Director of Stores) management and manning as an RFA and renamed *Oligarch*.

6 July: *Nucula* reduced to storage hulk.

7 July: *Boardale*, 8,406 grt, completed by Harland & Wolff at Govan for the Admiralty. *Aldersdale* launched.

8 July: *Boardale* maiden voyage – Glasgow, Port Said and Abadan.

5 August: *Arndale* launched.

16 August: *British Star* comes under in-house Admiralty (Director of Stores) management and manning as an RFA and renamed *Olynthus*.

2 September: *Broomdale* launched.

17 September: *Aldersdale*, 8,400 grt, completed by Cammell Laird at Birkenhead for the Admiralty.

18 September: *Aldersdale* – maiden voyage from the Clyde to Port Said.

20 September: Humanitarian aid – hospital ship *Maine* with additional RFA and RN ratings sailed from Malta to Valencia to evacuate refugees.

28 September: *Arndale*, 8,503 grt, completed by Swan Hunter & Wigham Richardson at Newcastle for the Admiralty.

29 September: *Arndale* – maiden voyage River Tyne on passage to Trinidad, Gibraltar and Port Said. *Abbeydale* signs on a Chinese crew at Singapore.

1 October: Tankers in reserve – held in state of readiness for national emergency – Lloyds's surveys, maintenance of class – Lloyd's agree to the classification of the vessels remaining undisturbed provided all overdue survey will be carried out before the vessel is put into service, also notification be given to their local representative when the biannual docking will be carried out in order that he will inspect the vessel.

19 October: *Bishopdale* recorded as now having a Chinese crew.

20 October: Hospital ship *Maine* arrives Marseilles after a fire occurred on upper bridge; considerable damage done.

3 November: *Broomdale*, 8,334 grt, completed by Harland & Wolff at

The small coastal store carrier RFA *Robert Middleton.* (World Ship Society)

Glasgow for the Admiralty; she became the first RFA to be fitted with a pair of gantry kingpost and net defence derricks for oiling at sea trials; later became first tanker to be fitted with conical heating coils in her cargo tanks.

7 November: RFA *Boardale* registered in London. *Olna* management transferred from Davies and Newman to the Admiralty.

15 November: *Bacchus* II used as a bombing target for the RAF and sunk off Alderney Light.

24 November: Outline of requirements for a new naval hospital ship submitted to Third Sea Lord.

14 December: *War Krishna* reverted to Admiralty management.

1938

1938: Merchant Navy Officers Pension fund formed. DEMS and anti-gas training for RFA personnel. First edition of BR 875, *Regulations and Instructions relating to registered Royal Fleet Auxiliaries* (the RFA Handbook) prepared; although prior to this a document known as the 'RFA Instructions' is sometimes referred to but no formal trace of it has been found. *British Star* comes under in-house Admiralty (Director of Stores) management and manning as an RFA, renamed RFA *Olynthus* (1). RFA *Hickorol* has a completely new tank section built in at Grangemouth; re-enters operational service

January: RFA *War Bahadur* is struck by a freak wave SW of Ireland and is severely damaged; did not proceed to sea again.

1 January: Camouflaging in time of war – the marine artist Cecil King, second in charge of 'Dazzles Painting Section', stated 'however, well dazzled a ship, her true course was given away by centring and symmetry of her masts' and he suggested trials on an Admiralty vessel adjusted to enable masts to be off centre – this was later applied to the design of the *Ranger* class.

2 February: RFA *War Bahadur*, after repairs, became fuel hulk at Devonport Naval Base.

17 February: Admiralty received a request from the French Government for information regarding size of tankers and whether there were regulations governing size and tonnage and what arrangements existed for time chartering.

1 April: RFA *Fortol* brought out of lay-up for operational service.

29 June: RFA *Robert Middleton* launched.

28 July: RFA *Robert Dundas* launched.

25 August: RFA *Robert Middleton*, 1,087 grt, completed by Grangemouth Dockyard Co at Grangemouth for the Admiralty as a coastal store carrier; initially manned on Yard Craft Agreement; to replace RFA *Nora*.

October: Reserved fittings for naval hospital ships: first set bought in 1935 with a regular approval in Naval Estimates until 1939; current status – one set in India and six sets at Sheerness.

12 October: *Argo* arrived Rosyth; reduced to a hulk for temporary stowage of munitions.

18 October: *Kimmerol* to Portsmouth for Trade Defence Exercise.

25 October: *Erato* (later to become RFA *Cairndale*) launched.

2 November: RFA *Robert Dundas*, 1,110 grt, completed by Grangemouth Dockyard Co at Grangemouth for the Admiralty as a coastal store carrier; initially manned on Yard Craft Agreement; to replace RFA *Argo*.

15 November: *Bacchus* II, after being used as a bombing target, sunk over the Hurd Deep, 10 miles off Alderney by gunfire from cruiser HMS *Dunedin*. RFA house flag – it was decided not to follow the general custom of the Merchant Navy of assigning a house flag or particular distinguishing markings for funnels of RFAs.

National emergency

Records show that in December 1938 the following RFA tankers were to be held in a state of readiness:

Rosyth – *Belgol, Celerol, Mixol* and one 'War' class
Scapa – one 'War' class
Devonport – *Fortol* and *Hickorol*
Portsmouth – *Distol*
Sheerness – two 'War' class
Dover – one 'War' class
Harwich – one 'War' class

CHAPTER 4

The Second World War, 1939–1945

1939

1939: CB 4029 (B) (39) Volume 2 Instructions concerning the supply of fuel in war – Particulars of RFAs published. *Berta* transferred to Anglo Saxon Petroleum Co Ltd (Lisbon) and renamed *Shell Dezoito*. RFA *Nora* replaced by RFA *Robert Middleton*; then reduced to a hulk for the temporary storage of ammunition on the Medway. *Kimmerol* and other oilers in the *Creosol* class were moved from Yard Craft manning to standard RFA manning conditions. To improve her stability RFA *Mixol* had 300 tons of steel removed. *Slavol* was stationed at Port Said to be the tanker at the disposal of the Red Sea Escort Force

26 January: *Erato*, 8,129 grt, completed by Harland & Wolff at Belfast for Anglo-Saxon Petroleum Co Ltd (Shell tankers); after running trials this motor tanker was taken over by the Admiralty for service as a freighting tanker; renamed RFA *Cairndale*.

16 March: Armament – *Oleander*, Portsmouth on paravane trials.

25 March: *Cedardale* launched.

2–21 April: *War Mehtar* at Rosyth and placed in semi-commission (two officers and eight ratings) on yard craft agreement.

RFA *Black Ranger*: this fleet attendant tanker is representative of the first Admiralty-designed tanker since 1914. (RFA Archive)

25 April: Introduction of costing arrangements for repairs to Admiralty tankers.

29 April: *Cairndale* sailed from Colombo on passage to Singapore towing lighter *C451*.

May: *War Nawab* placed in semi-commission at Portsmouth – two officers and eight ratings on yard craft agreement.

5 May: Turkish authorities informed HM Government that they were to be informed when Admiralty vessels proceeding to the Black Sea, on charter, pass through the Straits.

25 May: *Cedardale*, 8,132 grt, completed by Blythswood Shipbuilding at Glasgow for the Anglo-Saxon Petroleum Co Ltd (Shell tankers); this motor tanker was taken over by the Admiralty for service as a freighting tanker; renamed RFA *Cedardale*.

27 May: RFA *Cedardale* commences maiden voyage Greenock to Abadan.

31 July: *British Lady*, 6,098 grt, launched for British Tanker Co by Sir J L Thompson & Sons Ltd, steam turbines double reduction geared by Metropolitan Vickers, Manchester; purchased by the Admiralty, with former owners British Tanker Co, London as managers, she served in northern waters, mainly Scapa Flow, as a depot ship with some escort work; some RFA personnel were based aboard.

28 August: *Black Ranger*, *Blue Ranger*, *Brown Ranger*, *Gold Ranger*, *Green Ranger* and *Gray Ranger* ordered.

September: Defensively Equipped Merchant Ships (DEMS) and convoy system introduced. *War Sepoy* becomes port oiler at Dover. *Bacchus* (2) reportedly transmits a distress signal on a U-boat attack when crossing the Bay of Biscay. *War Nizam* withdrawn from sea-going service; laid up at Rosyth partially manned.

3 September: Britain, France, Australia and New Zealand declare war on Germany – Second World War.

5 September: *Empire Silver* (later to

RFA *Birchol*, a 1,000-ton harbour tanker lost by grounding in November 1939. (World Ship Society)

RFA fleet list and disposition, 1939
(including ships under construction)

	Status	Disposition
RFA *Abbeydale*	oiler	Chatham
RFA *Aldersdale*	oiler	–
RFA *Appleleaf*	oiler	Hong Kong
RFA *Arndale*	oiler	–
RFA *Bacchus*	store freighter	Chatham
RFA *Belgol*	oiler	Devonport in reserve
RFA *Birchol*	oiler	Sheerness
RFA *Bishopdale*	oiler	–
RFA *Boardale*	oiler	–
RFA *Boxol*	oiler	Malta
RFA *Brambleleaf*	oiler	Malta
RFA *Broomdale*	oiler	–
RFA *Cairndale*	oiler	–
RFA *Cedardale*	oiler	–
RFA *Celerol*	oiler	Devonport in reserve
RFA *Cherryleaf*	oiler	Malta
RFA *Distol*	oiler	Devonport in reserve
RFA *Ebonol*	oiler	Devonport
RFA *Elderol*	oiler	Portsmouth
RFA *Elmol*	oiler	Sheerness
RFA *Fortol*	oiler	Devonport in reserve
RFA *Francol*	oiler	Hong Kong
RFA *Hickorol*	oiler	Devonport in reserve
RFA *Kimmerol*	oiler	Portsmouth
RFA *Larchol*	oiler	Sheerness
RFA *Limol*	oiler	Devonport
RFA *Maine*	hospital ship	–
RFA *Mixol*	oiler	Devonport in reserve
RFA *Montenol*	oiler	Devonport
RFA *Olcades*	oiler	Portsmouth
RFA *Oleander*	oiler	Portsmouth
RFA *Oligarch*	oiler	Portsmouth
RFA *Olna*	oiler	Portsmouth
RFA *Olwen*	oiler	Portsmouth
RFA *Olynthus*	oiler	Portsmouth
RFA *Orangeleaf*	oiler	Bermuda
RFA *Reliant*	fleet supply ship	Malta
RFA *Scotol*	oiler	Portland
RFA *Serbol*	oiler	Gibraltar in reserve
RFA *Slavol*	oiler	Trincomalee
RFA *Thermol*	oiler	Gibraltar in reserve
RFA *Viscol*	oiler	Gibraltar
RFA *War Afridi*	oiler	Devonport
RFA *War Bahadur*	oiler	Devonport in reserve
RFA *War Bharata*	oiler	Devonport
RFA *War Brahmin*	oiler	Devonport
RFA *War Diwan*	oiler	Devonport in reserve
RFA *War Hindoo*	oiler	Devonport
RFA *War Krishna*	oiler	Devonport
RFA *War Mehtar*	oiler	Devonport
RFA *War Nawab*	oiler	Devonport
RFA *War Nizam*	oiler	Devonport
RFA *War Pathan*	oiler	Devonport
RFA *War Sepoy*	oiler	Devonport
RFA *War Sirdar*	oiler	Devonport
RFA *War Sudra*	oiler	Devonport

Robert Dundas coastal store carrier being completed, initially Yard Craft and then RFA agreement
Robert Middleton coastal store carrier being completed, initially Yard Craft and then RFA agreement

RFA *Derwentdale* (1), freighting tanker. (RFA Archive)

'Dale (1)' class

MERCANTILE-DESIGNED TANKERS THAT FALL IN FOUR GROUPS (19 SHIPS)

A group (pre-war British Tanker Company type 'three twelves')
RFA *Abbeydale* RFA *Arndale* RFA *Aldersdale*

B group (pre-war British Tanker Company type 'three twelves')
RFA *Bishopdale* RFA *Broomdale* RFA *Boardale*

C group (pre-war Shell type 12,000-ton tankers)
RFA *Cairndale* RFA *Cedardale*

D group war construction MoWT standard tankers
RFA *Darkdale* RFA *Dewdale* (1) RFA *Denbydale* RFA *Dingledale* RFA *Derwentdale* (1) RFA *Dinsdale*

E group war construction MoWT standard tankers (steamships)
RFA *Eaglesdale* RFA *Ennerdale* (1) RFA *Easedale* RFA *Echodale* (motorship) RFA *Eppingdale* (cancelled – *Empire Gold*)

Builder: Swan Hunter & Wigham Richardson, Newcastle
Machinery: One 4 cyl two-stroke single-acting Doxford ICE by William Doxford Ltd; 2,850 bhp; single screw; 11.5 knots
Dimensions (loa/bp x beam): 481.5/466.3ft x 62ft
Tonnage measurements: 8,299 grt, 12,235 dwt
Displacement: 17,210 tons
Complement: 44 (59 if Lascar crewing)

Remarks: +100A1; +LMC British Tanker Company design. These motor tankers were not sister-ships and the type of diesel engine differed, for example RFA *Derwentdale* was fitted with an 8 cyl four stroke single acting B&W built by Harland & Wolff.
This information is based on RFA Abbeydale *motor tanker.*

RFA *Bishopdale*, freighting tanker clearly showing the 'gun tubs' for her defensive armament. (World Ship Society)

Builder: Furness Shipbuilding, Haverton Hill (yard no 340)
Machinery: Steam 3 cyl triple expansion by Richardson, Westgarth of West Hartlepool; 3,650 ihp; single shaft; 11.5 knots
Dimensions (loa/bp x beam x draught): 479/463.5ft x 61.2ft x 16.5ft
Tonnage measurements: 8,630 grt, 12,040 dwt
Displacement: 16,820 tons
Complement: 70

Remarks: +100A1; +LMC, ordered by the Ministry of Shipping (MOS122) and handed over to the Admiralty upon completion. These ships had steam engines because the UK's diesel engine manufacturing capacity was full. These ships were generally termed as 'troublesome'.
This information is based on RFA Easedale *steam tanker*

RFA *Easedale* displaying the classic tanker layout. (World Ship Society)

become *Denbydale*) ordered by Ministry of Shipping (MOS2)

18 September: The water tankers *Freshet* and *Freshwater* ordered.

25 September: *Olna* was under orders of the cruiser HMS *Ajax*, when she grounded, no damage recorded.

October: *War Krishna* – a number of Chinese firemen refused to sail – placed in detention quarters and Egyptian firemen engaged. Water tanker *Spa* ordered.

1 October: *Olwen* in Montevideo due to mechanical defects.

7 October: Oiling at sea – RFA *Prestol* conduced trials with the destroyer HMS *Fury* off Scapa Flow.

9 October: *Nasprite* ordered.

12 October: *Black Ranger* laid down.

15 October: *Orangeleaf* refuelled cruiser HMS *Achilles* off Coquimbo.

25 October: Admiralty approved a contribution the British Sailors' Society of £3.00 per annum for each RFA supplied with a library.

26 October: *Blue Ranger* laid down.

27 October: *Brown Ranger* laid down.

November: *War Krishna* conducted paravane trials with long and short wires. Battle of the River Plate – RFA *Olynthus* supporting the cruiser force was reportedly signalled 'if the *Graf Spee* comes your way, let her through'; although there is no record of this in the official despatch.

29 November: Marine loss – RFA *Birchol* – 57.06N 0007.13.45W (off Uist, Hebrides, Scotland), this tanker was lost by stranding in fog, she was abandoned, some stores were salvaged – one rating injured.

4 December: *Olwen* refuelled the cruiser HMS *Achilles*.

11 December: *Derwentdale* (1) laid down.

15 December: During a lull in the battle of the River Plate, RFA *Olynthus* refuelled the cruiser HMS *Ajax* – a very difficult operation requiring hurricane hawsers and covered by the cruisers *Achilles* and *Exeter*.

26 December: *Empire Silver* (later to become *Denbydale*) laid down.

1940

1940: Tanker Tonnage Allocation Committee replaces duties of the Tanker Tonnage Committee in dealing with Service requirements. *Nucula* became an active harbour hulk in Auckland, New Zealand.

Thermol had over 100 tons of steel removed to improve her stability. Operation Puma – plans formulated and forces placed in being for the 'taking of the Atlantic Islands' (the Azores and Cape Verde Islands) – *Olwen* and *Abbeydale* on alert.

8 January: *Empire Granite* (later to become the diesel-engined RFA *Echodale*) laid down.

RAS(L): Second World War unidentified tanker deploying a fuel hose astern. (RFA Archive)

12 January: Anglo Saxon Petroleum Co Ltd (Lisbon) tanker *Shell Dezoito*, 2,397 grt, was requisitioned for Admiralty service; built by Harland & Wolff at Belfast in 1927 she was renamed RFA *Berta* and undertook fleet attendant duties on the south coast – Dartmouth, Plymouth and Falmouth.

12 February: *Olwen* to oil Force G and HMS *Shropshire* carried out an investigation of the discontent amongst *Olwen*'s crew.

15 February: *MOS9* (later to become *Ennerdale* (1)) laid down.

19 February: *Boxol* arrived Malta; *Ebonol* arrived Hong Kong.

7 March: *Nasprite* laid down.

23 March: *Freshwater* launched.

26 March: *Freshet* laid down.

4 April: Humanitarian aid – *Appleleaf* (1) assisted Norwegian *Produce* (1,171/1905) which had run aground on the North Reef, Parcel Islands, 37 crew rescued.

6 April: *Arndale* – Falkland Islands and fleet attendance operation in the South Atlantic.

17 April: Motor tanker *Papendrecht*, 10,746 grt, completed by N V Rotterdam Droogo Maats completed for Van Ommeren (later

Special Service Freighters (Decoy Ships)

In 1939 the Admiralty requisitioned a number of merchant ships that were converted for service as 'Admiralty Special Service Freighters' – Decoy ships (Q ships) – manned by special service crews, with the exception of two, these were heavily armed ships operating under the various cover names but they had one thing in common – they flew the Red Ensign when at sea but when entering and when in harbour they wore the Blue Ensign and appeared under RFA cover names:

RFA cover name	*Service*	*Commissioned as*
RFA *Antoine*	1939–41	HMS *Orchy*
RFA *Brutus*	1939–41	HMS *City of Durban*
RFA *Chatsgrove*	1939	HMS *PC74*
RFA *Cypurs*	1939–41	HMS *Cape Sable*
RFA *Edgehill*	1939–40	HMS *Willamette Valley*
RFA *City of Dieppe*	1939–46	converted for service as a special freighter
RFA *City of Tokio*	1939–46	converted for service as a special freighter
RFA *Lambridge*	1939–41	HMS *Botlea*
RFA *Lode*	1939–41	HMS *Beauly*
RFA *Maunder*	1939–41	HMS *King Gruffyd*
RFA *Prunella*	1939–40	HMS *Cap Howe*

'Ranger' class

ADMIRALTY-DESIGNED FLEET ATTENDANT TANKERS

RFA *Black Ranger* RFA *Gold Ranger* RFA *Blue Ranger*
RFA *Green Ranger* RFA *Brown Ranger* RFA *Gray Ranger*

Machinery: One 4 cyl two stroke, single acting Doxford ICE by William Doxford, Sunderland; single shaft; 3,500 bhp; 13 knots; the B group ships had one 6 cyl Burmeister & Wain four stroke single acting ICE build by Harland & Wolff, Belfast

Dimensions (loa/bp x beam x draught): 355/339.7ft x 48ft x 20.2ft

Tonnage measurements: 3,313 grt, 3,950 dwt

Displacement: 6,704 tons full load **Complement:** 40 + DEMS gunners

RFA *Black Ranger* as a defensively equipped merchant ship in camouflage 1943. (RFA Archive)

Remarks: +100A1; +LMC, the 'Ranger' class were the first RFAs designed since the First World War and they were originally intended to replace the 2,000-ton *Belgol* class. They had a cargo capacity of 3,213 tons enabling 2,582 tons of oil fuel, 541 tons of diesel oil and 90 tons of petrol to be carried and pumped. As built they were provided with extensive protection – 100lb steel over the petrol tanks, 4-inch thick plastic armour around the bridge. Defensive armament was in accordance with current DEMS practice – 1 x 4-inch LA, 1 x 12 pdr HA/LA and two Lewis machine guns. During the war the armament changed, and of course varied from ship to ship. The typical fit was 1 x 4-inch LA, 1 x 40mm Bofors and 4 x single 20mm Oerlikons.
For replenishment at sea this class was originally fitted with the stirrup astern method but this was replaced by the 'buoyant' hose method using 5-inch rubber hose. 40ft derricks were fitted for the abeam method. An unusual feature of their design was the offsetting of the funnel and the foremast and wartime guises of a dummy funnel forward and a very low genuine funnel aft.1
The details are based on RFA Gold Ranger *as built*

to become RFA *Empire Salvage*).

21 April: *Boardale* arrived Scapa Flow for operations off Norway.

27 April: The cruiser HMS *Exeter* damages *Aldersdale*, serving in northern waters. *Cherryleaf* (1) damaged at Sierra Leone after the hospital ship *Oxfordshire* dragged her anchor.

30 April–1 May: Marine loss – RFA *Boardale* – Aasan Fjord, off Narvik, Norway; this tanker was lost by navigation error when on passage Clyde to Narvik, abandoned after grounding; *circa* 18.40 she caught fire and sank; the Master was stated to be roughly to blame for the loss – no casualties reported.

May: Operation – Dunkirk evacuation – RFA *War Sepoy* is Dover port oiler. *Berta* bombed in the Dover Straits – no damage recorded, one officer injured. *Olcades* off Narvik in convoy NS3.

10 May: Winston Churchill became Prime Minister.

14 May: *Gold Ranger* laid down.

16-18 May: *Broomdale* – bombed, one rating injured and transferred to an HM Ship for medical treatment then to the hospital ship *Atlantis* for passage to the UK.

25 May: *Olcades* grounded on an uncharted rock in Trincomalee Harbour, sustained some damage.

26 May: *Oleander* (1) – Harstad Bay, Northern Norway, damaged by a near miss during an air attack.

3 June: Admiralty acquired for RFA service the small 497 grt Dutch motor tanker *Ingeborg*; launched 30 December 1936 by Jos L Meyer, Papenburg for Algemeen Vrachtkantoor NV, Rotterdam; retained her name.

3–4 June: Evacuation of Dunkirk complete.

9 June: *Ingeborg* taken over for fleet attendant duties in UK waters.

1,500-ton class oilers (1940).
In April 1940 approval was given to build six 1,500-ton fleet attendant tankers. Two intended to replace two of the old 1,000-tonners and the rest to replace larger fleet attendant tankers for freighting but eventually to replace other 1000 tonners. 3,200 tons full load displacement, 263ft oa x 38.5ft x 16ft draft, 1,200 ihp steam engines, 10 knots, 2,000 miles endurance, cargo – 1,500 tons oil fuel, 100 tons diesel, 50 tons petrol. There were no slips available in the UK for building and capacity for building was sought in Canada but shipyards could not cope. In May 1940 it was decided to abandon the idea.

8 June: War loss – RFA *Oleander* (1) – Harstad Bay, Northern Norway – on 26 May 1940 damaged by a near miss during an air attack; vessel was beached and attempts made to salvage her cargo then recorded as lost; three ratings injured – first RFA war loss of Second World War. *Robert Dundas* placed under full RFA manning.
14 June: *Robert Middleton* placed under full RFA manning.
24 June: *Gray Ranger* laid down.
July: *Olwen* (1) allocated for Operation Sackbut – a proposed occupation of the Cape Verde Islands.
6 July: *Freshet* launched.
19 July: War loss – RFA *War Sepoy* – 51.06.42N 001.19.45E (Dover Harbour, England) this tanker was damaged beyond repair during an air raid; – one officer injured; one death (Master) recorded on the Tower Hill Memorial.
23 July: *Empire Oil* (later to become RFA *Darkdale*) launched.
25 July: *War Sepoy* – received further damaged during an air attack; broke in two and burnt out.
August: Oiling at sea – RFA *Arndale* conducted trials with the cruisers HMS *Hawkins* and HMS *Cumberland* in the South Atlantic.
12 August: *War Nawab* shot down an enemy aircraft.
13 August: *War Nawab* assisted in shooting down another enemy aircraft.
14 August: *Scotol* – bombed at Portland, one officer injured.
20 August: Prime Minister Winston Churchill made his famous 'Never in the field of human conflict…' speech to the House of Commons.
27 August: *Black Ranger* launched.
7 September: *War Sepoy* – hulk filled with concrete sunk as a blockship in Western Entrance, Dover Harbour; this entrance was not reopened until 26 April 1964.
10 September: *Freshwater* and *Freshet*, 278 grt, water tankers, completed by Lytham Shipbuilder & Engineering Co at Lytham for the Admiralty.
23 September: *Green Ranger* laid down.
26 September: *Spa* laid down.
October: Seaman's Welfare Board established, supported by Port Welfare Committees.
19 October: *Empire Silver* launched.
31 October: *Olna* (1) and RFA *Brambleleaf* (1), escorted by cruiser HMS *Coventry*, arrived Suda Bay, Crete to establish a fuelling base.
12 November: The Europaische Tankreederei GmnH, Hamburg tanker *Eurofield* rendezvoused with *Admiral Scheer* and the naval tanker *Nordmark* for repairs and to refuel the naval vessels; *Eurofield* was the former Admiralty tanker *Beechleaf* (October 1916).
14 November: *Papendrecht* seized by German naval forces in Rotterdam; renamed *Lothringen*, she was later modified for service as a naval supply vessel with oiling at sea facilities, deployed as a unit of Operation Rheinubung – the *Bismarck*, *Prinz Eugen* sortie.
15 November: *Empire Oil*, 8,147 grt, completed by Blysthswood Shipbuilding at Glasgow for the Ministry of War Transport; taken over by the Admiralty and renamed RFA *Darkdale*.
28 November: *Nasprite* launched.
29 November: *Empire Granite* launched as *Echodale*.
10 December: *Freshet*, 278 grt, water tanker, completed by Lytham Shipbuilder & Engineering Co at Lytham for the Admiralty.
12 December: *Brown Ranger* launched.
15 December: *Cairndale*, Gibraltar – diesel oil cargo on board reduced to 200 tons until the arrival of and replenishment by *British Union*.
22 December: *Broomdale* returned to the Falkland Islands to load cargo and *Arndale* ordered to the River Plate.

1941

6–13 January: Operation Excess – convoy operation to Piraeus and Malta, Force A sailed from Alexandria with RFA *Brambleleaf*.
8 January: *Broomdale* transfers stocks of fuel to RFA *Arndale* in the River Plate.
27 January: *MOS9* (later to be *Ennerdale* (1)) launched.
28 January: *Black Ranger*, 3,417 grt, completed by Harland & Wolff at Govan for the Admiralty and joins the Fleet Fuelling Service as a fleet attendant tanker.
29 January: *Blue Ranger* launched.
30 January: *Empire Silver*, completed by Blythswood Shipbuilding Co at Glasgow for the MoWT; taken over by the Admiralty for service as a freighting tanker, renamed RFA *Denbydale*.
11 February: *Nasprite*, petrol carrier, 975 grt, completed by Blythswood Shipbuilding Co at Glasgow for the Admiralty at a cost of £97,207.
12 February: *Nasprite* joins the Fleet Fuelling Service.
15 February: *Easedale* laid down.
17 February: *Dewdale* launched.
March: British ships begin to be 'degaussed' against magnetic mines.

RFA *Freshbrook*, water tanker. (RFA Archive)

Oiling at sea – Director Plans at the Admiralty recommends 'development of the floating hose'. *Abbeydale* in South Atlantic to relieve *Arndale*. Operation Pilgrim (formerly Puma) plans modified and forces made ready for the 'taking of the Atlantic Islands (the Azores, the Canaries and Cape Verde Islands) – *Olwen* and *Abbeydale* and the LSGs *Dewdale* and *Ennerdale* on alert.

4 March: *Empire Granite* completed by Hawthorn Leslie at Hebburn for the MoWT (*MOS14*); taken over by the Admiralty as freighting oiler RFA *Echodale*.

12 March: *Gold Ranger* launched.

18 March: Water tankers *Freshener* and *Freshlake* ordered.

24 March: *Cairndale* fuelled Force H at sea, although no records remain that detail this.

25 March: Oiling at sea – Admiralty meeting 'Oiling of Capital ships and Cruisers at Sea' (chaired by Vice Chief of Naval Staff) to determine British requirements and policy on oiling at sea and a study of German methods in comparison with RN stirrup method.

26 March: Oiling at sea – Commander-in-Chief Home Fleet ordered to carry out preliminary trials, using 'Dale' class and 2,000-ton class RFA oilers, to determine what additional gear and fittings required in each class of oiler and in HM Ships and what flow rates can be expected with stirrup method and 5-inch hose (metallic).

27 March: *Dingledale* launched at Govan for MoWT.

8 April: Oiling at sea – modified stirrup method using 5-inch hose undertaken at Scapa between HMS *Galeta* and RFA *War Diwan*.

10 April: *Brown Ranger*, 3,417 grt, completed by Harland and Wolff at Glasgow for the Admiralty and joins the Fleet Fuelling Service as a fleet attendant oiler.

12 April: Oiling at sea – trials of underway oiling at sea by modified Stirrup method at Scapa Flow with RFA *Celerol* and HMS *Exeter* using 5-inch hose. *Derwentdale* (1) launched at Belfast for MoWT.

17 April Oiling at sea – *Aldersdale* at Scapa Flow to carry out Oiling at sea trials in open sea with HMS *Exeter* in order to conduct a comparison with the trials undertaken on the 12th with a smaller oiler.

19 April: *Aldersdale* and *Oligarch* allocated to fleet attendant duties in Norwegian waters.

22 April: Evacuation of British forces from Greece commences.

22 April: War loss – *Olna* – Suda Bay, Crete – this tanker was damaged and set on fire by air bombing, she was beached and badly burnt out; fell into German hands on evacuation of Crete on 31 May 1941; at the end of the war she was found as a wreck at Scaramanga, fit only for scrap; officers repatriated to UK and Chinese crew repatriated to Singapore – one rating injured, dying on 4 June as a direct result of injuries.

4–5 May: *Denbydale* bombed at Liverpool, no injuries reported.

25 May: *Cairndale* sailed from Gibraltar to act as the oiler for Force H, the squadron hunting the *Bismarck*.

27 May: *Gray Ranger* launched.

29 May: Oiling at sea – RFA *Belgol* and RFA *Celerol* conduct trials with destroyers using the trough method.

30 May: War loss – RFA *Cairndale* – 35.19N 008.33E (west of Gibraltar), this tanker was serving as the Force H oiler when the Italian submarine *Guglielmo Marconi* torpedoed her – casualties two officers and two ratings killed and four ratings injured (three deaths are recorded in The Tower Hill Memorial register).

4 June: The German support tanker *Gedania* (later to become *Empire Garden*) is captured.

5 June: *Blue Ranger*, 3,467 grt, completed by Harland and Wolff at Glasgow for the Admiralty and joins the Fleet Fuelling Service as a fleet attendant oiler.

6 June: Oiling at sea – *Belgol* conducted trials with the destroyer HMS *Inglefield*.

14 June: *Dewdale*, 8,298 grt, completed by Cammell Laird at Birkenhead for the Admiralty.

RFA *Blue Ranger*, fleet attendant tanker. (World Ship Society)

The Arctic Convoys

Between 1941 and 1945 the supply convoys to Northern Russian ports with their supporting operations illustrate one of the most arduous aspects of war at sea – hostile weather conditions and a determined enemy. Royal Fleet Auxiliaries and tankers of the Convoy Escort Oiler Service were heavily involved in escort support duties. In this war zone was one of the most famous convoys of the Second World War – PQ17 – and the RFA was to suffer losses including the new tanker *Gray Ranger* that was fitted with experimental oiling-at-sea equipment.

Operation Dervish – 12 August 1941 – RFA *Aldersdale*.
Operation Gauntlet – 19 August 1941 – RFA *Oligarch*.
Convoy QP1 – 28 September 1941 – RFA *Black Ranger* joined 4 October.
Convoy PQ1 – 29 October 1941 – RFA *Black Ranger*.
Convoy PQ14 – 26 March 1942 – RFA *Aldersdale*.
Convoy PQ15 – 10 April 1942 – RFA *Gray Ranger*.
Convoy PQ16 – 21 May 1942 – RFA *Black Ranger*.
Convoy PQ17 – 27 June 1942 – RFA *Aldersdale* and RFA *Gray Ranger*.
Convoy QP13 – 26 June 1942 – RFA *Gray Ranger* joined from PQ17.
24 July 1942 – an escorted RFA *Black Ranger* was an *en route* fuelling station to some warships taking ammunition and stores to Northern Russia; stores needed by PQ17's surviving escort vessels.
Convoy PQ18 – 2 September 1942 – RFA *Black Ranger* and RFA *Oligarch*. RFA *Blue Ranger* and RFA *Gray Ranger* supplied supporting fuelling facilities.
Convoy QP14 – 13 September 1942 – RFA *Black Ranger* and RFA *Gray Ranger*; RFA *Oligarch* joined later.
Convoy JW51A – 15 December 1942 – RFA *Oligarch*.
Convoy RA51 – 30 December 1942 – RFA *Oligarch*.
Convoy JW52 – 17 January 1943 – RFA *Oligarch*.
Convoy RA53 – 1 March 1943 – RFA *Oligarch*.
Convoy JW63 – 30 December 1944 – RFA *Blue Ranger*.
Convoy RA17 – 11 January 1945 – RFA *Blue Ranger*.
Convoy JW64 – 3 February 1945 – RFA *Black Ranger*.
Convoy RA64 – 17 February 1945 – RFA *Black Ranger*.
Convoy JW64 – 11 March 1945 – RFA *Blue Ranger*.
Convoy RA65 – 23 March 1945 – RFA *Blue Ranger*.
Convoy JW68 – 27 April 1945 – RFA *Black Ranger* and RFA *Blue Ranger*.
Convoy RA66 – 29 April 1945 – RFA *Black Ranger* and RFA *Blue Ranger*.

15 June: The German support tanker *Lothringen* is sighted and attacked by aircraft from HMS *Eagle*; the slightly damaged tanker is then intercepted and captured by HMS *Dunedin* with her oiling-at-sea gear and 5-inch rubber hoses intact; prize crew took her to Bermuda where the Collector of Customs, Greenock instructed that her cargo is taken into custody as a prize cargo but not the ship itself; temporally registered by the MoWT as *Empire Salvage*.

19 June: *Freshbrook*, water tanker, laid down.

2 July: *Airsprite* ordered.

4 July: *Gold Ranger*, 3,313 grt, completed by the Caledon Shipbuilding and Engineering Co at Dundee for the Admiralty; joined Fleet Fuelling Service as a fleet attendant oiler. *Empire Salvage* – Lt Commander RN (retd) appointed as Master.

11 July: *Ennerdale* (1), 8,219 grt, completed by Swan Hunter & Wigham Richardson at Newcastle for the MoWT (*MOS9*); taken over by the Admiralty as RFA *Ennerdale* (1).

14 July: *War Pindari* bombed at Skaalefjord off Solmunde, no injuries recorded.

15 July: *Blue Ranger* in collision with ss *Iris*, in fog, off the Clyde; *Iris* sunk, *Blue Ranger* leaking forward returned to Greenock with survivors.

22 July: *Freshmere*, *Freshpool* and *Freshwell*, water tankers, ordered.

25 July: Oiling at sea – RFA *Celerol* conducted oiling-underway exercise with the cruiser HMS *Shropshire* at Scapa Flow; the oiler was towed.

27 July–7 August: Operation FB – *Oligarch* and *War Sudra* supporting Force A which destroyed facilities on Spitsbergen.

August: Oiling at sea – *Gold Ranger* conducted trough rig trials with HMS *Berwick*.

2 August: Oiling at sea – *Montenol* successfully completed trials using the stirrup method.

4 August: *Darkdale* arrived St Helena.

8 August: Oiling at sea – *War Diwan* undertook trials at Scapa Flow with the cruiser HMS *Galatea*. *Denbydale*, *Dewdale* and *Ennerdale* allocated to Exercise Leapfrog in preparation for Operation Pilgrim – a proposed action against the Canary Islands.

12 August: *Dewdale* and *Ennerdale* allocated to Operation Pilgrim.

18 August: *Oligarch* supported Operation Gauntlet – the naval raid on Spitzbergen.

21 August: *Green Ranger* launched.

23 August: Oiling at sea – *Rapidol* in proposed arrangements for trials with OS and SL convoys.

24–27 August: Operation Gauntlet – *Oligarch* supporting evacuation of Soviets from Spitzbergen.

30 August: *Derwentdale* (1), 8.398 grt, completed by Harland & Wolff at Belfast for the MoWT, transferred to the Admiralty. *Rapidol* in company with HMS *Dunedin* rendezvoused with the battlecruiser HMS *Repulse*; she was to be employed for oiling at sea trials as soon as available.

September: *Spabeck*, water tanker, ordered. *Airsprite*, petrol carrier, laid down. *Bishopdale* on three occasions successfully oiled (stopped and at right angles) using troughs with

HM Ships *Eagle* and *Formidable*.

1 September: Oiling at sea – RFA *Gray Ranger* fitted with arrangements for improving existing oiling-at-sea methods using both buoyant (rubber) hose and a self-rendering winch.

2 September: *Derwentdale* sailed from Belfast on passage Clyde, Halifax, Trinidad, Simonstown, Alexandria and Bombay.

4 September Oiling at sea – *Empire Garden* (captured 4 June) conducts oiling-at-sea trials in the Clyde area.

6 September: *Maine*, hospital ship – bombed at Alexandria, three ratings killed, one officer, 10 RFA and two RN ratings injured.

10 September: *Dingledale* 8,185 grt completed by Harland & Wolff at Govan for the MoWT, transferred to the Admiralty.

12 September: *Petrella* bombed in Mediterranean, chief engineer killed, one engine room rating injured.

18 September: *Berta* suffered slight damage aft after a near miss during an air attack, no casualties reported.

24–30 September: Operation Halberd, supply convoy from Gibraltar to Malta, with fuelling force provided by RFA *Brown Ranger* with close escort corvette HMS *Fleur-De-Lys*.

25 September: *Gray Ranger*, 2,557 grt, completed by the Caledon Shipbuilding and Engineering Co at Dundee for the Admiralty; joined the Fleet Fuelling Service fitted with new oiling at sea arrangement for buoyant hose, special bollards and with a new steam drive Clarke-Chapman self-rendering winch.

29 September: Serious casualty – RFA *Denbydale* – Gibraltar; Italian submarine *Scire* penetrated Bay of Gibraltar, launching three Siluro a Lenta Corsa (SLC) – slow running human torpedo/frogman teams; this tanker was severely damaged, partially sinking; spent remainder of her life as a fuelling and accommodation hulk at Gibraltar – no casualties reported.

October: Oiling at sea – *Black Ranger* conducted stirrup rig trials in North Atlantic waters.

RFA *Black Ranger*, fleet attendant tanker. (World Ship Society)

1 October: Oiling at sea – German oiling-at-sea gear from *Empire Garden* (ex German fleet supply ship *Gedania*) landed at Greenock; proportion, including German rubber hoses, transferred to RFA *Gray Ranger* at Leith together with a report of the recent trials; some rubber hose transferred to 'Dale' class oilers as they had ample supply of compressed air. Two officers ex RFA *Reliant* and ex RFA *Slavol* killed when the *Pass of Balmaha* was the target of enemy action; both officers had been transferred on C-in-C's instructions to make up the ship's complement.

5 October: *Empire Salvage* sailed Halifax on passage to the Clyde.

17 October: *Derwentdale* carrying landing craft sailed from Trinidad for Simonstown.

20 October: Oiling at sea – production of rubber hose of British manufacture was suspended and trials of German type flexible hose (which embodied a different principle) for oiling at sea were to be carried out.

21 October: Oiling at sea – RFA *Black Ranger* reported on stirrup method of oiling at sea operations in Arctic waters. *Empire Salvage* is declared as urgently required for service as a fleet tanker. *Empire Norseman* (later to be RFA *Dinsdale*) launched Belfast for MoWT.

22 October: War loss – RFA *Darkdale* – 15.54.58S 5.43.15 W (St Helena), *U68* at *circa* 00.15 torpedoed this tanker, when at anchor; only survivors were the Master, Chief Engineer and seven ratings, all of whom were ashore – casualties 11 officers including two radio officers, 27 ratings and three DEMS gunners (37 deaths recorded on The Tower Hill Memorial).

28 October: Oiling at sea – trials in the Clyde area and some conducted at Scapa Flow with *Empire Salvage* and RFA *Gray Ranger*, much of it involved use of captured German rubber hoses and equipment.

30 October: The loss of the *Darkdale* and the lack of an alternative fuelling port for ships of limited endurance between Freetown and the Cape were raised with the Admiralty as a problem.

5 November: *Freshbrook*, water tanker, launched at Lytham.

6 November: *Freshener*, water tanker, laid down.

8 November: *Spa*, water tanker, launched at Dartmouth.

17 November: Oiling at sea – decision made that 'Ranger' class were unsuitable for oiling at sea in the Atlantic. *Demeter* – staffed by RFA personnel to 25 July 1945.

18 November: *Empire Metal* (later to be RFA *Eaglesdale*) launched at Haverton Hill for MoWT.

19 November: War loss – RFA *War Mehtar* – 52.35.45N 02.9.30E (off Great Yarmouth, England) – this tanker was on passage Grangemouth

to Harwich with 7,000 tons of Admiralty fuel oil when torpedoed by Schnellboot *S104* of the 2nd German E-boat flotilla; the crew of 45 were saved; unsuccessful attempts made to salvage the ship – casualties one officer and three ratings injured. *Rapidol* with the corvette HMS *Bergamot* sailed with ocean escort to joint convoy SL93, transferred to convoy OS11 with Freetown Escort Force for passage back to Freetown.

4 December: *Green Ranger*, 3,313 grt, completed by the Caledon Shipbuilding and Engineering Co at Dundee for the Admiralty; joined the Fleet Fuelling Service as an aviation spirit carrier.

6 December: Oiling at sea – RFA *Blue Ranger* was on the Clyde for preliminary trials of new British type flexible hose produced by Goodyear; 600ft of hose was made available and priority was given to these trials prior to trials in the Atlantic with a 'Dale' class oiler.

7 December: Pearl Harbor, base of the US Pacific Fleet, attacked by Japanese carrier-borne aircraft.

7–8 December: Britain and the USA declare war on Japan and Japanese aircraft attack Singapore and Hong Kong.

8 December: Oiling at sea – *Empire Salvage* undertook trials with *Blue Ranger* and with destroyers.

12 December: Captured – RFA *Ebonol* – Hong Kong – this tanker was scuttled to avoid capture, subsequently salvaged by the Japanese and renamed *Enoshima Maru*; recovered at Batavia in 1945 – four officers taken prisoners of war (PoW); chief engineer died in PoW camp 11 September 1942; the 26 ratings are recorded as missing or PoWs.

18 December: *Easedale* launched for MoWT.

22 December – 1 January 1942: Operation Anklet – second commando raid on the Lofoten Islands supported from Scapa Flow with RFA *Black Ranger* and RFA *Gray Ranger*.

25 December: Surrender of Hong Kong to the Japanese.

31 December: Oiling at sea – RFA *Gray Ranger* working with HMS *Bedouin* reported satisfactory results when using German rubber hose; arrangements made for RFA *Eaglesdale* to undertake trials with rubber hose.

1942

1942: Oiling at sea – RFA *Rapidol* conducted trials of shipboard equipment for handling rubber hose; this proved unsatisfactory and arrangements were made to fit RFA *Abbeydale* with a continuous set of rollers. Oiling at sea – RFA *Abbeydale* serving in the Mediterranean reportedly undertook the first simultaneous refuelling of three ships – one on either beam and one astern. *Olcades* was on freighting duties when crankshaft trouble reduced her to hulk service in Bombay; her Chief Engineer, with ship's engineers and two fitters from Mazagan repaired the defect, involving handling weights of 20 tons under tropical conditions and ship was back in service by 1943. *Bacchus* converted, Liverpool, into a naval stores issuing ship.

January: *Empire Salvage* is fitted with defensive equipment (armament and degaussing) and a gyro compass.

9 January: *Eaglesdale*, 8,030 grt, completed by Furness Shipbuilding at Haverton for the Admiralty.

12 January: *Derwentdale* left Alexandria for Benghazi with 15 LCMs embarked. *Gold Ranger*, fitted for oiling at sea, embarked 1,000 tons of oil, sailed UK to Freetown in convoy OS17.

16 January: *Orangeleaf* in convoy FTT6 when in collision with *Botnia*, undamaged.

19 January: One officer ex RFA *Bishopdale* was killed when the *Lady Hawkins* was subject to enemy action.

22 January–2 February: Oiling at sea –

Requirement for a Fast Fleet Oiler

In 1942 the Royal Navy was developing a requirement for a Fast Fleet Oiler. By November 1943 the 1944 Programme was in the course of preparation and by February 1944 a Staff Requirement existed in draft form. The problem was to find capacity to build the ships. The position was unacceptable and to overcome the problem compromises were reached and two Shell tankers were to become 'stopgap' fast tankers named *Olna* and *Oleander*. The end of the war came before *Oleander* was converted and she reverted to Shell ownership.

RFA *Orangeleaf* (1), 'Fast Leaf' tanker. (World Ship Society)

a number of trials were undertaken during this period in the North Atlantic with RFA *Dingledale* and the cruiser HMS *Hermione*; the modified stirrup method was used.

29 January: *Gold Ranger* refuelled from *Dewdale*.

February: Oiling at sea – *Eaglesdale* fitted for trials. Operation Pilgrim plans involving five RFAs stood down.

12 February: *Easedale*, 8,630 grt, completed by Furness Shipbuilding at Haverton for the Admiralty.

15 February: Surrender of Singapore to the Japanese.

16 February: Captured – *Ruthenia* – Singapore – this fuel hulk was scuttled; subsequently salvaged by the Japanese; she was renamed *Choran Maru*; recovered 1945.

19 February: Oiling at sea – *Eaglesdale* prepared for trials in Clyde area.

23 February: *War Sirdar* bombed and damaged by Japanese aircraft at Batavia, her cargo was transferred to *Celerol*.

28 February: War loss – *War Sirdar* – 12.39N 109.37E (Sunda Straits off NW Batavia, Java) – 25 February 1942 direct hit during air raid – no casualties; 27 February 1942 sailed in convoy Batavia to Tjilatjap; 08.00 on 28 February 1942 she grounded on a reef with an HM Ship standing by; she was bombed and machine-gunned; ordered to abandon; 07.45 all hands landed Jung Island; 1 March 1942 all hands taken off by Dutch minesweeper; the Master to Australia on leave; officers repatriated to the UK in SS *Strath Hallion* from Sydney; salvaged by the Japanese, renamed *Konan Maru*; 1943 renamed *Honan Maru*; 23 March 1945 sunk by US submarine *Bluegill* – no casualties recorded.

4 March: War loss – *Francol* – 11.00S 109.00E (near Tjilatjap, 300 miles south of Java) – this tanker was on passage Batavia for Fremantle when sunk as a result of an air attack and by gunfire from a Japanese naval surface squadron – three officers missing, four taken PoW, 13 survivors (four deaths recorded on the Tower Hill Memorial; Lloyd's Official Records list date as 3 March 1942, position 11.30S 109.3E, and two crew prisoners of war. International Red Cross gave sinking date as 4 March 1942). Oiling at sea – *Eaglesdale*, out of Londonderry, conducted extensive trials of captured German equipment and of independent work already carried out with 5-inch rubber hose; the success of the trials resulted in the general introduction of the rubber hose and deck rollers.

15 March: *Aldersdale*'s bows badly damaged by ice in Northern waters.

16 March: *Freshener* launched at Lytham. *Empire Salvage* fitted with aviation spirit stowage.

18 March: *Freshlake*, water tanker, laid down.

26 March: *Plumleaf* – war loss – Parlatorio Wharf, Malta – this tanker was damaged during an air attack, her after end went aground, but she remained lying upright; 4 April 1942 she received further damaged during heavy air attacks by II German Air Corps and Italian formations; she sank to deck level in about 46ft of water and after refloating on 28 August 1947 she was towed to Catania for scrapping; no casualties. *Slavol* – war loss – 32N 25.57E (NE of Sollum) – this tanker was on passage Alexandria to Tobruk with a cargo of fuel oil, when torpedoed and sunk by *U205*; 18 surviving Lascars repatriated to Bombay – casualties four officers and one Radio Officer killed, 31 Lascar ratings killed, one officer injured (five deaths recorded on the Tower Hill Memorial).

30 March: Oiling at sea – trials with *Abbeydale*.

April: *Spabrook*, water tanker, ordered. Force Q, RFA *Gray Ranger* with convoy PQ15.

RFA *Gray Ranger*, lost on convoy QP14 in September 1942. (RFA Archive)

Amphibious Operations 1942–1944

In addition to the great Normandy landings of 1944 British and Allied forces were engaged in a wide range of amphibious landings and RFA landing ships and tankers were there in direct support:

Operation Ironclad, Diego Suarez, Madagascar – 5 May 1942

RFA *Derwentdale*, landing ship gantry (LSG), left Durban 25 April in assault convoy Y, arrived at beachhead 5 May.

RFA *Easedale*, oiler, left Durban 25 April in assault convoy Y supporting destroyers and smaller ships *en route* to the beachhead.

Operation Stream, Majunga, Madagascar – 10 September 1942

RFA *Easedale*, oiler, left Mombasa 3 September in convoy F, arrived Majunga 18 September.

Operation Jane, Tamatave, Madagascar – 18 September 1942

RFA *Easedale*, oiler, left Mombasa 3 September in convoy F, arrived Majunga 18 September.

Operation Torch, invasion of North Africa – 8 November 1942

RFA *Abbeydale*, oiler, joined convoy KMS2 on 10 November and arrived Arzeu 11 November.

RFA *Brown Ranger*, oiler, with an escort formed Force R, left Gibraltar 5 November as fuelling support for Force H.

RFA *Derwentdale*, LSG, left the Clyde on 22 October in assault convoy KMS1, arrived Arzeu Z beachhead on 8 November.

RFA *Dewdale*, LSG, left the Clyde on 22 October in assault convoy KMS1, arrived Algiers 9 November to refuel destroyers and escort vessels; left 10 November, arrived Bougie 11 November to provide fuelling support to the fleet; damaged by air attack on 12 November and severely holed by a direct hit on 20 November in Algiers.

RFA *Dingledale*, oiler, with RFA *Brown Ranger* formed Force R, which left Gibraltar on 5 November to support Force H.

RFA *Ennerdale*, LSG, left the Clyde on 22 October in assault convoy KMS1, suffered defects in her Landing Craft handling gear on arrival Algiers beachhead on 8 November

RFA *Nasprite*, petrol carrier.

RFA *Viscol*, oiler.

Operation Husky, invasion of Sicily – 10 July 1943

RFA *Cedardale*, oiler, left Benghazi 8 July as part of Force R providing refuelling support to destroyers.

RFA *Derwentdale*, LSG, left Glasgow 11 June and then sailed from the Clyde on 22 June in assault convoy KMS18B, 9 July transferred to convoy KMF18 for early unloading; arrived Barkl West beachhead 10 July.

RFA *Ennerdale*, LSG, embarked landing her landing craft at Port Said, left Alexandria 3 July in assault convoy MWS36, arrived allocated beachhead 10 July.

RFA *Nasprite*, petrol carrier, left Malta to arrive her assigned beachhead 10 July.

RFA *Pearleaf*, oiler, detached from following-up convoy MWS37 to Benghazi to become part of Force R on 9 July.

Operation Avalanche, Salerno invasion, Italy – 9 September 1943

RFA *Derwentdale*, LSG, carrying 15 landing craft left Bizerta 7 September in assault convoy FSS2, arrived Salerno 9 September, 15 September aerial bombing near-miss, suffered engine room damage, towed to Malta.

Operation Shingle, Anzio, and Italy –22 January 1944 – no traceable record of the RFAs involved.

Operation Anvil (later **Operation Dragoon**), invasion of southern France – 15 August 1944

RFA *Celerol*, oiler, carrying diesel and lubricating oil, left Maddalena 14 August, failed to locate her assigned convoy SM2 and sailed unescorted arriving her assigned beachhead on 15 August.

RFA *Dewdale*, LSG, carrying 14 landing craft, fuel oil, diesel and fresh water, left Naples 12 August in assault convoy SM1, arrived assigned beachhead 15 August and near missed by a glider bomb.

RFA *Ennerdale*, LSG carrying 14 landing craft, 4,000 tons fuel oil, 1,035 tons diesel and 2,500 tons fresh water, left Naples 12 August in assault convoy SM1A, arrived assigned beachhead 15 August.

11 April: *Empire Norseman*, 8,214 grt, completed by Harland & Wolff at Belfast for the MoWT renamed *Dinsdale* when allocated to the Admiralty as compensation for the loss of *Cairndale*.

17 April: *Dinsdale* suffered engine room breakdown owing to an accumulation of sand in her engine intakes that prevented her sailing as planned. *Freshbrook*, 278 grt, water tanker, completed by Lytham Shipbuilder & Engineering Co at Lytham for the Admiralty; cost £29,330.

18 April: *Empire Salvage* surveyed at Newcastle and registered in London for service with the Admiralty as RFA *Empire Salvage*.

24 April: *Spa*, water tanker 720 grt, completed by Phillip & Sons at Dartmouth for the Admiralty.

25 April: *Gray Ranger* formed Force Q for fuelling support to convoy PQ15.

May: *Boxol*, Malta, defuelled cargo from the badly damaged British-crewed American tanker *Ohio*. *Empire Salvage* takes up fleet attendant duties.

5 May: Amphibious operations – Operation Ironclad, the occupation of Diego Suarez in Madagascar – *Derwentdale* (carrying 12 LCMs) and *Easedale* took part.

8 May: *Gray Ranger* at Lerwick with HMS *Ledbury* to replenish their

diesel fuel stocks.

11 May: *Black Ranger* detailed for Force Q, convoy PQ16.

14 May: *Derwentdale* for UK after discharge of personnel at Bombay.

21 May: *Montenol* – war loss – 36.41N 22.45W (eastern Atlantic – 40 miles ESE off Santa Maria, Azores) this tanker was in convoy OS28 to the Far East via the Cape, when torpedoed by *U159*; of the crew of 56 plus three DEMS ratings – three were lost; it was impractical to tow the damaged ship so she was finally sunk by gunfire from HM Ships; some of the Lascar survivors repatriated to Bombay – casualties two ratings killed and one died later from his injuries (this ship is not recorded on the Tower Hill Memorial). *Dinsdale* sailed from Trinidad on passage to Durban.

31 May: *Dinsdale* – war loss – 01.00S 030.15W (South Atlantic); this tanker was on passage Trinidad for Port Elizabeth with a cargo of aviation spirit when 120 miles SSW off St Paul's Rock she was torpedoed at *circa* 01.30 by the Italian submarine *Cappellini*; the submarine reportedly used three torpedoes; ship was abandoned and her survivors were landed in the UK – casualties one officer and four ratings killed, one officer injured out of a crew of 59 (four deaths recorded on the Tower Hill Memorial).

June: Convoy PQ17 with *Gray Ranger* as convoy oilers and RFA *Aldersdale* with Force Q; *Gray Ranger* damaged by ice and forced to return to base for repairs, *Aldersdale* became the convoy oiler. Oiling at sea – convoy refuelling of escorts first tried by the US with old four-funnel destroyer *Babbitt*.

10 June: *Brambleleaf* – serious casualty off Mersa Alun (eastern Mediterranean); this tanker was in convoy AT49, Alexandria to Tobruk; torpedoed and damaged by U-boat attack, safely towed to Alexandria and after partial repair entered service as an oil hulk, salvage award made to the crew by MoWT; 15 September 1944 stern half sunk suddenly in Alexandria harbour; of the survivors the Master and a junior engineer went to RFA *Cherryleaf*; one junior engineer went to RFA *War Krishna* and another went to the Hospital Ship RFA *Maine*, remainder repatriated to UK – casualties two officers, five ratings killed, six ratings injured.

12–16 June: Operations Vigorous and Harpoon – supply convoy from Alexandria to Malta and simultaneous one from Gibraltar to Malta with Force Y (Tanker Force) *Brown Ranger* and close escort.

30 June: *Aldersdale* joined convoy PQ17.

4 July: War loss – *Aldersdale* – 77.00N 22.00E (approximately) (Barents Sea), the tanker was the convoy oiler to PQ17 – damaged by an air attack by German bomber group KG30, crew abandoned ship; study was made to see if she could be towed – but impractical; attempts then made to sink her by gunfire and depth charges; 7 July 1942 the abandoned wreck torpedoed and sunk by *U457*; the crew were landed at Archangel; the Master, two officers and 8 DEMS ratings returned to UK August 1942; 11 officers, including three radio officers returned to UK September 1942 followed by most of remaining crew – no casualties recorded. *Spa* in collision with the cruiser HMS *Phoebe*.

16–17 July: *Blue Ranger* with destroyer HMS *Douglas* as Force Q sailed from

RFA *Montenol*, a 2,000-ton tanker torpedoed and lost March 1942. (World Ship Society)

RFA *Spa*, water tanker. (RFA Archive)

'Dale' class

LANDING SHIPS GANTRY
RFA *Derwentdale* RFA *Dewdale*
RFA *Ennerdale*
Machinery: One 6 cyl Burmeister & Wain 4 stroke single acting ICE built by J G Kincade, Greenock; single screw; 3,500 bhp; 11.5 knots
Dimensions (loa/bp x beam): 483/–ft x 59ft
Tonnage measurements: 8,265 grt, 11,387 dwt
Displacement: 16,782 tons full load
Complement: 70 + 16 DEMS gunners + accommodation for 260

The landing ship gantry RFA *Dewdale* displaying her landing craft under complex gantries, extensive armament facilities and fitted with early radar. (World Ship Society)

Remarks: These were the RFAs which formed part of Britain's Combined Operations forces and were the RFA's pioneers of what is today commonplace – supporting amphibious operations.

During 1940 a scheme was devised in which 48.5ft, 36-ton Landing Craft Mechanised Mark 1s (LCM(1)) could be carried on the deck of large ships and hoisted out and lowered using large davits or gantries. The scheme was to be applied to three tankers building for the Admiralty – the RFAs *Derwentdale*, *Dewdale* and *Ennerdale*. Each tanker was to become a landing craft carrier and be fitted with two 32-ton gantries with a lift of 32ft, one forward and one aft the central bridge structure and modified to carry 15 LCM(1). The landing craft would be stowed on rollers in three rows on deck with minimum interference to the original function of the ships. Owing to the shortage of tanker tonnage it was agreed that the ships, when not freighting LCM(1)s, would be available for use as tankers, so they remained RFAs. It was also felt that the ships of assault convoys would require attendant tankers and these three ships would go towards meeting this requirement. In reality, after their conversion, they were almost constantly used in ferrying landing craft.

In their initial conversion no accommodation was provided for the landing craft crews and *ad hoc* arrangements had to be provided. Later in a further conversion accommodation for LCM crews and a maintenance party had to be provided but could only be accomplished with a reduction in the tanker's capacity. Further conversion again reduced the tanker capability and arrangements made for the bulk 3,600 tons carriage of fresh water.

Finally they were provided with radar, 'talk between ship' (TBS) radio, paravane and degaussing equipment, protection plating and plastic armour and extensive defensive armament – 1 x 4.7-inch QF gun, 3 x 2 pdr Pom Poms, 6 x 20mm Oerlikons and a number of machine guns.

This information is based on RFA Derwentdale *(1)*

Hvalfjord for PQ18, then proceeded to Scapa as PQ18 was cancelled.

22 July: *Freshmere*, water tanker, laid down. *Freshener*, 278 grt, water tanker, completed by Lytham Shipbuilding & Engineering Co at Lytham for the Admiralty.

4 August: *Bishopdale* struck a mine, no casualties, returned to harbour.

10–15 August: Oiling at sea – Force W (Operation Berserk) a sea/air exercise in the Atlantic; reports show RFA *Abbeydale* had a new and inexperienced crew which resulted in complete disorder; the stirrup method of oiling was workable but rate was slow, with lack of hawsers, parted lines and burst hoses with oil spraying everywhere. Operation Pedestal – Malta convoy – the main Oiling Group supporting this convoy was known as Force R – *Dingledale* and *Brown Ranger* with a close escort of four corvettes, refuelled 24 destroyers and the cruiser HMS *Cairo*.

12 August: *War Afridi* damaged the cruiser HMS *Liverpool* at Rosyth.

September: *Danmark* – 5,419 grt Danish motor tanker built in 1931; January 1940 became a serious war casualty; taken for conversion into a stationary fuel hulk by Grangemouth Dockyard Co; all amidships accommodation was mainly intact, as were the pipelines in the cargo tanks and on deck but no steam pipes to operate the cargo pumps; the dry cargo hold, abaft the forepeak tank, was arranged as an engine/boiler room and uptake were led into a single funnel that in turn led through the forecastle deck; towed to Scapa Flow for service as an RFA-managed oil fuel hulk with RFA Chief Officer, Third Officer, Chief Engineer and Third Engineer.

8 September: *Blue Ranger* with *Oligarch* sailed from Hoxa Sound to Spitzbergen as Force D for PQ18.

9 September: *Spa* in collision with the battleship HMS *Howe*.

12 September: Chief Engineer of RFA *Maine* being repatriated to the UK was killed when the *Laconia* was torpedoed.

13 September: *Dingledale* suffered a fire in her bridge, chartroom and radio room – arson suspected.

22 September: *Gray Ranger* – war loss – 71.23N 11.03W (Arctic waters south of Mayen Island) – this tanker was the escort oiler with convoy QP14 *en route* from Russia, when torpedoed and sunk at *circa* 06.26 by *U435*; 27 September 1942 Master, Chief Engineer, seven DEMS and 11 ratings picked up and landed Scapa; 27 September 1942 six officers including Radio Officer, four DEMS and 14 ratings picked up landed Greenock; all other survivors landed during the course of September – casualties three officers including Radio Officer killed, three ratings killed and one officer injured.

October: *Abbeydale* refitted as a DEMS at Gibraltar.

1 October: 24 ratings of RFA *Green Ranger*, 29 ratings of RFA *Eaglesdale* and one officer ex RFA *Arndale* being repatriated to the UK – nine ratings killed and eight injured when the *Mendoza* was torpedoed.

RFA *Airsprite*, a fine example of these small spirit tankers built in 1941. (RFA Archive)

5 October: *Spa* in collision with the battleship HMS *King George V* at Scapa Flow.

12 October: *War Sudra* damaged whilst going alongside *Prestol* at Lyness.

22 October: Amphibious operation – Operation Torch – the Allied landings in French North Africa – *Derwentdale*, *Ennerdale* with *Brown Ranger* and *Dingledale* (Force R).

27 October: *Danmark* fuelling hulk at Scapa staffed by RFA to 3 October 1944.

30 October: A rating of RFA *Easedale* being repatriated to the UK was killed when the *Abasso* was the target of enemy action.

November: Oiling at sea – RFA *Abbeydale* serving in the Mediterranean undertook the first recorded multi-RAS with two ships abeam and one astern. Oiling at sea – RFA *Brown Ranger* serving in the Mediterranean reportedly repeated *Abbeydale*'s simultaneous refuelling of three ships – one on either beam and one astern; although bearing in mind the design of the 'Ranger' class this report seems improbable. Task Force 11, part of the Task Force 16 ANZAC Squadron, included RFA *Bishopdale*.

6 November: The La Riviera Societa Anonina di Nav, Genoa, tanker *Portofino* bombed and sunk by British aircraft at Benghazi; the tanker is the former Admiralty tanker *Roseleaf* (May 1916).

8 November: *Ennerdale* damaged by enemy action, no casualties.

9 November: Oiling at sea – *Derwentdale* undertook trials with the destroyer HMS *Amazon*.

11 November: Operation Torch – *Dewdale* arrived, reportedly shot down two enemy aircraft.

14 November: *Freshlake*, 278 grt, water tanker, completed by Lytham Shipbuilder & Engineering Co at Lytham for the Admiralty.

20 November: *Dewdale* – bombed by aircraft at Bassin de Mustapha, Port d'Alger, one rating injured.

23 November: *Freshmere* launched at Lytham.

26 November: *Freshpool* laid down.

December: Oiling at sea – statement issued by Commander-in-Chief Western Approaches – 3.5-inch canvas hose was used as a temporary measure for the modified trough method; instructions issued to Masters of oilers allocated to the Escort Oiling Service; canvas hose used until sufficient oilers are equipped to handle rubber hose.

22 December: *Airsprite* launched. *Thermol* in collision with the tug HMS *Brigadier*.

28 December: *Ennerdale* arrives Liverpool for repairs and conversion into an LSG.

29 December: *Dewdale* – further damage caused by a mine at Algiers.

1943

1943: Oiling at sea and North Atlantic convoys – The Admiralty recognised that trade protection in the North Atlantic would be considerably assisted if escorts could be refuelled

RFA *Seafox*: formerly a commissioned aircraft transport (small), later as an RFA she was used for ferrying naval aircraft and general stores in UK waters. (World Ship Society)

at sea as was being done in the OS and SL convoys. By January 1943 11 commercial tankers were fitted with derricks and platforms for oiling at sea; additionally 20 tankers also have what is known as 'commercial outfits only' enabling oiling at sea by the trough method using metallic hoses. Oiling at sea – Commander-in-Chief Eastern Fleet stressed the importance of providing a fast oiler equipped to US standards for oiling at sea; he asked to carry out trials in 'Dale' class by trough method using double line of 5-inch rubber hose; RFA *Echodale* was to carry out similar trials in the UK. Oiling at sea – RN aircraft carriers commenced fitting out for oiling at sea over the stern. *Olcades* back in service and with the Eastern Fleet as an oiling-at-sea tanker until 1946. *War Sirdar* was taken by the Japanese Army for service as an oiler and renamed *Honan Maru*. Operation Pilgrim – Azores plans reactivated with RFAS *Dewdale* and *Derwentdale* allocated. Admiralty make a decision to take up two 15-knot tankers of standard design to augment the RFA tanker fleet – these became the first of the 'Wave' class.

January: *Orangeleaf* with convoy FTT6, damaged in collision with *Bothnia*.

4 January: *Celerol* in collision with the Norwegian vessel *Namsos*. *Gold Ranger* sailed from East Indies to act as fleet attendant oiler at Durban.

5 January: *Oligarch* loaded full cargo of furnace fuel oil and sailed in convoy RU57 for Loch Ewe.

21 January: *Dewdale*, temporary repairs completed at Algiers.

February: Oiling at sea – 60–70 commercial tankers fitted for as convoy escort oilers; Masters report to Merchant Ships' Technical Committee that they prefer trough method and that it could be simpler with longer derricks, but astern method is best in rough weather.

3 February: *Wave Emperor* and *Wave Governor* ordered.

7 February: *Seafox* ordered.

16 February: *Airsprite*, petrol carrier, 965 grt, completed by Blythswood Shipbuilding Co at Glasgow for the Admiralty; carrying high octane for coastal forces.

21 February: *Empire Gold* registered in Middlesborough under the MoWT, and currently under refit at Palmer's, Hebburn, is to be transferred to Director of Stores at the Admiralty for manning and management as an RFA; Registrar of Shipping was requested to re-register this vessel at Port of London as the Admiralty vessel RFA *Eppingdale*, under section 80 of the Merchant Shipping Acts 1906.

22 February: RFA Master, Chief Officer, Chief Engineer with two engineers appointed to *Eppingdale*; transfer to Admiralty cancelled.

March: *Dewdale* again bombed and damaged at Algiers.

1 March: Oiling at sea – trials conducted with a full length of rubber hose that could be accommodated on stirrup rail equipment.

11 March: *Freshpool* launched at Lytham.

12–14 March: The ex-captain of RFA *Arndale*, being repatriated to the UK, was killed when the *Empress of Canada* was torpedoed.

18 March: *Freshwell*, water tanker, laid down.

19 March: *Altengamme*, the former Admiralty tanker *Briarleaf* (1916), is confiscated by the Hamburg Prize Court.

22 March: *Freshmere*, 278 grt, water tanker, completed by Lytham Shipbuilder & Engineering Co at Lytham for the Admiralty.

23 March: *Empire Sheba* (to become RFA *Wave King*) laid down.

30 March: Oiling at sea – RFA *Abbeydale* conducted oiling at sea trials with stirrup rails.

April: *Dewdale* arrived Liverpool for permanent repairs to damage and a refit.

RFA *Dingledale*, one of the 'D' group of war-built standard tankers.

13 April: *War Bharata* sustained damage during a collision with *Attendant* at Scapa Flow.

May: Force R, *Oligarch* carrying munitions for destroyers of Force H.

14 May: *Spabeck*, water tanker, laid down.

19 May: *Wave Emperor* laid down.

24 May: *Belgol* – bombed when in Sunderland, Chief Engineer injured, one rating and one DEMS gunner injured by burns – letter of their Lordship's of Admiralty appreciation of commendable services to the Chief Engineer.

25 May: *Oligarch* carrying depth charges, ammunition, etc in Force R for the destroyers of Force H.

28 May: *Thorpe Bay*, a hulk at Scapa Flow had had an RFA Chief Officer, Second Officer and Second Engineer appointed until 10 October 1944.

29 May: *Wave Regent* and *Wave Sovereign* ordered.

30 May: *Celerol* in convoy KMS15 Liverpool to Gibraltar.

17 June: *Empire Venus* (later to be RFA *Wave Monarch*) laid down.

21 June: *Spabeck* launched at Dartmouth, named *Rivulet*.

28 June: *Dewdale* repairs and refit completed.

July: Operation Husky, British element of Invasion of Sicily – RFA LSGs *Derwentdale* and *Ennerdale*, invasion also supported by *Cedardale* and *Nasprite*.

1 July: *Oligarch* – serious casualty – eastern Mediterranean – this tanker was torpedoed and proceeded to Tobruk under own power; used in harbour to fuel destroyers; after minor repairs, escorted in convoy UGS13, to Alexandria for use as a fuel hulk. Officers appointed to other RFAs, ratings repatriated to the UK – no casualties.

3 July: *Freshpool*, 278 grt, water tanker, completed by Lytham Shipbuilder & Engineering Co at Lytham for the Admiralty. *Rivulet*, water tanker 720 grt, completed by Phillip & Sons at Dartmouth for the Admiralty as *Spabeck*, cost £75,188.

6 July: *Freshwell* launched at Lytham.

7 July: *Freshburn* laid down.

23 August: *Oligarch* arrived Alexandria for partial repair for service as a fuelling hulk.

10 July: *Ennerdale* bombed and damaged off Sicily during the Allied landings. *Cedardale* and *Pearleaf* served at Benghazi with Force R.

13 July: *Ennerdale* – air attack at Sicily, shell exploded on No 8 port wing tank lid – one officer killed.

August: Operation Pilgrim – Azores invasion plans, with RFAs *Dewdale* and *Derwentdale*, stood down.

3 September: *Empire Bounty* (later to be RFA *Wave Victor*) launched.

7 September: Amphibious operations – *Derwentdale* sails from Bizerta as part of the southern attack force for Operation Avalanche – the Salerno landings.

8 September: Unconditional surrender of Italy.

15 September: *Derwentdale* severely damaged by aerial bombing at Salerno; engine room damaged; was beached to enable transfer of her cargo before being towed to Malta.

15 September: *Wave Governor* laid down.

16 September: *Spabrook* laid down.

October: *Empire Salvage*'s defensive armament is upgraded and she is fitted with gun positions, kite gear, alarm bells by Palmers Hebburn Co Ltd. Operation Alacrity (secret plan to establish Allied bases in the Azores), *Dewdale*, landing ship gantry at Horta.

25 October: *Dingledale* damaged at Freetown when HMS *Stork* was going alongside.

30 October: *Freshwell*, 278 grt, water tanker, completed by Lytham Shipbuilder & Engineering Co at Lytham for the Admiralty.

2 November: *Empire Law* (later to be RFA *Wave Conqueror*) launched.

5 November: *Freshford* laid down. Oiling at sea – *Echodale* conducted trials in the Clyde area.

29 November: Director of Victualling informs Director of Stores that it is the practice in victualling stores issuing ships to give keys of the refrigerated rooms to the Chief Engineer. This established the responsibility of the Chief for the refrigeration-plant in RFA *Reliant* and other ships carrying victualling and naval stores. Repairs to RFAs to be dealt with in future under Emergency Repair Agreement conditions.

31 December: *Seafox* laid down.

1944

1944: Gyro compasses fitted to all ocean-going RFAs. Royal Fleet Auxiliary personnel serving with a 'Mass Invasion of Europe' clause in their agreement were known as 'V men' (Refer ADM1/18960). *Oligarch* is refitted in which dummy funnel was fitted amidships to give the appearance of a dry cargo boat. Oiling at sea – the first 'Wave' ships were to be fitted with abeam-fuelling rigs of one 60ft derrick both port and starboard with a safe working load of 2 tons; astern fuelling was enabled by two stern chutes.

28 January: *Empire Sheba* and *Empire Venus* taken over by the Admiralty, these MoWT names cancelled.

February: Operation FX – supporting passage of convoy JW57 to Russia included *Rapidol*.

7 February: *Empire Bounty*, 9,1289 grt, completed by Furness Shipbuilding at Haverton-on-Hill for MoWT; under commercial management of Anglo Saxon Petroleum Co, London.

9 February: *Empire Milner* (later to be RFA *Wave Liberator*) launched.

12 February: *Buffalo Park* (later to be RFA *Fort Charlotte*) launched. *Boxol* arrived Naples for fleet attendant duties.

20 February: *War Nizam* – air raid near Southend-on-Sea, one seaman killed and one injured when returning from shore leave. *Rapidol* in Operation FX – the passage of Arctic convoy JW57 to Northern Russia.

23 February: The Ogura Sekiyu Kabushika Kaisha, Tokyo, tanker *Ogura Maru No 3* torpedoed and sunk by the US submarine *Cod* 100

nautical miles north of Morotsi Island in the Moluccas; this tanker was the former Admiralty tanker *Limeleaf* (October 1916).

28 February: *Fort Dunvegan* launched.

March: *Empire Law*, 8,127 grt, completed by Furness Shipbuilding at Haverton-on-Hill for MoWT; under commercial management of Anglo Saxon Petroleum Co, London.

11 March: *Fort Constantine* hull launched by Vancouver Dry Dock Co for completion at another yard. *Abbeydale* at Algiers reduced to care and maintenance status.

18 March: The battle-damaged *Derwentdale* towed from Malta to Bizerta and laid up on a care-and-maintenance basis.

23 March: *Freshford* launched at Lytham.

30 March–April: Operation Tungsten – carrier-launched attack by the Fleet Air Arm on the German battleship *Tirpitz* in Norwegian waters, support tankers *Blue Ranger* and *Black Ranger* supported the naval force.

1 April: *Freshburn*, 278 grt, water tanker, completed by Lytham Shipbuilder & Engineering Co at Lytham for the Admiralty.

2 April: The Chatham Dockyard-based ferry *Nimble* becomes RFA-manned as the Medway Ferry Service on duties between Chatham-Sheerness-ship in the Medway area, in connection with assembly for Operation Overlord.

5 April: *Buffalo Park*, 'Victory' type standard ship, 7,214 grt, completed as a refrigerated victualling stores issuing ship by Vancouver Ship Repairs Ltd at North Vancouver for the Canadian Government (Park Steamship Co); under commercial management of the Eastern & Australian Steamship Co.

6 April: *Wave King* launched.

14 April: *Fort Dunvegan*, 'Victory' type standard ship, 7,225 grt, completed as a refrigerated victualling stores issuing ship by Burrard Dry Dock Co at North Vancouver for MoWT; under commercial management of Ellerman & Bucknall Steamship Co.

Broomdale slightly damaged when *Fort Stikine* blew up in Bombay Harbour destroying 12 ships, setting fire to the western part of the city, death toll unknown.

21 April: *Empire Paladin* (later to be RFA *Wave Commander*) launched.

24 April: The LST(3) that was later to become RFA *Empire Gull* is ordered.

25 April: *Fort Constantine*, 'Victory' type standard ship, 7,221 grt, completed as a refrigerated victualling stores issuing ship by Burrard Dry Dock Co at North Vancouver for MoWT; under commercial management of Ellerman & Bucknall Steamship Co.

28 April: Oiling at sea – *Arndale* in collision with cruiser HMS *Ceylon* during operations.

May: *Spaburn*, water tanker, ordered.

20 May: *Empire Salisbury* (later to be RFA *Wave Master*) launched.

June: *Empire Milner*, 8,135 grt, completed by Furness Shipbuilding at Haverton-on-Hill for MoWT; under commercial management of Anglo Saxon Petroleum Co, London. Amphibious operations – RFA officers and Naval Stores Department staff were involved in the planning of the fuel requirements for Operation Neptune – the Normandy invasion; only two RFA vessels were directly involved, RFA *Rapidol* and the coastal store ship RFA *Robert Dundas*.

27 June: War risk serious casualty – *Abbeydale* 36.53N 01.55E, some 80 miles west of Algiers, *U73* torpedoed her; vessel nearly broke in two, but remained afloat owing to empty cargo tanks; crew abandoned ship with a number of volunteers remaining aboard to effect towing arrangements. Taken in tow following morning by HMSV *Salveston*; towed to Algiers with minesweeper HMS *Mutine*. Remaining crew returned to the ship; both halves were later rejoined at Taranto Dockyard. No casualties recorded (one death recorded on The Tower Hill Memorial).

6 July: *Reliant* (1) in collision with USS *Robert M T Hunter* at Naples. *Wave Monarch* launched.

15 July: RFA *Echodale*, at Trincomalee is the first ship to dock in the new AFD 23; the floating dock collapsed some days later with the battleship HMS *Valiant*.

18 July: *Freshford*, 278 grt, water tanker, completed by Lytham Shipbuilder & Engineering Co at Lytham for the Admiralty.

20 July: *Empire Protector* and *Wave Regent* launched.

21 July: *Wave King* taken over by the Admiralty.

22 July: *Wave King*, 8,158 grt, completed by Harland & Wolff at Govan for service with the Admiralty.

28 July: *Derwentdale* towed to the UK for repairs and her engines were replaced with parts salvaged from *Denbydale*.

1–10 August: *Rapidol* damaged, crew undertake efficient repairs, remained at Cherbourg.

15 August: Amphibious operations – *Dewdale*, *Ennerdale* and *Celerol* participate in Operation Dragoon – Allied invasion of the south of France.

22 August: *Freshtarn* launched.

23 August: *Empire Paladin*, 8,141 grt, completed by Furness Shipbuilding at Haverton-on-Hill for the MoWT; under commercial management of Athel Line Ltd.

24 August: *Spabrook* launched.

27 August: *Derwentdale* arrives on the Tyne for repairs.

28 August: Secret report on the expansion of the RFA Service from the Director of Stores.
RFA *Broomdale* – accidentally torpedoed by HM Submarine *Severn*, holed in No 1 and No 2 port tanks, one Lascar rating injured; repairs took several months.

29 August: *Fort Rosalie* (1) laid down.

31 August: *Fort Grand Rapids* (later to become RFA *Fort Beauharnois*) launched.

September: Radar is introduced into the RFA – tankers to be employed in Eastern waters were made a priority

RAS(L): RFA *Wave Chief* refuelling HMS *Blake*. This is a post-1945 photo but gives a good impression of the techniques acquired during the war. (RFA Archive)

fit.

4 September: *Freshpond* laid down.

11 September: *Fort Sandusky* laid down.

15 September: Oiling at sea – *Empire Salvage* at Scapa for five days of trials.

27 September: Admiralty places a contract with Lobnitz, Renfrew for four small 'Ol' class harbour tankers.

28 September: *Queensborough Park* (later to become RFA *Fort Duquesne*) launched.

29 September: *Abbeydale* – death of one rating is recorded in The Town Hill War Memorial Register.

October: *Empire Bounty* (later to become *Wave Victor*), 8,128 grt, completed by Furness Shipbuilding at Haverton on Hill, placed under management of Anglo Saxon Petroleum Co. *Abbeydale* under tow to Taranto for repairs – broken in two due to bad weather.

1 October: The Nippon Tanker Kabushika Kaisha, Yokohama, tanker *Zuiyo Maru* is torpedoed and sunk by the US submarine *Cabrilla* operating off the Philippines – the tanker is the former Admiralty tanker *Boxleaf* (December 1916).

7 October: *Spaburn* laid down.

14 October: *Abbeydale* – after part arrives Taranto in tow for repair.

16 October: *Wave Emperor* launched.

18 October: *Empire Protector*, 8,156 grt, completed by Furness Shipbuilding at Haverton-on-Hill for MoWT; under commercial management of Anglo Saxon Petroleum Co, London. *Abbeydale* – fore part arrived in tow at Taranto.

29 October: *Fort Grand Rapids*, 'Victory' type standard ship, completed as *Cornish Park*, 7,233 grt, by West Coast Shipbuilders Ltd at Vancouver as a victualling stores issuing ship for the Canadian Government (Park Steamship Co), under commercial management of Alfred Holt & Co.

31 October: *Montebello Park* (later to become *Fort Langley*) launched.

November: British Pacific Fleet established – Commander-in-Chief Admiral Sir Bruce Fraser and included Rear Admiral Fleet Train (RAFT) Rear Admiral D B Fisher who was afloat in HMS *Montclare*. East Indies Fleet established – Commander-in-Chief Admiral Sir Arthur Power (ashore in Colombo).

3 November: *Wave Monarch*, 8,158 grt, completed by Harland & Wolff at Govan for service with the Admiralty.

16 November: Oiling at sea – RFA *Echodale* and battleship HMS *Howe* conducted successful trials off Trincomalee using two 5-inch buoyant hoses. *Empire Mars* (later to be RFA *Wave Duke*) launched

18 November: *Fort Rosalie* (1) launched. Operation Outflank – Eastern Fleet task force from Trincomalee comprising RFA *Wave King* and escorts.

25 November: *Queensborough Park*, 'Victory' type standard ship, 7,222 grt, acquired by the MoWT, completed by West Coast Shipbuilders at Vancouver as a refrigerated victualling stores issuing ship; under commercial management of Alfred Holt Ltd. *Fort Sandusky* launched.

27 November: Oiling at sea – RFA *Wave King* and HMS *King George V* conducted successful trials using two 5-inch buoyant hoses.

30 November: *Wave Governor* launched.

December: *Empire Salisbury*, 8,199 grt, completed by Sir James Laing at Sunderland for MoWT; under commercial management of the Eagle Oil Co. Proposed to fit radar to RFA *Reliant*.

5 December: *Blue Ranger* in collision with HMS *Kent*.

10 December: *Wave Monarch* taken over by the Admiralty.

12 December: *Spabrook*, water tanker, 720 grt, completed by Phillip & Sons at Dartmouth for the Admiralty; cost £78,712.

14 December: RFA *Bishopdale* – San Pedro Bay, Leyte Gulf, Philippines when dived-bombed by Japanese aircraft that crashed into No 3 wing tank and exploded, she was just securing alongside a US Navy cruiser; two ratings killed, two ratings injured, one later died of the injuries sustained.

Normandy Landings

Operation Neptune was the codename for the naval part of the Allied invasion of Europe – the Normandy landings – Operation Overlord. D-Day was itself 6 June 1944 but the build-up commenced considerably earlier and the aftermath did not officially cease until early July. Despite Operation Neptune's billing as the 'greatest amphibious operation in history', surprisingly few Royal Fleet Auxiliaries were involved.

RFA *Rapidol*, harbour tanker, left the Solent in convoy ETM6W with an ETA Juno beach area of 12 June.

RFA *Robert Dundas*, coastal store carrier, left Plymouth in convoy ECM5 on passage to the Omaha beach area; arrived in the area on 24 June.

The victualling stores issuing ship RFA *Fort Beauharnois* seen here unloading, probably whilst under commercial management. (World Ship Society)

16 December: RFA *War Diwan* – war loss – River Scheldt estuary; this tanker was mined when *en route* to Antwerp; she broke in two and finally one half had to be sunk by gunfire; survivors taken aboard HMS *Franklin* and landed Ostend; they returned to Tilbury on 18 December 1944 – casualties one officer and four ratings killed, one officer injured (four deaths recorded on the Tower Hill Memorial); wreck of after part lies 51.25.31N 3.27.21E, forward part lies 51.25.45N 3.29.37E.

20 December: LST(3) that was later to become RFA *Empire Gull* is laid down.

22 December: *Freshtarn*, water tanker, 278 grt, completed by Lytham Shipbuilder & Engineering Co at Lytham for the Admiralty.

28 December: *Hyalina* (later to be RFA *Olna* (2)), launched for the Anglo Saxon Petroleum Co, London (Shell Tankers); taken over by MoWT for conversion and service by the Admiralty; sister ship *Helicina* also taken over.

1945

1945: *Cornish Park* acquired by the MoWT; renamed *Fort Beauharnois*, under commercial management of Alfred Holt, Liverpool. *Buffalo Park* acquired by the MoWT; renamed *Fort Charlotte*, under commercial management of Eastern and Australian Steamship Co. *Fort Dunvegan* placed in reserve. *Queensborough Park* acquired by the MoWT, renamed *Fort Duquesne*, under commercial management of Alfred Holt, Liverpool. Oiling at Sea – the Master of RFA *Wave Governor* suggested that abeam-method working parties on lower deck are in danger and working ability severely affected in, for example, heavy weather. He recommended that a spar deck be constructed on a level with 'flying bridge' capable of taking all oiling-at-sea trough-method gear and winches. HMS *Olna* attached to the British Pacific Fleet – then transferred to RFA as their first

RFA *Fort Langley*, armament stores issuing ship, seen here fitted with bow paravane frame. (World Ship Society)

turbo-electric driven ship. *Ingeborg* returned to her owners Algemeen Vrachtkantoor NV of Rotterdam. *Enoshima Maru* recovered at Java and towed to Hong Kong by *Gold Ranger*; name reverted to *Ebonol* (1). *Petronel* sold commercially and later renamed *Pass of Glencoe*. *Choran Maru* (ex *Ruthenia*) recovered at Singapore and used to transport PoWs under her original name. *Olna* (1) found as a wreck at Scaramanga, fit only for scrap. *Brown Ranger*, serving with British Pacific Fleet – reported some unrest amongst her crew and some naval ratings provided as a working party to assist with refuelling operations

January: Task Force 69 – fuelling force for Operation Meridan.

4 January: Operation Lentil – the Pangkalan Brandan carrier air strike on oil refineries – aircraft carriers HMS *Indomitable*, *Victorious*, *Indefatigable* and escorts supported by an underway replenishment group.

15 January: After arriving in Sydney the C-in-C British Pacific Fleet reported available to CinC US Fleet Admiral Ernest King.

16 January: British Pacific Fleet – main body, as Force 63, departed Trincomalee – included HM Ships *King George V*, *Indomitable*, *Illustrious*, *Victorious*, *Indefatigable* and escorts; the underway replenishment group comprised RFA *Arndale*, RFA *Wave King* and one unidentified oiler escorted by the cruiser HMS *Ceylon* and the destroyer HMS *Urchin*.

20 January: Force 69 – RFAS *Echodale*, *Empire Salvage* and *Wave King* with escort HMS *Urchin* form the underway replenishment group supporting Operation Meridan I.

24 January: Operation Meridan I – Force 63 (supported by Force 69) – delivered a naval air strike on the Palembang oil refinery.

29 January: Operation Meridan II – Force 63 supported by an underway replenishment group conducted a second strike on the Palembang oil refineries.

19 February: Storing at sea – the US Navy ammunition ships *Shasta* and *Wrangell* conducted the first successful trial in alongside transfer of ammunition at sea.

March: *Brown Ranger* reprogrammed as a fleet water tanker; seven ratings refused duty, removed by armed guard, found not guilty under the terms of their articles of agreement. *Olna* (ex *Hyalina*), 12,660 grt, completed by Swan hunter & Wigham Richardson Ltd at Wallsend; to be commissioned as the fleet oiler HM Ship *Olna* for service with British Pacific Fleet. *Arndale* and *Wave King* sail from Sydney for Manus, escorted by minesweeper *Whyalla*.

8 March: *Wave Governor*, 8,190 grt, completed by Furness Shipbuilding at Haverton-on-Hill for Admiralty service.

15 March: British Pacific Fleet, re-titled as Task Force 57 to fit in with US Navy practice, directed to participate in Operation Iceberg, the invasion of Okinawa – RFAS *Arndale*, *Brown Ranger*, *Cedardale*, *Dingledale*, *Wave King*, *Wave Monarch* and distilling ship *Bacchus* (2) attached.

23 March: Task Force 57 – a carrier task group comprising HM Ships *Indomitable*, *Victorious*, *Indefatigable*, *Illustrious* and escorts supported by an underway replenishment group escorted by detached destroyers sail from Ulithi Atoll, Caroline Islands for Okinawa area.

28–30 March: British Pacific Fleet Train – designated Task Force 112 – including the RFA oilers *Wave King*, *Wave Monarch*, *Arndale*, *Cedardale* and *Dingledale* replenishing Task Force 57; other supporting tankers and store ship were mercantile fleet auxiliaries – *Aase Maersk*, *San Adolfo*, *San Amado*, *San Ambrosio* and *Robert Maersk*.

28 March: *Honan Maru* (ex *War Sirdar*) torpedoed and sunk by the submarine USS *Bluegill*.

April: *Empire Mars*, 8,1,99 grt, completed by Sir James Laing at Sunderland for MoWT, under commercial management of British Tanker Co. *Bacchus* (2) and *Brown Ranger* at Leyte with Task Force 57.

7 April: *Fort Rosalie* (1), Canadian type standard ships, 7,374 grt, completed as an ammunition freighter by United Shipyards Ltd at Montreal

RAS(L): unidentified Second World War tanker refuelling the destroyer HMS *Wessex*. (ANRS)

for Canadian Government (Park Steamship Co), under commercial management of Ellerman Lines, London.

11–16 April: Operation Sunfish – a photographic reconnaissance survey and anti-shipping sweep off southern Malaya with Force 63 including HMS *Queen Elizabeth* and the escort carriers HMS *Emperor*, *Khedive* and escorts; the underway replenishment group, Force 70 comprised the oiler RFA *Easedale* and her escort frigate *Lossie*.

15 April: *Gold Ranger* allocated to Operation Dracula as Rangoon base tanker.

23–30 April: British Pacific Fleet and the Fleet Train at San Pedro Bay for rest, maintenance and storing; in addition to RFA oilers attached to the replenishment groups, the naval stores issuing ships RFA *Bacchus* and the water tanker RFA *Brown Ranger* were present.

27 April: *Hyalina*, 12,660 grt, completed by Swan Hunter & Wigham Richardson Ltd at Wallsend; commissioned as HMS *Olna* with a crew of 183.

29 April: *Blue Ranger* part of Operation Judgement – attack on U-boat depot ship at Kilbotn.

May: Operation Dracula – entry into Rangoon – *Echodale* and *Gold Ranger* deployed in support. Oiling at sea – HMS *Olna* arrives at Scapa Flow for RAS trials prior to deploying to the British Pacific Fleet.

4 May: Operation Judgement, last air strike by Home Fleet on Kilbotn anchorage by RN carriers with Naval Air Squadrons (NAS) supported by RFA *Blue Ranger*.

7 May: Unconditional surrender of Germany, hostilities cease in the Atlantic.

8 May: VE Day.

9 May: Royal Naval forces arrived Copenhagen; Kriegsmarine's replenishment ship *Nordmark* allocated to the British by the Inter-

RFA *Nimble*

FERRY

Pennant: X76 **Official number:** 123015
Builder: Hawthorn & Co, Leith (yard no 110)
Machinery: Steam 6 cyl triple expansion by Wm Kemp, Glasgow; single shaft; 13 knots
Dimensions (loa/bp x beam x draught): 194/–ft x 26ft x 6.5ft
Tonnage measurements: 392 grt, – dwt, – net
Displacement: – tons full load **Complement:** 16
Remarks: Originally built as *Roslin Castle* for Galloway Steam Packet Co, Leith in 1906 and purchased by the Admiralty in March 1908 for £15,500. She was renamed *Nimble* and entered service as a tender based at Sheerness.

RFA *Nimble* – the Medway Ferry Service. (J Smith collection)

RFA *Wave King* heavily armed and fitted with radar for service with the Pacific Fleet Train. (World Ship Society)

Amphibious operations in the Far East

Operation Dracula, seizing the Port of Rangoon, Burma – 2 May 1945.

RFA *Easedale*, oiler, at sea for refuelling support to the main naval force.

RFA *Gold Ranger*, oiler, left Trincomalee 26 April for follow-up convoy KRS1, on passage to Rangoon.

RFA *Olwen*, oiler, at sea for refuelling support to main naval force.

Operation Zipper, Malaya – 9 and 12 September 1945. These ships were originally part of Operation Zipper but were diverted as a result of the Japanese surrender.

RFA *Dewdale*, LSG, planned to arrived at the Zipper beachhead on 9 September but diverted, left Trincomalee 28 August on passage to Singapore.

RFA *Easedale*, oiler, diverted to Penang.

RFA *Ennerdale*, LSG, carrying 14 landing craft, left Madras 1 September in assault convoy JME1S, arrived her assigned beachhead 9 September.

Allied Repatriations Commission (Allied Central Investigation Unit No T56); inspected and refuelled.

10 May: Operation Dukedom – *Eaglesdale* Force 70.

13 May: Operation Dukedom – *Olwen* (1) in Force 69, in support of Royal Navy units that intercepted and sank the Japanese heavy cruiser *Haguro*.

15 May–8 June: *Wave Governor* at Harland & Wolff yard for fitting with defensive armament facilities and oiling at sea facilities; fitted with Type 268 radar.

16 May: *Empire Salvage* is immobilised for one month due to a long overdue change of crew and boiler clearing.

18 May: *Montebello Park*, 'Victory' type standard ship, completed as the air stores issuing ship *Fort Langley*, 7,285 grt, by Victoria Machinery Depot Co at Victoria for Canadian Government (Park Steamships Co), under commercial management of Alfred Holt, Liverpool.

25 May: *Birchol* (2) laid down.

31 May: *Wave Regent*, 8,184 grt, completed by Furness Shipbuilding at Haverton-on-Hill for MoWT and handed over for service with the Admiralty.

30 May: *Abbeydale* taken in hand for rejoining and permanent repairs at Taranto.

6 June: *Nordmark* left Copenhagen for Rosyth, manned by German naval crew under RN control, escorted by HM Ships *Diadem* and *Oribi*.

25 June: *Nordmark* arrived Palmer's Yard, Hebburn for survey and consequent repairs and conversion; allocated to the British Pacific Fleet.

July: Oiling at sea – *Brown Ranger* and *Bacchus* (2) are used to carry and issue replacement rubber hoses for lost and damaged ones, in order to relieve the shortage of oiling-at-sea equipment within the British Pacific Fleet.

9 July: LST(3) that was later to become RFA *Empire Gull* launched at Lauzon as HMS *LST 3523* for service in Royal Navy.

17 July: *Berta* released from government service.

25 July: *Demeter* paid off.

27 July: *Empire Herald* (later to be *Wave Prince*) launched.

28 July: *Orangeleaf* left Aden bound Singapore.

August: RFAs forming logistics support group attached to the British Pacific Fleet *Arndale, Bishopdale, Cedardale, Dingledale, Easedale, Serbol, Rapidol, Brown Ranger, Green Ranger, Wave Emperor, Wave Governor, Wave King, Wave Monarch, Empire Salvage, Bacchus* (2) and HMS (later RFA) *Olna*. *Arndale* extensively damaged by fire – refitting at Brisbane.

1 August: *Fort Sandusky*, Canadian type standard design, 7,375 grt, ammunition freighter, completed United Shipyards at Montreal for Canadian Government, under commercial management Ellerman Lines, London.

6 August: First atomic bomb dropped on Hiroshima, Japan.

9 August: Second atomic bomb dropped on Nagasaki, Japan.

13 August: Water tankers *Spalake* and *Spapool* laid down.

14–15 August: Unconditional surrender of Japan announced by Prime Minister Attlee and US President Truman.

14–18 August: Oiling at sea – *Broomdale* conducts trials.

23 August: HMS *Olna* – report on the manning, decommissioning and converting to RFA manning and transferring her to Director of Stores.

28 August: *Freshpool* launched.

September: RFA *Dewdale* (1) was the first RFA to enter Singapore after its re-occupation.

2 September: Formal Japanese unconditional surrender ceremony in Tokyo Bay.

27 September: *Ebonol* (2) laid down.

29 September: *Berta* returned to her owners.

October: *LST 3523* completed. *Danmark* towed from Scapa Flow to the Clyde and laid up off Kilcreggan.

3 October: Records show that a decision of Admiralty tanker requirements reviewed the future of *Olna* and *Oleander* (ex *Helicina*)

6 October: *Ingeborg* released from Admiralty service.

22 October: *Empire Naseby* launched.

November: *Ebonol* (1) instructions issued that only essential repairs should be carried out to enable vessel to function as the port tanker at Singapore.

5 November: *Freshburn* ceased to be classed as an RFA.

9 November: *Freshet* ceased to be classed as an RFA. *Broomdale* arrived Shanghai.

14 November: *Broomdale* Tokyo on fleet attendant duties.

20 November: *Empire Evesham* (to become *Wave Sovereign*) launched.

21 November: *Empire Tesbury* (later to be *Rippledyke*) launched.

British Pacific Fleet Train

The term Fleet Train was introduced during the Second World War for the non-combatant support of an operational force or the fleet, consisting of depot, maintenance, repair, replenishment and stores support ships. The major British one was the British Pacific Fleet Train (BPFT) supporting Allied naval units in the closing stages of the War in the Pacific, set up in 1944 under the command of Rear Admiral Fleet Train. Known as Task Force 112, the BPFT was in the main to carry commodities from the rearward base at Sydney, Australia to the intermediate base at Manus, the Admiralty Islands or to Leyte Gulf in Philippines, where the RN had begun to use the harbour. Tankers had to go right forward to the operational areas in order to RAS. BPFT was a collection of *circa* 60 ships of many nationalities, assembled not without a good deal of argument with the MoWT. A similar but must smaller Fleet Train was built up in Indian Ocean to serve East Indies Fleet as the Eastern Fleet had been renamed after formation of the British Pacific Fleet.

On 15 August (VJ Day) BPFT included the following RFAs:

RFA *Olna*	tanker
RFA *Wave Emperor*	tanker
RFA *Arndale*	tanker
RFA *Wave Governor*	tanker
RFA *Bishopdale*	tanker
RFA *Wave King*	tanker
RFA *Cedardale*	tanker
RFA *Wave Monarch*	tanker
RFA *Dingledale*	tanker
RFA *Green Ranger*	tanker
RFA *Eaglesdale*	tanker
RFA *Rapidol*	tanker
RFA *Serbol*	tanker
RFA *Bacchus*	distilling ship
RFA *Brown Ranger*	water carrier

HMS *Olna* was also deployed

RFA *Ennerdale* after the post-LSG refit and retaining her early radar fit. (World Ship Society)

War in the Pacific ends.

Tokyo Bay, 2 September 1945, was the scene of the formal surrender ceremony. Two Royal Fleet Auxiliaries were amongst the Allied ships present in Tokyo Bay, *Wave King* and *Dingledale*, whose Masters and Chief Engineers were invited on board the USS *Missouri* to witness the signing of the Japanese surrender document.

RFA *Abbeydale* broken in two after being torpedoed and awaiting repair 1945. (ANRS)

December: *Nordmark* classed as a Fleet Attendant Tanker (Fast), Devonport crew.

4 December: *Ennerdale* (1) detonated a magnetic mine in the Malacca Strait, seriously damaged and had to returned to the UK for repair. *Wave Governor* – general deck, engine room and defensive protection work carried out under Lend-Lease (US War Shipping Administration, New York).

5 December: *Appleleaf* laid up at Rosyth for disposal.

10 December: HM Treasury approved the transfer of *Wave Governor* to Admiralty ownership.

12 December: *Oakol* (2) laid down.

22 December: *Freshpond* ceased to be classed as an RFA.

RFA *Spapool*, water tanker. (World Ship Society)

RFA *Empire Salvage*

FLEET ATTENDANT TANKER
Pennant: A159
Official number: 159160
Port of registry: London
Callsign: –
Builder: Rotterdam Dry Dock, Rotterdam (yard no 220)
Machinery: one 8 cyl four stroke, single acting ICE by Stork & Co; 3,700 bhp; 12 knots
Dimensions (loa/bp x beam): 514/488ft x 73ft
Tonnage measurements: 10,953 grt, 15,597 dwt
Displacement: 21,450 tons full load
Complement: 78
Remarks: Completing as the motor tanker *Papendrecht* when requisitioned by German naval forces; renamed *Lothrigen* (J T Essberger, managers); modified and entered service as a support tanker; deployed as a unit of Operation Rheinubung – *Bismarck*, *Prinz Eugen* sortie; June 1941 intercepted and captured by the Royal Navy, taken to Bermuda as a Prize; registered as *Empire Salvage*; allocated to the Admiralty for service as a fleet attendant tanker; 2 April 1946 handed back to the Dutch authorities.

Papendrecht ex *Empire Salvage*. (Van Ommerm Archive)

CHAPTER 5

Peace, Wars and RAS, 1946–1982

1946

1946: Ministry of War Transport duties transferred to Ministry of Transport. *Olcades* took over 'Ruthenia' Jetty at Woodlands Oil Fuel Jetty, Jahore Causeway, Singapore and remained there until the oil fuel lines were restored at the Base. *War Afridi* became a floating fuel storage depot at Hong Kong. *War Nawab* reduced to a fuelling hulk at Devonport, yard craft conditions. *Bacchus* (2) reconverted to a naval stores freighter at Hong Kong. *Derwentdale* reconverted to a freighting tanker. *Freshwater* became the first of the 'Fresh' class water tankers to cease being classed as an RFA on transfer to the Director of Victualling for dockyard manning; three of the 'Fresh' class of water tankers that were yet to complete were delivered to the Director of Victualling and therefore did not become RFAs. *Petrella* sold commercially and renamed *Captain Mikes*. *Empire Law* acquired by the Admiralty and renamed *Wave Conqueror* remained under the commercial management of Anglo Saxon Petroleum Co Ltd.

5 January: *Spaburn* launched at Dartmouth.

10 January: HM Treasury approve formal transfer of HMS *Olna* to Admiralty ownership.

17 January: *Empire Evesham* (later to become *Wave Ruler* (1)) launched for the Ministry of War Transport.

18 January: *Dingledale* transferred to Admiralty ownership.

23 January: *Empire Salvage* is assigned to Force C to establish British naval port facilities at Kure and Sasebo, Japan.

28 January: HMS *Olna* arrived at Swan Hunter's on the Tyne for docking and repairs; to be made suitable for management and manning as a RFA, for example, survey, load line, Lloyd's classification, tonnage certificates and radio licence; registered as RFA *Olna*, London.

6 February: *Empire Evesham* (to become *Wave Ruler* (1) taken over by Admiralty; under management.

15 February: *Oligarch* handed over for disposal.

19 February: *Empire Flodden* (later to be *Wave Baron*) launched for the Ministry of Transport. *Birchol* (2) launched.

28 February: *Spapool* launched at Bristol. *Wave Sovereign*, 8,182 grt, completed by Furness Shipbuilding at Haverton-on-Hill for Admiralty service.

March: *Empire Tesbury* (later to become the Admiralty's *Rippledyke*), 975 grt, completed by Bartram & Sons at Sunderland for Ministry of Transport and placed under commercial management of Anglo Saxon Petroleum Co Ltd.

8 March: *Empire Herald* (later to become *Wave Prince*), 8,175 grt completed by Sir James Laing at Sunderland for the Ministry of Transport and placed under commercial management British Molasses Co.

20 March: *Olna* (2) transferred into the RFA.

April: *Wave Baron*, 8,174 grt, completed by Furness Shipbuilding at Haverton-on-Hill for the Admiralty, under commercial management of Gow, Harrison & Co, Glasgow. *Empire Evesham* (later to become *Wave Ruler*) 8,138 grt, completed by Furness Shipbuilding at Haverton-on-Hill for Ministry of Transport, under commercial management of Eagle Oil Co.

2 April: *Empire Salvage* is handed back to the Dutch authorities for eventual return to her commercial owners

Naval Hospital Ships

For the major part of the first half of the twentieth century the Royal Navy found it necessary to maintain at least one Hospital Ship in permanent commission and these have been operated as civilian crewed (non-combatant) Royal Fleet Auxiliaries but with a Naval Fleet Surgeon in charge of the hospital ship aspect of the vessel.

These ships were protected vessels, declared as Hospital Ships by the International Committee of the Red Cross (ICRC) Geneva, under the provisions of international law. This restricts the ship's use in military situations; for example, it cannot operate forward in a combat zone and personnel treated aboard cannot be pressed back into combat. Declared ships have to be painted to comply with the International Colour Scheme for Hospital Ships.

RFA *Berbice* 1920–1; ICRC No 18; 2,370 tons gross steam ship completed in 1909; 1920 purchased by Admiralty for service as a hospital ship; 1922 sold.

RFA *Maine* (1) 1901–14; 2,780 tons gross steam ship completed as *Swansea* in 1887; marine loss.

RFA *Maine* (2) 1914–16, 4,688 tons gross steam ship completed as *Heliopolis* in 1906; 1914 renamed *Maine* and reserved for conversion into a hospital ship – this conversion did not take place.

RFA *Maine* (3) 1920–48, ICRC No 1; 4,981 tons gross steam ship completed as *Panama* in 1902; purchased by Admiralty in 1921 for service as a hospital ship; sold for breaking up in 1948.

RFA *Maine* (4) 1948–54, 7,515 tons gross steam ship completed 1925 as *Leonardo Da Vinci*; 1941 renamed *Empire Clyde*, 1947 purchased by Admiralty for service as hospital ship; 1954 sold for breaking up.

Wave class

FAST STANDARD TANKERS, MINISTRY OF WAR TRANSPORT TURBINE DESIGN

RFA *Wave Baron**
(ex *Empire Flodden*)
RFA *Wave Chief**
(ex *Empire Edgehill*)
RFA *Wave Commander*
(ex *Empire Paladin*)
RFA *Wave Conqueror*
(ex *Empire Law*)
RFA *Wave Duke*
(ex *Empire Mars*)
RFA *Wave Emperor*
RFA *Wave Governor*
RFA *Wave King*
(provisionally *Empire Sheba*)
RFA *Wave Knight** (1)
(ex *Empire Naseby*)
RFA *Wave Laird* (ex *Empire Dunbar*)
RFA *Wave Liberator*
(ex *Empire Milner*)
RFA *Wave Master**
(ex *Empire Salisbury*)
RFA *Wave Monarch*
(provisionally *Empire Venus*)
RFA *Wave Premier*
(ex *Empire Marston*)
RFA *Wave Prince** (ex *Empire Herald*)
RFA *Wave Protector*
(ex *Empire Protector*)
RFA *Wave Regent*
RFA *Wave Ruler** (1)
(ex *Empire Evesham*)
RFA *Wave Sovereign**
RFA *Wave Victor** (ex *Empire Bounty*)

RFA *Wave Emperor.* (World Ship Society)

Machinery: Two steam turbines, double reduction gearing to single screw; two water tube boilers; 6,800 bhp; bunkers 1,680 tons; 15 knots; 50+ tpd consumption
Dimensions (loa/bp x beam): 492.5/473ft x 64.3ft
Tonnage measurements: 8,181 grt, 11,900 dwt
Displacement: 16,483 tons full load
Complement: 61 – accommodation for gun crews
Remarks: +100A1 +LMC. At the beginning of 1943 it was decided to take up two 15-knot Ministry of War Transport standard design tankers for RFA service. Later 18 other tankers of the same design were taken on completion. Cargo capacity was 9,680 tons packaged as 7,950 tons oil fuel, 750 tons diesel oil and 980 tons spirit.The 21st and final vessel in the class was sold commercially to J I Jacobs Ltd and named *Beechwood.*

Replenishment at sea was to be one of the main tasks for these tanker and they were fitted for fuelling by the trough (abeam) and stirrup (astern) methods with 2 x 2-ton 60ft derricks – one port and one starboard in the after well deck and with an astern fuelling facility.

* During their careers these ships were modified and updated, *eg* radar was fitted and eight of them were modified to deploy as fast fleet replenishment tankers with extra accommodation amidships and aft, some funnels were heightened and 70ft derricks with modern RAS facilities fitted.

The details are based on RFA Wave Sovereign *as built*

Phs van Ommeren (Nederland) BV.

3 April: *Empire Dunbar* (later to become *Wave Laird*), launched.

4 April: *Empire Edgehill* (later to become *Wave Chief*), 8,097 grt, launched by Harland & Wolff at Glasgow for Ministry of Transport.

11 April: Oiling at sea – *Black Ranger* at Portland/Portsmouth conducting trials.

12 April: *Spaburn*, water tanker, 718 grt completed by Phillip & Sons at Dartmouth for the Admiralty at a cost of £80,859.

14 April: *Oligarch* scuttled in deep water at the southern end of Sinai in the Red Sea, loaded with obsolete ammunition.

May: It was considered that *Northmark* (ex German *Nordmark*) might become an RFA-manned oiler but the expense of modification to service as a long-term civilian manned vessel was considered unjustifiable; follow-up proposal was taken up to operate her as an HM Ship for conducting experiments in RAS.

15 May: *Ebonol* (2) launched.

27 May: *Teakol* (3) laid down.

31 May: *Empire Naseby* (later to become *Wave Knight*), 8,187 grt, completed by Sir James Laing & Sons at Sunderland for Ministry of Transport, under commercial management of Tankers Ltd.

June: *Dewdale* at Portsmouth, reconverted into a freighting tanker.

14 June: *Spapool*, water tanker, 720 grt, completed by Charles Hill & Sons at Bristol for the Admiralty; cost £76,000.

12 June: *Birchol* (2), 1,440 grt, completed by Lobnitz & Co at Renfrew for Admiralty service.

25 June: *Petrella* handed over to the Ministry of Transport for disposal; sold commercially and renamed *Captain Mikes.*

Empire Mars later RFA *Wave Duke*. (World Ship Society)

27 June: *Empire Marston* (later to become *Wave Premier*), 8,175 grt, launched.

July: *Abbeydale* – repairs completed at Taranto.

7 August: *War Bahadur* handed-over to the Ministry of Transport for disposal.

8 August: *Ebonol* (1) – instruction issued that no further repair work to be undertaken and to be disposed of.

9 August: *Brambleleaf* released to the Ministry of Transport for disposal.

10 August: *Spalake* launched at Bristol.

21 August: *Ebonol* (2) 1,440 grt, completed by Lobnitz & Co at Renfrew as *Cedarol* for Admiralty service, because *Ebonol* (1) had been recovered from the Japanese.

27 August: *Wave Chief* taken over by the Admiralty.

28 August: *Oakol* (2) launched.

30 August: *Wave Chief*, 8,097 grt, completed by Harland & Wolff at Glasgow and placed on commercial charter.

September: *War Bahadur* arrived Blyth for demolition.

2 September: *Pearleaf* handed-over to MoT for disposal.

3 September: Replenishment-at-Sea meeting held by Director of Naval Equipment in Bath, discussed new 'Ranger' class oiler design.

30 September: *Wave Laird*, 8,187 grt, completed by Sir James Laing at Sunderland.

12 October: *Wave Victor* ownership taken over by the Admiralty for service as RFA.

21 October: *Cherryleaf* handed over to the Ministry of Transport for disposal.

Agency Service

The duties of the RFA Agent is performed by clerical and administrative staff of the Naval Stores Department, and its successors, located at HM Naval Bases at home and overseas. At commercial ports, commercial agents are engaged. Role – receive advance notice of a ship's arrival, arrange pilots and tugs where necessary, that berths or anchorages are allocated, customs clearance. Inform Master of local conditions and regulations, entry and port facilities. Services rendered include reception of mail, co-ordinate supply of victuals and stores, fuel, water, cash, crew replacements, laundry, dockyard services for repair, transport and medical, dental and welfare services, payment of bills, discharge and embark cargoes, and a boat service (if necessary).

22 October: Corfu Channel incident – RFA *Maine*, hospital ship, grounded and damaged when proceeding to support the HM Ships *Saumarez* and *Volage* damaged by Albanian mines when 44 RN personnel killed and 42 injured.

28 October: *War Nizam* handed over to Ministry of Transport for disposal and laid up on the Tyne.

November: HMS *Seafox*, naval aviation stores carrier, 711 grt, launched on 16 May, completed by James Pollock, Son & Co, Faversham.

1 November: *Oakol* (2), 1,440 grt, completed by Lobnitz & Co at Renfrew for Admiralty service.

8 November: *Thermol* transferred to the Ministry of Transport for disposal.

11 November: Oiling at sea – report by Admiralty Experimental Works, Haslar on 'interaction between ship' during replenishment a sea, based on models of the tanker *Olna* and the battleship HMS *King George V*.

14 November: *Teakol* (2) launched.

16 November: *Empire Mars* acquired by the Admiralty and renamed *Wave Duke*.

23 November: *Empire Protector* acquired by the Admiralty and renamed *Wave Protector*.

28 November: *Spalake*, water tanker, 672 grt, completed by Phillip & Sons at Dartmouth for the Admiralty; cost £76,000.

RFA *Olna* (2)
FAST FLEET TANKER
Pennant: A116 **Official number:** 180853
Port of registry: London **Callsign:** MQTR
Builder: Swan Hunter & Wigham Richardson Ltd, Wallsend (yard no 1689)
Machinery: British Thomson-Houston, turbo-electric; three Babcock & Wilcox water tube boilers; 13,000 shp; single screw; 2,130 ton bunkers; 17 knots; 100 tpd consumption
Dimensions (length oa/bp x beam): 583.5/561.8ft x 70.2ft
Tonnage measurements: 12,660 grt, 17,520 dwt, 7,412 net
Displacement: 25,096 tons full load **Complement:** 183 RN, later 77 RFA

The large diesel-electric fleet oiler RFA *Olna* (2). (World Ship Society)

Remarks: +100A; +LMC, ordered by Anglo-Saxon Petroleum Co Ltd as *Hyalina*, hull had been designed after exhaustive serials of model experiments at Nation Physical laboratory; taken over by Ministry of War Transport when under construction. Completed May 1945.

Olna was a large tanker and she was extensively modified for naval service. Initially commissioned as an HM Ship with a Devonport crew, commanded by a Lieutenant Commander RNR. She entered service with state-of-the-art oiling at sea equipment – cargo capacity of 8,993 tons fuel oil, 2,977 tons diesel oil, 2,348 tons spirit and 236 tons of lubricants in 16 tanks; nine cargo pumps in three pump rooms, fitted with an oiling at sea platform above the upper deck to the starboard side, eight steam winches, four 4-ton and one 5-ton derricks, trough and buoyant hose oiling at sea rigs. Extensively armed with one 4-inch gun aft, four single 40mm Bofors, eight 20mm Oerlikons on sponsons, upper deck stowage for depth charges on port side and 60lb protection plating on the deck and side in the area of the petrol storage tanks, degaussing arrangements and paravane gear. During her long RFA career she underwent a number of modifications to her RAS equipment. Sister-ship *Helicina* was also taken over by MoWT for Admiralty service, to have been named *Oleander*; conversion not completed before end of War and she was returned to her original owners.

29 November: *War Nawab* reduced to an oiling hulk at Devonport; sold commercially, name unchanged.
December: *Spalake*, water tanker, 720 grt, completed by Charles Hill & Sons at Bristol for the Admiralty. *British Lady* placed on the disposal list. *Empire Paladin* (later to become *Wave Commander*) purchased by the Admiralty. *Empire Milner* acquired by the Admiralty and renamed *Wave Liberator*. *Empire Salisbury* (later to become *Wave Master*) acquired by the Admiralty.
6 December: *Wave Premier*, 8,175 grt, completed by Furness Shipbuilding at Haverton-on-Hill for the Admiralty.
30 December: *Olwen* laid up at Trincomalee for disposal.
31 December: *War Krishna* laid up at Trincomalee.

'Ranger' Class Oilers (1946)
At a Replenishment-at-Sea meeting held on 3 September 1946 by the Director of Naval Equipment in Bath, the Director of Stores reported that new 'Rangers' (3,500 tons) were about to be designed, fitted with limited oiling-at-sea capacity – one 7-inch astern rig and one portside abeam rig.

1947

1947: 'Spa' class water tankers – in his post-war policy the Director of Stores indicated a reluctance to dispose of these tankers; suggested that Director of Victualling operate them, place them in reserve or bareboat charter them to commercial companies; *Spalake* and *Spapool* were then bareboat-chartered to the War Office for service as water boats in the Mediterranean and Far East. The Admiralty oiler *Thornol* placed under the management of Metcalf Motor Coasters Ltd, London, until 1948. Auxiliaries allocated pennant numbers with flag superior A (known as the 1947 scheme). *Nucula* sold as scrap in New Zealand for £1,520. *Olwen* (1) sold M Esmailji Abdulhusein Co, Karachi; later renamed *Mushtari*. *Prestol* and *Petrobus* took part in the Clyde Home Fleet Review. *War Krishna* sold commercially, name unchanged. *War Nizam* sold commercially, renamed *Basinghall*. *Thermol* sold J Harker & Co, Hull and renamed *Brodcodale H*. *Cherryleaf* (1) sold British Oil Shipping Co Ltd and renamed *Alan Clore*. *Brown Ranger* supported the battleship HMS *Vanguard* during the Royal Tour to South Africa
1 January: Admiralty purchased the hospital ship *Empire Clyde* (ex *Leonardo Da Vinci*) for further service; renamed RFA *Maine*.
10 January: *Kimmerol* laid up at Trincomalee; handed-over to MoT

for disposal, sold to C E Rust and name remained unchanged until further sale. *Empire Herald* (later to become *Wave Prince*), under commercial management of British Molasses Co, transferred to Admiralty ownership.

14 January: *Teakol* (2), 1,440 grt, completed by Lobnitz & Co at Renfrew for the Admiralty.

28 January: *Empire Naseby* transferred to Admiralty management and renamed *Wave Knight* (1).

12 February: *Empire Herald* transferred to Admiralty management and renamed *Wave Prince*.

14 February: *War Pathan* handed over to Ministry of Transport for disposal.

7 March: *Empire Evesham* acquired by the Admiralty and renamed *Wave Ruler* (1), transferred from Eagle Oil management.

April: *LST 3523* renamed HMS *Trouncer* in reserve.

17 April: *Orangeleaf* handed over to Ministry of Transport for disposal.

18 April: *War Pathan* sold commercially.

23 April: *Distol* handed-over to STO Bombay for disposal.

30 May: *Empire Paladin* renamed *Wave Commander*; remained under commercial management of British Molasses Co.

June: Oiling at sea – *Northmark* due Portsmouth for repairs including building an oiling-at-sea deck, enlarging the crew accommodation, installing goal-post rigs and generally incorporating ideas from experience by the British Pacific Fleet; Chatham crew.

2 June: Admiralty authorised the Seafarers' Education Society to place libraries onboard RFA vessels and *Brown Ranger* was the first supplied the following day.

July: *War Krishna* handed over to Ministry of Transport for disposal. *Northmark* renamed as HMS *Bulawayo*.

1 August: *Scotol* sold to Hemsley, Bell & Co, Southampton, renamed *Hemsley I*.

RFA *Teakol*, 1,500-ton harbour tanker. (RFA Archive)

HMS *Bulawayo*

FLEET OILER

Pennant: X51 **Official number:** 118493
Port of registry: London **Callsign:** GSDV
Commissioned: As *Westerwald*, a Kriegsmarine replenishment ship
Builder: Schichau, Elbing
Machinery: Steam turbine with double reduction gearing; two Wagner boilers; two shafts; 21,590 shp; 21 knots (designed)
Dimensions (length oa/bp x beam): 585/549ft x 72.5ft
Tonnage measurements: 10,848 grt
Displacement: 22,000 tons full load
Complement: 133 German, 292 British
Remarks: Although she never served as a RFA, HMS *Bulawayo* was an important ship in the history of the development of RAS practices and knowledge. Germany designed large fleet replenishment tankers designed to support warships at sea with fuels, fresh water and limited dry stores including ammunition; sister-ship of the *Altmark*; September 1955 for disposal and handed over to the British Iron and Steel Corporation; October 1955 to W H Arnott Young, Dalmuir for breaking-up.

HMS *Bulawayo*, former German 'AOR' *Westerwald*, later renamed *Nordmark*, served as a front line support ship to the *Admiral Scheer*, and the raiders *Thor*, *Kormoran* and U-boats; taken over by the Royal Navy at Copenhagen where her name was initially 'anglicised as *Northmark*. As HMS *Bulawayo* she was the backbone of extensive post-war replenishment at sea trials that influenced the future design and practices of Royal Fleet Auxiliary fleet tankers. (ANRS)

Tugs and Salvage Vessels

After the Second World War many of the tugs and salvage vessels that were either White Ensign or on a T124 variant manning reverted to full civilian manning. *Circa* 1947 some of the HM Rescue Tugs and Salvage Vessels were registered as merchant ships and as RFAs – manned by Director of Stores (Navy) with operational and management in all other respects, including repair and seaworthiness, undertaken by the Director of Boom Defence, later Director of Boom Defence and Marine Services, and even later Director General Dockyards and Maintenances (Marine Services Division), later Director of Marine Services (Navy). During their careers many crewed on various yard craft, home trade or dockyard D606 agreements. In 1970 they transferred to the newly-formed Royal Maritime Auxiliary Service. Those tugs and salvage vessels that served as RFAs are listed in the Fleet List, although it is difficult to be precise on their RFA dates.

The tug RFA *Cautious* was completed in 1940 as HMS *Prudent.* (World Ship Society)

The 1,050-ton coastal salvage vessel RFA *Swin.* (World Ship Society)

September: *Black Ranger* took part in the Home Fleet Review on the Clyde.

16 September: *Fort Duquesne* transferred to the Admiralty as an RFA – took part in Home Fleet Review.

18 September: *Cedarol* renamed *Rowanol* to reduce confusion with *Cedardale.*

29 September: *Spalake* and *Spapool* bareboat chartered to the War Office.

October: *Plumleaf*, Malta, wreck towed to Sicily by tug *Marauder*, accompanied by *Sea Salvor* for demolition.

10 October: *Fort Charlotte* transferred to the Admiralty. *War Pathan* renamed *Basingbank. War Bharata* handed over to Ministry of Transport for disposal.

25 October: *War Pindari* handed over to Ministry of Transport for disposal.

7–29 October: Oiling at sea – HMS *Bulawayo* at Portland for RAS trials conducted with HMS *Duke of York*, HMS *Superb* and HMS *Dunkirk* and involved a study of interaction, speed trials, RAS (Liquid) trials abeam and astern with 7-inch hoses and quick release couplings, RAS (Stores) trials with light and heavy jackstays, light jackstays for casualties.

18 November: *Empire Salisbury* renamed *Wave Master*, management transferred from Eagle Oil Shipping.

20 November: *Fort Rosalie* (1) transferred to the Admiralty for service as an RFA, converted, at Portsmouth Dockyard, into an armament stores issuing ship.

15 December: *Appleleaf* arrived Troon for demolition.

23 December: *Pearleaf* arrived Blyth for demolition.

1948

1948: Merchant Navy Welfare Board established. *War Bharata* sold to Verano Steamship Co, London (F V Andlow, managers), renamed *Wolf Rock. War Pindari* sold to John Harker Ltd, renamed *Deepdale H. Distol* sold to Kuwait Oil Co Ltd for use as a water tanker, renamed *Akhawi. Ebonol* (1) sold to Chinese concern, name unchanged. *Mixol* sold to the Whitebrook Shipping Co (Counties Ship Management Ltd, managers), London, renamed *Whitebrook. War Sudra* handed over to Ministry of Transport for disposal, sold to Oak Steam Ship Co, London, name unchanged.

25 January: *Orangeleaf* arrived Briton Ferry for demolition.

February: *Danmark* arrived Dublin, renamed *Shelfoil*; remained there for a number of years. *Hickorol* sold to Hemsley, Bell & Co, Southampton, renamed *Hemsley II.*

12 March: *Reliant* (1) to Ministry of Transport for disposal.

1 April: *Wave Baron* transferred to Admiralty management.

5 April: *Boxol* sold to Oscar Shipping Co Ltd, London, renamed *Portnall.*

13 April: *Rapidol* sold to Moller's Ltd, Hong Kong, initially name remained, renamed in 1950 as *Louise Moller*.

16 May: *Wave Commander* transferred to Admiralty management.

19 May: *Reliant* (1) sold to Maltese Cross Steamship Co, London, renamed *Anthony G.*

5 June: *Thornol* sold to Metcalf Coaster Ltd, London.

11 June: *Fort Charlotte* transferred to Admiralty, at Gibraltar for RFA service; converted at Portsmouth Dockyard into a naval stores/victualling stores issuing ship.

22 September: *Fort Beauharnois* transferred to Admiralty; converted into a naval stores/victualling stores issuing ship.

1 October: Oiling at sea – *Wave Sovereign* in collision with 'Battle' class destroyer HMS *Sluys* – slight damage.

11 October: *Nimble* – Director of Ships and Transport arranges disposal; purchased by Lloyds Albert Yacht and Motor Packet Service, Southampton. MV *Chungking* (later to become *Retainer*) laid down.

31 December: *Fort Dunvegan* transferred to the Admiralty.

RFA *Fort Rosalie* (1), armament stores issuing ship. (RFA Archive)

1949

1949: Admiralty decision that all RFAs listed below should be fully equipped with bow paravane gear: 'Wave' class, 'Ranger' class, 'Dale class', *Fort Charlotte*, *Fort Duquesne*, *Fort Rosalie*, *Prestol*, *Bacchus*, *Maine*, *Olna*, *Nasprite*, *Belgol*, *Celerol*, *Fortol*, *Serbol*, 'Robert' class; the paravane gear was to be removed from the following ships (the *Birchol* class were not fitted): *Elderol*, *Elmol*, *Larchol*, *Limol*, *Philol*, *Petrobus*. HMS *Bulawayo* dry-docked, Portsmouth for refit which included alterations to the accommodation, introduction of canteen messing and installation of two cargo lifts; work up in Solent and at Invergordon; classed as a Fleet Oiler. *War Hindoo* became a fuelling hulk at Malta. *Fort Constantine* transferred to the Admiralty.

13 January: *Fort Sandusky* transferred to the Admiralty for RFA service; converted into an armament stores issuing ship at Portsmouth Dockyard.

4 February: *Wave Premier* commences Arctic endurance trials with HM Ships *Vengeance*, *Gabbard*, *St Kitts*, *Artful*, *Loch Armaig* and MTBs *3012*, *2016* and *2017*.

14 February: *Nimble* arrived Boom for breaking-up.

12 March: *Ruthenia* returned to Singapore and was sold for scrap.

7 June: *Changchow* (later to become *Resurgent*) laid down.

18 June: *Ruthenia* arrived Dalmuir for partial dismantling, final demolition carried out at Troon.

September: *Argo* allocated to British

Victualling stores issuing ship RFA *Fort Dunvegan*. (World Ship Society)

Iron & Steel Corporation (BISCO) for demolition.

7 September: *War Brahmin* laid up in reserve on the River Fal.

November: *Gold Ranger* accompanied RRS *John Biscoe* to the South Shetlands and Deception Island in Antarctica.

5 December: *Fort Constantine* transferred to Admiralty management in RFA service.

7 December: RRS *William Scoresby* – Admiralty Board approve that she should be run through the Director of Stores with manning and management; management fees is indicated as £675.00.

1950

1950: All guns and mountings at present onboard RFAs to be landed at ship's base port. Stiffening, pedestals and platforms to be retained. *Spabeck* remained an RFA and was earmarked for special service; to Vickers Armstrong Ltd, Barrow for conversion into an HTP (high test peroxide) fuel carrier – to support what was a 'top secret' project with the *Explorer* class submarines; special tanks were built-in her existing cargo tanks to enable the carriage of up 111 tons of special fuel and 17 tons of Avcat; these tanks and the cargo pumps were manufactured from pure aluminium. Function bands painted on funnels: red band = ammunition

'Fort' (1) class

STANDARD DESIGN DRY CARGO SHIPS

RFA *Fort Beauharnois* (ex *Cornish Park*)
RFA *Fort Charlotte* (ex *Buffalo Park*)
RFA *Fort Constantine* (ex *Earls Court Park*)
RFA *Fort Dunvegan*
RFA *Fort Duquesne* (ex *Queensborough Park*)
RFA *Fort Langley* (ex *Montebello Park*)
RFA *Fort Rosalie* (1) (ex *Waverley Park*)
RFA *Fort Sandusky* (ex *Simcoe Park*)

Machinery: Steam 3 cyl triple expansion; two water tube boilers; 2,500 ihp; single shaft; 11 knots
Dimensions (loa/bp x beam): 439/424ft x 57.2ft
Tonnage measurements: 7,253 grt, 7,508 dwt, – net
Displacement: – **Complement:** 115
Remarks: +100A1; +LMC +RMC, the 'Fort' class war construction standard design cargo freighters were ordered and built for the Canadian Government under management of the Park Steam Ship Co, they were also the first major block of dry cargo ships to come onto the sea-going inventory of the RFA.

FORT ROSALIE

Built by
United Shipyards Limited
Montreal, Canada

Keel laid August 29, 1944 — Launched November 18, 1944
Completed July, 1945

Fort Rosalie was built by Bienville in 1716 on the present site of Natchez, Mississippi, and named after Mme Pontchartrain, wife of the French Prime Minister.

Cadillac, Governor of Louisiana, desperate over the poverty of the colony, the advance of the British and the hostility of the Natchez, planned to subdue the Indians. His dislike of Bienville, whom he succeeded, prompted him to clear two issues at once. Accordingly he ordered Bienville to defeat the Natchez, permitting him only fifteen men for this task. Bienville obeyed the orders, took his fifteen men, built Fort Rosalie, and with a plan both brilliant and cunning, defeated the large war-like tribe.

This deception of the Natchez only increased the trouble. A violent hostility resulted which led up to the Natchez Massacre of 1729 in which Fort Rosalie was destroyed and most of its garrison murdered. Almost immediately rebuilt, the post passed into British hands in 1763, then into Spanish hands in 1779 and finally into the hands of the Americans in 1798, only being demolished in 1805.

To commemorate this early fort in the joint history of North America, this cargo ship has been named the

SS FORT ROSALIE

Wartime Shipbuilding Limited
Montreal, Canada

Above: The 'Fort' class ships carried a framed plaque in their wardrooms that described the history of the ship's name.

RFA *Fort Charlotte* at Hong Kong, displaying a white funnel band of a victualling stores ship. (RFA Archive)

ships, white band = victualling ships.

17 January: *Fortol* laid up in Devonport.

19 January: *Chungking* launched.

20 March: *Eddybeach* laid down.

20 April: RRS *Discovery II*, owned by the National Oceanographic Council, is transferred to the Director of Stores for RFA manning and maintenance.

18 May: *War Brahmin* sailed from River Fal for Devonport.

25 June: Start of Korean War and United Nations operations.

31 July: *Changchow* launched.

Chungking, 9,398 grt, cargo liner, completed by Scotts' Shipbuilding Co, Greenock for the China Navigation Co.

November/December: Aviation – *Fort Duquesne* fitted with a small helicopter landing platform by Malta Dockyard in preparation for helicopter trials.

3 December: *Fort Duquesne* sailed Malta on passage to Hebburn on Tyne.

RFA Pensions

1 January 1948 revised regulations made for a scheme of retiring allowances and gratuities for RFA personnel engaged on Board of Trade agreements serving under NMB conditions, retrospective to 1 January 1938. Applied to Masters, Chief Officers, Second Officers, Third Officers and Fourth Officers, Chief Engineers, Second Engineers, Third Engineers, Fourth Engineers, Fifth Engineers, Junior Engineers, Electrical Engineers and Radio Officers employed directly by the Admiralty; Scheme was also extended to cover all officers covered by Merchant Navy Officers' Pension Fund from 1 January 1938.

1 August 1950 revised regulations made for a scheme of retiring allowances and gratuities for RFA engaged on MoT agreements serving under NMB conditions was extended to cover Refrigerating Engineers and Electricians. It also introduced Widows' and Children's' Pension Scheme and of Dependants' Scheme. Officers service in RFA Tugs and Salvage Vessels operated by the Director of Boom Defence and Marine Salvage and manned by Director of Stores personnel were included.

Non-Registered RFA Duties

The Admiralty had a number of smaller vessels that were not registered RFAs, but during the course of their career individual RFA officers, particularly those with Foreign Trade Certificates, were appointed to them. For example, in 1937 an RFA Engineer First Class was appointed to the tug *C405* based at Trincomalee; and between 1946 and 1951 RFA Masters were loaned to a number of the Naval Armament Vessels that had to take passage outside UK coastal waters or from an overseas station to UK waters.

C Craft

The Naval Stores harbour craft were usually allocated a number bearing the prefix C. This descended from the days when the Coaling Officer operated the fuelling craft. Many of these craft were operated by the Naval Stores Department under the Director of Stores (Navy). C numbers were allocated to, for example, dumb barges, coal lighters, dumb coal lighters, self-propelled diesel lighters, self-propelled stores lighters, launches and tugs. A number were registered as RFAs and many wore the 'green stripe' that indicated the Naval Stores Department. Those traced as having served as RFAs are listed in the Fleet List, although it is difficult to be precise on their RFA dates.

The small lubricating oil carrier RFA *C653*. (RFA Archive)

Korean War

Between 25 June 1950 and 27 July 1953 the following RFA assets were deployed:

RFA *Birchol*
RFA *Echoldale*
Fort Langley (MFA)
RFA *Fort Sandusky*
RFA *Gold Ranger*
RFA *Wave Chief*
RFA *Wave Knight*
RFA *Wave Premier*
RFA *Wave Regent*
RFA *Brown Ranger*
RFA *Fort Charlotte**
RFA *Fort Rosalie*
RFA *Green Ranger*
RFA *Wave Baron*
RFA *Wave Duke*
RFA *Wave Laird*
RFA *Wave Prince*
RFA *Wave Sovereign*

RFA *Maine* (hospital ship) was also deployed.

* *Fort Charlotte* was the naval stores issuing ship based at Sasebo.

During this war RFAs steamed 300,000+ miles. About one third of the RFA fleet contributed to the war effort carrying fuel and stores to the Far East and distributing it to ships in operational zones. 90,000 tons of fuel transferred by RAS(L). RFA *Wave Chief* – 66 RAS operations, pumped 27,000 tons of oil and aviation fuel; RFA *Fort Rosalie* in 18 months supplied 9,000 tons of munitions until relieved by *Fort Sandusky*.

1951

1951: Captain S G Kent RFA appointed Commodore RFA. *Portnall* reacquired by the Admiralty during the Korean War and name reverted to *Boxol*.

January: Aviation – around 180 helicopter landing and take-off trials conduced on RFA *Fort Duquesne* with Dragonflies from NAS 705. Replenishment at sea – *Fort Duquesne* conducted trials with a prototype Clark Chapman 1-ton automatic tensioning winch.

10 January: *Fort Duquesne* sails Hebburn to Portland.

23 January: *Eddycove* ordered.

7 February: *Tatry* (later to become *Surf Patrol*) launched for Polish Ocean Lines.

15 February: *Changchow*, cargo liner, 9,398 grt, completed by Scotts Shipbuilding Co Ltd for the China Navigation Co.

17 February: *Fort Duquesne* on passage Portland to Gibraltar conducted helicopter trials with HMS *Savage* in Portland/Plymouth area.

6 March: *Fort Constantine* sailed Bermuda with the final stores from the Royal Naval Dockyard which had ceased to exist on 1 March.

19 March: *Fort Dunvegan* entered RFA service as a store carrier.

23 March: *Eddybay* laid down.

27 March: *Eddymull* ordered.

April: *Surf Pilot* – the 10,519 grt tanker *Kurosio Maru*, sunk in January 1945, was salvaged in 1947 and rebuilt by Hong Kong & Whampoa Dockyard; renamed *Yung Hao* of the China Tanker Co; requisitioned by Admiralty at Hong Kong to prevent Korean War use by Chinese; although in poor condition she was towed to Singapore (HMS *Terror*) by *Salvalour*, escorted by HMS *Charity*; it is

The first helicopter trials undertaken in 1951 with a Westland Dragonfly on RFA *Fort Duquesne*. (RFA Archive)

'Eddy' class

ADMIRALTY-DESIGNED FLEET ATTENDANT TANKERS

RFA *Eddybay* RFA *Eddybeach*
RFA *Eddycliff* RFA *Eddycreek*
RFA *Eddyfirth* RFA *Eddyness*
RFA *Eddyreef* RFA *Eddyrock*
RFA *Eddycover* (cancelled)
RFA *Eddymull* (cancelled)

Machinery: Steam 3 cyl triple expansion by Lobnitz, Renfrew; two Scotch boilers; single screw; 1,750 ihp; 12 knots; 18 tpd consumption
Dimensions (loa/bp x beam): 287.7/–ft x 44.2ft
Tonnage measurements: 2,157 grt, 2,200 dwt
Displacement: 4,165 tons full load
Complement: 38
Remarks: +100A1 +LMC. Four cargo tanks served by four main pumps and limited dry cargo capacity and magazine served by two 3-ton and two 1-ton derricks. Small tankers built for fleet attendant duties, with the fast post-war changing of the RFA's role, two of the planned ships were cancelled and within a short time they refocused on harbour and coastal duties. With the exception of the enduring RFA *Eddyfirth* the active service life of this class was by RFA standards very short.
The details are based on RFA Eddyfirth *as built*

RFA *Eddybay*, harbour tanker. (RFA Archive)

RFA *Surf Pioneer* (ex *Beskidy*).

reported that she was to be have been renamed *Surf Pilot* and to be used by the Admiralty as a RFA station tanker; there is no evidence of this and she was laid up at Singapore.

12 April: *War Afridi* hulked at Hong Kong.

23 April: *Beskidy* (later to become *Surf Pioneer*) launched for Polish Government (Polish Ocean Lines, Gdynia, managers).

24 April: *Eddybeach* launched.

May: HMS *Seafox* withdrawn from commissioned service.

6 June: *Empire Tesbury* transferred to the Admiralty at Singapore; renamed *Rippledyke* and operated on charter to various companies.

14 July: *Tatry* requisitioned by the Admiralty, renamed *Surf Patrol*; *Beskidy* requisitioned, renamed *Surf Pioneer*.

17 July: *Surf Patrol*, 7,742 grt, completed by Bartram & Sons at Sunderland under RFA manning and management.

7 October: At noon, first Commodore RFA (Captain S G Kent OBE) hoisted his Broad Pendant at Rosyth in RFA *Fort Dunvegan*.

28 November: *Surf Pioneer*, 7,742 grt, completed by Bartram & Sons at Sunderland under RFA manning and management.

29 November: *Eddybay* launched.

December: SS *Fort Amherst* purchased for conversion and service as a naval armament freighter.

8 December: *Eddybeach*, coastal tanker, 2,157 grt, completed by Caledon Shipbuilding at Dundee.

1952

1952: *Olcades* sold to BISCO for demolition after a serious fire at Singapore. *Eddycove* and *Eddymull* cancelled. *Blue Ranger* wins the annual Bulawayo Cup for the most conspicuous efficiency in replenishment-at-sea in the Mediterranean area.

24 January: *Seafox*, small aircraft transport, 711 grt, after conversion to meet Lloyd's requirements for merchant ships, enters RFA service.

6 February: Death of HRH King George VI.

29 February: *Changchow* and *Chungking* purchased by the Admiralty, remaining on charter to Messageries Maritimes until December; the Admiralty used the MoT to supervise the charter with Butterfield & Swin acting as managers.

5 April: *Wave Ruler* (1) caught fire whilst anchored off Greenock; ship's crew and local firemen fought for two hours to suppress the fire.

7 April: *Prestol* placed in reserve at Devonport.

25 April: *Eddybay*, 2,153 grt, completed by Caledon Shipbuilding at Dundee.

28 April: *Eddyfirth* laid down.

23 May: *Wave Conqueror* whilst anchored off Immingham was badly damaged aft after being hit by the Norwegian *Belray* (2,901/1926), she was towed to North Shields for repairs.

15 July: *Fort Amherst*, 3,496 grt, hull survey satisfactory, renamed RFA *Amherst*, small naval armament freighter with passenger accommodation reduced to 12 for Admiralty service; her original Scotch boilers were replaced by two water tube boilers constructed in 1945 for a 'Loch' class frigate

5 August: *Tide Austral* laid down.

25 August: *Eddycliff* launched.

RFA *Amherst*, sporting bow paravane frame. (World Ship Society)

3 October: Operation Hurricane 1 – first British test atomic bomb explosion, Monte Bello Islands, off NW Australia; RFAs in support: RFA *Fort Beauharnois*, RFA *Fort Constantine*, RFA *Fort Rosalie*, RFA *Wave Ruler*, RFA *Wave Prince*, RFA *Wave Sovereign*, RFA *Gold Ranger*.
November: *Chungking* delivered to the Admiralty.
16 December: *Eddyrock* launched.
19 December: *Chungking* renamed *Retainer* and chartered out commercially to British India Steam Navigation Co.

1953

1953: *Fort Duquesne* wins the annual Bulawayo Cup for the most conspicuous efficiency in replenishment-at-sea in the Mediterranean area.
19 January: *Eddycreek* launched.
February: Humanitarian assistance – severe flooding of UK east coast and Dutch coast after abnormally heavy tides; Naval helicopters sent to Holland for flood relief and worked with RFAs (unidentified) and coastal craft of the Rhine Squadron.
10 February: *Eddycliff*, 2,173 grt, completed by Blythswood Shipbuilding at Scotstoun.
20 February: Uniforms – St Edward's Crown adopted for badges and buttons.
March: *Changchow* delivered to the Admiralty. *Eddybay*, *Eddycliff* time-chartered to Shell in UK waters.
3 April: *Brambleleaf* arrived Spezia for demolition.
16 April: *London Loyalty* (later to become *Brambleleaf* (2)) launched.
18 April: *Olcades* arrived Blyth for demolition.
25 April: *Changchow* renamed *Resurgent* and chartered to Buries

'Tide' class

ADMIRALTY-DESIGNED LARGE FLEET REPLENISHMENT TANKER

RFA *Tide Austral* (became HMAS *Supply*)
RFA *Tiderace* (became RFA *Tideflow*)
RFA *Tiderange* (became RFA *Tidesurge*)
RFA *Tidereach*

Builder: Swan Hunter & Wigham Richardson, Wallsend (yard no 1847)
Machinery: Two Pametrada steam turbines by Wallsend Slipway; double reduction geared to single screw; superheated Babcock & Wilcox water tube boiler; 15,000 shp; 17 knots
Dimensions (loa/bp x beam): 583.2/561ft x 71ft
Tonnage measurements: 13,516 grt, 16,848 dwt
Displacement: 26,000 tons full load
Complement: 100 – accommodation overall for 146
Remarks: +100A1 +LMC +RMC, ice class 3, class VII; these were the first Admiralty design, purpose-built fleet replenishment tankers – high-value units intended for enduring front-line support; their design introduced into the RFA the hard-learned lessons of the Second World War and set the example for further hardworking ships. Sometimes known as the 'early Tides', these tankers were fitted with the state-of-art abeam rigs with automatic tensioning winches and astern fuelling rigs; cargo capacity 8,500 tons FFO, 4,600 tons dieso and 1,900 tons Avcat.
The details are based on Tidereach *as built*

RAS(L): three 'Tides' – RFAs *Tidesurge*, *Tideflow* and *Tidereach*, 1964. (RFA Archive)

Eddycliff displaying her unusually low freeboard when fully loaded. (RFA Archive)

The Admiralty-owned RFA *Resurgent* (formerly the *Changchow*) chartered out for commercial service before undergoing her conversion into a fleet replenishment ship. (World Ship Society)

Markes.

21 May: Presidential Citation – President Syngman Rhee presented a Presidential Citation to RFA *Maine*, hospital ship, for her work during the Korean War.

28 May: *Eddyreef* launched.

Laurelwood (later to become *Cherryleaf* (2)) launched.

2 June: *Tidereach* laid down.

7 June: *Eddyrock*, 2,172 grt, completed by Blyth Drydock and Shipbuilding at Blyth.

15 June: Coronation Fleet Review, Spithead – RFA *Fort Dunvegan*, RFA *Amherst*, RFA *Olna*, RFA *Eddybay*, RFA *Black Ranger*, RFA *Wave Victor* and RFA *Robert Middleton*.

30 June: *Limol* laid up at Pembroke Dock.

July: *Boxol* laid up at Pembroke Dock.

1 July: *Tiderange* laid down.

30 August: *Tiderace* laid down.

9 September: *Somersby* launched.

10 September: *Eddyfirth* launched.

11 September: *Eddycreek*, 2,223 grt, completed by Lobnitz at Renfrew.

October: *Seafox* reclassified as a victualling stores issuing ship.

Replenishment at sea – Exercise Main Brace with RFA *Wave Knight*.

22 October: *Eddyness* launched.

23 October: *Eddyreef*, 2,219 grt, completed by Caledon Shipbuilding at Dundee.

5 November: *Fort Langley* previously

Bulawayo Cup

The Bulawayo Cup was awarded annually to the RN or RFA vessel that, in the opinion of the 'committee' had in the previous year displayed the most conspicuous efficiency in fleet replenishment at sea, in the Mediterranean area. The Cup was awarded from 1951 to 1960:

1951	HMS *Vigo*
1952	RFA *Blue Ranger*
1953	RFA *Fort Duquesne*
1954	RFA *Fort Duquesne*
1955	HMS *Aisne*
1956	RFA *Retainer*
1957	RFA *Fort Duquesne*
1958	RFA *Tideflow*
1959	RFA *Fort Langley*/ RFA *Fort Duquesne*
1960	RFA *Tide Austral*/ RFA *Fort Duquesne*

RAS(L) from a 'Ranger' class tanker. (ANRS)

RFA *Maine* (4)

NAVAL HOSPITAL SHIP
Pennant: –
Official number: 159356
Port of registry: London
Callsign: GCFB
Builder: Ansaldo San Giorgio, La Spezia (yard no 192)
Machinery: Six steam turbines with double reduction gearing to two shafts by Ansaldo, Sampierdarena; four water tube and two Scotch boilers; 1,120 shp; 13 knots
Dimensions (loa/bp x beam): 447/–ft x 52.4ft
Tonnage measurements: 7,517 grt, – dwt, 4,205 net
Displacement: –
Complement: RFA + medical staff

The hospital ship RFA *Maine* (4), formerly *Empire Clyde*. (World Ship Society)

Remarks: +100A1; +LMC, ordered by Transatlantica Italiana Societe Anonima di Navigazione, Genoa and on 28 December 1924 launched as *Leonardo Da Vinci*; May 1925 completed, followed by maiden voyage Naples, Palermo, Boston, New York; 1925 Ansaldo Group's bankers went bankrupt resulting in collapse of the whole group; shares taken over by Credito Italiano and a new company formed – Compagnia Italiana Transatlantica (CITRA); 1926–9 laid up; 1934 as a result of further financial difficulties ship was transferred to Tirrenia Line; 1936 suffered serious fire and had to reconstructed; 11 February 1941 captured by HMS *Hawkins* at Kismayu, her engines sabotaged; 14 February 1941 handed over to Ellerman Lines, London for management and sailed for Mombasa for repairs; 1942 taken over by Ministry of War Transport, converted into an army hospital ship, renamed *Empire Clyde* and placed under the management of City Line; May 1945 taken over for use as a naval hospital ship with a 288-bed general hospital facility; 1947 purchased by the Admiralty; 1 January 1948 registered as an RFA and on 26 January renamed RFA *Maine* (4); 5 March 1954 it was announced that she was to be disposed of; 26 April 1954 operational service ended at Hong Kong; 25 May 1954 sold to Hong Kong breakers for demolition.

run commercially, arrived Hong Kong from Sasebo, then passage to Leith for a refit.

28 December: *Laurelwood*, 12,400 grt, completed by Sir J Laing at Sunderland for Molasses & General Transport Co.

1954

1954: Captain W Brunswick Brown appointed Commodore RFA. Engineer Cadetship scheme introduced. 'Battle of the River Plate' film was made and RFA *Olna* (2) played the role of the German oiler refuelling '*Graf Spee*' played by HMS *Bermuda* and USS *Salem*. *Fort Duquesne* wins the annual Bulawayo Cup for the most conspicuous efficiency in replenishment-at-sea in the Mediterranean area. Replenishment at sea – automatic tensioning winches ready for service when Clark Chapman supplied 2-ton winches for fitting in *Tidereach* and in *Retainer*, also seen the introduction of the 'lattice' type of derrick..

10 January: *London Loyalty*, 12,100 grt, completed by Furness Shipbuilding at Haverton-on-Hill for London & Overseas Freighting Ltd.

17 January: *Wave Victor* suffered a serious engine-room fuel fire when off Illfracombe and had to be abandoned; the fire was finally extinguished the following day but the vessel was nearly lost.

23 February: *Fort Langley* taken over by the Admiralty.

4 March: *Somersby*, cargo liner (designed to carry 12 passengers), 8,396 grt completed by Sir James Laing at Sunderland for Ropner Shipping Co.

30 March: *Eddyrock* to Singapore to relieve *Oakol*.

April: *Wave Victor* towed to North Shields for repairs to severe fire damage.

25 April: *Eddyfirth*, 2,221 grt, completed by Lobnitz at Renfrew.

May: *Fort Langley* transferred to the Admiralty for RFA management, converted into an armament stores issuing ship.

18 May: *Tidereach* original launch date postponed.

26 May: *Maine*, the last permanent

British hospital ship, is sold.
2 June: *Tidereach* launched.
July: *Retainer* taken in hand for partial conversion into a fleet replenishment ship.
1 July: *Tiderange* launched.
13 July: *Wave Commander* in collision in fog off Gibraltar with the BP tanker *British Unity* (8,416/1939) which was badly holed; *Wave Commander* was escorted to Gibraltar by *Wave Duke*.
30 August: *Tiderace* launched.
1 September: *Tide Austral* launched for the Commonwealth of Australia, Department of the Navy.
11 September: *Tiderace* towed to the Tyne for installation of her engines.
11 October: *Eddyness*, 2,172 grt, completed by Blyth Dry Dock and Shipbuilding Co at Blyth.
28 October: *London Integrity* (later to become *Bayleaf* (2)) launched.

RFAS *Retainer* and *Resurgent*

ARMAMENT SUPPORT SHIPS

Pennant: A280
Official number: 184366
Port of registry: London
Callsign: GGTM
Builder: Scotts' Shipbuilding & Engineering Co, Greenock (yard no 654)
Machinery: One 6 cyl two stroke, single acting Doxford ICE by the builder; 6,500 bhp; bunkers 925 tons; 16 knots
Dimensions (loa/bp x beam): 477.2/459.7ft x 62.2ft
Tonnage measurements: 9,357 grt, 14,400 dwt
Displacement: 14,400 tons full load
Complement: 112 + 34 naval stores staff
Remarks: +100A1; +MBS, +RMC (for refrigerated machinery) class 1 ships built as the sisters *Chungking* and *Changchow*, purchased by the Admiralty and converted for service as fleet replenishment ships fitted for service as fleet replenishment ships fitted with small cargo platforms for VERTREP. There were five holds and 'tween decks – No. 1: 600-ton capacity with a 11 x 16ft hatch served by 2 x 5-ton derricks and an electric lift; No 2: 1,300-ton capacity with a 11 x 25ft hatch served by 2 x 10-ton derricks and an electric lift; No 3: 900-ton capacity with a 11 x 19ft hatch served by 2 x 7-ton derricks; No 4: 300-ton capacity with a 14.2 x 15.9ft hatch served by 2 x 10-ton derricks and an electric lift; and No 5 500 ton capacity with a 11 x 20ft hatch served by 2 x 5-ton derricks. They were capable of carrying a range of armament stores, frozen and dry provisions, fresh provisions (covering between 1,500 and 2,000 man months), NAAFI stores, medical stores, 200 survivors kits. She was fitted with and tested the new 2-ton automatic tensioning winches.
The details are based on RFA Resurgent

The fleet replenishment ship RFA *Retainer* (formerly the China Navigation Co cargo passenger liner *Chungking*). (World Ship Society)

1955

1955: Captain T H Card appointed Commodore RFA. *Spabeck* based at Vickers Armstrong Ltd, Barrow-in-Furness where she was used for transporting High Test Peroxide (HTP) fuel for the experimental submarines HMS *Explorer* and HMS *Excalibur*, a technology made redundant by the advent of the nuclear-powered submarine.
8 February: *Southern Satellite* (later to become *Orangeleaf* (2)) launched.
10–15 March: Exercise Sea Lance – joint Home and Mediterranean Fleet exercise in the western Mediterranean – aircraft carriers HM Ships *Centaur* and *Albion*, seven *Daring* class destroyers, one fast minelayer, 11 destroyers, six frigates, fleet tug and Fleet Air Arm and RAF aircraft. RFA support was provided by RFAS *Fort Duquesne*, *Brown Ranger*, *Green Ranger*, *Blue Ranger* and *Wave Sovereign*.
April: Conversion of *Retainer* into a fleet replenishment ship completed.
28 April: *London Integrity*, 12,123 grt, completed by Furness Shipbuilding at Haverton-on-Hill for London & Overseas Freighters.
17 May: *Tide Austral*, fleet replenishment tanker, 13,168 grt, completed by Harland & Wolff at Belfast for loan to the Admiralty for operation as a RFA for three years.
8 June: *Southern Satellite*, 12,481 grt, completed by Furness Shipbuilding at Haverton-on-Hill for Christian Salvesen.
27 July: *Denbydale* arrived Blyth for demolition.
30 August: *Tidereach*, fleet replenishment tanker, 13,146 grt, completed by Swan Hunter & Wigham Richardson, Wallsend for the Admiralty.
4 October: HMS *Bulawayo*, fleet tanker, handed over to the British Iron and Steel Corporation for scrapping.

1956

1956: *Green Ranger* chartered for trading on Canadian coast, one voyage was undertaken in convoy with icebreaker. *Retainer* wins the annual Bulawayo Cup for the most conspicuous efficiency in replenishment-at-sea in the Mediterranean area.

7 January: Serious manning shortages on replenishment at sea tanker led to the introduction of a Replenishment-at-Sea allowance.

24 January: *Tiderace*, fleet replenishment tanker, 11,980 grt, completed by J L Thompson & Son at Sunderland for the Admiralty.

4 February: Oiling at sea – *Blue Ranger* in collision with the destroyer HMS *Chieftain* during bad weather.

1 March: *Wave Prince* hit by the Shell tanker *Volvella* (20,731/1956) whilst alongside on the Tyne; the Shell tanker had broken adrift from Wallsend in a gale and had careered five miles down the river colliding with seven ships *en route*.

26 March: *Tiderange*, fleet replenishment tanker, 13,146 grt, completed by Sir James Laing at Sunderland for the Admiralty.

24 April: *George Lyras* (later to become *Appleleaf* (2)) launched.

May: Operation Mosaic 1 – British nuclear trials at Monte Bello Island off Australia – RFA *Eddyrock*.

August: MV *Somersby* chartered by the Admiralty for three months. Humanitarian assistance – earthquake shocks in Greece, naval vessels sent to assist with relief (unidentified RFAs).

9 August: *Wave King* struck a rock off Brazil and was refloated badly damaged; subsequently laid up at Portsmouth.

September: *Fort Constantine* converted into a naval stores/victualling stores issuing ship. *George Lyras*, 11,570 grt, completed by Bartram & Sons at Sunderland for Marine Enterprises Ltd (Lyras brothers, London). Humanitarian assistance – earthquake shocks in Cyprus, naval vessels sent to assist

Suez 1956 (Operation Musketeer)

	*Operational order 27.10.1956**	*Admiralty press release of ships 30.10.1956*	*C-in-C's Final Report on the operation*	*Army special order 81/1957**
Tiderace	•	•	•	•
Tiderange	•	•	•	•
Olna	•	•	•	•
Retainer	•	•	•	•
Fort Sandusky	•	•	•	•
Wave Master	•	•	•	•
Wave Laird	•	•	•	•
Wave Conqueror	•	•	•	•
Wave Sovereign	•	•	•	•
Eddybeach	•	•	•	•
Blue Ranger	•	•	•	•
Brown Ranger	•	•	•	•
*Surf Pioneer**	•	•	•	•
Spaburn	•	•	•	•
Spapool	•	•	•	•
Fort Duquesne	•	•	•	•
Amherst	•	•	•	•
Bacchus	•	•	•	•
Tidereach			•	•
Wave Victor			•	•
Wave Protector			•	•
Fort Charlotte			•	•
Fort Dunvegan			•	•
Eaglesdale			•	•
Echoldale			•	•
Dewdale				•
Gold Ranger				•
Wave Premier				•
Succour				•
Kinbrace				•
Sea Salvor				•

**Surf Pioneer* was used as a water tanker.
The following RFAs were also deployed: RFAs *Warden, Samsonia, Mediator* and *Kingarth*.

The ocean salvage vessel RFA *Sea Salvor* deployed for Suez. (RFA Archive)

(unidentified RFAs). Introduction of Station Allowances for UK-manned RFAs.

23 September: First night flight by a naval helicopter – HMS *Albion* to RFA *Echoldale*, east of Gibraltar.

October: HMS *Trouncer* is one of 12 LST (3)s to be recalled to service as a result of the Suez Crisis; she was transferred to commercial management by the Ministry of Transport and renamed *Empire Gull*.

31 October: Operation Musketeer – Suez conflict commences – RFA assets deployed:

Task Force 324 (Red Sea Group – Operation Toreador) included RFA *Wave Sovereign*.

Task Force 325.8 (logistics group supporting the carriers) included RFAs *Fort* Sandusky, *Olna*, *Retainer*, *Tiderace*, *Tiderange*.

Operation Grapple

In 1957, task force supporting operation and fleet for the British H-bomb test at Christmas Island in Pacific Ocean. *Fort Beauharnois* was the first RFA to fly a RN Senior Officer's flag – Commodore, Grapple Squadron, Christmas Island. Between now and 1960 the following ships were directly employed:

RFA *Reliant*	RFA *Wave Prince*	RFA *Gold Ranger*
RFA *Wave Chief*	RFA *Wave Victor*	RFA *Green Ranger**
RFA *Somersby*	RFA *Olna* (2)	RFA *Tiderange*
RFA *Fort Beauharnois*	RFA *Wave Ruler*	RFA *Wave Sovereign*
RFA *Fort Rosalie*	RFA *Fort Constantine*	RFA *Wave Master*
RFA *Wave Baron*	RFA *Wave Knight*	RFA *Salvictor*

*RFA *Green Ranger* served as a water tanker.

1957

1957: Captain T Elder appointed Commodore RFA. By the end of 1957 the Admiralty order a detailed investigation into a nuclear-powered installation for a fleet replenishment tanker. Yarrows carried out the work under the designation Y.502. Tenders were invited for an installation for a single screw tanker of 65,000 tons deadweight. In November 1961 the government decided not to go ahead on the grounds of economy. *Spabeck*, based at Faslane, laid up between experiments of the submarines HMS *Explorer* and HMS *Excalibur*. Fort Duquesne won the annual Bulawayo Cup for the most conspicuous efficiency in replenishment-at-sea in the Mediterranean area.

6–7 March: *Wave Ruler* – 'Gregory Trials' – after loading at Portsmouth.

April: Humanitarian assistance – earthquake in south-west Turkey, naval vessels sent to assist with relief (unidentified RFAs).

July: *Resurgent* returned to Admiralty service. *Retainer* converted into an armament stores issuing ship.

31 July: *Green Ranger* in collision with the Norwegian *Buccaneer* (5,675/1950) off Beachy Head in fog.

August: *Resurgent* taken in hand for conversion into an armament stores issuing ship.

3 August: *Somersby* purchased by the Admiralty.

11 August: First RFA appointments to *Somersby* which entered service on freighting duties with name unchanged, duties included destoring of Trincomalee Naval Base.

21 September: Humanitarian aid – *Wave Master* assisted in the search for the missing German sailing vessel *Pamir*.

11 November: *Wave Protector* replaced *War Hindoo* as the oil storage hulk and jetty at Ras Hanzir in Grand Harbour, Valetta, Malta.

December: Humanitarian assistance – widespread floods in Ceylon, naval vessels sent to assist with relief (unidentified RFAs).

1958

1958: After some time undertaking charter work *Green Ranger* was placed in operational reserve at Devonport until 1962. *Rippledyke*, after a period on charter to the Bulk Oil Co, was RFA-manned for passage to Gibraltar where she was to used as an oil hulk. Oceanlink, a five-nation South East Asia Treaty Organisation (SEATO) exercise conducted north of Singapore with RAN, RNZN, USN and Pakistan included RFAs *Fort Charlotte*, *Wave Knight* and the US oiler *Kawishiwi*. *War Afridi* broken up at Hong Kong.

4 January: *Wave Conqueror* which had defective engines was laid up at Sheerness for disposal.

February: *Somersby* taken in hand by Smith's Dock, North Shields, for stage one of her conversion into an air stores issuing ship.

13 February: *Ennerdale* laid up at Devonport for disposal.

9 May: *War Hindoo* arrived Blyth for demolition.

June: *Larchol* sold commercially for scrap, but resold the following year.

8 June: *Prestol* arrived St David's Harbour for scrapping.

22 June: *Belgol* arrived Rosyth for demolition.

27 June: *Fortol* sailed Devonport in tow after handover to breakers.

28 June: *Tiderace* renamed *Tideflow* to remove confusion with her sister ship *Tiderange* which was renamed *Tidesurge*.

30 June: *Serbol* arrived Blyth for breaking up.

17 July: *Celerol* arrived Bo'ness for breaking up.

August: *Corheath* (later to become *Plumleaf* (2)) laid down. *Seafox* placed on disposal list as for sale.

2 August: Replenishment at sea – *Resurgent* conducts trials on the Tyne with HMS *Blackwood*.

6 August: *Fortol* arrived Rosyth for demolition.

28 August: The conversion of *Resurgent* into an armament stores issuing ship is completed.

September: *Somersby*'s initial conversion completed.

RFA *Reliant* (2)

AIR STORES SUPPORT SHIP

Pennant: A84 **Official number:** 180097
Port of registry: West Hartlepool **Callsign:** GRLK
Builder: Sir James Laing & Sons, Sunderland (yard no 801)
Machinery: One 6 cyl 2 stoke Doxford ICE by R & W Hawthorn, Leslie Co; 7,500 bhp; single shaft; bunkers 1,298.5 tons; 50 days at 16 knots
Dimensions (length oa/bp x beam): –/440ft x 61.4ft
Tonnage measurements: 8,438 grt, 9,290 dwt
Displacement: 13,737 tons full load
Complement: 110 RFA and storekeeping personnel (Chinese ratings)
Remarks: +100A1 +LMC +RMC class 1 ship open shelter flush-deck passenger liner of welded construction, single funnel amidships, four masts with prominent crosstrees.

During her first stage conversion by Smith's Dock, North Shields much internal reshaping was undertaken with the adding of another steel deck, refitting the holds with specially designed shelving, storage bins and trays and 700 tons of ballast; extra accommodation was created and fully air conditioned for tropical service; naval radio equipment fitted; generating capacity increased and RAS fittings and automatic tensioning winches added. Her operational loading as an air stores support ship was over 30,000 different patterns of aircraft and naval stores ranging from ½-inch washers to 2-ton flight deck tractors. This operational loading enabled her to support aircraft carriers at sea and to enable the new concept that carriers should be able to spend greater time at sea independent of shore bases.

During her second stage conversion at Henry Robb, Leith her capability was improved with refrigeration machinery being installed together with 30,300 cu ft of insulated storage. Her operational loading increased to 40,000 different patterns of victualling, NAAFI, aircraft and naval stores – she was restored as an air stores/victualling stores issuing ship. She was also fitted with a large 49ft long x 52.5ft wide helicopter cargo platform (a dump deck) fitted over the poop deckhouse. In 1969 after a period in reserve she restored as a stores support ship with an operational loading that including victualling stores, NAAFI stores and clothing.

There were six holds and 'tween decks – three forward of the machinery space and three aft:

No 1: 19,308 cu ft capacity with a 6ft 9in x 21ft 6in hatch served by two 48ft 10-ton derricks, two 45ft 5-ton derricks and two 3-ton electric winches;
No 2: 70,338 cu ft capacity with a 18ft 3in x 21ft 6in hatch served by two 52ft 5-ton derricks and automatic tensioning winch (with a winchman's shelter);
No 3: 97,891 cu ft capacity (including nine refrigerated spaces) with a 11ft x 27ft hatch served by two 40ft 5-ton derricks with two 3-ton electric winches;
No 4: 22,030 cu fit with 13ft x 21ft 6in hatch served by two 35ft 11-ton derricks and two 3-ton winches
No 5: 59,721 cu ft capacity with a 22ft x 21ft 6in hatch; and
No 6: 23,711 cu ft capacity with an 11ft x 14ft 3in hatch, both served by four 44ft 10-ton derricks, automatic tensioning winch (with a winchman's shelter) and six 3-ton electric winches.

She was extensively equipped for replenishment at sea with six RAS points – forward heavy rigs to port and starboard and with light jackstays to port and starboard; after heavy rig to port and starboard; she carried two 42ft naval storing tenders and had a limited VERTREP capability. Known in the RFA as 'The Yacht' – to retain this appearance she was excluded from painting up a black top funnel band.

The 'RFA yacht' *Reliant* was fitted for service as an air stores support ship.

RFA *Tideflow* preparing for a RAS(L) with her aft starboard derrick rig. (RFA Archive)

13 September: Humanitarian aid – *Wave Knight* in company with HM Ships *Bulwark*, *Puma*, *Loch Killisport* and *St Bride's Bay* salvage MV *Melika* and MV *Fernand Gilbert* which had collided and were on fire in Gulf of Oman.

17 September: *Melika* salvage – *Cedardale* ordered to assist in salvage of valuable cargo and took 23,000 tons of crude oil onboard.

23 September: *Somersby* renamed *Reliant* (2) at Rosyth; then to Chatham Dockyard for storing as an air stores issuing ship with over 30,000 patterns of air, general and naval stores.

25 September: *Black Ranger* defuelled the reserved fleet at Barrow and then deployed to Portland as the first 'FOST Work-up' tanker.

October: The term Technical Advisers, first used *circa* 1920, was retitled as Marine Superintendent and Deputy Marine Superintendents. The Technical Assistants were retitled as Marine Engineering Superintendent and Deputy Engineering Superintendents.

22 October: *Wave Commander* laid up in Swansea for disposal.

4 November: *Reliant* (2) sailed Chatham for deployment on the Far East Station, as the Navy's first air stores issuing ship capable of replenishing aircraft carriers at sea.

December: *Wave Conqueror* sold to H G Pounds for service as an oil hulk at Le Havre, name unchanged.

1959

1959: *Elderol* sold for scrap. *War Brahmin* renamed *Olterra* for a film about Italian frogmen and their operation against Gibraltar in which RFA *Denbydale* was severely damaged. New uniform hull and superstructure colour scheme adopted. RFA Circular Letter detailed a Company Service Contract scheme for Signalmen. Cyprus emergency – *Blue Ranger* and *Brown Ranger* working in the waters around the Island. The ranks of Senior Master and Senior Chief Engineering Officer are instituted in the RFA.

6 January: *Wave Liberator* laid up in Bombay with unrepaired collision damage.

5 February: *Easedale* laid up at Devonport for disposal.

24 February: *Petrobus* arrived Grays, Essex for breaking up.

April: *Wave Emperor*, after a period of lay-up at Portland, is placed on the disposal list.

2 April: *Wave Liberator* sold for scrap.

12 April: *Echoldale* laid up at Devonport for disposal.

14 April: *Ennerdale* arrived Faslane for breaking up.

17 April: *George Lyras*, 11,588 grt motor tanker, taken over by the Admiralty from Marine Enterprises Ltd, on bareboat charter as a freighting tanker renamed RFA *Appleleaf* (2).

30 April: *Wave Governor* laid up at Rosyth.

First Cod War Afloat Support (31 August 1959 – 20 July 1961)
UK v Iceland fishery dispute involving HM Ships, maritime patrol aircraft and the following RFAs:
RFA *Wave Baron*
RFA *Wave Chief*
RFA *Wave Ruler* (1)
RFA *Wave Victor*
RFA *Wave Sovereign*
RFA *Wave Laird*
RFA *Wave Master*
RFA *Wave Prince*
RFA *Black Ranger*
RFA *Olna* (2)
RFA *Tideflow*
RFA *Tidesurge*
Wave Ruler (1) spent 38 continuous days at sea and was damaged due to poor weather conditions.

Review of RFA Manning Levels
In 1959 RFA manning levels were reviewed and it was decided that there should be a distinction between RAS-capable ships and other RFAs. RAS capable ships themselves fell into several categories with various manning policies:

- Fleet replenishment ships – fully fitted and manned for RAS; permanently manned with full RAS complement even if temporarily on freighting duties.
- Stand-by fleet replenishment ships – fully fitted but not manned, *ie* with normal freighting crew with a nucleus of RAS-experienced officers and petty officers.
- Transfer at sea ships – capable of limited RAS with freight crew.

Bareboat Charter

A bareboat charter (*aka* a demise charter) is a contract under which the shipowner merely provides the ship. The charterer, *eg* the Admiralty, leases the ship for a period of time, which may range from a few weeks to 20 years. During this time the charterer becomes totally responsible for the operating of the vessel – appointing the crew, paying all expenses incurred, carrying out repairs, refits, surveys etc, providing the cargo and running the ship where he wants to within any limits set by the shipowner or Classification society. A number of vessels have been taken up on bareboat charter and operated by the Admiralty as RFAs, a practice that commenced in 1958/59 with the 'Leaf' class.

3 May: *Wave Regent* laid up at Devonport for disposal.
4 May: *Wave Liberator* arrived Hong Kong for demolition.
6 May: *Dewdale* laid up at Devonport for disposal.
9 May: *Wave Commander* arrived Inverkeithing for breaking up.
10 May: *Dingledale* laid up at Devonport for disposal.
15 May: *Laurelwood* is bareboat-chartered by the Admiralty; renamed RFA *Cherryleaf* (2).
19 May: *Derwentdale* laid up at Rosyth for disposal.
22 May: *London Loyalty* bareboat-chartered by the Admiralty; renamed RFA *Brambleleaf* (2).
25 May: *Southern Satellite* bareboat-chartered by the Admiralty; renamed RFA *Orangeleaf* (2).
9 June: *Wave Premier* laid up at Rosyth for disposal.
16 June: *London Integrity* bareboat-chartered by the Admiralty; renamed RFA *Bayleaf* (2).
6 July: *Fort Beauharnois* played a large part in the salvage of the British cargo vessel *Beaverank* (5,600/1956).
23 August: *Limol* arrived Briton Ferry for breaking up.
1 September: *Elderol* arrived Llanelly for breaking up.
2 September: *Boxol* arrived Llanelly for breaking up.
18 September: *Abbeydale* and *Arndale* laid up.
15 October: *Pearleaf* (2) launched.
November: *Eaglesdale* sold commercially for £65,000, to be renamed *N. Tisar*.
15 November: *Cedardale* laid up at Hong Kong for disposal.
December: *Derwentdale* sold

RAS(L): 'Wave' class tanker. (ANRS)

commercially for £65,000, renamed *Irvingdale I*.

9 December: *Dingledale* sold commercially for £65,000 and renamed *Royaumont*.

23 December: *Dewdale* arrived Antwerp for breaking up.

Radio on RFAs – the Commercial Radio Room

The sinking on 14 April 1912 of the RMS *Titanic* led directly to the universal introduction of radio for Safety of Life at Sea. All ocean going British registered merchant ships, including RFAs were required by law to maintain and operate a marine radio station that conformed to the requirements of the Merchant Shipping (Radio) Rules and Merchant Shipping (Direction Finding) Rules, by the provisions of international conventions for the SOLAS and be licensed by the British Post Office (and its successor organisations). Additional rules stipulated the qualifications and watchkeeping duties of the Radio Officers. It was usually Admiralty and hence RFA practice that Marconi International Marine Co supplied the commercial radio installation on a hire and maintenance agreement. This agreement would also cover the ship's associated aerial systems and the portable lifeboat equipment. Such installations were subject to annual inspection by a Radio Inspection and a Radio Safety Certificate issued.

The Communications Branch was generally staffed as:

Senior Radio Officer or First Radio Officer – watchkeeper – naval radio office and communications, compiling complans, tactical and aircraft.

Radio Officer (A) or First Radio Officer – maintainer – responsible for the efficient working of all communications equipment.

Radio Officer (B) or Second Radio Officer – watchkeeper – commercial radio room, emergency equipment.

Junior Radio Officer or Third Radio Officer – watchkeeper.

Junior Radio Officer or Fourth Radio Officer – watchkeeper.

1960

1960: *Tide Austral/Fort Duquesne* shared the annual Bulawayo Cup for the most conspicuous efficiency in replenishment-at-sea in the Mediterranean area. *Fort Dunvegan* is converted into a temporary air stores issuing ship at Hong Kong and *Reliant* (2) returns to the UK for stage two of her conversion to be undertaken.

January–February: *Eddycreek* used as Gan Station Tanker, under Far East Fleet, to provide fuel facility for the Royal Air Force.

2 January: After a period laid up *Broomdale* arrived Bruges for breaking up.

8 January: First appointment of Commodore Chief Engineer RFA.

15 January: *Pearleaf* (2), 12,353 grt, completed by Blythwood Shipbuilding at Scotstoun for Jacobs & Partners Ltd.

23 January: *Brown Ranger* under orders of Flag Officer Royal Yachts.

28 January: *Pearleaf* (2) is placed on a 20-year bareboat charter to the Admiralty.

February: *Wave Monarch* sold commercially, name unchanged.

2 February: *Cedardale* sold for demolition at Hong Kong.

5 February: *War Brahmin* arrived Spezia for breaking up.

18 February: *Easedale* sold commercially, name unchanged.

March: *Wave King* sold for scrap. *Rippledyke* placed on the disposal list.

29 March: *Plumleaf* (to have been *Corheath*) launched.

30 March: *Wave Victor* arrived Gan to act as a fuelling hulk for military aircraft as air transportation supersedes troopships.

12 April: *Arndale* arrived Willebrock for breaking up. *Rippledyke* arrived Genoa for demolition but was resold for further service as a suction dredger.

16 April: *Wave King* arrived Barrow for breaking up.

May: Investigation into the operation of the RFA by the 'Way Ahead' sub-working party considered the question of White Ensign manning of RFA hulls. RFA *Reliant* (2) becomes the first RFA to fly a Commander-in-Chief Flag.

RFA *Pearleaf* (2) was taken over by the RFA upon completion of her trials and went through a series of modifications from product freighter to RAS-equipped support tanker. (RFA Archive)

24 May: Introduction of the RAS Proficiency Bonus payment for deck and engine-room ratings.

8 June: *Wave Premier* sold for £63,000 for demolition at Rosyth.

19 June: *Wave Emperor* arrived Barrow for demolition.

29 June: *Wave Regent* arrived Faslane for demolition.

20 July: *Wave Governor* sold to breakers for £64,500.

29 July: *Plumleaf* (2), 12,548 grt, completed by Blyth Dry Dock and Shipbuilding Co at Blyth for Cory Tanker Ltd.

31 July: End of the Malayan Emergency.

August: *Reliant* (2) returns to the UK for second stage of her conversion, work to be undertaken by Henry Robb, Leith.

9 August: *Wave Governor* handed over to shipbreakers at Rosyth.

13 August: *Surf Pioneer* laid up at Devonport in reserve.

24 August: *Plumleaf* (2) bareboat-chartered by the Admiralty for RFA service, initially for 19 years.

6 September: *Abbeydale* handed over for demolition at Barrow-in-Furness.

November: *Brown Ranger* becomes the Clyde Port Oiler under control of FO Submarines.

18 November: *Black Ranger* in collision with the submarine HMS *Thule* which accidentally tried to surface underneath her during exercises; a subsequent signal sent to *Black Ranger* reportedly read 'Only Thules rush in where Rangers fear to tread'.

1961

1961: RFA circular letter issued details for a Company Service Contract for UK Petty Officers and ratings in foreign-going tankers and stores issuing ships. Duration of contact two years with NMB standard pay rates plus efficiency pay and RFA allowances, such as, contract allowance, signalling allowance, RAS proficiency bonus, station allowances, eastern bonus, extra leave on RAS ships, pension and gratuities including widows and children. All ratings could be transferred between ships and Petty Officers had to provide themselves with a uniform. A number of Chief Stewards were granted officer status. *Fort Duquesne*/*Tide Austral* share the annual Bulawayo Cup for the most conspicuous efficiency in replenishment-at-sea in the Mediterranean area. RFA Second Officer attended the Lieutenants course at RN Staff College, Greenwich

28 February: Improved 'Tide' class ships *Tidepool* and *Tidespring* ordered.

March: *Appleleaf* officially opened the new Henderson Graving Dock at Immingham. *Reliant* (2) conversion into an air stores/victualling stores issuing ship completed and stored for a further Far Eastern deployment.

1 April: Gan Station Tanker, RFA *Wave Victor* reduced to hulk status.

16 April: *Hebe* laid down.

Exercise Sharp Squall: RFA *Tidesurge* receiving fuel from RFAS *Wave Ruler* (left) and *Wave Prince* (right) in the English Channel on Friday 20 October 1961 – 3,444 tons of fuel transferred. (RFA Archive)

Improved 'Tide' class

ADMIRALTY-DESIGNED LARGE FLEET REPLENISHMENT TANKER

RFA *Tidepool* **Pennant:** A76 **Official number:** 304559
RFA *Tidespring* **Pennant:** A75 **Official number:** 304379
Port of registry: London
Builder: Hawthorn Leslie Shipbuilders, Hebburn-on-Tyne (yard no 753)
Machinery: Two Pametrada steam turbines by Hawthorn Leslie; double reduction geared to single screw; selectable superheated Babcock & Wilcox water tube boilers; 15,000 shp; bunkers 2,248 tons; 17 knots
Dimensions (length oa/bp x beam): 583.8/562ft x 71ft
Tonnage measurements: 14,129 grt, 18,900 dwt
Displacement: 27,400 tons full load
Complement: 110 + Naval air detachment of up to 24 – accommodation overall for 131

RFA *Tidespring*, a large fleet replenishment tanker with extensive helicopter facilities. (RFA Archive)

Remarks: +100A1 +LMC, ice class 3, class VII; based on Admiralty design, purpose-built 'Tide' class fleet replenishment tankers, they had similar abeam replenishment at sea rigs with automatic tensioning winches and astern fuelling rigs but were the first front-line RFAs to provide a single spot 50 x 70ft landing platform for Royal Navy Wessex helicopters and stressed to ferry fixed-wing aircraft up to 30,000lb, and hangar arrangements for one Wessex with a second aircraft capable of being stowed on the forward end of the flight deck. Operational use in peacetime was not intended to exceed the occasional refuelling of helicopters based in HM Ships with the wartime role envisaging limited reinforcement of the Fleet's ASW strength with helicopters probably embarked for short periods supported by a small RN party. Basic aviation facilities include Avcat refuelling and defuelling, supply of luboil and hydraulic fluid, glide path indicator and supporting lights, securing and fire-fighting facilities. Aviation maintenance facilities and spares would be embarked with the flight. When a Sea King helicopter was operationally deployed on a 'Tide' class tanker, up to four portable workshops (known as flying packs) based on the ISO container design would be deployed in support of the aircraft. Cargo capacity – 9,500 tons FFO, 5,500 tons dieso and 2,000 avcat, they carried a limited range of dry cargo in their forward hold. Had a distinctive stove pipe (Welsh hat) extension on their funnel.
The details are based on RFA *Tidepool as built*

July: Kuwait crisis – *Fort Dunvegan, Fort Sandusky, Wave Master, Gold Ranger, Olna, Resugent, Tidereach, Wave Ruler* (1), *Fort Charlotte, Retainer, Reliant* (2), *Orangeleaf* (2) and *Pearleaf* (2) involved in supporting the operation. *Fort Dunvegan* converted into a naval stores/victualling stores issuing ship at Hong Kong.

July–August: *Olna* (2), *Retainer, Reliant* and *Tidereach* in support of the carrier HMS *Victorious.*

24 July: *Tidespring* laid down.

16 September: *Eddybay* arrived Gibraltar to act as a petrol hulk for the RAF.

20 September: *Echoldale* arrived Spezia for breaking up.

October: *Blue Ranger* supporting Royal Yacht *Britannia* off West Africa.

November: Humanitarian assistance – after floods in Kenya carrier group of HM Ships and RFAs including LSLs (unidentified) provided relief.

December: *Sir Lancelot* (LSL 01), a new 'War Office' design of landing ship prepared by the Sea Transport Department of the Ministry of Transport, ordered from Fairfield Shipbuilding & Engineering Company, Govan. Special squadron on South Atlantic cruise – HMS *Lion* with RFA *Wave Prince* – Port Stanley, Valparaiso, Panama Canal to Trinidad to February 1962.

14 December: *Tidepool* laid down.

1962

1962: The term 'Front Line Support Ships' first appears in the Statement on Defence Estimates, covering replenishment oilers, stores supports ships, armament supply ships that are responsible for transferring fuel, ammunition and stores to fighting ships underway, so that they can remain independent of shore facilities. Ships' Badges for RFAs first authorised officially by the Ships' Badges Committee. Captain A E Curtain OBE RD appointed Commodore RFA. RFA *Tidesurge* featured as No 15 of 16 Ships of the

British Navy Kelloggs 'cigarette' cards.
March: *Sir Lancelot* laid down.
7 March: *Hebe* launched.
13 April: *Bacchus* (2) arrived Singapore for disposal.
23 April: *Fort Beauharnois* laid up in Malta.
May: *Hebe*, stores freighter, 4,823 grt, completed by Henry Robb at Leith for British India Steam Navigation Co.
3 May: *Tidespring* launched.
12 May: *Eddybeach* sailed from Gibraltar where she was the last station tanker.

Ships' Badges
The shape of official RFA badges was approved as pentagonal. Irrespective of shape, the badge has a rim of stylised rope and is surmounted by the Naval Crown. Below the Crown is a panel bearing the ship's name in capital letters. Ships' Badges are used for decorative purposes, *eg* bridge front, brow gangway awnings with RFA 'NAME', ceremonial harbour lifebuoys, official ship's stationery.

It is generally understood that ships' badges were first authorised for Royal Fleet Auxiliary ships *circa* 1962. Some badges include a motto. For Example, RFA *Argus*: motto 'Oculi Omnium' – 'The eyes of all' – Psalm 145.

4 June: *Bacchus* (3) launched.
18 June: *Hebe* bareboat-chartered to the Admiralty for 19 years.
July: *Fort Beauharnois* placed on the disposal list.
3 July: RRS *Discovery* launched by Hall, Russell & Co Ltd, Aberdeen for the National Institute of Oceanography – manning and management by Director of Stores with the RFA.
August: Naval Stores Department, Fuel Division (later to become Fuel and Tanker Branch) moved to new

Bacchus class (also called *Hebe* class)

ADMIRALTY-DESIGNED STORE FREIGHTER

RFA *Bacchus*	**Pennant:** A404	**Official number:** 304368
RFA *Hebe*	**Pennant:** A406	**Official number:** 304252

Port of registry: London
Builder: Henry Robb, Leith (yard no 483)
Machinery: One 5 cyl Sulzer SRD68 two stroke turbocharged ICE by Swan Hunter & Wigham Richardson Ltd; single screw; 5,500 bhp; bunkers 630 tons; 15 knots; 18 tpd consumption
Dimensions (loa/bp x beam): 379/–ft x 55ft
Tonnage measurements: 4,823 grt, 5,200 dwt
Displacement: 8,173 tons full load
Complement: 36 – accommodation for 54

The general stores carrier RFA *Bacchus* (3). (World Ship Society)

Remarks: +100A1 +LMC +RMC, ice class 3, class VII; these motor ships were on bareboat charter from British India Steam Navigation Co (BISN Co); built to an Admiralty design, to employ CHACON containers and used for transporting general cargo including refrigerated cargo, two grades of lubricating oil (210 tons) and fresh water (490 tons). They were managed by the Director of Stores with responsibility for crewing, stores, bunkers, running costs and maintenance, and operated by the Director of Movements as part of the Naval Freighting Service. In 1973 on the takeover of BISN Co their ownership was assigned to P&O Strath Services. The 1980 Defence White Paper stated – both ships retained to support amphibious operations, converted to meet Royal Marines requirements and carry explosives. Deck stiffening for defensive weapons.

There were three holds and 'tween decks, all forward of the machinery space with a capacity of 230,000 cu ft; the hatch covers were MacGregor 'single pull' rolling steel – No 1 with a 22.5 x 16ft hatch served by two 48ft 5-ton derricks; No 2 with a 65 x 24ft hatch served by two 55.5ft 5-ton, two 54.5ft 5-ton and one 61.75ft 25-ton derrick; No 3 with 40 x 24ft hatch served by two 48.5ft 5-ton, two 52.5ft 5-ton and one 61.75ft 20-ton derrick. A 'tween deck had a 10 x 20ft hatch served by the 52.5ft 5-ton derrick on No 3 hold, this deck had two refrigerated spaces each of 2,000 cu ft. No 1 hold had a special cargo locker of 7,850 cu ft and a 'lock-up space' of 3,300 cu ft. This class had no replenishment at sea capability.

The details are based on RFA Bacchus *as built.*

Royal Research Ships (RRS)

In November 1949 the Admiralty purchased the *Discovery II* and the *William Scoresby* for the Oceanographic Research Council. The Director of Stores undertook management of both ships and the ships were maintained, officered and run as RFAs with the prefix RRS. In 1962 the new 2,665 grt *Discovery* was also officered and managed under the same conditions until 1968 when local manning commenced and full operational management was taken over by the Natural Environment Research Council which was setting up a research ship base at Barry Docks, South Wales. Officers serving on the *Discovery* followed the uniform regulations of the National Institute of Oceanography.

The Royal Research Ship *Discovery.* (NIO)

headquarters in Empress State Building, Fulham – '*the mad house*'. RFAs ordered to paint up pennant numbers in-line with the practice of HM Ships.

14 August: *Bacchus* (2) sold commercially and renamed *Pulau Bali.*

7 September: *Tide Austral* handed over to the Royal Australian Navy and commissioned as HMAS *Supply* – Portsmouth.

7 September: RRS *Discovery II* returned to Plymouth to pay off and was laid up.

23 September: *Wave Master* laid up at Singapore for disposal.

16 October: *Overseas Adventurer* (later to become *Cherryleaf* (3)) launched.

8 November: *Fort Beauharnois* arrived Spezia for demolition; she had been replaced by *Hebe. Bacchus* (3), stores freighter, 5,823 grt, completed by Henry Robb at Leith for British India Steam Navigation Co and bareboat-chartered by the Admiralty for RFA service for 19 years.

9 November: *Eddybay* laid up at Gibraltar.

RFA *Tidereach* in a multiple replenishment with the frigate HMS *Yarmouth* (left), and the cruisers HMNZS *Royalist* (right) and HMS *Belfast* aft, South China Sea April 1962. (RFA Archive)

CHACON
(Chatham container)
Designed and developed in 1947 at Chatham Naval Dockyard by the Superintending Naval Stores Officer, Mr Montgomery, the CHACON is a wooden construction package box of approximately 7 x 7 x 5ft. This box holds a 4-wheeled trolley that is provided with shelves and are loaded by hand at various Naval Store Depots in the UK. These store items are then placed in bins or trays then they slide into the shelves on the trolleys.

CHACON can be handled by forklift trucks, derricks, cranes and on portage rollers. Initially they were developed for shipment of stores to Singapore, complete in their stacks of trays. Refrigerated containers were a later development. The store freighters RFAS *Bacchus* and *Hebe* for example, carried CHACONs.

17–18 November: Marine loss – *Green Ranger* – this tanker was under tow by the tug *Caswell*, on passage from Plymouth to Cardiff for refit; in Force 10 NW gale the tow parted and she was blown ashore off Mansley Cliff, Hartland Point, North Devon; running crew taken off safely.
8 December: *Green Ranger*'s hull broke in two and became a total loss.
11 December: *Tidepool* launched.
18 December: *Fort Constantine* laid up at Devonport.
29 December: During a berthing operation at Chatham assisting *Hebe*, the tug *TID97* was damaged and sank.

1963

1963: First training course for RFA Petty Officers
18 January: *Tidespring*, large fleet replenishment tanker with aviation facilities, 14,129 grt, completed by Hawthorn Leslie at Hebburn on Tyne; she replaced *Wave Master*.
24 January: *Regent* and *Resource*, fleet replenishment ships ordered.
29 January: *Eddyness* laid up at Devonport.
February: *Overseas Adventurer* (later to become *Cherryleaf* (3)) 13,721 grt, completed by at Rheinstahl Nordseewerke at Emden for London and Overseas Bulk Carriers Ltd.
4 February: *Olynthus* (2), *Oleander* (2) and *Olna* (3), large fleet replenishment tankers ordered.
April: RFA allocated to freighting duties and their RAS capabilities in April, were recorded as *Wave Chief*, *Appleleaf* (astern only), *Bayleaf* (astern only) *Brambleleaf* (astern only), *Cherryleaf* (astern only), *Orangeleaf* (abeam and astern), *Pearleaf* (astern only) and *Plumleaf* (astern only).
30 April: *Wave Master* towed to Jurong for demolition.
May: *Fort Duquesne* as air stores support ship with *Tidesurge* and *Retainer* accompany HMS *Ark Royal* from UK to Middle East. *Amherst* withdrawn from service and placed on disposal list.
25 May: RRS *Discovery II* arrived Passage West for breaking up by Haulbowline Industries Ltd.
June: *Wave Protector* and *Eddybay* on the disposal list. *Amherst* sold for demolition in Antwerp.

RAS(L): RFA *Tidespring* refuelling the carrier HMS *Centaur* and HMS *Devonshire*, 1963. (RFA Archive)

'Sir' class (also known as 'Knights of the Round Table' class)

WAR OFFICE DESIGNED RO-RO LANDING SHIPS LOGISTIC (LSL)

RFA *Sir Lancelot*	**Pennant:** L3029 (LSL01)	**Official number:** 305889
RFA *Sir Galahad* (1)	**Pennant:** L3005 (LSL02)	**Official number:** 309790
RFA *Sir Bedivere*	**Pennant:** L3004 (LSL03)	**Official number:** 309987
RFA *Sir Geraint*	**Pennant:** L3027 (LSL04)	**Official number:** 334551
RFA *Sir Tristram*	**Pennant:** L3505 (LSL05)	**Official number:** 334639
RFA *Sir Percivale*	**Pennant:** L3036 (LSL06)	**Official number:** 335624

The landing ship *Sir Lancelot* in the traditional white hull with blue band colour scheme of a British troopship. (World Ship Society)

Port of registry: London
Machinery: Two 12 cyl Sulzer 12MD-51 two stroke turbocharged ICEs by Denny; two screws; 9,520 bhp; 17 knots; bow thrusters fitted
Dimensions (loa/bp x beam x draught): 415/366.3ft x 59.8ft x 12.8ft mean
Tonnage measurements: 6,390 grt, 2,180 dwt
Displacement: 5,639 tons full load
complement: 68 RFA – military lift accommodation 340 + 16 tanks, munitions and fuel or up to 60 4-ton trucks and Landrovers.
Remarks: +100A1 +LMC, class I troopships; based on a staff requirement to replace the difficult and expensive to run wartime-build landing ships tank (LST) the design of the prototype *Sir Lancelot* at an estimated cost of £3.5 million, was approved August 1960. These six ships were built for the MoD (Army) for the rapid and secure movement of troops and their equipment. British India Steam Navigation Co, on behalf of the Board of Trade Sea Transport Division, was responsible for placing the contracts, supervision of construction and management of these vessels. *Sir Lancelot* was the prototype – following extensive trials the five further ships built were of similar size but with numerous differences – a modified layout, different cranage and they used 10 cyl Mirrlees National Monarch diesel engines. They were painted in traditional British troopship colours with a white hull with a blue horizontal band.

Fitted with bow and stern ramps, these small, highly versatile workhorses transferred to the MoD(Navy), Directorate of Supplies and Transport (Fuel and Movement) management as RFAs during the early 1970s. Tasked by MoD(Army) Directorate of Movements they have seen world-wide service in NATO exercises, routine peacetime operations, humanitarian operations and in war. It is in war as an integral part of the UK's Amphibious Forces that they worked their hardest and suffered their most with *Sir Galahad* and *Sir Tristram* lost during the Falklands War of 1982. *Sir Tristram* has been rebuilt, a new *Sir Galahad* was built and *Sir Bedivere* has undergone a major 'slip life extension program (SLEP). LSLs have been modified to 'mothership' the 'plug in' containerised RN Fleet Support Units and units like 539 Assault Squadron, Royal Marines.

Superstructure is built of aluminium and they have an after 76ft x 59ft flight deck fitting for day and night operations. Also the 100ft x 42ft vehicle deck forward of the bridge can be used as helicopter deck. The LSLs are homeported at Marchwood Military Port on Southampton Water and operate with the 20 Maritime Regiment, Royal Corps or Transport now the 17 Maritime & Port Regiment RLC. These Army LSL teams assist with embarkation including loading/discharge of cargo.

This class has no replenishment at sea capability. In 1975 the Royal Australian Navy based HMAS *Tobruk* on this design.

The details are based on the prototype RFA Sir Lancelot *as built*

25 June: *Sir Lancelot* launched at Govan for the Ministry of Transport.

28 June: *Tidepool*, large fleet replenishment tanker with aviation facilities, 14,129 grt, completed by Hawthorn Leslie at Hebburn on Tyne; she replaced *Wave Sovereign*.

July: UK to Far East passage of the aircraft carrier HMS *Victorious* with RFAS *Reliant*, *Resurgent*, *Tidespring* and *Wave Ruler*.

11 July: RFA *Olynthus* (2) laid down.

August: *Nasprite* on the disposal list. *Eddybeach*, *Eddycliff* and *Eddycreek* all placed on the disposal list.

16 August: *Wave Protector* sailed Malta in tow for demolition at La Grazie.

20 August: *Tidepool* in the English Channel supporting the Canadian aircraft carrier HMCS *Bonaventure*.

27 August: *Oleander* (2) laid down.

30 August: *Naess Scotsman* (later to become RFA *Ennerdale* (2)), launched at Kiel for commercial owners.

September: International maritime exhibition at Helsinki visited by RFA *Tidepool* and HMS *Scott*.

10 September: *Eddybay* arrived Portsmouth in tow for demolition but was resold to Belgian breakers in 1964.

25 September: *Philol* laid up on the Medway.

October: *Airsprite* laid up in reserve at Devonport.

12 November: Gan Station Tanker, RFA *Wave Sovereign* to relieve RFA *Wave Victor*.

December: *Eddycreek* sold to P R

Marchwood Military Port

Marchwood Military Port (MMP), established in 1942, is situated on the western side of Southampton Water, opposite Southampton Docks. The port consists of a number of jetties. The largest is 220m long and 33m wide and is capable of accepting vessels up to 16,000 tons. It has a sophisticated Ro/Ro facility capable of handling vessels with various ramp configurations, and the jetty also has two 35-tonne rail-mounted cranes and railway access. The second jetty, built during the Second World War, is 190m long, has rail access and is capable of accepting vessels of up to 8,000 tons with limited Ro/Ro facilities. In 1986 a port rebuild was undertaken to improve jetty arrangements. The site is the only military port in UK, and has significant ammunition and explosives handling capability. It is the home port for the RFA's LSLs. Since 1948 the post has been administered by a 'Port Regiment' – 17 Port and Training Regiment Royal Engineers, then 17 Port Regiment Royal Corps of Transport now by the 17 Port and Maritime Regiment Royal Logistics Corps assisted in wartime by a specialist TA Port Squadron. Their role is to load and discharge service and civilian shipping in support of military administration, exercises and operations world-wide. In 2000 it was renamed Marchwood Sea Mounting Centre.

Mexeflote

The LSLs' amphibious warfare ability is enhanced by their capability to provide what is technically called 'Class 60 load carrying pontoon equipment'. A 120ft, 90-ton multi-purpose pontoon (called a Mexeflote – derived from Military EXperiment Equipment), two can be carried by each LSL where they are winched vertically flat on the ship's side. To launch they are lowered, or dropped, into the water and are powered by two Hydromaster 6 cyl 75hp outboard diesels, which are lowered onto the pontoons. These are then used as a raft to ferry able beach or to form a jetty or causeway between the ship and shore, should the ship not be above to beach. They are crewed by specially trained personnel from the 17 Maritime & Port Regiment, Royal Logistics Corps (RLC).

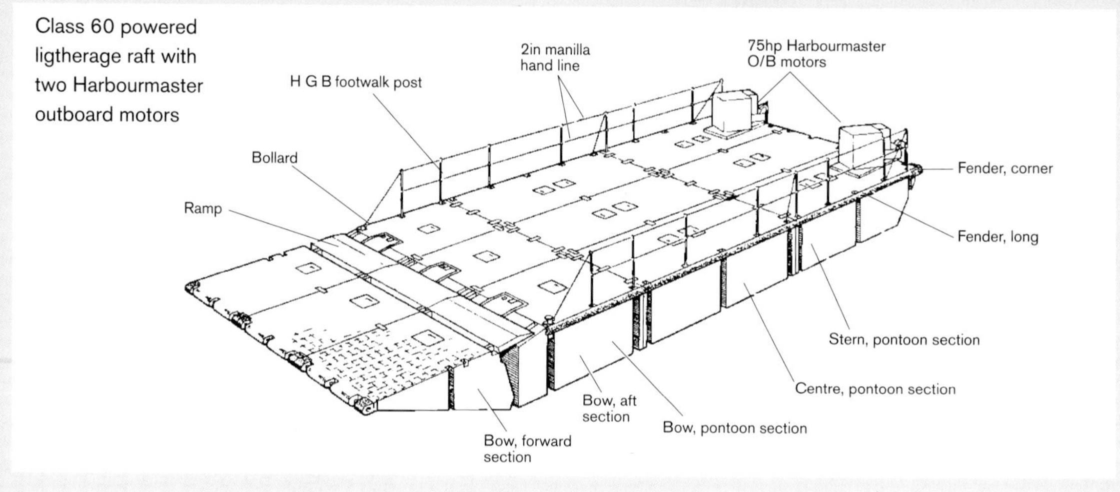

Abela of Genoa, name unchanged. *Eddyreef* on the disposal list.

1964

1964: Captain E Payne CBE appointed Commodore RFA. Order-in-Council 121 from Statutory Rules & Orders 1911 No 338 amended by Statutory Instruments 1964/489. 767 NAS at Culdrose training Wessex helicopters for service on RFAs. *Eddybeach* sold commercially and renamed *Mykinai*. *Eddycliff* sold commercially and renamed *Knossos*. *Eddycreek* on passage Naples to Genoa for scrapping when driven ashore in a gale, east of Capri Island. Persian Gulf – RFA support to HM Ships providing anti-smuggling, piracy and security tasks.

8 January: *Halcyon Breeze* (later to become RFA *Derwentdale* (2)) launched.

16 January: *Sir Lancelot*, 6,390 grt, completed by Fairfield Shipbuilding and Engineering at Glasgow for Ministry of Transport, placed under the commercial management of the British India Steam Navigation Co.

5 February: *Nasprite* arrived Antwerp for demolition at Willebroek.

14 February: Gan Station Tanker, RFA *Wave Victor*, returned.

March: *Eddyreef* sailed Devonport in tow to Belgian breakers. Malaysia – start of confrontation with Indonesian rebels.

1 March: Humanitarian aid – RFA *Hebe* standing by for the evacuation of British nationals after overthrow of the Government of Zanzibar.

April: *Halcyon Breeze* (later to become *Dertwentdale* (2)), 42,504 grt, completed by Hitachi Zosen at Inoshima for Caribbean Tanker Ltd (Court Line Ltd, managers). *Sir Galahad* (1), *Sir Bedivere*, *Sir Geraint*, landing ships logistic, ordered. RFA Radio Officers began to attend the Long Course at HMS *Collingwood*.

1 April: The Admiralty became an integrated part of the unified Ministry of Defence and became known as Navy Department; Board of Admiralty became known as Admiralty Board.

19–22 May: Aviation – *Tidespring* carried a detachment of two Wessex helicopters from 814 NAS.

19 June: *Resource* laid down.

2 July: *Olna* (3) laid down.

10 July: *Olynthus* (2) launched at Hebburn. *Oleander* (2) launched at Wallsend.

August: *Wave Knight* (1) after a period of lay up is placed on the disposal list at Devonport. *Naess Scotsman* (later to become *Ennerdale* (2)) 30,112 grt, completed by Kieler Howaldstwerke AG for Anglo-Norness Shipping Co (Naess Denholm Col Ltd, managers).

18 August: *Engadine*, air training ship, ordered.

29 August: *Eddybay* arrived Antwerp for demolition.

4 September: *Regent* laid down.

19 October: *Wave Knight* (1) arrived Antwerp Roads *en route* to Willebroek for demolition.

28 November: *Blue Ranger* ran aground on Haisboro Sands but refloated without any serious damage.

7 December: *Lyness*, *Stromness* and *Tarbatness*, stores support ships, ordered.

> **Indonesian Confrontation**
> This confrontation was an undeclared war that originated in 1962 and continued until the Bangkok agreement of August 1966. It was a border conflict over the disputed island of Borneo (in which is situated the Kingdom of Brunei, Sarawak and British North Borneo, later to be renamed as Sabah) between British-backed Malaysia and Indonesia ruled by the dictator President Sukarno. By 1964 Indonesian troops began to raid areas in the Malaysian peninsula. Commonwealth forces from Britain, Australia and New Zealand were deployed. The Royal Navy established patrols and coastal surveillance and the Malacca Strait Patrol to prevent insurgents from landing in Singapore and Borneo. RN units from the Far East fleet and units of an inshore squadron were supported by RFAs such as *Gold Ranger*, *Eddyrock*, *Fort Charlotte*, *Wave Sovereign* and *Tidereach*.

RFA *Tidespring* deploying a Wessex HAS3 helicopter. (World Ship Society)

1965

1965: Approval given for RFA ratings to use restaurants and bars operated by the NAAFI in town and fleet clubs and fleet canteens and use of NAAFI services shops.

January: Indonesian Confrontation – RFA support to HM Ships providing patrols off East Malaysia, Singapore and in Malacca Straits to 11 August. *Birchol* (2) and *Teakol* (3) laid up at Devonport. 'Cadet' replaced the term 'Apprentice' for officers under training. *Airsprite* transferred to the Ministry of Transport for disposal.

1 January: Royal Naval Supply and Transport Service formed.

February: *Oakol* (2) laid up at Devonport.

22 February: *Sir Galahad* (1) (LSL 02) laid down.

5 March: *Edenfield* (later to become RFA *Dewdale* (2)), launched.

11 March: *Airsprite* sold for scrap.

14 March: *Airsprite* arrived Antwerp for demolition at Willebroek.

April: *Sir Tristram* (LSL 05) and *Sir Percivale* (LSL 06) ordered. Merger of the Royal Army Service Corps and Transportation elements of the Royal Engineers to form the Royal Corps of Transport.

1 April: Secretary of State for Defence becomes the Registered Owner of RFAs in accordance with Merchant Shipping Act.

May: Operation Seahorse – SEATO maritime operation in South China Sea; the replenishment support provided by RFAs *Tidereach*, *Tidepool*, *Retainer* and *Reliant*.

21 June: *Olynthus* (2) fleet replenishment tanker with aviation facilities, 18,603 grt, completed by Hawthorn Leslie (Shipbuilders) at Hebburn for MoD(Navy).

2 July: *Edenfield*, 35,805 grt, completed by Harland & Wolff at Belfast for Hunting (Eden) Tankers Ltd.

7 July: *Lyness* laid down.

28 July: *Olna* (3) launched at Hebburn.

'Ness' class

MOD(NAVY)-DESIGNED STORES SUPPORT SHIPS

RFA *Lyness*	**Pennant:** A339	**Official number:** 309818
RFA *Stromness*	**Pennant:** A344	**Official number:** 309912
RFA *Tarbatness*	**Pennant:** A345	**Official number:** 334594

Port of registry: London

Machinery: One 8 cyl two stroke Sulzer 8RD76 turbocharged ICE by Wallsend Slipway; single screw; 12,800 bhp; 18.5 knots

Dimensions (length oa/bp x beam): 523/490ft x 72ft

Tonnage measurements: 12,359 grt, 7,782 dwt

Displacement: 16,792 tons full load

Complement: 110 RFA + 50 strong stores working party – accommodation for 176

Stores support ship RFA *Tarbatness*. (World Ship Society)

Remarks: +100A1 +LMC +RMC, ice class 3, class VII; designed to meet MoD(N) requirement as front-line multi-RAS stores ships, they proved to be an effective and innovative design.

Lyness was stored as an air stores support ship carrying some 10,000 different items of naval and victualling stores but with over 80,000 different items of aircraft and naval stores to meet the needs of aircraft carriers and their escorts. Both *Stromness* (known as the 'Super Sampan') and *Tarbatness* each carried varying quantities of up 40,000 different items of general naval stores, dry and refrigerated food. They also carried up to 350 tons of potable water. The cargo was carried in four temperature-controlled holds served by three 5-ton and four 2-ton lifts that moved stores to a 320ft x 38ft covered clearway deck with 12ft wide access to the 2-ton jackstay RAS transfer stations served by 1- and 2-ton jackstay points and automatic tensioning winches. Stores were moved internally using a range of forklift trucks, power pallet transports and mechanical handling aids. These ships were fitted with heavy lifting gear – a 25-ton derrick (starboard aft) and a 12-ton derrick (port aft).

These ships were very VERTREP-capable with their day and night landing, single spot, 110ft x 60ft flight deck that could accept helicopters up to 40,000lb. Support facilities were limited because there was no hangar or workshop arrangements. The flight deck was served by a stores lift and the ships had two 42ft self-propelled naval storing tenders.

All three ships of this class were sold to the US Navy's Military Sealift Command and are still operational.

The details are based on RFA Stromness *as built*

One of the longest-surviving RFAs, the *Helmsley I* was originally RFA *Scotol* (ANRS)

RFA *Empire Gull* in her black-hulled livery. (J Smith collection)

RFA *Robert Middleton* with an interesting deck cargo. (J Smith collection)

RFA *Wave Baron* empty and well down by the stern, photographed at Gibraltar. (J Smith collection)

RFA *Tidereach.* (J Smith collection)

RFA *Engadine*, the Navy's first purpose-designed helicopter training ship. (RFA Archive)

The sister-ships RFA *Olna* and *Olwen*. (World Ship Society)

The Chilean Navy's *Almirante Jorge Montt*, formerly RFA *Tidepool*, one of a number of vessels whose active life was extended well beyond their RFA service. (ANRS)

RFA *Tidespring* passing under San Francisco's Golden Gate bridge. (J Smith collection)

RFA *Regent* at South Georgia during the Falklands War, 1982. (J Smith collection)

RFA *Fort Grange* during her long spell of duty at Split. (J Smith collection)

RFAs *Tidespring* and *Diligence* in the Gulf during 1991. (RFA Archive)

RFA *Sir Percivale* displays the original troopship colour scheme of a white hull with blue band and buff funnels and masts. (Brian Hargreaves)

Left: RFA *Sir Lancelot* beached with bow ramp down, showing the original configuration of the class. (RFA Archive)

Above: RFA *Sir Tristram* at sea with a full deck load and Mexeflotes secured to her hull. (RFA Archive)

RFA *Sir Galahad* (2) at Dartmouth with the splendid backdrop of Britannia Royal Naval College. (RFA)

The modified RFA *Sir Bedivere* at sea. (RFA)

An unusual view of the 40,000-tonne support tanker RFA *Brambleleaf* taken from a low-flying helicopter. (RFA Archive)

One of the latest additions to the RFA fleet, *Largs Bay* under construction at Swan Hunter, Tyneside. (Dr Ian Buxton)

Above: The small fleet tanker RFA *Gold Rover* in a lively sea. (RFA)

Left: An aerial shot of the carrier *Invincible*, the AOR RFA *Fort Victoria* and the frigate *Coventry.* (RFA Archive)

Right: RAS between RFA *Orangeleaf* and RFA *Olmeda.* (RFA)

The 34,000-tonne AOR RFA *Fort Victoria* conducting a RAS serial during Operation Telic. Note that the normal high-visibility colour of the lifeboats has been suppressed. (J Allix)

Above: The LSL RFA *Sir Percivale* operationally loaded during Operation Telic. (J Allix)

Left: The AOR RFA *Fort George.* (MoD(N))

Above: Seamanship at its best as the 34,000-tonne fleet oiler RFA *Wave Knight* conducts a RAS only metres from the frigate HMS *Sutherland.* (RFA)

Left: AOR RFA *Fort Victoria* during Operation Telic: the first operational deployment of the new Merlin MH1 helicopters (of 814 Naval Air Squadron). (J Allix)

Trafalgar Day 1993 in the Adriatic – Admiral of the Fleet, HRH Duke of Edinburgh being introduced to marine engineering staff by Second Engineer Officer Peter Henney of RFA *Fort Grange*. (RFA Archive)

Trafalgar Day 1993 in the Adriatic – Admiral of the Fleet, HRH Duke of Edinburgh enjoying a moment on the bridge of RFA *Fort Grange* with the ship's Master, Captain Peter Nelson RFA (RFA Archive)

Royal visit to RFA *Fort Austin* at Portland, 26 June 1981. RFA CPO Bosun Steve Duncan BEM presented to HM The Queen. (RFA Archive)

Royal visit to RFA *Fort Austin* at Portland Naval Base on 26 June 1981. HM The Queen with Commodore Sam Dunlop RFA and his flight commander Lt Cdr Thorpe of 824 Naval Air Squadron. (RFA Archive)

Above: Men and women serving on the aviation training and primary casualty receiving ship RFA *Argus* are welcomed home by the band of Her Majesty's Royal Marines. (RFA Archive)

Left: Future seafarers of the RFA – Sea Cadets from the training ship *Fort Grange* on a visit to their affiliated ship the RFA *Fort Grange* with her Master Captain Roberts RFA. (RFA Archive)

Women at sea – undergoing the rigours of vital fire-fighting training at the Navy's Phoenix NBCD School. (RFA Archive)

Women at Sea – officer cadet training on the bridge of RFA *Fort George* on passage in the Indonesian archipelago, 1997. (RFA Archive)

Wilkinson Sword of Peace presentation 25 July 1997 – jointly awarded to RFA *Sir Galahad* for her humanitarian support to the UN sponsored operations in Angola in1995 (RFA Archive)

The Fitzroy Memorial. Dedicated on 8 June 1985, this 8ft obelisk of Cornish granite bears the name of those members of the RFA who died at Fitzroy Cove. The plinth bears the crests of the RFA s *Sir Galahad* and *Sir Tristram* and the inscription 'Faithful until Death' in English and Chinese. (RFA Archive)

RFA Sea Flags – see Appendix C for details

RFA Ensign

Admiralty Blue Ensign

Red Ensign

RFA Jack

Ships' Badges – see Appendix E for details

RFA *Brambleleaf*

RFA *Gold Rover*

RFA *Orangeleaf*

RFA *Sir Galahad*

Funnel badges – see Appendix E for details

STANAVFORLANT

STANAVFORMED

Commander Amphibious Task Group

COMFRA

Official RFA crest, approved by The Queen

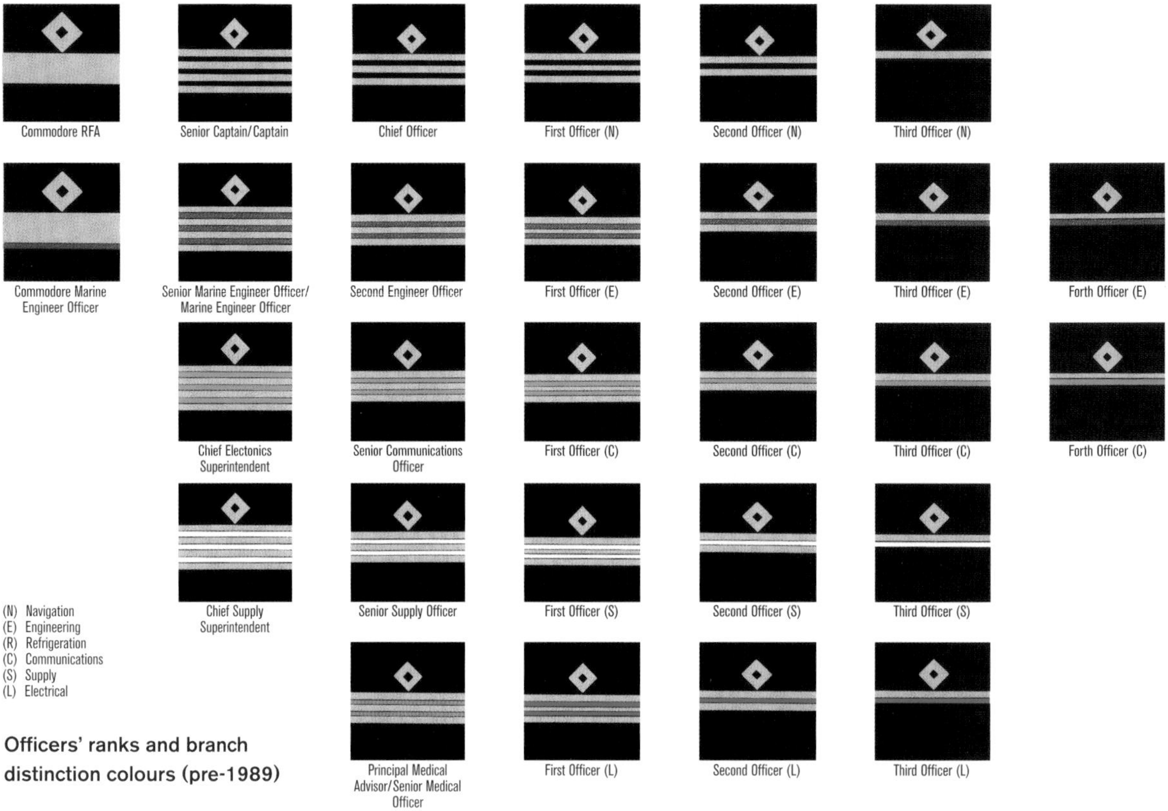

Commodore RFA
Senior Captain/Captain
Chief Officer
First Officer (N)
Second Officer (N)
Third Officer (N)
Commodore Marine Engineer Officer
Senior Marine Engineer Officer/ Marine Engineer Officer
Second Engineer Officer
First Officer (E)
Second Officer (E)
Third Officer (E)
Forth Officer (E)
Chief Electonics Superintendent
Senior Communications Officer
First Officer (C)
Second Officer (C)
Third Officer (C)
Forth Officer (C)
Chief Supply Superintendent
Senior Supply Officer
First Officer (S)
Second Officer (S)
Third Officer (S)
Principal Medical Advisor/Senior Medical Officer
First Officer (L)
Second Officer (L)
Third Officer (L)
(N) Navigation
(E) Engineering
(R) Refrigeration
(C) Communications
(S) Supply
(L) Electrical

Officers' ranks and branch distinction colours (pre-1989)

Ord/Able Rate
Leading Hand
Petty Officer
Chief Petty Officer
Engineering
Deck
Communication
Supply
Medical
RFA

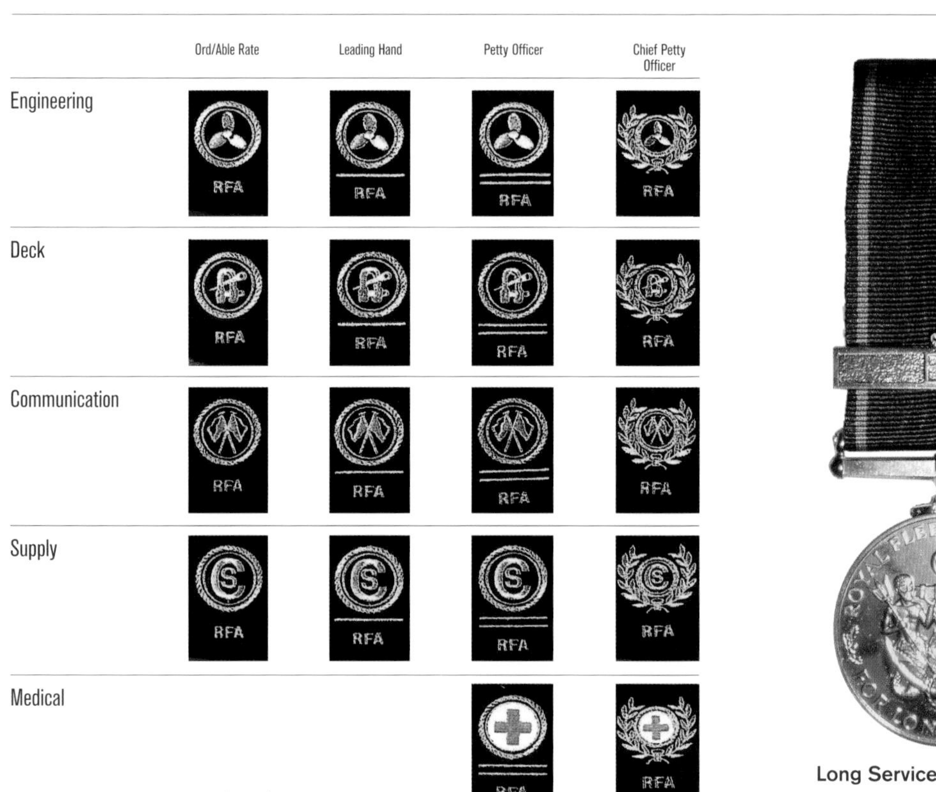

Ratings' insignia 2001 (RFA)

FOR LONG SERVICE

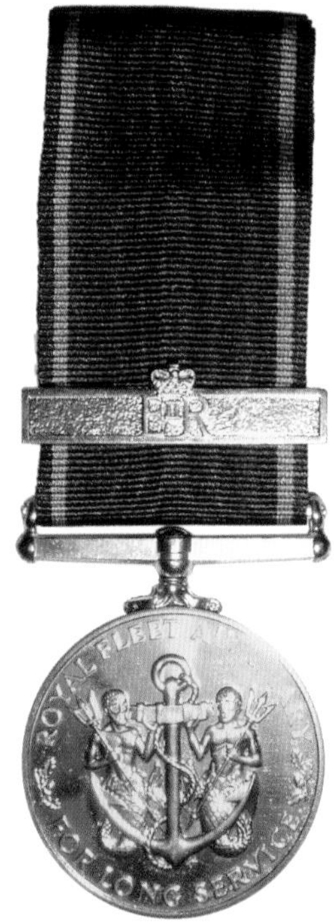

Long Service medal –
see Appendix B for details (J Allix)

Olynthus class

ADMIRALTY-DESIGNED LARGE FLEET REPLENISHMENT TANKERS

RFA *Oleander* **Pennant:** A124 **Official number:** 305440
Port of registry: Newcastle
RFA *Olna* (3) **Pennant:** A123 **Official number:** 308070
RFA *Olynthus* **Pennant:** A122 **Official number:** 307787
Ports of registry: London

In August 1967 redesignated the *Olwen* class when *Oleander* was renamed *Olmeda* and *Olynthus* was renamed *Olwen* (2); sometimes quoted as the 'O' or 'Ol' class
Builder: Hawthorn Leslie (Shipbuilders) Ltd (yard no 756)
Machinery: Two Pametrada steam turbines; two Babcock & Wilcox selectable superheat boilers; single reduction gearing to single screw; 26,500 shp; bunkers 3,825 tons; 21 knots max; 160 tpd consumption; bow thrust propeller fitted
Dimensions (loa/bp x beam): 648/–ft x 84ft
Tonnage measurements: 18,582 grt, 24,134 dwt
Displacement: 36,027 tons full load
Complement: 99 – 32 RN aviation support
Remarks: +100A1 +LMC +RMC, ice class 3, class VII; designed to provide close frontline support of marine and aviation fuels, three grades of luboil, fresh water and limited dry and refrigerated provisions. Built for £3 million. This class was fitted with seven abeam fuelling rigs with automatic tensioning winches and two astern rigs managed from a central control room. Aviation facilities provided by an 81ft x 56ft flight deck and a hangar with space for two aircraft, limited maintenance facilities but support could be provided from portable workshops based on ISO containers. Refuelling facilities and Avcat storage for 1,250 gals. This decks was served by a 1-ton stores lift. Flight deck code ON. The hangar is to the port side of the funnel with a garage and stowage space to starboard. There is a forehold for dry cargo and munitions with a capacity of 900 tons, including 20 tons for refrigerated cargo, served by a 10-ton derrick.
The details are based on RFA *Olna as built*

RFA *Olna* (3) underway at sea.(RFA Archive)

Royal Naval Supply and Transport Service

Until 1965, the logistic support for the Royal Navy was provided by four separate and largely independent directorates – Director of Stores (Navy) with its origins dating back to 1786 and where day-to-day management of the personnel and ships the Royal Fleet Auxiliary was undertaken; Director of Armament Supply (Naval) with its origins dating back to the sixteenth century; Director of Victualling with its origins dating back to 1546, and Director of Fuel, Movements and Transport (Naval) with origins dating back to the Napoleonic and Crimean Wars.

The need for rationalisation and for integrated Afloat Support was so obvious that in 1965 these directorates merged to become the Royal Naval Supply and Transport Organisation (RNSTS) under the leadership of a senior Civil Servant – the Director General Supply and Transport (Naval) reporting to the Chief of Fleet Support.

Through its supply depots and afloat support to the primary role of the RNSTS was world-wide support of the Royal Navy in an efficient and effective way with general stores (for example, timber, flags, paints, gases and greases), with specialist stores (for example, weapons equipment stores, marine engineering equipment, mechanical spares), victualling stores (for example, fresh, frozen and dry provisions, protective clothing, uniforms and fresh water), armament stores (for example, strategic and tactical weapons, pyrotechnics, small arms and ammunition) and fuel (for example, diesel fuel, naval aviation fuels, lubricating oils). It was centrally responsible for the supply of food to the Royal Navy, the Army and the Royal Air Force. In 1996 the RNSTS ceased and much of its role (excluding RFA management) was integrated into the Ministry of Defence's new Naval Bases and Supply Agency.

In April 2001 this Agency and the Defence Sea Mounting Centre at Marchwood were absorbed into the new Warship Support Agency (WSA) as part of the Defence Logistics Organisation. The RFA shipborne stores team of non-industrial and industrial civil servants now come from the WSA.

In 1983 Her Majesty the Queen approved the design of the RNSTS flag. This flag is not an Ensign: it is flown at RNSTS stores and establishments within the UK and overseas.

Catering Superintendent
During the 1960s (precise date uncertain) the first Catering Superintendent was appointed to RFA Headquarters. The all-important catering at sea is conducted under his auspices and he advises on equipment and purchases, carries out inspections of ships' catering arrangements and above all is responsible for the selection and training of staff (catering officers, cooks and stewards) to the Merchant Navy Training Board job specifications.

RFA *Regent* and her sister ship *Resource* were the first front line RFAs to deploy a permanent helicopter. (Wessex HU5) flight. (RFA Archive);

8 August: *Black Ranger*, *Olynthus* (2), *Resurgent*, *Rowanol* and *Wave Prince* take part in the Clyde Royal Review; *Wave Prince* is then laid up at Devonport.
9 August: *Engadine* laid down.
5 October: *Stromness* laid down.
19 October: *Oleander* (2), fleet replenishment tanker with aviation facilities, 18,565 grt, completed by Swan Hunter & Wigham Richardson at Wallsend for MoD(Navy).
28 October: *Sir Bedivere* (LSL 03) laid down.

1966

1966: Captain G O W Evan CBE DSC appointed Commodore RFA. CB 4587 Particulars of RFAs published. Royal Fleet Auxiliary revised designations. *Spabeck*, HTP fuel carrier, is placed on sale list, Devonport. RFAs *Regent* and *Resource* first RFAs to be allocated permanent flights – Wessex HU5 helicopters from NAS 829
8 January: *Sir Geraint* laid down.
February: *Sir Tristram* laid down.
4 February: *Cherryleaf* (2) bareboat charter ended, returned to her owners; sold Aeas Cia Nav SA, Liberia and renamed *Agios Constantinos*.
8 February: *Regent* planned launch date postponed. *Resource* officially named but launching delayed due to high winds.
11 February: *Resource* launched at Greenock.
March: *Spabeck* on the disposal list at Plymouth.
1 March–13 June 1975: Beira Patrol established to prevent the flow of crude oil into the port of Beira following UK Security Council decision to apply oil embargo on Rhodesia – RFA support to one aircraft carrier, two frigates; the endurance record of 90 continuous days is held by *Tidespring*.

Electronics Superintendent
First appointment made in 1966, borne on the staff of RFA Headquarters with responsibility for organisation and working of the Communications Department and for electronic equipment in RFA vessels and the technical supervision of Radio Officers and Communications ratings in the RFA fleet.

9 March: *Regent* launched at Belfast.
12 March: Humanitarian aid – *Oleander* – assisted in the rescue of 37 crew from the blazing Liberian tanker *World Liberty* (18,226/1949) which had been in collision with the Norwegian tanker *Mosli* (34,395/1964) in the Red Sea.
April: *Sir Percivale* laid down.
1 April: *Olna* (3) fleet replenishment tanker with aviation facilities, 18,582 grt, completed by Hawthorn Leslie (Shipbuilders) at Hebburn for £3 million for MoD(Navy).
7 April: *Lyness* launched at Wallsend.
15 April: *Tarbatness* laid down.
19 April: *Sir Galahad* (1) launched at Linthouse for the Ministry of Transport.
14 May: *Spabeck* arrived Antwerp *en route* to Willebroek for demolition.
June: Fleet Manager RFA, borne on HQ Staff of DFMT(N) with rank of Assistant Director introduced to ensure that approved operating programme of RFAs, the policies and procedures for ship maintenance, organisation and

Support Oilers
The term freighting tanker was used to describe a product tanker intended primarily for the collection and freight of fuel oil and aviation fuels from ports of origin for discharge into the Admiralty stocks. In 1966 it was decided that this term would be dropped and such vessels modified and rerated as Support Oilers.

manning and authorised targets for refit times and costs were achieved – later this responsibility was divided into Fleet Manager (Tankers) and Fleet Manager (Dry Cargo and LSLs). *Blue Ranger* laid up in reserve at Devonport.

13 June–December: Beira Patrol supporting UN Security Council oil embargo on Rhodesia – RFA support to two frigates or destroyers.

19 June: Humanitarian aid – *Olna* rescued 26 survivors from the Liberian *Zaneta* (7,176/1943) which had developed leaks and sank in the Arabian Sea off the Kuria Muria Islands, survivors landed in Aden.

July: Humanitarian relief – RFAs (LSL and tankers) supporting Britannia aircraft standing by for evacuation of British civilians from East Pakistan.

20 July: *Sir Bedivere* launched at Hebburn for the Ministry of Transport.

15 September: *Engadine* officially named but launching delayed due to high winds.

16 September: *Engadine* and *Stromness* launched.

20 September: *Pearleaf* – rescued the crew of the Italian tanker *Mare Nostrum* (2,050/1954) which had run aground on Hallaniya Island in the Kuria Muria group and landed them in Bahrain.

November: *Olna* (2) withdrawn from service, placed on the sale list at Devonport.

12 December: *Sir Tristram* launched at Hebburn for the Ministry of Transport.

17 December: *Sir Galahad* (1), landing ship logistic, 4,473 grt, completed by Alex Stephen & Sons at Glasgow for the Ministry of Transport for operation under commercial management of BISN.

22 December: *Lyness* air stores support ship, 14,113 grt, completed by Swan Hunter & Wigham Richardson at Wallsend for the Admiralty; replaced RFA *Fort Duquesne.*

Beira Patrol
On 11 November 1965 Southern Rhodesia unilaterally and illegally declared independence; the UN Security Council called for an economic blockade and in April 1966 full mandatory sanctions were imposed. The British commenced a naval blockade to stop the flow of oil. This began on 1 March 1966 off the port of Beira in the Mozambique Channel (aka MOZCHAN). Between March 1966 and June 1975 the RN ships maintaining this demanding patrol were supported at various times by in all 16 RFA tankers and 10 stores support ships. The patrol averaged 14 days with R&R in Capetown, Durban, Mombasa, Mauritus and the Seychelles.

Tidepool, continuously at sea for 81 days, supported HMS *Eagle* on her peacetime-record patrol of 71 days at sea, during which time the tanker issued 41,000 tons of oil fuel and aviation fuel and embarked 44,000 tons from support tankers. However, the endurance record is held by *Tidespring* which left the UK in May 1967 and arrived Singapore in September with 90 continuous days on the Beira Patrol, steaming 33,000 nautical miles and replenishing ships at an average of six per week. The final RFA deployment was *Tidesurge.*

1967

1967: NATO's Standing Naval Force Atlantic (STANAVFORLANT) formed as a permanent peacetime multinational naval squadron; the RFA occasionally contributes the supporting oiler. All HM Ships and RFAs east of Suez were designated as Eastern Fleet and came under the control of Commander Far East. Short Miscellaneous Air Courses (SMAC) become available for RFA officers and ratings, *eg* SMAC 18 on flight deck control and fire fighting and SMAC 18A on helicopter acquaint for ship's masters. Expo '67 in Montreal, Canada – visit by British ships and International Naval Review at Halifax, included RFA *Tidepool. Philol* broken up in Belgium. *Fort Langley* converted at Chatham Dockyard for the freighting of missiles and other Polaris material supporting the Royal Navy's fleet of Polaris submarines

January: Introduction of a centralised pay scheme for officer's salaries with pay being settled monthly.

6 January: *Olna* (2) sold to Spanish shipbreakers, left Plymouth in tow for Castellon, sale value reported as £125,000.

19 January: *Olna* (2) arrived for breaking up at Castellon.

26 January: *Sir Geraint* launched at Linthouse for the Ministry of Transport.

February: Humanitarian assistance – *Hebe* freighted Oxfam relief stores to Cochin to assist in famine relief.

28 February: *Tarbatness* launched at Wallsend 24 hours later than planned owning to high winds.

March: *Eddyrock* laid up at Singapore for disposal.

30 March: *Stromness*, stores support ship, 12,359 grt, completed by Swan Hunter & Wigham Richardson at Wallsend for MoD(Navy); intended to replace RFA *Fort Charlotte.*

April: *Wave Sovereign* on the disposal list. *Fort Duquesne* placed in reserve at Chatham.

May: *Wave Sovereign* broken up at

Singapore. Oiling at sea – *Olna* (3) refuelled *Clan Mactaggart* (8,035/1949) at sea after the commercial ship had suffered from a 'go-slow' by the bunkering firm in Aden.

16 May: *Regent*, fleet replenishment ship, 18,029 grt, completed by Harland and Wolff at Belfast for MoD(Navy).

18 May: *Sir Bedivere*, landing ship logistic, 4,473 grt, completed by Hawthorn Leslie at Newcastle for the Ministry of Transport for operation under commercial management of BISN.

23 May–10 June: Arab-Israel (Six-Day) War – homeward bound RFA support with HMS *Victorious* waited at Malta and the HMS *Hermes* group with RFA support in the Red Sea, following announcement by Egypt of blockade of the Straits of Tiran.

5 June: *Resource*, fleet replenishment ship, 18,029 grt, completed by Scotts Shipbuilding and Engineering at Greenock for MoD(Navy).

6 June: With the abolition of the post of CinC Mediterranean Fleet RN vessels and RFAs in the Mediterranean passed to CinC Home Fleet; he became responsible for all HM Ships and RFAs in the sea areas west of Suez which became known as the Western Station and title changed to CinC Western Fleet.

9–23 June: Humanitarian assistance – Nigerian civil war – RFAs supporting HMS *Albion* standing by to evacuate British nationals.

Aden Task Force

Between 11 October 1967 and 25 January 1968 Task Force 318, including four aircraft carriers, two assault landing ships, one guided missile destroyer, one submarine and five LSTs was formed to cover final British military withdrawal from Aden. RFAs involved:

RFA *Dewdale* (2)
RFA *Appleleaf*
RFA *Olna**
RFA *Retainer*
RFA *Stromness**
RFA *Reliant**
RFA *Resurgent**
RFA *Fort Sandusky**
RFA *Tidespring*
RFA *Tideflow**

* ships engaged in the final Fleet Review

The mobile reserve tanker RFA *Dewdale* ex commercial tanker *Edenfield*. (RFA Archive)

17 June: *Halcyon Breeze* (to become RFA *Derwentdale* (2)), proceeded to Wallsend for modifications.

27 June: *Eddyrock* sold commercially, name unchanged.

29 June: *Fort Duquesne* arrived in the Scheldt for demolition at Tamise; replaced by *Lyness*.

12 July: *Sir Geraint*, landing ship logistic, 4,473 grt, completed by Alex Stephen & Son at Linthouse for the Ministry of Transport for operation under commercial management of BISN.

5 August: *Olynthus* (2) renamed RFA *Olwen* (2) to reduce confusion with the submarine HMS *Olympus*.

10 August: *Tarbatness*, stores support ship, 12,381 grt, completed by Swan Hunter & Wigham Richardson at Wallsend for MoD(Navy).

28 August: *Olynthus* class of fleet replenishment tankers is redesignated as the *Olwen* class.

14 September: *Sir Tristram*, landing ship logistic, 4,473 grt, completed by Hawthorn Leslie at Hebburn for the Ministry of Transport for operation under commercial management of BISN.

20 September: *Edenfield*, motor tanker on seven-year bareboat charter from Hunting (Eden) Tankers to MoD(Navy), after conversion Cammell Laird sailed from Birkenhead, renamed RFA *Dewdale* (2) (length oa 774ft, 35,805 grt, 63,588 dwt), a mobile reserve tanker for East of Suez service; her black hull due to the use of bitumastic paint was retained.

October: *Naess Scotsman*, motor tanker on seven-year bareboat charter to MoD(Navy) from Anglo-Naess Shipping Co Ltd, arrived Palmers Hebburn for conversion, renamed RFA *Ennerdale* (2), (length oa 710ft, 30,112 grt, 49,209 dwt) mobile reserve tanker for East of Suez service. *Spapool* commissioned under the White Ensign to sail from Singapore to Mombasa.

4 October: *Sir Percivale* launched at Hebburn for the Ministry of Transport.

'R' class

ADMIRALTY-DESIGNED FLEET REPLENISHMENT SHIPS

RFA *Regent* **Pennant:** A486
Official number: 305574
Port of registry: Belfast
RFA *Resource* **Pennant:** A480
Official number: 334496
Port of registry: London
Builder: Harland & Wolff, Belfast (yard no 1658)
Machinery: Two AEI geared turbines, two Foster Wheeler ESD double-cased boiler with superheaters; double reduction gearing to a single 5-bladed propeller; 20,000 shp; bunkers 2,900 tons; 16 knots (21 max); 84 tpd consumption; four 1,250 kW steam-driven turbo generators.
Dimensions (loa/bp x beam): 640/599.3ft x 77ft
Tonnage measurements: 18,029 grt, 19,000 dwt
Displacement: 22,890 tons full load
Complement: 125 RFA + 44 RNSTS + 11 Naval Air Department

The armament, explosives, food and stores ship RFA *Resource.* (RFA Archive)

Remarks: +100A1 +LMC +RMC, ice class 3, class VII; these steam ships were the first to have been specially designed by Director General Ships as AFES (ammunition, food, explosives stores ships) carrying a high value cargo of armament (including nuclear depth charges), naval and victualling stores together with a range of NAAFI stores, medical and survival kits. Designed with a bulbous bow, the hull was of all-welded construction with four decks, a five-tier bridge block amidships and a four-tier poop aft with 80 x 60ft flight deck and hangar facilities to operate, maintain and fuel their own Wessex HU5 helicopter for vertical replenishment.

There were seven holds with a storage capacity of 4,690 tons. Each hold and the flight deck was served by a cargo lift and there were 10 derricks. There was a special rig at No 7 hold for handling Seaslug missiles deployed on the 'County' class destroyers. No 3 hold had arrangements for refrigerated cargo. Two cargo fresh water tanks contained a total of 378 tons. They had extensive replenishment at sea capability with at least 8 RAS points, some fitted with the GEC RAS rigs (known as Snoopy'). Foremast two 6-ton derricks, kingpost with one 3-ton and one 10-ton derrick, kingpost with two 3-ton derricks, derrick post with 3-ton derricks and a kingpost with one 5-ton and one 3-ton derrick. All winches were electric and there were six 2-ton automatic tensioning winches. Internally cargo handling was undertaken by electrically driven fork lift trucks and pallet transporters.

This class had naval standard Nuclear, Bacteriological, Chemical and Damage Control (NBCD)with pre-wetting and citadel arrangements, extensive fire fighting and flooding arrangements, degaussing, Agouti measures to reduce propeller noise, Type 182 towed torpedo decoy and deck stiffening for defensive armament.

Both ships reportedly cost a total of £15 million. They were managed by the Director of Fuel, Movements and Transport (Naval) for crewing, fuel, repairs and maintenance, with the onboard stores organisation managed by the Supply and Transport Officer (N).

Affectionately known within the service as 'Regret' and 'Remorse'.

The details are based on RFA Regent *as built.*

November: *Fort Charlotte* on the disposal list at Singapore. *Fort Langley* commences a Polaris material support shuttle service between the US Naval Supply Center, Charleston, South Carolina and the Armament Depot, Coulport, Scotland.

23 November: *Halcyon Breeze*, motor tanker on seven-year bareboat charter to MoD(Navy) from Caribbean Tankers Ltd; after conversion by Swan Hunter (Drydocking) sailed Wallsend renamed RFA *Derwentdale* (2) (length oa 796.5ft, 42,503 grt, 73,375 dwt), mobile reserve tanker for East of Suez service; became the largest-ever ship in the RFA fleet.

4 December: *Oleander* (2) renamed RFA *Olmeda* to reduce confusion with the frigate HMS *Leander*.

6 December: *Naess Scotsman* on bareboat charter to MoD(Navy) is

renamed RFA *Ennerdale* (2), mobile reserve tanker, after conversion by Vickers Ltd, Hebburn.

14 December: *Engadine*, helicopter training ship, 6,360 grt, completed by Henry Robb, Leith for MoD(Navy) at a cost of £2.5 million.

1968

1968: Captain J Dines CBE RD RFA appointed Commodore RFA. *Fort Dunvegan* broken up in Kaohsiung. Guinea Gulf Patrol commenced and was operated until the reopening of the Suez canal – this was in effect an RFA refuelling patrol off St Helena to RAS transiting HM Ships; this patrol which was, in the main, maintained by 'Wave' and 'Rover' class ships used Freetown to load and Simonstown to load and for repairs

January: *Fort Charlotte* sold to Singapore breakers; replaced by *Stromness*. Major defence cuts announced – Royal Navy to lose its aircraft carriers and general run-down from the Middle and Far East.

January: *Blue Rover*, *Green Rover* and *Grey Rover* ordered.

15–21 January: Humanitarian assistance – RFA *Sea Salvor* and four RN minesweepers off NW Sicily post-earthquake.

22 January: RFA *Tidereach* supporting HMS *Cambrian*, Rodrigues Islands, internal security platoons landed to stop disturbances.

25 January: End of Aden Task Force 318 deployment.

27–31 January: Humanitarian assistance – Israeli submarine

RFA *Engadine*

ADMIRALTY-DESIGNED HELICOPTER TRAINING SHIP

Pennant: K08 **Official number:** 334674
Port of registry: London **Callsign:** GRBU
Builder: Henry Robb, Leith (yard no 500)
Machinery: One 5 cyl Sulzer RD68 ICE by Wallsend Slipway & Engineering Co; 5,500 bhp; 16 knots
Dimensions (loa/bp x beam): 424.25/286ft x 58.8ft
Tonnage measurements: 6,360 grt, 4,520 dwt
Displacement: 8,960 tons full load
Complement: 63 + attached 32 RN contingent
Remarks: +100A1; +LMC class 1 ship fitted with Denny Brown stabilisers; 160 x 58 (max) ft flight deck with two landing spots and an integrated hangar, Avcat storage, stores, workshop facilities and air weapons storage; capable of operating two Wessex or one Sea King helicopter, although she was designed to carry up to six Wessex anti-submarine helicopters; FD code EN; 7,000 items of naval stores covering the spares allowance for two to six Wessex helicopters and a single Wasp; 1969 refitted with a small hangar atop main hangar to enable handling pilotless target aircraft (PTA). During 1983/84, with post-Falklands lessons incorporated she was refitted at Gibraltar to enhance her helicopter capabilities by widening and extending her flight deck by 39 ft, electronic support measures and 'chaff' launchers. She was fitted with five RAS points and helicopter in-flight refuelling (HIFR) capable.

Administration aboard *Engadine* rested with the Master who was in command of the ship. The senior naval officer aboard was to be known as the Naval Adviser to the Master and was in command of the RN contingent with responsibility for running the Air Department and in particular for advice to the Master on aircraft operations and in conjunction with the Master the discipline of RN personnel who were embarked on detached duty from HMS *Osprey*. She entered service under the full command of the MoD(Navy) with operational command exercised by the Commander-in-Chief Western Fleet and delegated to Flag Officer Sea Training (FOST).

Helicopter support ship RFA *Engadine*. (RFA Archive)

missing in Eastern Mediterranean – RFA *Wave Baron* available to support HM Ships tasked to assist in a vast air and sea search for the Israeli submarine *Dakar*.

February: *Ennerdale* (2) conversion completed.

28 February: *Green Rover* and *Grey Rover* laid down.

23 March: *Sir Percivale*, landing ship logistic, 4,473 grt, completed by Hawthorn Leslie at Hebburn for the Ministry of Transport for operation under commercial management of BISN.

1 April: Alec Rose (later Sir Alec) sailing single-handed around the world in his yacht *Lively Lady* was escorted round Cape Horn by RFA *Wave Chief*.

18 April–28 May: Aden – RFA support to HM Ships *Eagle* and *Albion* forming a standby force during talks with Aden Government.

9 May: RFA *Tideflow* working with USS *America*.

July: Exercise Coral Sands – a military and amphibious exercise that took place around Australia involving 50 ships, 18,000 personnel – RFAs in support *Fort Rosalie*, *Reliant*, *Tarbatness*, *Tidespring*, *Gold Ranger* and *Pearleaf*.

December: Announced that from 1970 manning and management of the 'Sir' class Army Logistic landing ships and one LST (*Empire Gull*) would be transferred from British India Steam Navigation Co to the RFA.

19 December: *Green Rover* launched at Hebburn.

30 December: *Blue Rover* laid down.

RFA *Lyness* (bottom) and the tanker RFA *Olwen* (second from top) in the Arabian Sea fuelling and storing the guided missile destroyer HMS *Devonshire* and the carrier HMS *Hermes*, January 1968. (RFA Archive)

RFA *Brown Ranger* dwarfed by the tanker RFA *Olna* and the store ship RFA *Lyness*. (RFA Archive)

1969

1969: Royal Fleet Auxiliary funnel function bands cease to be painted on ships. HRH Prince of Wales visited RFA *Resource* during presentation of Colours to the Royal Navy. *Engadine* fitted with a small hangar on top of her main hangar to house 12 PTA drones. *Bacchus*, *Olna* and *Orangeleaf* carry out successful trials of a new victualling system and it is extended to rest of the RFA fleet during 1970. RN/RFA joined the Marine Society's British Ship Adoption scheme. Ships' Clerks were retitled as Ships 'Accounts Officers – responsible for a ship's business, upkeep of books and accounts, ordering stores and provisions. *Reliant* (2) is restored as a stores support ship. *Olmeda* was the only ocean-going unit available to the CinC to shadow a Soviet squadron off north of Scotland

21 March: Platbritrex – Royal Naval exercise with Uruguayan naval units in the south Atlantic with Argentine Navy observers aboard HM Ships – RFA *Lyness* and RFA *Olwen*; *Lyness* was used to accommodate a floating exhibition of naval and marine equipment.

17 April: *Grey Rover* launched at Hebburn.

June: Humanitarian aid – *Ennerdale* (2) was diverted to refuel the South African warship *Simon van der Stel en route* to Gough Island in the south Atlantic to search for two missing meteorologists, two bodies were recovered; as a result she was the first RFA to be awarded the Wilkinson Sword of Peace.

16 June: The RFA Ensign – a Blue Ensign defaced with a vertical gold anchor – approved by HM the Queen in 1968 was introduced fleet wide.

July *Birchol* (2), *Oakol* (2) and *Teakol* (3) on the disposal list.

2 July: Aviation – *Engadine* had her first deck landing by a Westland Sea King helicopter.

28–29 July Western Fleet Review – HM the Queen reviewed the Western Fleet off Torbay, Devon – RFAS *Resource*, *Engadine*, *Lyness* and *Olmeda* were involved.

August: CB 4587 Particulars of RFAs revised edition published. *Fort Constantine* on the disposal list.

15 August: *Green Rover*, small fleet oiler, 7,503 grt, completed by Swan Hunter & Wigham Richardson at Hebburn for the MoD(Navy) at a cost of £3 million.

18 September: *Birchol* (2) arrived Antwerp for demolition.

22 September: *Teakol* (2) arrived Antwerp for demolition.

24 September: *Oakol* (2) sailed Devonport in tow after being sold

commercially for food storage purposes at Bruges; name unchanged.

October: Cook Bicentenary – RN and RFA ships visited New Zealand and Australia to mark the 200th anniversary of the first landing – RFA *Tidereach*, RFA *Tidesurge* and RFA *Stromness*.

24 October: *Fort Constantine* arrived Hamburg for demolition; replaced by *Bacchus* (3).

November: *Wave Duke*, *Wave Laird*, *Surf Patrol* and *Surf Pioneer* on the disposal list.

6 November: *Fort Langley* arrived at Devonport for destoring and lay-up.

11 November: *Blue Rover* launched at Hebburn.

December: *Wave Baron* laid up Devonport. *Surf Patrol* sold commercially and renamed *Marisurf*. *Eddyness* on the disposal list.

18 December: Last RFA officers leave the RRS *Discovery* as full manning and management is undertaken by the owners – National Environmental Research Council.

25 December: *Wave Duke* arrived Bilbao for demolition.

29 December: Humanitarian aid – *Tidepool* sent her doctor to treat casualties after the Shell tanker *Mactra* (104,772/1969) had suffered an explosion during tank cleaning in the Mozambique Channel.

1970

1970: Marchwood Military Port on Southampton Water is the baseport for the RFA landing ships logistics and RFA *Empire Gull*. MoD(Navy) announced that the *Olwen*, 'Ness', Improved 'Tide' and 'Rover' classes were suitable for embarking and launching Pilotless Target Aircraft (PTA) operations.

In order to comply with current custom in commercial shipping companies the titles of Superintendents were restyled as:
Chief Marine Superintendent
Deputy Marine Superintendent
Marine Superintendent
Marine Engineering Superintendent
Chief Technical Superintendent
Deputy Marine Superintendent
Technical Superintendent
Assistant Marine Superintendent
Deputy Technical Superintendent

January: *Appleleaf*, end of bareboat charter, ship returned to owners; sold commercially and renamed *Damon*.

3 January: *Sir Lancelot* transferred to RFA manning and management.

14 January: *Sir Bedivere* transferred to RFA manning and management.

28 January: *Bishopdale* sold to Spanish breakers.

February: *Empire Gull* transferred to RFA manning and management.

17 February: *Bishopdale* arrived Bilbao for demolition.

24 February: *Eddyness* sailed Devonport in tow for Spanish breakers.

28 February: *Surf Pioneer* arrived Burriana for demolition.

5 March: *Sir Geraint* transferred to RFA manning and management.

6 March: *Sir Percivale* transferred to RFA manning and management.

7 March: *Sir Galahad* (1) transferred to RFA manning and management. *Wave Laird* arrived Gandia for demolition.

10 April: *Grey Rover*, 7,513 grt, completed by Swan Hunter at Hebburn for the MoD(Navy).

14–15 April: *Ennerdale* (2), *Tarbatness* and *Tideflow* with five HM Ships in South Atlantic and Indian Ocean for Apollo XIII spacecraft incident, alternative splashdown positions.

RFA *Empire Gull*

LANDING SHIP TANK MK 3

Pennant: L3513
Official number: 168231
Port of registry: London
Callsign: MVRD
Builder: Davie Shipbuilding, Lauzon, Levis (yard no 970)
Machinery: Two 4 cyl triple expansion by Canadian Pacific Railways Co; two water tube boilers; 5,500 ihp; twin screw; bunkers 950 tons; 10 knots
Dimensions (loa/bp x beam): 347/–ft x 54ft
Tonnage measurements: 4,258 grt, 2,412 dwt
Displacement: 2,300 tons full load
Complement: 63 – accommodation for 80 troops

The Mark 3 tank landing ship RFA *Empire Gull*. (World Ship Society)

Remarks: +100A1 +LMC +RMC; LST mark 3 of rivet and weld construction; bow doors; 224ft hold with two hatches (48 x 12ft) (26 x 14ft) served by two derricks; black hull due to the use of bitumastic paint; 1957 modified to carry heavy tanks; after return to UK waters her hold was specially adapted for the carriage of munitions and she was regularly employed on the cross-channel Marchwood to Antwerp-Zeebrugge route

Rover class

ADMIRALTY-DESIGNED SMALL FLEET REPLENISHMENT TANKERS

RFA *Green Rover* A268
RFA *Grey Rover* A269
RFA *Blue Rover* A270
RFA *Gold Rover* A271
RFA *Black Rover* A273

Machinery: Two 16 cyl Ruston Hornsby AO16 two stroke, single acting, turbocharged ICEs; single reduced geared to single controllable pitch propeller; 16,000 bhp; 19 knots; bow thrust units (see 'remarks' on new engines)

Dimensions (loa/bp x beam): 461/441.8ft x 63ft

Tonnage measurements: 7,503 grt, 6,931 dwt

Displacement: 11,520 tons full load

Complement: 55

RFA *Gold Rover*. This small fleet tanker is representative of one of the most successful designs of tanker used by the RFA. (RFA Archive)

Remarks: +100A1, +LMC, ice class 3, class VII; these small versatile fleet tankers were originally capable of carrying parcels of FFO, dieso, aviation fuel, mogas, luboil and fresh water. In addition 340 tons of dry cargo including munitions and refrigerated stores. The cargo hold is served by a 20-ton lift and two 5-ton derricks. Fitted for abeam and astern fuelling, automatic tensioning winches and with 2-ton stores jackstays; they are also fitted with a large single spot (51 x 99ft) flight deck for day and night operation but without a hangar so can only refuel an embarked helicopter. They have proved to be the worldwide fleet workhorses of the RFA for a number of years. Comfortable, powerful, fast and handle very well in a wide range of sea conditions.

The *Blue Rover*, *Green Rover* and *Grey Rover* were originally fitted with the Ruston AO 16 cyl Paxman diesels but these were unsatisfactory and were replaced by 16 cyl four stroke Crossley Pielstick PC2V ICEs during 1973/74.

Two of the class have been sold for further service with overseas navies.

Black Rover *and* Gold Rover *are marginally different in details, the details above are based on RFA* Green Rover *as built.*

15 July: *Blue Rover*, 7,513 grt, completed by Swan Hunter at Hebburn for the MoD(Navy).

1 June–4 August: Marine loss – *Ennerdale* (2) – this mobile reserve tanker was outward bound from Port Victoria, struck a submerged object, later described as an uncharted coral pinnacle; ship abandoned, no casualties reported; sank position 04.29.36S 55.31.32E (230 degrees 1.25 miles off Mamelle Light, Seychelles); neither the vessel nor her cargo of thousands of tons of fuel oil was salvaged; one RN frigate, one submarine and four RFAs stand by to deal with the oil pollution.

21 July: *Fort Langley* arrived Bilbao for demolition.

Chief Marine Superintendent

The appointment of Chief Marine Superintendent (CMS) was that of the senior Captain working ashore in RFA headquarters as the 'uniform head of the RFA'.

Feb 1951 – Nov 1958	Captain H M Sinclair RFA
Nov 1959 – July 1965	Captain D J S Newton RFA
July 1965 – June 1967	Captain H G Carkeet RFA
July 1967 – Mar 1971	Captain N R McLeod RFA
April 1971 – May 1975	Captain I B Roberts, RFA
June 1975 – April 1979	Captain J Ditchburn RFA
April 1979 – Oct 1981	Captain S McWilliam RFA
Nov 1981 – Sept 1986	Captain C G Butterworth RFA
Oct 1985 – 1989	Captain B H Rutterford RFA

The Navy Board approved for the posts of Commodore RFA and that of Chief Marine Superintendent to be merged from 27 June 1986. The first new merged 'uniform head of the RFA' was Commodore B H Rutterford RFA . Today this rank is titled as Commodore (X) RFA.

August: *Spa* on the disposal list at Greenock.

28 August: *Olmeda* was flagship for Flag Officer Far East Fleet.

September: The Portland (FOST) tanker *Black Ranger* was placed in reserve at Devonport and *Grey Rover* was attached to FOST.

October: Humanitarian aid – RFA *Tideflow* and a US Navy helicopter in a joint operation off South Vietnam to land a badly-injured sailor from the British cargo ship *Trevaylour*.

4 October: Gan Station Tanker, RFA *Wave Ruler* arrived to replace *Wave Victor* as the fuelling hulk for military aircraft.

9 October: *Spa* arrived Passage West, Cork for breaking up.

December: Maritime careers convention in London supported by RFA *Blue Rover* moored in the River Thames.

19 November–11 December: Humanitarian assistance – Operation Burlap – to East Pakistan following extensive damage and flooding by a cyclone – UK military relief operation with RFAs *Sir Galahad*, *Resource*, *Olwen* and *Stromness* with HM Ships *Triumph*, *Intrepid* and *Hydra* with 3 Commando Brigade, Royal Marines.

3 December: *Rowanol* destored and reduced to hulk status at Devonport.

Chief Technical Superintendent

The appointment of Chief Technical Superintendent (CTS) was that of the senior uniformed Marine Engineer working ashore in RFA headquarters.

September 1947 – 1962	F E Langer OBE
1962 – July 1964	G J Matthews OBE
July 1964 – July 1973	H E A Brain OBE
February 1973 – September 1979	D G Edgar
September 1979 – December 1982	D Webb
December 1982 – 1989	A C Foster

In 1989 the ashore post of CTS was merged with the senior seagoing appointment of Commodore Chief Engineer – the status was upgraded to Assistant Director status with executive functions as The Commodore Marine Engineering Officer RFA – today this rank is titled as Commodore (E) RFA.

The Navy Board approved for the posts of Commodore RFA and that of Chief Technical Superintendent to be merged from 27 June 1986. The first new merged 'uniform technical head of the RFA' was Commodore A C Foster RFA. Today this rank is titled as Commodore (E) RFA.

Harrier vertical landing on the flight deck of RFA *Green Rover* on the River Thames at Greenwich in September 1971. (Hawker Siddeley)

1971: Captain H O L'Estrange DSC RD RFA appointed Commodore RFA. With the abolition of Commander Far East Fleet the Western and Eastern Fleets simply became 'the Fleet' under Commander-in-Chief Fleet; programming of fleet RFAs then rested with an RFA officer appointed as Operations Room Logistics Officer and later renamed as the Fleet Logistics Officer.

Accounts Officers

The RFA officer structure responsible for a ship's business, upkeep of all books and accounts, ordering of ship's stores and provisions. 1 January 1971 after an agreement between MoD and the Merchant Navy & Airline Pilots Association – a new joint structure to integrate Catering and Accounts duties under title 'Purser' came into effect.

February: RFA *Blue Rover* supports the Royal Yacht *Britannia* in the Pacific.
March: *Rowanol* on the disposal list.
1 March: During a refit on the Clyde the *Retainer* was holed by the ore carrier *St Margaret* (5,225/1941).
10 April: *Wave Victor* sailed Gan in tow for demolition in Singapore; was reported to be lying hulked in Manila Bay in March 1975.
2 June: *Wave Prince* placed on disposal list.
4 August: Operation Lymelight – live BBC Television programme from the English Channel that included RFAs *Olmeda* and *Regent*.
17 September: Aviation – a deck landing demonstration of the new Harrier VSTOL 'Jump Jet' in the London river using *Green Rover*.
November: *Black Rover* and *Gold Rover* ordered. *Blue Ranger* on the disposal list at Devonport. *Fort Grange* and *Fort Austin* ordered.
1–31 December: Operation Bracken – Task Force 318 with one aircraft carrier, 11 other HM Ships and 12 RFAs is formed in the Persian Gulf to ensure safe and orderly withdrawal from British bases in the area.
8 December: *Robert Dundas* laid up at Chatham for disposal.
10 December: *Rowanol* arrived Zeebrugge for demolition.
13 December: *Sir Caradoc* laid down as *Grey Master*.
16 December: *Wave Prince* arrived Burriana for demolition.

Retitling of RFA Superintendents, 3 January 1971

Present style	*New style*
Marine Superintendent	Chief Marine Superintendent
Deputy Marine Superintendent	Marine Superintendent
Marine Engineer Superintendent	Chief Technical Superintendent
Deputy Marine Engineer Superintendent	Technical Superintendent
Assistant Marine Engineer Superintendent	Deputy Technical Superintendent

1972

1972: Captain G A Robson CBE RFA appointed Commodore RFA. Project Stornaway – RAF station urgently required 1,500 tons of aviation fuel – RFA *Blue Rover* anchored off and a 22-mile pipeline was laid; total RFA discharge time 13 hours.
9–15 January: *Tideflow* visits Tristan da Cunha.
16 January: *Blue Ranger* sold commercially; renamed *Korytsa*.
26 January–7 February: British Honduras – HMS *Ark Royal* task group supported by one RFA ordered to area to provide anti-invasion force, the British amphibious force comprised HMS *Fearless* and RFAs *Sir Bedivere*, *Sir Geraint* and *Sir Tristram*.
10 February: *Wave Baron* placed on the disposal list.
13 February: *Fort Sandusky* destored and laid up at Rosyth for disposal.
15 March: *Brambleleaf* (2) arrived Rosyth on her final freighting run as an RFA.
April: Withdrawal from Malta – following Mr Mintoff's ultimatum, the evacuation of British forces from Malta commenced; RFA *Bayleaf* freighted oil fuel from Malta to UK storages; RFA *Sir Geraint* freighted large quantities of service equipment and belongings; RFA *Lyness* provided stores support at Malta, after a new agreement was signed and the withdrawal terminated; after the withdrawal terminated virtually nothing was left so RFA *Lyness* provided stores support for HMS *Angelo* (shore base), the RN, RMAS *Layburn* (locally deployed) and RAF and Army personnel in the Malta area. Humanitarian aid – Rodriguez Island, 350 miles east of Mauritius was battered by a cyclone, aid was airlifted in from *Tidespring*, *Stromness* and HMS *Hydra*.

RAS(L): RFA *Blue Rover* using both her derrick rigs to refuel the repair ship HMS *Triumph* and frigate HMS *Minerva*, January 1972. (RFA Archive)

13 April: *Brambleleaf* (2), bareboat charter ends, returned to her owners; renamed *London Loyalty*.
23 April: *Wave Baron* arrived Bilbao for demolition.
1 May: *Fort Rosalie* (1) destored and laid up at Rosyth for disposal.
June/July: *Engadine* with a party of geologists, supported by Sea King helicopter from 819 NAS, erected a navigation beacon light on the Island of Rockall, a rocky peak 280 nautical miles west of the Hebrides; 15-day operation.
3 June: *Robert Dundas* arrived Grays, Essex for demolition.
July: Replenishment at sea – GEC trials of their RAS equipment on *Lyness* supporting HMS *Ark Royal* in UK waters. Internal security duties in Northern Ireland with Operation Motorman and the move of an infantry battalion to Londonderry using RFA LSLs.
11 August: *Sir Caradoc* launched at Brevik as MV *Grey Master* for commercial owners
September: *Sir Lamorak* launched at Floro as *Anu* for commercial owners. Strong Express – large NATO exercise in the north Atlantic involving some 60 ships, 70 aircraft and included a number of RFAs. The logistics group included RFAS *Olwen*, *Olna*, *Tidespring*, *Plumleaf*, *Engadine*, *Lyness*, *Regent* and *Retainer*.
7 September–31 December: Iceland – HM Ships with RFA support deployed for patrol duties outside Icelandic-claimed waters.
October to December: Operation Zealous – ships required on standby off East Africa in case of requirement to evacuate British nationals from Uganda – ex Beira patrol tankers RFAS *Tidepool*, *Tidesurge* and *Tidereach*.
November: Replenishment at sea – *Resource* undertakes acceptance trials of four production models of the GEC Mk 1 RAS Rigs; successful demonstration with HMS *Brighton* off Portland.
15 December: *Anu* completed.
22 December: *Gold Ranger* arrived Singapore to be laid up for disposal.

1973: *Pearleaf* – as a result of crew unrest up to 25 Chinese seamen disembarked at Plymouth and flew home. *Brown Ranger* presented with a Meritorious Unit Commendation by US Navy's Chief of Naval Personnel in recognition of her contribution to a Joint US/UK oceanographic operation (Task Group 81.3) in the North Atlantic. Humanitarian aid – *Olwen* rescued 20 people from the blazing Norwegian tanker *Fernwave* (9,200/1972) off the east Yorkshire coast and flew them to Bridlington. Humanitarian aid – 60 miles off Brest *Resource* and HMS *Intrepid* fought a fire in the 49,000-ton Liberian registered tanker *Naess Spirit*.
1 January–14 May: Iceland (Cod War) – HM Ships with RFA support deployed for patrol duties outside waters claimed by Iceland.
8 January: Aviation – *Engadine* is base for extended Lynx helicopter trials.
3 January: *Grey Master* completed.
February: *Overseas Adventurer* bareboat-chartered by MoD(Navy) for RFA manning and management; renamed *Cherryleaf* (3).
10 February: *Fort Rosalie* (1) and *Fort Sandusky* arrived Castellon for demolition.
22 February: *Bayleaf* (2) completed her final trip as an RFA.
March: *Bayleaf* (2), bareboat charter ends, returned to her owners; renamed *London Integrity*. *Black Ranger* laid up at Portsmouth for disposal.
7 March: *Gold Rover* launched at Wallsend.
26 March: *Reliant* (2) destored and laid up at Rosyth on a care and maintenance basis.
April: Humanitarian aid – Rodriquez Island (350 miles east of Mauritius) – *Tidespring* and HMS *Hydra* provided humanitarian support to the inhabitants when the island was battered by 130 mph gales for 18 hours.

30 April: *Appleleaf* (3) laid down.
15 May–13 November: Second Cod War Afloat Support – Anglo-Icelandic fishery dispute involving HM Ships, RFAs *Wave Chief* and *Blue Rover*.
June: *Tidepool* supported by a Wessex V helicopter from 846 NAS landing Royal Marines on Rockall.
1 June: *Tarbatness* towed *Dewdale* (2) to Durban after the tanker had suffered a fractured crankcase while on Beira Patrol duties.
11–18 June: *Sir Lancelot* alerted to provide assistance to the Sultan of Oman's forces beleaguered at Simba. *Stromness* acted as a helicopter base during relief operations.
July: *Black Ranger* sold commercially; renamed *Petrola XIV*. *Gold Ranger* sold commercially; name unchanged.
27 July: Humanitarian aid – *Olmeda* rescued a survivor from the sunken yacht *Sealegs* off the Lizard and landed two survivors in Penzance.
28 July: *Grey Rover*, serving as the Clyde Port Oiler, was struck underwater by the submerged Canadian submarine HMCS *Okanagan*.
August–September: Humanitarian aid – *Sir Tristram* with the survey ship HMS *Hecate* stood by a dramatic three-day rescue operation of men trapped in the deep submergence submarine *Pisces III*, off Atlantic coast of southern Ireland.

Cherryleaf (2), the former *Overseas Adventurer*, bareboat-chartered to the MoD(Navy) for RFA service. (RFA Archive)

Cod War: RFA *Wave Chief* refuelling the frigate HMS *Jupiter* off Iceland 1973. (RFA Archive)

3 September: Senior RFA officer appointed to serve on the staff at FOST Portland, start of planned RFA 'Sea Riders'.
9 September: Oiling at sea – the commercial tanker *British Tamar* fitted as a convoy escort oiler demonstrated with *Gold Rover* its adaptability in replenishment whilst underway at sea in a successful pump over.
October: Four RNR minesweepers (part of the 10th Minesweeping Squadron) given an Atlantic escort by RFA *Brown Ranger*.
8 October: Humanitarian aid – *Resurgent* came across the blazing and abandoned Cypriot *Nejma* (500/1965), boarded her, extinguished the blaze and towed the heavily-damaged ship to Majorca.
30 October: *Black Rover* launched at Wallsend.
November: *Blue Rover* suffered a serious engine room fire whilst supporting the Royal Yacht in the

RFA *Lyness* (right) in a RAS with tanker RFA *Olna* and HMS *Hermes*, when 300 tons of stores were transferred by jackstay in over 7 hours. (RFA Archive)

Pacific and had to be towed by the Yacht to Tahiti for temporary repairs.

5 November: Helicopter trials support unit for *Engadine* formed at RNAS Culdrose (HMS *Seahawk*).

9 November: *Fort Grange* laid down.

December: *Green Rover* re-engined.

1974

1974: Ship Safety Officers appointed for safety liaison under Health & Safety at Work Act 1974. *Sir Percivale* was presented with the AWRE ice bucket – a silver-plated ice bucket to mark her work on behalf of the AWRE Aldermaston.

February: *Reliant* (2) refitted at Rosyth for further operational service.

22 March: *Gold Rover*, small fleet tanker, 7,547 grt, completed by Swan Hunter at Wallsend, at a cost of £7.7m for MoD(Navy).

April: *Grey Rover* and *Blue Rover* re-engined.

7 April to 31 October: Operation Rheostat 1 – Minewarfare Task Group assistance to the Egyptian government for the clearance of war debris from the Suez Canal – involved RFA *Bacchus*.

May: *Reliant* (2) returned to operational service following one year in reserve and a refit at Wallsend followed by several months at FOST, Portland; restored as a stores support ship.

June–July: *Derwentdale* (2) discharged her final Admiralty cargo at Gibraltar and was restored for return to her owners Caribbean Tankers Ltd.

10 July–30 September: RFAs *Regent* and *Olwen* with a task force, including HMS *Hermes* with 41 Commando Royal Marines, stands by off Cyprus following a *coup d'etat* attempt and subsequent Turkish invasion; RFAs *Gold Rover* and *Olna* were also standing by.

23 July: *Brambleleaf* (3) laid down.

August: *Wave Chief* laid up at Rosyth for disposal.

23 August: *Black Rover*, small fleet tanker, 7,574 grt, completed by Swan Hunter at Wallsend, at a cost of £7 million for MoD(Navy).

September: Northern Merger – major NATO maritime exercise in European waters involved RFAs *Regent*, *Resource*, *Olmeda*, *Tidepool*, *Lyness* and *Pearleaf*.

October: Humanitarian aid – two Sea King helicopters (824 NAS) from HMS *Ark Royal* on a search and rescue operation use *Resource* as a refuelling station.

November: *Brown Ranger* laid up in Devonport for disposal.

13 November; *Wave Chief* arrived Inverkeithing for demolition.

12–19 December: Aviation – *Olmeda* conducts trials for FOST Portland with Wessex helicopters.

Seaslug missile being transferred to HMS *Kent.* (Hawker Siddeley)

1975

1975: *Gold Rover* flew flag of Flag Officer 2nd Flotilla when deployed in Pacific. Aviation – *Olna* with two Wessex V helicopters from 845 NAS supporting HMS *Tiger* serviced the light on Rockall. Aviation – *Tidespring* embarking a Wessex HU5 helicopter proves the Helicopter Despatch Service (HDS) concept.

1 January–25 June: Beira Patrol supporting UN Security Council oil embargo on Rhodesia – RFA support to one frigate or destroyer ends.

February: Aviation – *Engadine* conducted Harrier VSTOL trials.

6–14 February: *Olmeda* and HM Ships *Tiger*, *Ajax* and *Charybdis* stand by to east of Malta owing to the situation in Cyprus.

12 February: *Hudson Progress* (later to become *Orangeleaf* (3)) launched at Birkenhead and then laid up at Birkenhead incomplete.

March: General Council of British Shipping (GCBS) took over the role of the UK Chamber of Shipping and British Shipping Federation (originally founded in 1878) – as the central organisation representing all UK ship owners in all matters affecting seagoing personnel. Provides the employers' side of the National Maritime Board and Merchant Navy Training Board, National Sea Training School. The RFA is represented as the 'MOD shipowner'. *Robert Middleton* laid up at Rosyth for disposal, sold commercially, renamed *Myrina*.

10–11 March: Humanitarian aid – Operation Faldage, *Olna* and HMS *Blake* standby off KomPongSom, Cambodia to evacuate British nationals.

Third Cod War Afloat Support (24 November 1975–1 June 1976)
UK v Iceland fishery dispute involving HM Ships, Maritime Patrol Aircraft and the following RFAs:

RFA *Green Rover* vice *Blue*	3 weeks on patrol
RFA *Olwen*	11 weeks on patrol
RFA *Tidepool*	12 weeks on patrol
RFA *Tidereach*	1 week on patrol

29 March–26 April: Humanitarian aid – Operation Stella, *Green Rover* and HMS *Lowestoft* in evacuation of refugees from Vietnam.
April: *Brown Ranger* sold for scrap.
May: *Black Rover* accompanied HMS *Kent* on a three-day Borphorous/Black Sea passage; called at a number of ports; eight days notices of passage required by 1936 Montreaux Convention.
5 May: Humanitarian aid – *Orangeleaf* and HMS *Salisbury* on passage Cape to Clyde, deployed off Angola for possible evacuation of British nationals.
28 May: Demolition of *Brown Ranger* commenced at Gijon.
July: *Plumleaf* (2) was the first vessel to transit the newly-opened Suez Canal that had been blocked during the 1967 Arab-Israeli War.
25 June: Beira Patrol terminates; *Tidespring* holds the endurance record.
July: *Tidesurge* was the last fleet tanker to serve on the Beira Patrol.
24 July: *Hudson Cavalier* (later to become *Appleleaf* (3)) launched at Birkenhead; laid up at Liverpool after running builder's trials.
September: A party from *Olna* install seismic equipment on Rockall.
November: *Wave Ruler* (1) service at Gan terminated; remaining cargo transferred to *Tidesurge*. *Tideflow* laid up at Devonport for disposal. An RFA Bo'sun represented the RFA at the Royal British Legion Festival of Remembrance in the Royal Albert Hall.
December–January 1976: TASMANEX 75 – a joint RN Group 3 deployment with RAN, RNZN, USN and RCN; this 11-day exercise included RFAS *Gold Rover*, *Tidespring* and *Tarbatness*
9 December: *Fort Austin* laid down.
13 December–5 January 1976: *Olwen* (2) acted as support ship during the fisheries dispute with Iceland.
14 December: Humanitarian aid – *Engadine* rescued seven crew from the Cypriot motor vessel *Georgios B* (499/1950) which foundered off the Channel Islands.

1976

1976: Ship Badges were standardised with the pentagonal shape allocated to RFA badges. 'Sailor' – BBC television documentary covering the six-month Westlant deployment with HMS *Ark Royal* supported by *Lyness* – probably first public coverage of the RFA and its role. Rum Punch – RN/USN exercise deployed in the Caribbean included RFAS *Retainer*, *Tidereach* and *Blue Rover*. *Regent* suffers an engine-room fire – Birkenhead for repairs. *Resource*, *Olmeda* and *Olna* (3) – refitted with a new Kelvin Hughes radar outfit (one situation display, one 21/16C compass stabilised 16-inch display, two 19/12 12-inch relative displays interswitched through two scanners and two transmitters) designed to provide front line vessels with a higher degree of radar availability for long distance navigation, conning and pilotage while in convoy and surveillance and control of helicopter. Lord Shackleton's 'economic' Survey of the Falklands Islands; RFA *Tidesurge* assisted.
January: *Wave Ruler* (1) sold for scrap.
1 January–1 June: Cod War continues with RFA ships in support.
8 January: *Tideflow* placed on the disposal list.
22 January–24 February 1976: *Olwen* (2) acted as support ship during the fisheries dispute with Iceland.
25 February–4 April: *Tidesurge* and HMS *Eskimo* deployed to South Atlantic in view of a possible Argentinean adventure against the Falkland Islands.
March: *Wave Ruler* (1) sailed Gan in tow for the breakers. RAF Gan in the Maldives, Indian Ocean closed and with it the deployment of an RFA fuelling hulk; RFA *Sir Percivale* embarked the rear party and the last stores and equipment of RAF and Department of the Environment.
25 April: Replenishment at sea – *Grey Rover* conducted abeam refuelling trials with the BP tanker *British Tamar* (14,644/1973) that involved just the connection of hoses; *Blue Rover* conducted similar trials with *British Esk*.
May: *Tidesurge* laid up at Portsmouth for disposal.
7 May: *Reliant* (2) arrived Rosyth to destore and lay up for disposal.
10 May: *Tideflow* arrived Bilbao for demolition.
17–22 June: Humanitarian aid – RFAS

The port quarter view of *Sir Geraint* illustrates the beautiful lines of this fleet workhorse. (RFA Archive)

Grey Rover and *Stromness* and two RN frigates standing by off Lebanon to evacuate British nationals, RFA *Engadine* with 826 NAS on standby at Gibraltar.

6 July: *Astronomer* (later to become RFA *Reliant* (3)) launched at Gdansk, Poland for commercial owners.

19 July: Humanitarian aid – *Bacchus* rescued nine crew from the Greek motor vessel *Sea Wave* which sank off Crete after her cargo had shifted and shortly afterwards towed the coaster *Thuntank 10* to Vigo from the vicinity of Cape Torinana in NW Spain.

28 August: *Reliant* (2) placed on the disposal list and sale advertised in Lloyd's List.

29 December: *Wave Ruler* (1) hulk reported to be laid up off Johore Shoal in Singapore Roads in a very poor condition.

Harrier VSTOL aircraft landing on the flight deck of RFA *Stromness* in Chatham Dockyard. (ANRS)

1977

1977: Captain S C Dunlop DSO MBE RFA appointed Commodore RFA. *Wave Ruler* (1) broken up in Taiwan. Aviation – 772 NAS was providing Wessex HU5 helicopters for VERTREP duties on *Regent*, *Resource* and *Tidepool*.

20 January: *Astronomer* delivered at a cost of £9,665,336.

19 February: *Sir Lancelot* in collision with the Algerian *Djurdjura* (3,143/1977) in Southampton Water.

19 April: *Tidesurge* sailed Portsmouth in tow for Spanish breakers.

May: Operation Pallium – *Sir Geraint* deployed to Pitcairn Island with a detachment of Royal Engineers with machinery and material to improve landing facilities in Bounty Bay and to improve some roads; a postage stamp was issued to commemorate this operation. *Tarbatness* – Maltese crew replaced by UK personnel.

24 June: *Spaburn* and *Spalake* sold for demolition.

28 June: Queen's Silver Jubilee Review at Spithead – the following RFAs were involved: *Engadine* (press facility ship), *Lyness* (guest ship), *Sir Tristram* (guest ship) with RFAs *Gold Rover*, *Tidespring*, *Olwen*, *Stromness*, *Sir Geraint* and *Pearleaf* in the review lines.

23 August: *Reliant* (2) arrived Inverkeithing for demolition.

September: *Dewdale* (2) withdrawn from RFA service, returned to owners and reverted to the name *Edenfield*.

5 September: Replenishment at sea – the BP tanker *British Tamar*, earmarked for wartime duties as a convoy escort oiler, conducted an experimental and successful pump over of fuel with RFA *Gold Rover* whilst underway.

14 September: Aviation – Harrier GR3 landing trials on the flight deck of RFA *Stromness* at Chatham Naval Base.

October: Humanitarian aid – *Stromness* rescued a man attempting to cross the Atlantic in a rubber boat.

December: Soviet ships – the Soviet Navy's aircraft carrier *Kiev* was shadowed by RN frigates supported by *Green Rover*.

19 December: Operation Journeyman – increased covert naval presence in South Atlantic, off Falklands, during talks with Argentine government – RFA supporting two frigates and one SSN.

1978

1978: Order-in-Council 121 from Statutory Rules & Orders 1911 No 338 (amended by Statutory Instruments 1964/489) amended by SI 1978/1533. IMO drafts Standards of Training, Certification and Watchkeeping (STCW 78) to cover basic sea training covering fire fighting, sea survival and personal safety. Intention announced to convert the stores support ship *Tarbatness* into an amphibious assault ship for use by the Royal Marines; plans subsequently cancelled on ground of cost. Aviation – Gilbert, the Wessex V helicopter deployed on *Tidespring* wins Sopwith Pup Trophy for A Flight of 772 Naval Air Squadron; 824 NAS becomes parent unit for RFAs; 706 NAS conducted Sea King trials on *Fort Grange*. Commemorative postage stamp from Pitcairn Island features *Sir Geraint* on Operation Pallium (20p). Task Group 317.7 – left UK to deploy to Caribbean and North Atlantic with RFAs *Stromness*, *Green Rover* and *Tidespring*.

March: *Tidereach* laid up at Portsmouth for disposal.

9 March: *Fort Austin* launched at Greenock.

'Fort' (2) class

MOD(NAVY)-DESIGNED FLEET REPLENISHMENT SHIPS

RFA *Fort Austin*
Pennant: A386
Official number: 379796
RFA *Fort Grange*
Pennant: A385
Official number: 377548
Port of registry: London
(In 2000 *Fort Grange* was renamed RFA *Fort Rosalie* (2).)
Machinery: One 8 cyl Scott-Sulzer RND ICE; 23,200 bhp; single shaft; controllable pitch propeller; bow thrusters unit; 20+ knots
Dimensions (loa/bp x beam): 640/599.3ft x 77ft

Fleet replenishment ship RFA *Fort Austin*. (World Ship Society)

Tonnage measurements: 18,029 grt, 19,000 dwt
Displacement: 22,890 tons full load
Complement: 140 RFA + 44 store working party + 20 Naval Air Department
Remarks: +100A1 +LMC +RMC, ice class 3, class VII; these ships have been specially designed as AFES (ammunition, food, explosives stores ships) carrying a high-value cargo of armament (including 'special' (nuclear) weapons), naval and victualling stores together with a range of medical and survival kits.

They have extensive aviation facilities with a single-spot 115 x 56ft flight deck with hangar and flying control facilities to operate, maintain and fuel up to four Sea King for vertical replenishment and ASW support. This deck is served by two stores lifts. The roof of the hangar is strengthened for use as an emergency landing platform and helicopter in-flight refuelling (HIFR) capable.

Designed with a bulbous bow, the hull is of all-welded construction with four decks and the bridge block amidships. There are four holds with storage capacity of 3,600 tons; a number of cargo stores and room for 'special' (see above) stores are also provided. Two cargo fresh water tanks contain a total of around 500 tons. No 1 and No 4 holds are for explosives and stores and both are served by a 5-ton lift. Holds 2 and 3 are for refrigerated stores, explosives and naval stores and both are served by 5-ton store lifts. Internally there is a clearway deck and stores handling is by electrically-driven forklift trucks and pallet transporters.

They have modern replenishment-at-sea capability with at least six RAS points, some fitted with the GEC RAS MI and Mk II storing rigs and jackstay facilities. All winches are electric and there are six 2-ton automatic tensioning winches.

This class has naval-standard NBCD with pre-wetting and citadel arrangements, extensive fire fighting and flooding arrangements, degaussing, Agouti measures to reduce propeller noise, Type 182 towed torpedo decoy and deck stiffening for defensive armament.

The details are based on this class as built

April: *Retainer* destored at Rosyth and laid up for disposal. *Hebe* sailed from Hong Kong for the last time.

6 April: *Fort Grange*, fleet replenishment ship with aviation facilities, 16,049 grt, completed by Scott Lithgow, Cartsburn yard at Greenock for MoD(Navy).

10 April: Sea King helicopter (XV574 ex HMS *Tiger* ditched in the Persian Gulf on 30 March) is transferred to *Tidepool* at Malta for shipping back to the Royal Naval Aircraft Yard, Fleetlands.

May: *Orangeleaf* (2), end of bareboat charter, returned to owners and later scrapped.

June: NATO Council and Military Committee demonstration of STANAVFORLANT, off Portland – RFA *Grey Rover* was the press facility ship.

July: Westlant deployment – the final deployment of the aircraft carrier HMS *Ark Royal* supported by RFAS *Resource*, *Olmeda* and *Lyness*.

5–7 July: *Green Rover* and HMS *Juno* present off Virgin Islands, owing to internal security problems.

September: *Tarbatness* is complemented on a reduced level to undertake a four-month defence sales tour.

3 September: *Empire Gull* withdrawn from service and laid up at Portsmouth.

27 October: Plans announced for MoD to charter two destored tankers.

24 November: Commemorative postage stamps from Tristan da Cunha feature *Orangeleaf* (5p), *Tarbatness* (10p), *Tidereach* (20p) and *Reliant* (25p).

30 November: Marine loss – *Hebe* –

this store freighter was at Main Wharf, Admiralty Dockyard, Gibraltar; at around 23.00 a fire broke out extensively damaging the accommodation and bridge, one rating died; the 1979 Statement of Defence declared the vessel a constructive total loss and up for disposal; cost of loss estimated at £1 million; a crew member was later charged with arson and murder.

December: *Hebe* declared a constructive total loss, the bareboat charter terminated, returned to her owners, sold commercially; renamed *Good Guardian*.

4 December: Replenishment at sea – *Regent* back-RASed armaments from HMS *Ark Royal* – a preliminary destore prior to the carrier arriving in Devonport.

7–9 December: Humanitarian aid – Task Group 332.1, including *Grey Rover* on passage Karachi to Seychelles ordered to loiter off Iran owing to civilian unrest and possible evacuation of British nationals – overthrow of the Shah of Iran.

10 December: The STaT32 standard product tanker *Hudson Cavalier* arrived on the Tyne for conversion.

18 December: Commemorative postage stamps from Pitcairn Islands – a set of four with one (20c) depicting RFA *Sir Geraint* unloading material for their new jetty.

USNS *Sirius*, formerly RFA *Lyness* (US Navy)

1979

1979: Replenishment at sea – *Resource* was first to try out the shore test point for the RAS Mk2 rig at RN Armament Depot, Glen Douglas. RFA discipline covered by a new Merchant Navy Code of Conduct. Aviation – 772 NAS deploys flights on *Regent* (O), *Resource* (A) and *Olmeda* (B); 824 NAS deploys Sea King flights on *Fort Austin* (D), *Fort Grange* (A) and *Olmeda* (C).

January: *Tarbatness* undertakes her final deployment – supply run to Diego Garcia, support to the Royal Yacht and escorts during HM The Queen's Arab States Tour.

1 January: Flag Officer 3rd Flotilla under CINCFLEET was established to be responsible for the Royal Navy's major surface ships and for the aviation element of all ships.

5 January: Humanitarian aid – *Resource* with HMS *Alacrity*, one RAF Nimrod aircraft and two Wessex helicopters assist searching the area west of the Casquets Light Vessel after the loss of MV *Cantonad* which was on passage Lisbon to Denmark with a cargo of salt.

22 February: *Tidereach* sold for scrap.

March: *Olmeda* is first RFA to be fitted with satellite communications terminal.

14 March: Humanitarian aid – *Cherryleaf* and HMS *Mohawk* stand by off Grenada for evacuation of British nationals.

20 March: *Tidereach* arrived Bilbao for demolition.

30 March: Closure of Malta – up until now RFA *Bacchus* (3) busy freighting material in preparation of the closure, then a mini task group of RFAs *Sir Lancelot*, *Tarbatness*, *Olna* and HMS *London* left Malta; *Sir Lancelot* embarking 41 Commando RM.

5 April: Aviation – *Olwen* (2) carried out 12 successful Sea Harrier landings on her flight deck – the first RFA to land a Sea Harrier aircraft.

11 May: *Fort Austin*, fleet replenishment ship with aviation facilities, 16,054 grt, completed by Scott Lithgow, Cartsburn yard at Greenock for MoD(Navy).

8 June: *Hudson Cavalier*, STaT32 standard product tanker, 19,975 grt, officially bareboat-chartered by the MOD (Navy) and was renamed *Appleleaf* (3).

21 June: *Sir Geraint* in collision with the German tanker *Tarpenbek* (999/1972) in the English Channel in fog.

28 June–7 July: Unstable situation from local elections in St Lucia – *Cherryleaf* supporting HMS *Brighton* remained covertly nearby.

July: *Hudson Progress*, STaT32 standard product tanker completed for Lloyd's Industrial Leasing as *Balder London* (later to become *Orangeleaf* (3)).

16 July–October: Operation Culex was conducted following an influx of illegal immigrants in Hong Kong – *Bacchus* carried two hovercraft out from the UK, *Fort Grange* delivered one Sea King helicopter.

18 August: *Resurgent* arrived Rosyth for destore and lay-up for disposal.

29 August–5 September: Humanitarian relief – Hurricanes David and Frederic in Barbados and

Dominica area – *Cherryleaf* supporting HMS *Fife*.

24 September: *Retainer* sold to Davies & Newman, London on behalf of Sparreboom Shipbrokers, Rotterdam for breaking up.

19 November: *Retainer* arrived Barcelona for demolition.

December: Replenishment at sea – *Resource* undertakes a series of trials with the Mk2 RAS rig and trials RAS of Seawolf missiles, both with HMS *Broadsword*.

1980

1980: *Tidepool* supporting two Sea King aircraft serviced the light on Rockall. Humanitarian aid – RFA *Olmeda* as hospital guard ship, provided medical emergency support in Gulf of Oman to the tanker *Kristine Maersk*. *Cherryleaf* (3), end of charter, returned to her owners, reverts to original name *Overseas Adventurer*. Iran-Iraq conflict – Persian Gulf deployment of RFAs *Fort Austin*, *Olna* and *Olmeda*.

17 January: Due to Iranian crisis RN task force to Mediterranean to co-operate with US Navy included RFAs *Grey Rover* and *Fort Grange*.

28 January: *Stena Inspector* (later to become *Diligence*) laid down.

20 February: *Hudson Deep*, StaT32 standard product tanker, after conversion by her builders, bareboat-chartered by the MoD(N) and renamed RFA *Brambleleaf* (3), 20,440 grt.

29 February: *Empire Gull* sold for scrap.

18 March: *Empire Gull* arrived Santander for demolition.

1 April: *Tarbatness* laid up at Gibraltar.

3 April: *Stena Inspector* launched at Landskrona for commercial owners.

23 April: Maritime careers seminar hosted by *Sir Bedivere* when in the Pool of London alongside HMS *Belfast*.

12 May: *Black Rover* and HMS *Eskimo* in the Bahamas area after Cuban aircraft sink Bahamian ship *Flamingo* in a fishery dispute.

7 October: Operation Armilla (aka Armilla Patrol) commences, first RFAs to serve on this were *Olwen* and *Stromness*.

15 November: *Lyness* acquired by the US DoD on time charter for service with the US Military Sealift Command for 2–5 months

28 November: *Contender Bezant* (later to become *Argus*) launched at Venice for commercial owners.

7–8 December: Humanitarian relief – *Green Rover* in area off Cayman Islands, Hurricane Allen.

Armilla Patrol
Operation Armilla was established to maintain a visible British presence in the Gulf of Oman/Straits of Hormuz for the protection of merchant ships in the event of an escalation of the Iran-Iraq conflict. Initially serviced by units from TG318.0 returning from Far East deployments, but after the initial two groups, future deployments came from the UK. Armilla Patrol was designated as TG321.1 and each subsequent deployment designated in turn from this series, *eg* TG321.1.1, TG321.1.2. The first RFA deployment on Armilla was *Olwen* and *Stromness* from October to December 1980.

1981

1981: Armilla Patrol – Red Sea, Gulf of Oman and Persian Gulf – RFA tanker support to HM Ships providing a British presence in the region to protect British shipping.

12 January: *Stena Inspector*, ordered as a multi-purpose support vessel for North Sea operation, 6,500 grt, completed by Oresundsuarvett AB at Landskrona for Stena (UK) Line.

17 January: *Lyness* agreement with US DoD changed to a bareboat charter with the US Military Sealift Command.

18 January: *Lyness* renamed USNS *Sirius*.

18 March: *Resurgent* sold to Davies & Newman Ltd, London for £189,000 on behalf of Asturamerican Shipping Co, Panama for breaking up.

April: *Eddyfirth* laid up at Devonport for disposal.

13 May: *Resurgent* arrived Avilez where some superstructure was removed to lighten her.

15 May: *Resurgent* arrived Gijon for final demolition.

2 July: *Oktania* (later to become *Oakleaf* (2)) launched at Uddervalla for commercial owners and completed later that year.

6 July: First Tanker Safety Course for RFA Petty Officers first held at Warsash Nautical College.

31 July: *Contender Bezant*, container ship, 1,306 TEU, completed by Cantiere Navale at Breda, Italy for Sea Containers Ltd.

September: *Engadine*, with HRH Prince Andrew embarked, rescued a sailor from the submarine HMS *Ocelot* who had been washed overboard by a freak wave.

8 September: *Bacchus* (3) destored at Chatham and withdrawn from RFA service.

30 September: *Tarbatness* acquired on time charter by the US DoD for service with US Military Sealift Command.

1 October: *Bacchus* (3) sailed Chatham for the Tyne for drydocking at end of her charter, returned to her owners, sold to Lion Shipping Co (Pte) Ltd, Singapore; renamed *Cherry Lanka*. *Eddyfirth* for sale, invitation to tender issued; to Spence & Young for £50,000.

27 October: *Bayleaf* (3) launched at Birkenhead for commercial owners.

4 November: *Tarbatness* charter changed to a bareboat charter, following day renamed USNS *Spica*.

8 December: Humanitarian aid – *Engadine* rescued 28 seamen from the Jersey-registered motor vessel *Melpol* (568/1959) which was gutted by fire in the English Channel.

1982

1982: Emergency Life Support Apparatus (ELSA) introduced into RFAs.

February: *Stromness* commenced destoring prior to withdrawal from service as a defence economy measure.

1 March: USNS *Sirius* (ex RFA *Lyness*) purchased for US Military Sealift Command.

25 March: Meeting of the Naval Staff Advisory Group to consider naval implications of Argentine landing on South Georgia; CINCFLEET earmarks ships at Gibraltar for deployment.

25 March: *Bayleaf* (3), STaT32 standard product tanker, 20,086 grt, completed by Cammell Laird Shipbuilders at Birkenhead for bareboat chartering to the MoD(Navy).

28 March: *Eddyfirth* demolition commenced at Seville.

29 March: *Fort Austin* (Commodore S Dunlop CBE RFA) returning to the UK from Armilla patrol diverted to the South Atlantic with stores for HMS *Endurance.*

RFA *Bayleaf* (3). (World Ship Society)

April: Replenishment at sea – *Grey Rover* operated out of Portland during Operation Corporate – she conducted RAS trials with numerous ships that were taken up from the trade (STUFT). *Sir Bedivere* was recalled to the UK from the west coast of Canada. *Sir Tristram* diverted from Belize. *Bayleaf* (3) sailed direct from her builders to stretch her rigs with RFA *Grey Rover* off FOST Portland, then sailed for service in South Atlantic. National Maritime Board agreed a 'War Zone', the crews of merchant ships within or transitting this zone are paid a percentage basic War Bonus – not paid to RFAs in the Falklands War Zone.

2 April: Task Force formally instituted for Operation Corporate – recovery of the Falkland Islands. *Appleleaf* (3) diverted to Gibraltar whilst on passage from Curaçao to the UK, then sailed for South Atlantic. *Tidespring* sailed south from the Mediterranean and *Sir Tristram* sails from Belize.

4 April: *Tidepool* sold, for a report £1.8 million, to the Chilean Navy (as a

Falklands War: RFA *Olmeda* with the hospital ship *Uganda* and HMS *Hydra*, 2 June 1982. (RFA Archive)

The ocean tug RFA *Typhoon* later became a unit of the Royal Maritime Auxiliary Service. (World Ship Society)

RFA parties in Operation Corporate

A number of RFA Parties were formed and served upon STUFT during Operation Corporate in 1982, serving upon support tankers, storage tankers and fresh water tankers. Officially known as Liaison Teams they comprised primarily RFA Radio Officers, Deck Officers and Senior Rates; they were appointed to assist the merchant ships working with the fleet and during RAS operating. One RFA officer was lost with the MV *Atlantic Conveyor*.

defence economy measure) was on passage with a joint RFA and Chilean crew, when sale suspended for Operation Corporate and she sailed from Curaçao; Order-in-Council to requisition merchant shipping (what was to become known as 'ships taken up from trade (STUFT) was approved. *Sir Percivale* sailed from Marchwood Military Port.

5 April: Task Force ships sail from the UK – RFAS *Resource* (from Rosyth), *Olmeda* (from Devonport with A flight 824 NAS embarked) and *Pearleaf* from Portsmouth; *Sir Lancelot* from Marchwood; *Gold Rover* replenished with luboils by a commercial vessel. *Brambleleaf* (3) diverted from Armilla Patrol duties in the Gulf of Oman for service in South Atlantic. *Pearleaf* (2) sailed from Portsmouth to South Atlantic.

6 April: *Sir Geraint* (embarking 450 Royal Marines and three Gazelle helicopters) and *Sir Galahad* (embarking 350 Royal Marines) sail from Devonport. National Maritime Board convened and Warlike Operations Agreement reached covering compensation for death/injury and 150 per cent bonus for all Merchant Navy personnel, including RFA, within 200 nautical miles off the coasts of Argentina.

7 April: Amphibious Landing Group assembled at sea and sailed south – RFAS *Sir Galahad*, *Sir Geraint*, *Sir Percivale* (310 Royal Marines and troops), *Sir Lancelot* (troops and three helicopters embarked) and *Pearleaf*. *Stromness*, after restoring, left Portsmouth. *Regent* sailed from Rosyth with two Wessex 5 (848 NAS) embarked.

8 April: *Stena Inspector* requisitioned for service in support of Operation Corporate.

10 April: SS *Canberra* and MV *Elk* sail south; *Tidespring* (Captain S Redmond) arrived at Ascension Island and a small Task Group to retake South Georgia was assembled with special forces.

11 April: *Stromness* joined the Amphibious Landing Group; the escort oilers *British Esk* and *British Tay* sail south.

13 April: *Fort Austin* and *Tidespring* embark a full RN surgical support unit for the South Georgia Task Force; escort oiler *British Tamar* sailed south.

16 April: *Blue Rover* sails from Portsmouth. *Stena Inspector*, with a naval party embarked, sailed Portsmouth after conversion into a repair ship.

19 April: *Regent* sailed from Devonport and *Plumleaf* sailed from Portland; SS *Uganda* converted into a registered hospital ship sails from Gibraltar.

21 April: Operation Paraquat – the retaking of South Georgia commenced with *Tidespring* embarking special forces and two Wessex helicopters.

23 April: *Brambleleaf* joined Operation Paraquat.

26 April: *Tidespring* embarked 187 PoWs and Argentinean/Uruguayan civilians after the recapture of South Georgia.

29 April: *Sir Bedivere* sailed from Marchwood.

30 April: HM Government total exclusion zone around the Falklands came into effect

May: *Sir Lancelot* became special forces headquarters at San Carlos. *Contender Bezant* (later to become RFA *Argus*) requisitioned for service, sent to Devonport for conversion into an 'auxiliary aircraft carrier'.

3 May: RFA *Tidespring* sailed for

The Fitzroy Memorial

This RFA memorial cairn was first erected at Fitzroy Cove in 1982 and has since been rebuilt to include a brass plaque bearing the names of the RFA personnel lost in action during the Fitzroy landings of 8 June 1982.

Ascension Island with the PoWs and civilians.

10 May: *Olna* (3) with 848 NAS B flight embarked and *Engadine* with 847 NAS A flight and maintenance team embarked sail from UK.

11 May: *Fort Austin* and *Resource* take survivors from HMS *Sheffield*.

12 May: RMS *Queen Elizabeth II* sails south. *Tidespring* arrives at Ascension Island with 153 PoWs, 32 Argentinean civilian and two Uruguayan civilians.

13 May: *Balder London* requisitioned for service, sailed Portsmouth. *Fort Grange* sailed south with 824 NAS C flight embarked. Union Side of the National Maritime Board claims extension of the warlike operations bonuses zone to apply to RFA and Merchant Navy personnel out to the limits of the Lloyd's Underwriters' Exclusion Zone.

14 May: *Sir Bedivere* sails south from Ascension.

16 May; *Sir Percivale* successfully test fires an Army 105mm gun from her tank deck.
Fort Austin picks up a number of special forces and their equipment parachuted into the South Atlantic from a RAF Hercules transport aircraft.

18 May: Active Service declaration in the South Atlantic formally announced.

20 May: *Contender Bezant* sailed Devonport for service in South Atlantic.

21 May: Beachhead established in San Carlos Water; *Fort Austin* claims a kill on one Argentine aircraft.

24 May: *Sir Bedivere*, in San Carlos Water, hit by a 1,000lb bomb from an Argentine aircraft; the bomb hit the ship's 20-ton crane, cut through shell plating and bounced into the sea where it did explode; only minor damage to ship; the onboard Royal Marines Blowpipe Air Defence section claimed a 'probable' hit on an enemy aircraft.

24 May: *Sir Lancelot*, in San Carlos Water, twice hit by 1,000 bombs from an Argentine aircraft in two separate attacks; bombs fail to explode; significant damage; fire in troop accommodation; ship abandoned. *Sir Galahad*, in San Carlos Water, hit by a 1,000 bomb from an Argentine aircraft; bomb fails to explode; moderate damage and small fire in area of her vehicle deck.

25 May: *Atlantic Conveyor* lost – 12 lives lost including the ship's Captain and First Radio Officer Ron Hoole RFA who was attached to the ship. *Sir Lancelot*, in San Carlos Water, again hit by a bomb and gunfire from an Argentine aircraft; bomb fails to explode. *Stena Inspector* (later to become RFA *Diligence*) chartered by MoD(Navy) for service as a fleet repair ship, embarking Naval Party 2010, in South Atlantic.

26 May: Unexploded bomb removed from *Sir Galahad*.

28 May: *Astronomer* requisitioned for service during the Falklands Conflict and was converted for service as a helicopter support and repair vessel.

1 June: *Sir Galahad* returned to full operational service. *Brambleleaf*, with a full cargo of fuel sails from Portland for second tour in South Atlantic; PoWs on *Sir Percivale* are transferred to facilities ashore.

4 June: *Sir Percivale* makes passage to Teal Inlet.

5 June: *Sir Lancelot* repaired and power restored.

6 June: *Engadine* arrives in the Falklands Total Exclusion Zone.

8 June: War risk loss – *Sir Galahad* – transporting about 600 troops and equipment to Fitzroy Cove, Falklands Islands when bombed by Argentinian aircraft; one bomb went through an open hatchway on the foredeck and exploded on her tank deck causing major casualties amongst the Welsh Guards; a second bomb exploded in the galley killing an RFA rating and a third bomb went into the engine room causing further casualties; she was set on fire and abandoned; these raged for over a week; five of her RFA crew and 55 Welsh Guards were killed; 11 RFA crew injured and many of the military passengers; later sunk as a war grave; two RFA personnel are awarded the George Medal – Second Engineer Officer Paul Henry GM (posthumous) and seaman Chiu Yiu Nam GM. War risk constructive loss – *Sir Tristram* – transporting men and equipment to Fitzroy Cove when at 1315 she too was bombed by Argentinian aircraft; her after accommodation was burnt out and ship temporarily abandoned; two of her RFA crew were killed, many injured amongst her military passengers; she was towed to Port Stanley where she became an accommodation hulk for almost a year whilst awaiting a decision on her future; later brought back to the UK and rebuilt.

9 June: *Engadine* in San Carlos Water to act as a Wessex helicopter support ship and refuelling station.

14 June: Argentine armed forces in East and West Falkland Islands surrendered.

16 June: *Sir Percivale* becomes the first British ship to re-enter Port Stanley; she was followed by *Sir Bedivere*; National Union of Seamen indicated that a dispute over war bonus to RFA personnel existed with RFA Management (DSF(FMV).

18 June: *Olmeda* at South Georgia, embarks teams from 42 Commando Royal Marines for the recapture of South Thule.

20 June: Operation Keyhole – retaking of South Thule by a small task force – HMS *Endurance* and *Olmeda*.

23 June: Survivors from *Sir Galahad* and *Sir Tristram* landed at Ascension Island and then fly home to UK; 87 RFA Chinese rating survivors flown home to Hong Kong.

25 June: *Sir Galahad* (1) towed out to sea by RMAS *Typhoon* and after a short service she was sunk as a War Grave in position 052.12.39S 056.45.21W.

28 June: *Sir Percivale*, *Olmeda*, *Blue Rover* and *Resource* sail for the UK.

29 June: RFAS *Stromness* and *Tidespring* sail for home.

30 June: *Sir Geraint* sails for home.

Aviation – Pilotless Target Aircraft

RFA *Engadine* (1967) was designed and equipped to conduct Pilotless Target Aircraft (PTA) operations. She was originally equipped with 12 PTAs and had a PTA hangar built atop her main aircraft hangar. In 1970 it was announced that a number of RFA classes were considered suitable for embarking and launching Pilotless Target Aircraft operations – *Olwen*, 'Ness', Improved 'Tides' and 'Rover' classes.

PTAs are small lightweight radio-controlled recoverable aerial targets, *eg* the Chukar, an 11-foot turbojet and the Shelduck, a 12-foot piston-engine vehicle, operated by the RN Fleet Target Group. The specialised RN party embarked in a RFA would average one RN officer and eight ratings (Fleet Air Arm) with six targets plus launcher/ fuel/ spares/infra-red flares.
In her 1986 refit RFA *Olwen* had her flight deck altered to fit the 30-foot launcher for the British Aerojet Ltd unguided target rocket – the Petrel.

RFA *Olmeda* with PTA deployed on her flight deck, refuelling to port and dwarfing HMS *Falmouth*. (RFA Archive)

July: The converted container ship *Astronomer* relieved *Engadine* as helicopter support in the South Atlantic. Twenty-two of the 27 ships in the RFA Fleet were engaged in Operation Corporate and its supporting actions. First formal award of Battle Honours to RFAs – Falklands 1982. Revised 'low visibility' colour scheme adopted, *eg* black smoke bands removed from funnels.

7 July: *Engadine*, having performed 450 deck fuellings and received 1,606 deck landings, sails for UK with 825 NAS personnel and a damaged Sea King HAS2A embarked.

10 July: *Olmeda* disembarked her attached Flight to RNAS Culdrose.

12 July: *Olmeda* arrived Devonport after 96 days at sea without anchoring and having conducted 186 RAS operations.

26 July: Commemorative service held at St Paul's Cathedral, London in the presence of HM The Queen.

28 July: National Maritime Board Warlike Operation Bonus terminated at midnight.

29 July: *Gold Rover* assisted a special forces demonstration in Poole Bay.

13 August: *Tidepool* finally delivered to the Chilean Navy, renamed *Almirante Jorge Montt*.

1 October: USNS *Spica* (ex RFA *Tarbatness*) purchased for US Military Sealift Command for $10.5 million.

16 November: *Sir Bedivere* arrived Marchwood with the remains of 64 British servicemen for burial at home.

December: *Astronomer* chartered by MoD(Navy) for two years with the aim of a more permanent conversion into an aviation support ship using the US Arapaho system; In accordance with the charter party, six Harrison Line officers and eight ratings sailed with the RFA as part of her complement.

CHAPTER 6

Post-Falklands, 1983–2005

1983

1983: Captain J G M Coull RFA appointed Commodore RFA. RFA officers go on their first specialist operator and maintainer course to Kongsberg, Norway on the Albatross Dynamic Positioning System fitted in RFA *Dilgence.*

January–December: Armilla Patrol – Gulf of Oman and Persian Gulf – RFA tanker support to HM Ships providing a British presence in the region to protect British shipping. South Atlantic – reduction in British force levels in the Falklands Islands area – RFA support maintained to HM Ships present in the Falkland Island Protective Zone.

January: Negotiation commence with US Navy on their Arapaho system of converting commercial container ships into aviation support platforms.

14 January: *Grey Master* bareboat-chartered by the MoD(N) as a stop-gap replacement for RFA *Sir Galahad* (1).

14 January: *Lakespan Ontario* (ex *Anu*) bareboat-chartered by the MoD(Navy) as a stopgap replacement for RFA *Sir Tristram.*

February: *Brambleleaf* (3) purchased by the MoD(Navy).

1–4 February: Operation Matchstick – very low key operation to destroy the base on the South Atlantic island of Thule – RFA *Tidespring*, HMS *Ariadne* with two Sea Kings of 826 NAS – these aircraft were flights ZA126 *Tidespring* and ZA136 *Fort Austin.*

March: Indian Ocean – Armilla Patrol with USS *Midway* battle group and Ocean Express included RFAs *Appleleaf*, *Blue Rover* and *Regent.*

11 March: *Lakespan Ontario* formally renamed RFA *Sir Lamorak*, L3532, refitted at Glasgow for RFA service as a 1,566 grt, 18 knot, ro-ro ferry, 5,300 tons full load displacement, 24 RFA crew, two 8 cyl ICEs.

17 March: *Grey Master* formally renamed RFA *Sir Caradoc*, L3522, refitted at Falmouth for RFA service as a 2,049 grt, 16 knot, ro-ro ferry, 5,980 tons full load displacement, 24 RFA crew, four 9 cyl ICEs.

April: *Stromness* acquired on charter by the US DoD for service with US Military Sealift Command; renamed USNS *Saturn.*

25 April: *Astronomer* at Cammell Laird, Birkenhead for conversion into aviation support ship, introducing the Arapaho system of container ship conversion; the prototype US system being shipped to the UK.

16 May: *Sir Tristram* left Port Stanley in the Falklands, aboard the heavy-lift semi-submersible *Dan Lifter* (10,281/1982) for passage to the UK for rebuilding.

The ro–ro ferry RFA *Sir Caradoc.* (RFA Archive)

The battle-damaged RFA *Sir Tristram* on her way home after the Falklands War. (RFA Archive)

RFA *Reliant* (3)

HELICOPTER SUPPORT SHIP WITH ARAPAHO SYSTEM
Pennant: A131 **Official number:** 364436
Port of registry: Liverpool **Callsign:** GVOC
Builder: Stocznic im Lenina, Gdansk (yard no B463/201)
Machinery: One 10 cyl RND90 Sulzer ICE by H Cegielski, Poznan; single 6-bladed propeller; 29,000 bhp at 122 rpm; 22 knots; fixed pitch bow thrusters; cruising fuel consumption 60 tpd
Dimensions (loa/bp x beam): 670/–ft x 101ft
Tonnage measurements: 27,867 grt, 23,471 dwt
Displacement: 28,000 tons full load
Complement: 60 RFA + 150 attached Naval Part 2240 & RNSTS staff

The aviation support ship RFA *Reliant* (3). (RFA Archive)

Remarks: +1001A; +LMC with UMS +RMC ship with Denny-Brown-AEG stabilisers;
196 x 85ft flight deck with two landing spots and hangar facilities; air weapons storage.

Built as a cellular container ship with ro-ro facilities, owned by Charente SteamShip Co Ltd, managed by Harrison Line Ltd; she was temporarily chartered from trade during the Falklands War of 1982 for service as an aircraft transport – fitted with amidships flight deck, hangar forward, fuel system and workshops. At the end of 1982 she was chartered by the MoD(Navy) for a more permanent conversion to a helicopter support ship using the US Arapaho system. This was fitted by Cammell Laird, Birkenhead and is estimated to have cost £30 million with British modified modules for aviation supply, logistics and ordnance and a 600-ton aviation fuel facility. The ship's five main sections were (from aft) a large four-tier accommodation block, known as the 'Hilton'; the original accommodation providing accommodation, storage and recreational spaces for all the ship's crew – known as 'the Tower'; forward of the main superstructure was 'The Village' which provided full accommodation for embarked RN personnel including offices, a central galley, recreation spaces, laundry, sickbay, NAAFI and briefing facilities for aircrew; flight deck/hangar construction of portable galvanised steel mesh with hangar forward that was large enough to accommodate four Sea King helicopters with supporting safety equipment, avionics and mechanical workshops; and finally Stores – under the management of STO(N) was a complex range of victualling and naval stores for both ship's own consumption and for distribution to other units in the fleet. As a naval ship she did lack degaussing, sonar decoys and had no dedicated HQ1 or citadel arrangements. In July 1984 she was renamed RFA *Reliant* (3).

The Arapaho Concept

Developed by the US Naval Air Systems Command in conjunction with the UK, Australia, Canada, New Zealand, West Germany, The Netherlands and Chile. This was intended to rapidly fit a container ship with a self-supporting helicopter operating facility with stores, workshops and accommodation for both air and ground crews – a modern form of MAC ship. This was achieved by bolting on a specially designed kit developed around the standard ISO marine container.

Between 5–7 October 1982 a prototype was trialled on a US merchant container ship – the *Export Leader* – on loan from the Maritime Administration's James River Reserve Fleet. This 18,000-ton ship was outfitted with a flight deck, hangar, fuelling system, night lights, power supplies and damage control facilities. She successfully conducted trials with six types of military helicopter.

This USN system comprised 56 flight deck modules providing hangars for up to four Sea King helicopters, spare deck park and two operating spots – flyco, briefing room, workshops, power generating, fuel pumping and filtration and fire fighting equipment, ordnance, crew quarters and galley. Fitting – total of 12 hours! British negotiations with USN on their gear commenced in January 1983.

7–12 August: Humanitarian aid – *Green Rover* in area supporting HMS *Scylla*, which was providing support in Cayman Islands, Operation Allen.
10–16 August: Armilla Patrol tanker *Grey Rover* with HMS *Andromeda* and HMNZS *Waikato* diverted to the vicinity of the Chagos Archipelago (Indian Ocean) owing to illegal incursions.
19 September: *Green Rover* at the St Kitts-Nevis independence celebrations.
1 October: USNS *Saturn* purchased for service with US Military Sealift Command.
31 October: *Stena Inspector* purchased by MoD(Navy).
12 November: *Stena Inspector* arrived Clyde Dock Engineering, Govan for a £28 million conversion into a forward repair ship that would be

manned and managed as an RFA.
18 November onwards: Operation Offcut – naval support for British troops in multi-national force in the Lebanon, includes RFAs *Blue Rover*, *Grey Rover* and *Brambleleaf*, later joined by RFA *Reliant*.

1984

1984: RN Lieutenant Commander was appointed to the RFA to assist in weaponry matters – known as the RFA Defensive Weapons Officer.
January–December: Armilla Patrol – Gulf of Oman and Persian Gulf – RFA tanker support to HM Ships providing a British presence in the region to protect British shipping; Royal Marines air defence detachment with Javelin SAMs embarked. West Indies Guard Ship with RFA tanker primarily to support Belize, disaster relief, and general British presence in the area.
January–May: South Atlantic and Antarctica – RFA support maintained to HM Ships present in the Falkland Island Protective Zone.
11 January onwards: Humanitarian aid – *Reliant* (3) after a curtailed workup, with NP220 and 846 NAS, sailed Portland for service off the Lebanon and to relieve HMS *Fearless* and to assist in evacuation of British nationals; three Sea King Mk 4 helicopters from 846 NAS embarked – over 5,000 civilian evacuated in four weeks.
25 January: Humanitarian aid – *Regent* and *Olmeda* airlifted their doctors to the container ship *Kowloon Bay* and transferred a patient back to *Regent*.
8 February: Following decision to air-evacuate the entire 'BritForLeb' *Reliant* received some 115 men and 50 military trucks and armoured vehicles.
10 February: *Reliant* off the Lebanese coast took onboard some 518 civilians of 32 nationalities and air-shuttled them to Cyprus.
29 February: *Stena Inspector* conversion into a forward repair ship, primarily for service in the South Atlantic, completed.
1 March: *Contender Bezant* purchased for £18 million by Harland & Wolff Ltd, Belfast for conversion into an aviation training ship for resale to the MoD(Navy); to replace RFA *Engadine*.
12 March: *Stena Inspector* formally renamed RFA *Diligence* and accepted into service.
29 March: *Contender Bezant* arrived Belfast to begin her conversion.

The 'Arapaho' flight deck of RFA *Reliant* (3).

RFA Aviation Support Unit (RFAASU)
Formed at RNAS Culdrose (HMS *Seahawk*) on 1 October 1984, it was a centralised organisation responsible for all aviation support teams by maintaining, deploying and operating the Sea King ASW support facilities in RFAs. It provided the permanent RN parties in the 'Fort' (2) class ships and to support 'Tide' and 'Ol' detachments including containerised helicopter support facilities.

The RFAASU operated an emergency flight pool for aircrew and air engineering personnel. An Aviation Support Officer (AVSO) was the RN officer in charge of an Aviation Support Element and was responsible to OiC RFAASU for the efficient organisation of the air engineering department. FOF3 was Fleet Aviation Authority and he specified requirements for embarked parties, administered them when embarked and conducted the harbour and seagoing acceptance trials (HATs and SATs).

With effect from 1 May 1986 the RFA aviation ships – *Engadine*, *Reliant* (3) and *Argus* (with NP 4167) were allocated to the Third Flotilla (FOF3). RFA *Reliant* (3) with Naval Party 2240 was unique in that she was trialling the US Arapaho containerised helicopter carrier concept.

Computers in RFAs
In mid-1984 a programme commenced to install microcomputers in RFAs to relieve the Purser's staff of time-consuming tasks. This first system was a Rank Xerox 820-11 8 CP/M micro and initial trials were conducted on RFA *Resource* and RFA *Engadine*.

6 April *Reliant* (3) returned Devonport to destore prior to an assisted maintenance period.

May–December: South Atlantic and Antarctica – reduction in the level of RFA support maintained to HM Ships present in the Falkland Island Protective Zone to 'as required' plus forward repair ship *Diligence*.

24 May: *Blader London*, StaT32 standard tanker, officially bareboat-chartered from Lloyd's Industrial Leasing Ltd by MoD(Navy) for service as a freighting tanker and renamed RFA *Orangeleaf* (3), 19,976 grt.

June: 'Royal Fleet Auxiliary' march written and recorded by the Royal Marines Band.

1 June: Marchwood Memorial. Specifically dedicated to the RFA to mark the South Atlantic campaign of 1982. Unveiled at Marchwood Village, Hampshire.

Solid Stores Support by RFA Tankers

Policy established for the regular use of 'Rover', 'Ol' and 'Leaf' ships carrying limited solid stores in pre-prepared packs up to 100 in some ships and mechanical handling equipment provided. Provision for refrigerated stores in reefer containers and special arrangements for ammunition and munitions.

2–7 June: *Sir Bedivere* was control and accommodation ship at Caen for the 40th celebrations for D-Day.

9 August: RFA *Olwen* on duty in South Atlantic suffered a major accident when hit by a rogue wave – two RFA crew killed and four injured. The injured were transferred to the British Military Hospital at Port Stanley by a Sea King of 826 NAS.

10 August: *Sir Tristram* entered the dry dock of Tyne Ship Repairers where she was cut in two for a 14-month rebuilding programme.

6 September: *Sir Galahad* (2) ordered.

RFA *Diligence*

FORWARD REPAIR SHIP

Pennant: A132 **Official number:** 399182
Port of registry: London **Callsign:** GCPC
Builder: Oresundsvarvett AB, Sweden (yard no 276)
Machinery: Diesel electric with five Vee 16 cyl four stroke ICE, 18,000 bhp driving five 2,520 kW generators connected to four electric motors with single reduced gearing to a single controllable pitch propeller by Bofors Nohab, Trollnattan; two thrust propellers forward and two direction thrust propellers aft; fuel 3,150 tons; 15 knots
Dimensions (loa/bp x beam): 367.6ft/–ft x 68.10ft
Tonnage measurements: 6,544 grt, 4,941 dwt
Displacement: 10,595 tons full load
Complement: 39 RFA + 90-man Naval Party 2010 + accommodation for additional 147

The former offshore support ship *Stena Inspector* as the Navy's floating service station RFA *Diligence*. (RFA Archive)

Remarks: +100A1; +LMC +UMS Ice 1A class VII sophisticated multi-purpose ship fitted with the Albatross dynamic positioning system; extensively modified for RFA service with wide range of workshops for hull and machinery repairs, over-the-side supply of electricity, water, fuel, air, steam, 40-ton cranage, large range of naval stores, extensive accommodation, extensive firefighting gear, naval communications and defensive armament; she has support of nuclear submarines and fitted with MoD compression chamber with SUBMISS/SUBSUNK support; 83ft diameter 'Chinook' capable flight deck over the superstructure with one landing spot and refuelling facilities; FD code DL. On her transfer to the RFA a number of Stena officers remained with her for a short period in the South Atlantic to ensure the transfer of expertise.

Commonly known as 'The Resident Falkland Islands Support Ship' she plays an important role in the support of both surface ships and nuclear-powered submarines. When serving in the Middle East, supporting Mine Countermeasures Vessels, she is complemented with Naval Party 1600.

25 September: Falkland Islands 1982 Battle Honours presented to RFAs *Sir Bedivere*, *Sir Geraint* and *Sir Percivale* at Marchwood Military Port. Humanitarian aid – a team from *Grey Rover* extinguished a fire in Freeport, Bahamas aboard the motor yacht *Yankee Clipper*.

October: *Reliant* (3) at Portland with Sea Kings of 826 NAS for work up prior to deployment south to the Falklands Islands Protective Zone.

1 October: Aviation – Royal Fleet Auxiliary Aviation Support Unit formed at RNAS Culdrose (HMS *Seahawk*).

November: *Reliant* (3) after docking for essential defects and exhaustive work up programmes at Portland, deployed to the Falkland Island Protective Zone to provide ASW protection.

Chinese Ratings RFA

The employment of Hong Kong Chinese seamen in the British Merchant Navy goes back to the nineteenth century. Traditionally they were recruited from 'boarding house keepers' known as 'Compradores', who in return for a percentage of a man's wages, found him a ship and supported him while he was ashore. Many shipping companies employed their own 'Compradore'. With the Admiralty the employment of Hong Kong Chinese, Maltese and Seychelles ratings goes back to the inter-war period when station tankers were established and when locally recruited ratings were employed. For many years Hong Kong Chinese were used to crew RFA ships. In 1979 there were some 700 ratings manning nearly one-third of the RFA fleet, so the MoD(Navy) planned to reduce the number employed, the primary reasons being training and language difficulties. By 1985 the number had been reduced to 260. By 1986 the policy between the MoD(Navy) and the National Union of Seamen was to entirely replace all Chinese ratings with British sailors by the 1990s. By 1987 only 180 Hong Kong Chinese remained and in 1989 RFA *Sir Lancelot* paid off as the last RFA crewed by Hong Kong Chinese ratings.

1985

1985: Captain B H Rutherford RFA appointed Commodore RFA. RFA adopt a comprehensive boat policy with all RFAs being provided with rigid inflatable boats (RIBs) for rescue purposes; 11m work boats to be replaced with a 13m general purpose LCVP; in the 'Rover' class a Cheverton replaced the Crash boat. College of Maritime Studies Warsash commissioned to undertake a long hard look at the RFA; known as the Warsash Study it reviewed manpower utilisation and the Manpower Management Programme was a special project team to examine and work on systems, appointing, appraisal, career development, promotion, training and education; Training Control Officer appointed. The RFA Service newspaper *Gunline* is first published.

The Rebuilt *Sir Tristram*

Work undertaken by Tyne Shiprepair's Wallsend Drydocks. RFA *Sir Tristram* was lengthened by 29ft by the addition of a 120-ton midships section, the aluminium superstructure was replaced by steel and the superstructure rebuilt with new bridge communication facilities and accommodation, the flight deck enlarged to became 'Chinook' capable; new 25-ton crane, new goalpost mainmast and a new electronic pneumatic control system added to manage the main engines. Revised statistics: length oa 441.1ft, 5,800 tons displacement full load, complement 52.

Rebuilt after the Falklands War, RFA *Sir Tristram* passing through Tower Bridge in the Pool of London on her post-rebuild maiden trip. (RFA Archive)

January–December: Armilla Patrol – Gulf of Oman and Persian Gulf – RFA tanker support to HM Ships providing a British presence in the region to protect British shipping; RM air defence detachments embarked. West Indies Guard Ship with RFA tanker primarily to support Belize, disaster relief, and general British presence in the area.

January–May: South Atlantic and Antarctica – RFA support maintained, as required, to HM Ships present in the Falkland Island Protective Zone including deployment of RFAs *Diligence* and *Reliant*.

March: HM The Queen officially approved the Royal Fleet Auxiliary Service crest.

29 March: Approval given to charter *Oktania* to replace the ageing *Plumleaf* (3).

15 June: South Atlantic Campaign Memorial Service St Paul's Cathedral, London. Dedicated by HM the Queen.

12 July: *Sir Galahad* (2) laid down.

15 August: *Green Rover* transferred 1,350 gallons of fuel to Richard Branson's *Virgin Atlantic Challenger* during his abortive Blue Riband record attempt; boat sank four hours later.

September: Supply Officers Training Unit established to run Purser (3/O(S)) Induction Training Course.

3 September: Commemorative first day cover was issued to mark the 80th anniversary of the RFA and to support the *Sir Galahad* Lifeboat Appeal.

19 September: *Oktania* formally accepted on bareboat charter by the MoD(Navy).

14 October: RFA *Sir Tristram* visits the Pool of London.

Oakleaf was initially bareboat-chartered to the MoD(N), now owned by the Crown. (RFA Archive)

1986

1986: Directorate of Naval Manpower Audit instigate a review of the manning philosophy of the RFA and the tasking and role of RN parties and RNSTS embarked civilians. Commanding Officer Designate course is first run – a 13-week course held at HMS *Collingwood* and other RN establishments for RFA Captains and Chief Officers.

Ship Weapon System Authority (SWSA)
A new concept in which the SWSA treats the design, procurement, integration, installation and commissioning of all weapons and electronic systems on a RFA as a 'turnkey' operation. With this the shipbuilder is relieved of all direct responsibility for this high specialised activity, *eg* Harland & Wolff, Racal Marine Radar for MOD contract for RFA *Argus*.

RFA HQ post of Principal Medical Adviser was established. RFA Catering Superintendent retitled as Chief Supply Superintendent. First RFA officer undertakes the RN's Principal Warfare Officer course. First RFA Captain attends the 13-week RN Commanding Officers' Designate Course.

January: Humanitarian aid – Aden, evacuation of British and foreign nationals from civil war in People's Republic of Yemen involving Royal Yacht *Britannia* and RFA *Brambleleaf* from the Armilla Patrol.

20 January: *Sir Lamorak* charter expired, returned to owners and renamed *Merchant Trader*.

February: First two-week course by Bond Instrumentation for engineering and electrical officers, to gain insight into operational maintenance of electronic controlled machinery management systems and UMS systems being fitted in the 'Fort' class AORs, *Sir Tristram* and *Sir Galahad*.

3 February: Director General Ship Refitting is formed to represent the refitting and repair requirements of the various MoD directorates as customers of commercial dockyard facilities; within this is included the RFA Refits group, headed by the Deputy CTS.

11 February: *Fort Grange*, stationed in the Falkland Islands Protection Zone with four Sea King helicopters of 826 NAS, receives a visit from Prime Minister Thatcher.

17 February: *Oktania* arrived Falmouth for conversion.

March: Proposal to introduce the Consolidated Rating Salary for company service contract ratings – this consolidated average overtime payments and some stand-by and cargo handling payments; RFA allowances, such as RAS proficiency bonus, defensive weapons allowance, afloat support allowance and station allowance continued to be paid separately. New guidelines for avoiding industrial action in RFAs were agreed between the National Union of Seamen and RFA management; in any future disputes on NMB or other employers issues the RFA management would be given a seven-day appeal period; in previous disputes, such as that of 1981, RFAs were excluded on grounds of national security.

HMAS *Supply*, formerly RFA *Tide Austral*. (RAN)

April–December: Global 86 RN/RFA task group deployment with RFAS *Fort Grange*, *Bayleaf* and *Olmeda*.
11 April: *Pearleaf* (2) arrived Portsmouth for the final time to pay off.
23 April: *Fort Victoria* ordered.
1 May: Aviation-dedicated ships were allocated to the Third Flotilla and embarked flights administered by Flag Officer 3rd Flotilla – RFAS *Engadine*, *Reliant* (3) and *Argus*. *Orangeleaf* (3) completes an eight-month conversion by Tyne Shiprepair Ltd, into a full RAS tanker with abeam fuelling rigs and additional accommodation.
8 May: *Pearleaf* (2), end of charter, returned to her owners, sold commercially; renamed *Nejmat El Petrol XIX*.
25 May: *Reliant* (3) returned to Devonport and disembarked 826 NAS.
June: The senior sea-going post of Commodore RFA and senior post ashore of Chief Marine Superintendent merged under Commodore RFA. The senior sea-going post of Commodore Chief Engineer and senior post ashore of Chief Technical Superintendent merged under Commodore Chief Engineer RFA.
9 June: Humanitarian relief – Operation Jubilee – Jamaica following heavy rain – HMS *Ariadne* and RFA *Gold Rover*.
27 June: New system of standardised RFA ranks approved by the Admiralty Board. Final RFA Radio Officers' Long Course (RFA26) at HMS *Collingwood*. Title of Radio Officer replaced by Communications Officer.
July: *Reliant* (3) arrived Seaforth Container Terminal, Merseyside for the Arapaho container equipment to be removed for return to US Navy.
13–14 July: Humanitarian aid – *Bayleaf* rescued 15 crew from the Taiwanese cargo vessel *Hwa Lie* (1,411/1972) that sank 60 miles east of Hong Kong.
25 July: *Reliant* (3) arrived Birkenhead for restoration for mercantile service but was purchased by the MoD and placed on sale list; proposed sale to USA fell through.
11 August: *Oktania* conversion completed at a cost of approximately £5 million.
14 August: *Oktania* formally renamed RFA *Oakleaf* (2), displacement full load 49,648, 37,328 dwt, length oa 570ft, one Burmeister & Wain 4L80 MLE ICE, single shaft, crew 35.
September: First RFA weapons maintenance course introduced at

Revised RFA Rank Structure, 1986

On 27 June 1986, the Navy Board approved the introduction of a revised rank structure and titles for RFA officers. A more navalised standard ranks were established up to 2½ ring level. The Radio and Purser Branches were renamed as Communications Officers and Supply Officers respectively; in addition the new ranks of Senior Captain and Senior Marine Engineering Officer were introduced and the Chief Electronic Superintendent and Chief Supply Superintendent became entitled to wear four rings.

The Communication Branch reorganisation was:

4 rings	Chief Electronics Superintendent (formerly RFA Electronics Superintendent)
3 rings	Senior Communications Officer
2½ rings	1st Officer (C)
2 rings	2nd Officer (C)
1 ring	3rd Officer (C)
½ ring	4th Officer (C)

The Branch's light green distinction cloth was retained.

Electrical officers are part of the Engineering Department; responsible for the running and maintenance of the main and emergency electrical installations on board a RFA. The branch has been reorganised:

2½ rings	Senior Electrical Officer	*now* 1st Officer (L)
2 rings	1st Electrical Officer	*now* 2nd Officer (L)
1 ring	2nd Electrical Officer	*now* 3rd Officer (L)
½ ring	Junior Electrical Officer	*now* 4th Officer (L)

The Branch's dark green distinction cloth was retained.

The RFA Uniform

The standard Merchant Navy uniform was authorised by an Order-in-Council of 13 December 1921 – the Mercantile Marine (Uniform) Order 1921. However, over the years the RFA uniform developed away from the standard MN dress and during the 1980s the uniform became more navalised as it became known by naval regulation terms, for example, No 5J (Woolly pully rig) and of No 4 AWD with NBCD and tropical rigs

Certificated contract officers wore a full diamond above the uniform sleeve lace together with RFA cap badge and buttons. It is not possible to confirm the date when this was introduced, it is reported that a cap badge for RFA officers with the Tudor Crown was introduced *circa* 1925. The current version with St Edward's Crown was authorised in 1953. Again it is difficult to confirm, but it would appear that RFA cap badges for Petty Officers became available *circa* 1954.

In 1965, as the association between the RFA, RN and shore-based authorities increased, the RFA uniform rules were changed to permit all contract officers to wear the full diamond. It became obligatory for all contract officer to be in possession of uniform including mess kit and a uniform upkeep allowance became payable.

RFA Branch colours are Deck (navigation) branch (N) later (X) – no colour; Engineering branch (E), refrigeration (R) – purple; Electrical (L) – dark green; Radio (C) – light green; Pursers later Supply (S), later Logistics Supply (LS) – white; Medical – scarlet; new Communications (C) – blue.

RFA senior rates on company contract were expected to provide themselves with a Merchant Navy Petty Officer's uniform, the RFA Petty Officer's cap badge and RFA buttons were available through Naval stocks. When necessary uniforms were issued on loan. Increasingly during the 1980s the Working rig for ratings became No 8 (now No 4) AWD and now NBCD rig. A uniform upkeep allowance is payable. On particularly ceremonial occasions ratings have worn the tradition naval cap with an 'R.F.A' cap tally or one bearing the ships name, eg, 'R.F.A *Tidespring*'.

The RFA Uniforms Committee approved the introduction of a Ratings Uniform around 1987. The new dress (non-RN system) uniform incorporates unique Branch badges. Owing to financial constraints the introduction was shelved. However, this was resurrected when the Type Commander was established in 1993. Rating badges were approved for basic rate, leading hand, petty officer and chief petty officer and branch badges cover seamanship, marine engineering, supply/cook/steward, system engineering and communications. The shoulder flash ROYAL FLEET AUXILIARY is worn.

HMS *Collingwood* and *Cambridge*. Introduction of the Communication Officers' Long Course (RFA27). *Black Rover* affected by seamen's strike.

2 September: Oiling at sea – *Bayleaf*, on passage Sydney to Melbourne, conducts a RAS(L) with USS *Missouri* – first complete RAS of a battleship by the RFA for many years.

11 September: *Reliant* (3) offered for sale as lies at West Canada Dock, Liverpool.

29 September: Following the loss of RFA *Sir Galahad* in the Falklands in 1982, the RFA service set up the *Sir Galahad* lifeboat appeal – a fund to have a RNLI lifeboat named after the LSL, to be a memorial to those who lost their lives; the appeal raised over £148,292, and HRH Princess Alexandra named the new 'Tyne' class lifeboat *RFA Sir Galahad* at Tenby, South Wales, where she is stationed.

October: Royal Australian Navy 75th anniversary – multinational fleet review in Sydney Harbour included HM Ships *Illustrious*, *Manchester*, *Amazon*, *Beaver*, RFA *Fort Grange* and HMAS *Supply* (formerly RFA *Tide Austral*).

27 October: *Reliant* (3) sold to commercial owners and renamed *Admiralty Island*.

6 November: *Olwen* assisted in the search and rescue attempt from survivors of a ditched Chinook helicopter 2 miles east of Sumburgh Head in the Shetlands in which 45 people died.

7 November: *Plumleaf* (2) sailed Devonport on her redelivery voyage to her owners in the Far East.

16 November–8 December: Exercise Shining Sword (Saif Sareea) – Anglo-Oman exercise that practised a large scale and rapid strategic deployment of tri-service UK forces with HMS *Illustrious*, HMS *Intrepid* with escorts and Royal Marines supported by RFA *Fort Grange*, RFA *Olmeda* and RFA *Orangeleaf*.

13 December: *Sir Galahad* (2) launched at Wallsend.

17 December: *Plumleaf* (2) sold by Blue Funnel Bulkships Ltd to Cheng Yung Enterprises Ltd, arrived at Kaohsiung for demolition.

1987

1987: ICS25 integrated communications system fitted in RFAs *Olwen*, *Olna*, *Argus*, *Sir Galahad* and to be fitted in RFA *Olmeda* and all new construction and major refits. Uniforms – RFA Uniform Committee approved a new dress (non RN system) uniform for ratings incorporating unique Branch badges. Owing to financial constraints the introduction was shelved until around 1993. Rate of Petty Officer (Stores) introduced. British Maritime Technology undertook a study to investigate feasibility of a Ship Life Extension Programme (SLEP) on RFA *Sir Lancelot* when she was in refit at Smith Ship Repairers. Jordan Trophy

– to be presented twice annually to the 'best RFA for above water warfare for tactical and deliberate procedures'. Donated by Lieutenant Chris Jordan RN, the first RFA Defensive Weapons Officer.

1 February: *Diligence* undertakes a £2 million refit by Seaforth Welding, Liverpool prior to Gulf deployment with Armilla Patrol.

March: *Oakleaf* fitted with a computer installation for stores and stock management.

3 March: Humanitarian aid – *Engadine* with RN Sea Kings, rescued the crew from the Danish coaster *Hornestrand*, 34 miles off Portland Bill, after fire had broken out in her cargo of explosives.

11 March: Korean War Memorial – unveiled by HM The Queen at St Paul's Cathedral; memorial includes the RFA.

25 March: *Contender Bezant* formally renamed RFA *Argus*.

1 April: Direct General Ship Repairs organisation established to oversee all ship refitting work and alterations and additions – RFA Refits section staffed by Technical Superintendents, Technical Officers is established at MoD(Navy) Bath.

July: RFA HQ team set up to study implementation of Warsash Study. Pre-Joining Training (PJT) introduced on weapons and NBCD particularly for deployments such as Armilla Patrol and South Atlantic. National Maritime Board agreed a 'War Zone', the crews of merchant ships within or transitting this zone are paid a percentage basic War Bonus – not paid to RFAs in the Gulf War Zone.

19–21 July: *Sir Galahad* (2) conducted contractor's sea trials.

August: RFA Staff Officer post established with MOD Directorate of Naval Warfare (DNW(WR)). 4th MCM Squadron (four 'Hunt' class MCMV and HMS *Abdiel*) left Rosyth on passage to the Gulf supported by RFA *Regent*.

12 August: Operation Cimnel – mine clearance operation – HMS *Abdiel* and the four 'Hunt' class MCMVs arrived off Fujairah – *Diligence* to provide engineering and logistic support, *Regent* remains close by with logistic support and a helicopter.

13 August: *Diligence* recalled for service from around the Falkland Islands to act as support ship for the 'Hunt' class MCMVs during the Iran-Iraq war.

September: Alcohol abuse prevention – National Officer from Accept joined RFA *Resource* for a short acquaint voyage. RFA commence a period of RAS and fuel management training to Royal New Zealand Navy personnel prior to the commissioning of their replenishment tanker HMNZS *Endeavour*.

November: Purple Warrior – biggest single maritime operation for British forces since the Falklands War, controlled from a tri-service Joint Force HQ at HMS *Warrior* – involved 39 ships with HMS *Ark Royal* and HMS *Illustrious* – RFAS *Fort Austin*, *Resource*, *Olmeda*,

RFA *Sir Galahad* (2)

MOD(NAVY) DESIGNED LANDING SHIP LOGISTICS
Pennant: L3005
Official number: 713026
Port of registry: London
Call sign: GABN
Builder: Swan Hunter, Wallsend
Machinery: Two Mirrlees-Blackstone 9 cyl KM9 Major Mk3 ICE, each driving a controllable pitch propeller through a reduction gearbox, each 6,600 bhp; 1,260 ton bunkers; 18 knots; bow thrusters
Dimensions (loa/bp x beam): 461/–ft x 65.08ft
Tonnage measurements: 8,900 grt, 3,077 dwt
Displacement: 8,585 tons full load
Complement: 53 + troop lift of 339

RFA *Sir Galahad* (2) running builder's trials under the Red Ensign. (RFA Archive)

Remarks: +100A1 +LMC, UMS, class I passenger ship; this new Ro-Ro landing ship, unlike her sisters, is fitted with a 50-tonne 'bow visor' door and a 22-tonne capacity scissor lift amidship to enable helicopters landing on her forward deck to be lowered into the vehicle deck below. She has the capacity for 18 main battle tanks, 20 heavy wheeled vehicles and up to 40 ISO containers, with two 8.5-tonne cranes to port and starboard forward and a 25-tonne crane forward of the bridge structure. She is designed to carry Mexeflotes.

RFA *Argus*

AVIATION TRAINING SHIP AND PRIMARY CASUALTY RECEIVING SHIP

Pennant: A135 **Official number:** 384837
Port of registry: London **Callsign:** GDSA
Builder: Cantieri Navali, Breda SA, Venice, Italy
Machinery: Two Pielstick 18PC2-5V ICE by Lindholmen each developing 11,700 bhp via reduction gearing to twin screws; 22 knots; bow thrust unit
Dimensions (loa/bp x beam): 567.07/–ft x 100.08ft
Tonnage measurements: 26,421 grt, 12,221 dwt
Displacement: 28,480 tons full load
Complement: 79 RFA + 38-man RN Naval Party 4167+ accommodation for 137
Remarks: +100A1; +LMC class +UMS. Originally built as a container ship with a 1,108 TEU capacity; converted by Harland & Wolff, Belfast into an aviation training ship with a 369 x 92ft flight deck with five landing spots and two lifts to a below deck hangar 370 x 90 x 20ft capable of taking up to eight Sea Harriers and three Sea King helicopters; the flight deck was built from the former hatch covers that were turned over and filled with 6 inches of concrete and covered in steel and the hangar was fitted with four sliding watertight doors. Extra accommodation was provided in a seven-tier box-like structure added to the original superstructure; fitted with extensive command and control including CANE AIO system, air weapons facilities and limited maintenance workshops. Deck letter AS.

During the 1990 Gulf War she took on what was traditionally the RFA's role – that of operating hospital ships – when she was fitted out as a Primary Casualty Receiving Ship (PCRS) with 100-bed emergency medical facilities. This hospital complex required a full chemical warfare protection system and was based on a PortaKabin® Duplex system. A modular system based on 11 'building blocks' containing – casualty reception, triage, resuscitation and holding, operating theatre with two surgical tables, post-operative recovery, 10-bed Intensive Therapy Unit, X-ray facilities, sterile supply, blood and biochemical laboratories. Filtered air was supplied from six standard frigate air-filteration units.

RFA *Argus* is termed by the Royal Naval Medical Service as Third Line Support. During 2000/2001 she underwent a major refit of her permanent hospital facilities. Now based over three decks her 100-bed air conditioned hospital is in three categories – 10-bed intensive care, 20-bed high dependency and 70-bed wards, supported by three operating theatres, a specialist head injury theatre, CT scanner unit and the standard X-ray, sterile and laboratory facilities. Physiotherapy, pharmaceutical, dental and mental health facilities are also provided. Her medical staffing is complex and ranges from a basic team of eight to around 200 doctors, surgeons, QARNNS nurses, medical assistants, medical support staff and Royal Marines Bandsmen as stretcher-bearers and NBCD monitoring and decontamination. This includes support from the RNR and the QARNNS(R) with some specialities from the Army and RAF; for example, Laboratory Technicians come from the RFA Medical Services. An RAF air evacuation team may also be carried.

The aviation support ships RFA *Argus*, formerly the container ship *Contender Bezant*. (RFA Archive)

During Operation Telic (March–April 2003) RFA *Argus*, with four Sea King helicopters from 820 NAS embarked, operated as a PCRS in the Gulf providing vital surgical and medical support to injured Coalition and Iraqi forces and civilian personnel.

Olwen, *Sir Bedivere*, *Sir Geraint*, *Sir Lancelot*, *Sir Percivale*, *Sir Tristram*.

7–8 November: MoD(Navy) approved for the RFA to be represented at the Royal British Legion service of remembrance in the Royal Albert Hall and at the Cenotaph in London with one officer, one senior rate and up to eight ratings; first public appearance of the RFA ratings' uniform.

25 November: *Sir Galahad* (2), landing ship logistic (replacement), completed by Swan Hunter at Wallsend for MoD(Navy) at a cost of £40 million.

December: A three-day communications security course trialled by RFA with GCHQ Cheltenham.

18 December: *Fort George* ordered.

31 December: The Merchant Navy privilege of permitting wives to be carried on RFAs started to be phased out.

1988

1988: Ratings Consolidated Salary introduced for all contract rates and it involves improved pension arrangements and overtime and majority of allowances are consolidated and RFA introduced a Direct Entry adult rating scheme. Cubits semi-automatic navigational plotting aid introduced into the RFA. *Sir Lancelot* only remaining RFA with a Hong Kong Chinese crew.

1 January: All RFA Petty Officers and ratings who are defensive weapons qualified will be paid the Defensive Weapon Allowance regardless of whether their ship is actually fitted or not.

21 January: RFA Chaplain – the Chaplain of the Fleet agreed to the appointment of a RFA Chaplain, based at Portsmouth, this sea-going position was first held by the Rev. Roger Bennett on a two-year trial appointment.

3 March: *Argus* conversion completed at a cost of £45 million.

18 March: *Argus* formally accepted by MoD(Navy) to carry out extensive trials.

April: Consolidated Rating Salary agreed and included the introduction of the naval rate of Leading Hand.

May: *Green Rover* laid up in reserve at Portsmouth. Rating Helicopter Controllers – announced that the RFA was to introduce Rating Helicopter Controllers – aptitude assessment at HMS *Osprey*, three-week radar training at Warsash and one week transit controller training at *Osprey*; later the course was to include an aircraft controllers' module at HMS *Dryad*; both transit and tactical control training is available, the tactical control is one week at *Osprey*, three weeks at

Outback 88: the tanker RFA *Olwen* (centre) with RFA *Fort Grange* and the destroyer HMS *Edinburgh*. (RFA Archive)

RFA Officers

Insignia	Rank	Seaman	Specialisation suffix Marine Engineering	Systems Engineering	Supply
Broad band	Commodore RFA	X	E		
4 rings	Captain RFA	X	E	SE	S
3 rings	Chief Officer RFA	X	E	SE	S
2½ rings	First Officer RFA	X	E	SE	S
2 rings	Second Officer RFA	X	E	SE	S
1 ring	Third Officer RFA	X	E	SE	S
½ ring	Fourth Officer RFA		E	SE	
Lapel	Officer Cadet	X	E		

The Surgeon Chief Officer RFA is a 3 ringer.
The specialization suffixes (C) or (L) will be used in addition to SE to denote Communications and Electrical specialists within the Systems Engineer structure, for example, SE(C) and SE(L).
Fourth Officer in the RFA will be progressively phased out.

RFA Senior officers

New title	*Abbreviation*	*Current definition(s)*
Commanding Officer	CO	Captain
Chief Engineer Officer	CEO	Marine Engineer Officer (MEO)
Executive Officer	XO	Chief Officer (Choff)
Marine Engineer Officer	MEO	Senior Engineer Officer (SEO)
Systems Engineer Officer	SEO	new title
Communications Officer	SE(C)	First Officer (Communications) or (Senior) Radio Officer
Electrical Officer	SE(L)	First Officer (Electrical) or (Senior) Electrical Officer
Supply Officer	SO	First Officer (Supply) or (Senior) Supply Officer
Medical Officer	MO	Senior Medical Officer (SMO) or Doctor

Dryad plus the 11-week aircraft controller course.

June–December: Outback 88 – a group deployment to the Far East, Australia and the Indian Ocean to coincide with Australia's bi-centennial celebrations. HMS *Ark Royal* led the group including RFA *Olwen*, RFA *Orangeleaf* and RFA *Fort Grange*.

June: *Sir Caradoc* returned to her owners, sold the following month and renamed *Stamveien*. RFA deck officer loaned to the Royal New Zealand Navy to advise with RAS trials being conducted by their new replenishment tanker HMNZS *Endeavour*.

1 June: RFA *Argus* entered service as training ship based at Portland.

1 July: RFA *Diligence* transfers to Operation Calendar II (a continuation of Operation Cimnel) as Western European Union mine clearance operation gets underway –

3 September: *Diligence* involved in providing assistance to the Type 42 destroyer HMS *Southampton* after she had been in collision with the container ship *Tor Bay*.

13–20 September: Humanitarian relief – Hurricane Gilbert hits Grand Cayman and Jamaica – the tanker *Oakleaf* supports HMS *Active*.

15 September: *Fort Victoria*, lead ship of the new auxiliary oiler replenishment (AOR) design, laid down in the Building Dock at Harland & Wolff, Belfast.

7 November: *Diligence* transfers from Operation Calendar to Armilla Patrol.

7 December: Falklands Islands 1982 Battle Honour presented to RFA *Sir Galahad* (2) at Marchwood.

1989

February: *Engadine* handed over aviation training duties to RFA *Argus*, at Portland.

9 March: *Fort George*, AOR, laid down.

31 March: *Engadine* laid up at Devonport for disposal; *Sir Lancelot* paid off at Marchwood for disposal.

May: Captain R M Thorn RFA appointed Commodore RFA, rated Assistant Director level with executive authority. Supply Petty Officer – new grade introduced into the RFA, believed to have first been used destoring RFA *Sir Lancelot* in April.

1 June: Humanitarian aid – *Olna* assisted the blazing Greek tanker *Drastirios* (48,686/1968) 300 miles southeast of Fujairah. *Sir Lancelot* sold commercially and renamed *Lowland Lancer*.

26 June: *Argus* recovered a man lost

overboard from the Russian tanker *Apie*, 120 miles east of Madeira.

July: RFA *Argus* refitted to improve her aviation standards.

5 July: Replenishment at Sea – *Appleleaf* (3) undertakes her last operational RAS with HMS *Cornwall*.

1 August: New RFA officer common rank structure with specialisation suffixes and a navalised nomenclature for senior officer was approved by HM The Queen and new job titles for head of departments introduced.

8 August: Humanitarian aid – *Fort Austin* provided assistance in Bermuda in the aftermath of Hurricane Dean.

17–24 September: Humanitarian assistance – *Brambleleaf* supporting HMS *Alacrity* as West Indies Guardship provided assistance to Montserrat, St Kitts, Nevis and Tortola in the wake of Hurricane Hugo; resulted in the awards of one OBE and one MBE.

24 September: *Appleleaf* (3) bareboat charter expired, transferred to the Royal Australian Navy.

9 October: *Appleleaf* (3) officially renamed HMAS *Westralia*.

8 November Order-in-Council 1989, Merchant Shipping, Ships and Shipowners – The Merchant Shipping (MoD) Ships Order and letter of intent to the Department of Transport – 'this Order makes provision for the registration under the Merchant Shipping Acts 1894-1988 of ships belonging to the Secretary of State for Defence and in the service of the Ministry of Defence, and for certain modifications and exceptions in the application of those Acts to such ships. By section 47 of the Merchant Shipping Act 1988, this Order and the provisions of the Merchant Shipping Acts applied by it (both as modified by that section) apply also to United Kingdom registered ships in the service of the Ministry of Defence by reason of a charter by demise to the Crown. The Order does not apply to ships forming part of Her Majesty's Navy'.

The business end of RFA *Sir Galahad* (1). (RFA Archive)

Stores Personnel on RFAs

The shipborne stores personnel, under the management of a Stores Officer (STO(N)) is a team of non-industrial and industrial civil servants from the Naval Bases and Supply Agency (formerly Royal Naval Supply and Transport Service), seconded from dockyards and stores depots – normally serving afloat for tours of 12 to 18 months. Their responsibilities include the receipt, custody and issue of the 'cargo' until it leaves the RFA vessel. This means they manage the holds (warehouses), the environment of individual holds and the mechanical handling equipment that move stores to the RAS transfer points. This working party – SOG (Stores Officer Grades), storehousemen, clerical officers, fork lift drivers etc, sign Ship's articles like all other crew members and are absorbed into the Ship's company. Prior to 1965, each Department – Naval, Victualling, Armament Supply – ran its own separate world inside the RFA.

1990

1990: Armament – the fitting of laser weapons on RFAs was discussed. Aviation – Royal Fleet Auxiliary Support Unit created at HMS *Seahawk* to replace the RFA Aviation Support Unit.

January–December: South Atlantic and Antarctica – one RFA tanker support maintained, as required, to support British presence in the area.

9 February: *Engadine* sold commercially and towed to Falmouth, name unchanged.

4 May: *Fort Victoria* floated in the Harland & Wolff Building Dock, Belfast.

1 June–August: Operation Eldorado – precautionary deployment off Liberia of RFA *Tidespring* supporting HM Ships to undertake any evacuations from the civil war.

5 June: *Sir Percivale* sailed Devonport to act as support ship alongside in Freetown, providing accommodation and stores support for the British Army.

12 June: *Fort Victoria* formally named.

2 August Iraq invades Kuwait – RFA *Orangeleaf* on Armilla Patrol supporting HMS *York*.

4 August: United Nations Security Council passes Resolution 660

condemning the invasion.

8 August: Decision taken to deploy RFAs *Fort Grange*, *Olna* and *Diligence* to the Gulf; *Fort Grange* deploying a flight of two Sea King HC 4 aircraft of 846 NAS.

9 August: Operation Granby (the Gulf War) approved.

14 August: *Diligence* diverted from the South Atlantic for service in the Gulf.

17 August: *Olna* left UK, embarking two Sea King HAS 5 helicopters from C Flight, 826 NAS; aircraft later deployed to RFA *Sir Galahad* to assist in mine countermeasures.

22 August: *Fort Grange* left Devonport for the Gulf, with two Sea King HC4 helicopters 846 NAS embarked.

25 August: United Nations Security Council Resolution 665 approves military action to enforce economic sanctions on Iraq.

1 September: *Gold Rover* lost her rudder in severe weather in the South Atlantic and some of her crew were airlifted off.

4 September: *Diligence* arrived Mombasa for storing.

6 September: Terrorist activity – *Fort Victoria*, at Belfast, suffered a bomb blast in her engine room, no casualties.

27–28 September: RFAs *Sir Bedivere* (from Emden) and *Sir Tristram* (from Marchwood) plus some chartered merchant ships depart with equipment and supplies for the 7th Armoured Brigade

8 October: *Sir Galahad* sailed Marchwood Military Port for the Gulf.

10 October: *Sir Percivale* sailed Marchwood Military Port for the Gulf.

17 October: *Resource* sailed Emden with Army Emergency Munitions Reserves for service in the Gulf.

29 October: *Argus*, deploying as the Primary Casualty Evacuation Ship in the Gulf, suffered a steering gear breakdown and had to return to Devonport for repairs.

31 October: *Argus* sailed Devonport for the gulf, embarking four Sea King HC 4 helicopters from C and D flights of 846 NAS.

Women at Sea

In 1990 the RFA set up a study to cover employing Wrens on RFAs, women in RFA service and with STO(N) organisation. In 1991 during Operation Granby the senior medical officer on RFA *Argus* was female. In 1992 a female surgeon chief officer was appointed to RFA *Olwen* and in 1993 the first female officer cadets went to Warsash and later to the Cadet Training Unit on RFA *Fort Austin*.

Operation Granby

RFA ships deployed:

RFA *Olna*
RFA *Orangeleaf*
RFA *Bayleaf*
RFA *Resource*
RFA *Fort Grange*
RFA *Sir Galahad*
RFA *Sir Tristram*
RFA *Sir Percivale*
RFA *Sir Bedivere*
RFA *Diligence*
RFA *Argus*

The role of the Armilla Patrol is to enforce the embargoes on Iraq and protect shipping in the Gulf area from attack. The Royal Navy deploy a frigate, a destroyer and one RFA support vessel in the area. After the war RFA *Brambleleaf* became the duty RFA on a two-year deployment with rotated crew.

1991

1991: BR 875, the RFA Handbook, also known as 'The Bible' was rewritten in four volumes, – Administration – Operating Standards – Warfare – Ship maintenance and repairs. Formal award of Battle Honour – Gulf War 1991 – to 11 RFAs. RFA Way Ahead Study commissioned.

10 January: RFAs *Olmeda* and *Regent*

RFA Naval Support Unit (RFANSU)

The RFANSU was created in 1990 at RNAS Culdrose (HMS *Seahawk*) replacing the RFAASU to undertake a greater aviation support role and expand it to cover the 'Fort' class AORs and RFA *Argus*. Its primary purpose is to supply suitably qualified General Service and Fleet Air Arm personnel to work, maintain and operate all RN controlled departments on RFAs. To provide meteorological staff to RFAs as required supporting flying operations. It also provides a central organisation to administer and control personnel and equipment required to support in-service RFAs, including RFA Aviation Support Portable Workshops for the 'Tide' class.

This is the one point of contact between the RFA and RN for administration. Originally a small engineering support unit covering Sea King helicopters on the back of RFAs. Aim of this 150 strong team is to place small teams with ships to provide the kind of support that is present in the ship's company of an aircraft carrier but not in an RFA, and by being flexible ships can be kept at sea longer. Responsible for all RN personnel embarked in RFAS (including administration, *ie* pay, drafting, expenses, Divisional matters etc). Three teams cover the permanent positions on the AORs, adapted to support the Merlin helicopter. RFANSU 150 strong dealing with 8–10 ships.

Support goes further than helicopter controllers and air engineering – electrical and communications specialists – weapon engineering staff to look after defensive systems, such as, the Phalanx CIWS, Metoc staff for flying and RAS operations.

sailed UK for service in the Gulf.

23 January: *Bayleaf* sailed UK to relieve *Orangeleaf* in the Gulf.

22 February: HRH Prince Edward visited RFA headquarters at Empress State Building to visit the Casualty Cell.

1 March: *Fort George* launched at Wallsend.

8 March: Humanitarian aid – in the Adriatic Sea, RFA *Olmeda* stood by the motor vessel *Legend*, heavily laden with refugees from Albania.

20 April–15 July: Humanitarian relief – Operation Haven – RFAs *Argus* and *Resource* on humanitarian support to Kurdish refugees in the Turkey/Iraq frontier area, supported by Royal Marines Units, Lynx AH7 and Gazelle AH1 aircraft of 3 Commando Brigade Air Squadron and Sea Kings from NAS 845 and 846 and RAF Chinook helicopters.

May: *Diligence* returns to the South Atlantic.

8 May–3 June: Humanitarian relief – Operation Manna – RFA *Fort Grange* humanitarian relief operations in Bangladesh following major damage and flooding in wake of a cyclone.

August: 50th anniversary Arctic convoys – RFA *Tidespring* and the frigate HMS *London* were earmarked to visit Soviet Arctic ports to mark the anniversary of first Allied convoys to Murmansk and Archangel – cancelled owing to 'coup' in Soviet Union.

Operation Granby – RN helicopter sorties flow from RFAs

25 August 1990–16 January 1991 – blockade and build-up

Sea King 5	389	from RFA *Olna* and HMNethMS *Zuiderkruis*
Sea King 4	524	from RFA *Argus* (4 aircraft)
Sea King 4	313	from RFA *Fort Grange* (2 aircraft)

17 January 1991–28 February – Operation Desert Storm

Sea King 5	128	from RFA s *Olna* and *Sir Galahad*
Sea King 4	502	from RFA s *Argus* and *Fort Grange*

RFA *Fort Grange* with a Sea King helicopter on the emergency landing deck on her hangar roof. (RFA Archive)

31 August: Operation Granby completed and forces reduced – one RFA tanker supporting Armilla Patrol.

19 December: Navy Board agreed a set of proposals for the way ahead on the management of the RFA service.

1992

1992: Humanitarian support – *Resource* and *Fort Grange* were heavily involved in support to the Mileva Tomec and Rudine Institute orphanages in Split whilst based there until 2000. *Regent* laid up at Devonport with maintenance crew aboard. *Resource* laid up at Rosyth with maintenance crew aboard.

1 January: RFAs allocated BFPO numbers.

12 February: Changes to the management of the RFA made by ministerial announcement in the form of a Parliamentary Written Answer.

1 April: Scheme introduced to recognise and award Meritorious Conduct in the RFA. *Olmeda* introduces the Warsash Manning Trial with departmental flexible manning for ratings, brings communication ratings into the radio room; the maintenance manager concept introduced in 1991 was used with the introduction of the Systems Engineering concept; the ship's communications officer (part of the SE Branch) was to be assisted by a Yeoman and signalmen and three rating radio operators, the rate of Leading Hand was being trialled.

7 April: *Green Rover* purchased by her builders, who then sold her to the Indonesian Navy for further service; renamed *Arun*.

8 April: Humanitarian aid – *Gold Rover* and HMS *Campbeltown* assist the tanker *World Hitachi Zosen* which was on fire after a collision off West Africa.

9 April: *Arun* towed from Portsmouth to the Tyne for refurbishment –

30 April: NATO's Standing Naval Force Mediterranean

RFA *Fort Victoria* represents the new 'one stop shop' concept of the AOR (auxiliary oiler replenishment). (RFA Archive)

(STANAVFORMED) is activated to provide a continuous maritime presence; the RFA occasionally contributes the supporting oiler.

May: Orient 92 RN/RFA deployment with *Fort Austin* and *Olwen*, the first major deployment to the Far East since Outback 88.

29 June: *Fort Victoria* sailed from Belfast for contractor's sea trials – two years later than originally planned.

6 July: *Fort Victoria* arrived Birkenhead for completion and rectification of damage sustained during sea trials.

14–28 August: Humanitarian relief – *Orangeleaf* supported HM Ships *Cardiff* and *Campbeltown* in West Indies operation in the wake of Hurricane Andrew.

October: *Regent* is placed on the ship disposal list.

October–December: Operation Grapple – RFAs sailed to the Adriatic to support British element of the UN Protection Force in the former Yugoslavia – *Sir Bedivere* and *Resource*, reactivated from reserve, based in Croatian port of Split, *Argus* with a flight of four Sea Kings embarked.

1993

January–December: Operations Grapple and Hamden – Adriatic 1993–94 – British and allied forces ashore in Bosnia on peacekeeping and humanitarian aid duties needed support – Task Force 612 led by HMS *Ark Royal* with RFA *Fort Grange* embarking two Sea King Js from 820 NAS and RFA *Olwen* with two Sea Kings from 820 NAS, RFA *Argus* acting as an interim LPH with units, such as 29 Commando Regiment Royal Artillery, *Bayleaf*, *Orangeleaf* and *Olna* providing support at sea –

This aerial view shows the complex deck layout of the small fleet tanker *Blue Rover*. (RFA Archive)

Resource (later *Fort Grange*) and *Sir Percivale* replaced *Sir Bedivere* providing support facilities in Split.
15 January: *Regent* sold for scrap and renamed *Shahzadelal* for the delivery run to the breakers.
21 January: *Shahzadelal* sailed Devonport under her own steam for the breakers.
19 February: *Shahzadelal* arrived Alang for demolition.
March: *Blue Rover* purchased by the Portuguese Navy.
31 March: *Blue Rover* officially handed over to the Portuguese Navy at Portsmouth; renamed NRP *Berrio*.
1 April: The result of the RFA Way Ahead Study saw the reorganisation of the RFA with the demise of DST (SF) (Directory Supply & Transport) (Ships and Fuel) as a Civil Service post that (under various titles) has 'headed up' the RFA since August 1905 and introduction of the Type Commander (RFA Flotilla) role for the Commodore RFA within the CINCFLEET; headquarters remained in Empress State Building, London until new offices became available at Portsmouth Naval Base; the operational command of *Argus* was also handed back from Flag Officer Surface Flotilla (previously known as the Flag Officer Third Flotilla); the established titles of Marine Superintendent and Technical Superintendent were replaced by Chief Staff Officer.
5 April: *Fort Victoria* sailed Birkenhead, still incomplete.
7 April: *Fort Victoria* arrived Portsmouth for completion and defect rectification.
March: Aviation – Operation Hamden/Grapple – four Sea King 4s vice RFA *Argus* disembarked to *Fort Austin*.
May: Operation Hamden/Grapple – *Orangeleaf* replaced *Olwen* for a self-maintenance period. 50th anniversary of the Battle of the Atlantic, HM The Queen attended a service at Liverpool Cathedral and *Olmeda* was present.
4 May: *Argus* docks at Split.
15 July: *Fort George* completed and formally commissioned the following day.
4 August: *Fort Victoria* sailed from Portsmouth for trials after completion.
23 September–9 December: Humanitarian aid – Operation Snowdon – *Oakleaf* supported HMS *Active* in the international interdiction operation during

'Fort' (3) class

MOD(NAVY)-DESIGNED AOR

RFA *Fort George* **Pennant no:** A388
RFA *Fort Victoria* **Pennant no:** A387

Builder: Harland & Wolff , Belfast (A387) and Swan Hunter Shipbuilding (A388)

Machinery: Two 16 cyl Crossley Pielstick type 16 PC2.6 ICE; 23,600 hp; two shafts; 22 knots; bow thruster

Dimensions (loa/bp x beam): 667.7/607ft x 95.7ft

Tonnage measurements: 28,820 grt, 16,060 dwt

Displacement: 35,500 tons full load

Complement: 95 RFA + 24 civilian stores party + 90-man RN party

The auxiliary oiler replenishment RFA *Fort George.* (RFA Archive)

Remarks: +1001A; +LMC class +UMS, ice class. Officially known as AORs, these large versatile vessels are 'one-stop ships', that is they combine the role of fleet oiler and stores ship, designed to meet high and demanding naval standards with low radar cross section and acoustic signature.

Cargo capacity 10,000 cubic metres of fuel and 3,000 cubic metres of dry cargo including munitions. Fitted amidships with four dual-purpose RAS rigs and one Hudson reel for astern fuelling. Fitted with comprehensive command and control facilities – operations room, Type 996 surveillance radar and full NBCD arrangements. Hospital arrangements include a 12-bed hospital. These AORs have extensive aviation facilities with a large two spot flight deck, hangar and maintenance facilities capable of embarking and sustaining up to four large Merlin helicopters. These high-value units have defensive facilities that include 30mm cannon, two Phalanx CIWS and four Sea Gnat and the Type 182 decoy systems.

Uniforms

RFA uniform for ratings, first approved in 1987, was resurrected by the Type Commander and rate badges – basic rate, Leading Hand, Petty Officer and Chief Petty Officer approved with specialisation badges for Seamanship, Marine Engineering, Cook/Steward and Systems.

See colour plates for illustrations

political problems in Haiti.

1 December: Medical Administration Officer appointed to COMRFA staff.

1994

January: *Olmeda* laid up in Portsmouth for disposal. Personnel management of the RFA service has been delegated to RFA headquarters (aka RFA Bureau).

January–December: Operation Hamden – Adriatic – carrier group providing maritime support to British elements with the UN Protection Force in the former Yugoslavia with two RFAs (*Resource* replaced by *Fort Grange*) and one LSL based in Split.

April: RFA *Grey Rover* on patrol off South Georgia rescued single-handed yachtswoman Anne Lise Guy and her boat *Wildflower*.

24 April: *Fort Grange* on Operation Grapple based at Split; the LSL was withdrawn.

May: Captain N D Squire CBE RFA appointed Commodore RFA.

10 May: *Grey Rover* assisted the 28 surviving crew of the Chilean vessel *Firo Sure V* after a severe fire had killed two and injured many; escorted it back to Grytviken in South Georgia.

June: *Sir Bedivere* and *Sir Galahad* in Caen and *Sir Percivale* at the Spithead Review to mark the 50th anniversary of D-Day.

1 June: RFA Medical branch adopted the RN medical store system.

July: *Sir Bedivere* arrived Rosyth for her Ship Life Extension Programme (SLEP).

5 July: *Olmeda* sold for scrap and renamed *Niaxco* for the delivery run to the breakers.

19 July: *Niaxco* sailed Portsmouth under her own steam for the breakers.

17 August: *Niaxco* arrived Alang for demolition.

31 August: Official badge of the Commodore RFA approved.

3 September: Humanitarian aid – *Argus* rescues family from their yacht that had struck rocks whilst on passage Brittany to Milford Haven.

The 'Slepped' *Sir Bedivere*

Sir Bedivere's SLEP contract was placed with Babcock Rosyth Dockyard Ltd. Designed to extend her working life by up to 15 years, her hull was lengthened, substantial steelwork replaced, the bow doors strengthened and now hydraulically operated, additional accommodation added together with improved stowage and operational facilities, *eg* for securing ISO containers; a new 25-tonne crane in front of the bridge; the flight deck has been lowered and upgraded to handle the new Merlin helicopters and the forward helicopter deck is 'Chinook' capable. She has been re-engined with two 12 cyl Stork-Wartsila SW280 four stroke, turbo-charged ICE driving her original propellers at 17 knots; she has significantly improved machinery arrangements that includes a control and surveillance management system for unmanned operation. *Sir Bedivere* now has two bow thrusters, full NBCD citadel protection and meets the latest SOLAS requirements for a passenger ships, *eg* enclosed lifeboats. The most obvious aspect is that her superstructure, funnel and mainmast are angled to reduce the radar cross section. Her defensive armament has been upgraded and her lifeboat davits are able to handle LCVPs and she continues to lift and stow mexiflotes. Because of her age this was a difficult job which took longer and cost more than projected. Revised statistics – length oa 449ft, beam 59.8ft, 6,700 tonnes displacement full load, RFA crew 49, troop lift 340.

RFA *Sir Bedivere* seen here after being rebuilt in her 'ship life extension programme'. (RFA Archive)

17–30 September: Operation Spartan – *Oakleaf* supported HM Ships in UN Maritime interdiction operations off Haiti.

9 October–15 November: Operation Driver – deployment of Armilla patrol to the Northern Gulf – *Bayleaf* supporting three HM Ships.

10 November: Humanitarian aid – *Brambleleaf* and HMS *Leeds Castle* assisted in the rescue of a French transatlantic yachtsman.

12 December: *Resource* on Operation Grapple replaced *Fort Grange* at Split.

1995

1995: The International Convention on Standards of Training, Certification and Watchkeeping is amended and known as STCW 95.

January–December: South Atlantic and Falkland Islands – RFA support to HM Ships in the protection of British interests, included RFA tanker. Operation Hamden – Adriatic – carrier group providing maritime support to British elements with the UN Protection Force in the former Yugoslavia; first time RN force placed under NATO command in operational situation; *Resource* based in Split.

14–15 March: *Olna* rescues four crew from the motor vessel *Pelhunter* that later sank in the Ionian Sea.

30 March: The Westland Wessex HU5 helicopter (XT480) involved in evacuation of the burning *Sir Galahad* on 8 June 1982 became the 'gate guard display' at RNAS Fleetlands, painted in the original RFA *Regent* operational colours it wore around 1969 with fin code RF.

6 April–21 August: Humanitarian aid – Operation Chantress – *Sir Galahad* on four-month deployment in Lobito, Angola to provide assistance to UK elements of UN stabilisation forces.

21 July: FOST Portland closes and transfers to HMS *Drake*, Plymouth.

September: *Sir Tristram*, followed shortly by *Fort Grange*, both undertaking a 'continuation operational sea training' (COST) package, are the first RFAs to use FOST Plymouth.

6–15 September: Humanitarian aid – *Oakleaf* supporting HMS *Southampton* provided repair teams to Anguilla after Hurricane Luis had devastated the area.

1996

January–20 November: Operation Hamden – Adriatic – carrier group providing maritime support to NATO elements with the Implementation Force (IFOR) in the former Yugoslavia; first time RN force placed under NATO command in operational situation; *Resource* based in Split.

February: COMRFA takes the salute at the HMS *Raleigh*'s basic training passing out parade of new ratings to the Royal Navy.

18 March: *Celestine* (later to become *Sea Crusader*) laid down.

April: Exercise RUKUS906 – first joint exercises with Royal Navy, US Navy and Russian Navy were conducted of the UK south coast and *Black Rover* supported HMS *Gloucester*.

11–17 April: *Gold Rover* off Liberia to assist in evacuation of UK/US nationals from Monrovia; the RFA was under the tactic command of the US Joint Task Force.

7 June: *Celestine* launched at Sakaide, Japan for commercial owners.

28 June: Humanitarian aid – *Olwen* provided a boarding party to assist in flooding control in Russian cruise liner *Alla Tarasova* off Fraserburgh.

1 August: Joint Rapid Deployment Force (JRDF) formed.

18 August–18 November: *Diligence* in South Atlantic.

17 September: *Celestine*, Ro-Ro strategic sealift, 23,986 grt, length oa 528.2ft, completed by Kawasaki Heavy industries; main machinery two Kawasaki MAN ICE; bareboat charter to MoD(Navy) for two years signed.

10 October: *Celestine* handed over at Sakaide and renamed RFA *Sea Crusader*

16 October: Humanitarian aid – *Gold Rover* rescues three St Vincent nationals adrift in open boat.

21–23 October: HMS *Invincible*'s Sea Harriers conduct operations in Adriatic supported by RFAs *Oakleaf* and *Fort Grange*.

1997

1997: STCW 95 is amended, still known as STCW 95. UK forces supported the Stabilisation Force (SFOR) in the former Republic of Yugoslavia; RFA *Resource* based in Spilt (on Operation Grapple since 12 December 1994, replaced by *Fort Grange* on 5 April) to provide logistic support to the UK land forces attached to Operation Lodestar; the RFA conducted regular re-supply.

January–December: Armilla Patrol and Operation Bolton – Gulf of Oman and Persian Gulf – RFA tanker support to HM Ships providing a British presence in the region to protect British shipping and contribute to the UN embargo of Iraq imposed after the Gulf War.

13 January: Exercise Ocean Wave 97 – a 20-ship RN/RFA Task Group led by the carrier HMS *Illustrious* deployed to the Asia-Pacific region and included RFAs *Fort Austin*, *Fort George*, *Olna*, *Sir Galahad*, *Sir Percivale*, *Sir Geraint* and *Diligence*.

1 March: Replenishment at Sea – *Bayleaf* in collision with Royal Yacht *Britannia* during a RAS off Karachi.

12 March: *Wave Knight* (2) and *Wave Ruler* (2), new fleet oilers, ordered from Vickers Shipbuilding and Engineering Ltd (VSEL).

5 April: *Fort Grange* arrived Split to replace *Resource* as logistic support (accommodation ship and floating warehouse).

14 April: *Resource* at Split since 12 December 1994 is relieved by *Fort Grange*.

1 May: *Resource* arrived Devonport to destore for disposal, having been one of the few British units to have participated in all four phase of British operation in the Balkans –

UNPROFOR (UN Protection Force), UNCRO (UN Forces in Croatia), IFOR (the Implementation Force set up by the peace agreement) and SFOR (the Stabilisation Force).

May–29 August: Humanitarian aid – RFA *Black Rover* and HMS *Liverpool* in the vicinity of Montserrat during and after major volcanic eruptions; Operation Caxton – voluntary evacuation arrangements.

June: *Resource* sold to Electra Maritime (London) Ltd for scrap and renamed *Resourceful* for the delivery run to the breakers.

24 June: *Resourceful* sailed Devonport for the breakers.

2–10 June: RFA *Argus* off west Africa as a contingency covering Operation Tiller in Sierra Leone and at notice for possible evacuation of British nationals from the Congo (Brazzaville).

30 June: Hong Kong – final handover to the People's Republic of China; HMS *Chatham*, Hong Kong Squadron (HM Ships *Peacock*, *Plover*, *Starling*) and RFA *Sir Percivale* sail past the Royal Yacht *Britannia*. *Sir Percivale* was the last RFA out prior to the handover.

20 August: *Resourceful* arrived Alang for demolition.

26 August: Humanitarian aid – Bay of Biscay – RFA *Fort Austin* in company with HMS *Illustrious* stood by the French tanker *Once* with an engine-room fire.

10 October: Humanitarian aid – Bay of Biscay – RFA *Oakleaf* in company with HMS *Herald* provided medical assistance to injured yachtsman, who was transferred to RFA *Oakleaf* and then by helicopter to Spain.

14–30 October: Humanitarian aid – RFA *Orangeleaf* in company with HMS *Monmouth* and FS *Surcouf* – off West Africa (Pointe Noire) in readiness for evacuation during deteriorating political situation in the Congo.

14 November–31 December: Persian Gulf – HMS *Invincible* accompanied by RFA *Fort Victoria* deployed to enforce UN resolution against Iraq – Operation Bolton.

Aviation support ship and primary casualty receiving ship RFA *Argus*. (RFA Archive)

1998

1998: *Stena Ausonia* (later to become *Sea Centurion*) launched at Viareggio for commercial owners, resold before completion and renamed *Und Ege*.

1 January–17 April: Operation Bolton was the Mediterranean and later Gulf deployment that included HMS *Invincible* and RFA *Fort Victoria* in support of UN operations against Iraq; group joined with the Armilla Patrol ships including RFAs *Fort George*, *Bayleaf*, *Brambleleaf* and the forward repair ship RFA *Diligence*; the 'Fort' class RFAs deployed up to five Sea King helicopters.

2 February: Humanitarian aid – *Argus* rescued 13 survivors from the sunken Spanish container ship *Delfin Del Mediterraneo* (4,614/1979) 400 miles west of Gibraltar after her containers had shifted in heavy weather.

11 February–20 March: Humanitarian aid – Operation Resilient – RFA *Orangeleaf* supporting the West Africa Deployment Ship HMS *Monmouth*, later HMS *Cornwall*, standing by to evacuate UK nationals and assist UK High Commissioner during civil war in Sierra Leone.

May: *Sea Chieftain* officially named – due to enter service in April 1999 – contact later cancelled owing to delays at the shipyard.

6 May: Humanitarian aid – *Diligence* in the Gulf of Aden provided medical assistance to the *Leros Star* that had come under small arms fire off Somalia.

22 May: *Wave Knight* laid down.

12–25 June: *Oakleaf* supporting HMS *Cornwall* off coast of Sierra Leone.

12 July: Humanitarian aid – the MV *Anestine Mac* that had engine failure was towed to Montserat by *Black Rover*.

22–23 September: Humanitarian relief – *Black Rover* supporting HMS *Sheffield* in St Kitts and Montserrat following Hurricane Georges.

31 October–3 November: Humanitarian relief – *Black Rover* supporting HMS *Sheffield* in Honduran offshore islands following Hurricane Mitch.

2–4 November: Humanitarian aid – *Gold Rover* supporting HMS *Sutherland* acted as a helicopter refuelling point, off South Georgia, during evacuation of seriously ill woman from MV *Explorer*.

17 December: Humanitarian relief – *Sir Tristram* arrived Marchwood Military Port after a West Indies deployment that included Operation Tellar – relief operations off the coasts of Honduras and Nicaragua following destruction and floods caused by Hurricane Mitch. RFA *Sir Tristram* was supporting Royal Marines from 45 Commando and Dutch marines. RFA *Black Rover*, and HM Ships *Ocean* and *Sheffield* were also in the area.

1999

1999: *Olwen* (2) withdrawn from service as a defence economy measure. *Olna* (3) withdrawn from service as a defence economy measure and laid up at Gibraltar. Humanitarian relief – *Black Rover* and *Sir Tristram* shared the Wilkinson Sword of Peace Award for their outstanding contribution made to the humanitarian aid operations in Honduras and Nicaragua.

12 January–March: *Oakleaf*, *Gold Rover* and *Grey Rover* supporting (at various times) HM Ships off Sierra Leone.

28 January: *Und Ege* bareboat-chartered to MoD(Navy) and was renamed RFA *Sea Centurion*.

30 January–1 April: Operation Magellan – *Brambleleaf* and *Fort Austin* in the Persian Gulf in an RN/RFA group deployed as a precautionary move to counter continuing Iraqi intransigence over compliance with UK Security Council resolutions.

March: Captain P J Lannin RFA appointed Commodore RFA and Assistant Chief of Staff (Sustainability).

24 March–20 May: Operation Magellan – UK Maritime forces including RFAs *Argus*, *Bayleaf* and *Fort Austin* contribute to NATO's Allied Force in former Republic of Yugoslavia /Kosovo in support of KFOR.

May: *Wave Ruler* laid down.

October: *Sea Centurion*, Stena 4-Runner class Ro-Ro strategic sealift ship, 21,000 grt, length 598ft, completed by Societa Esercizio Cantieri spa, Italy; main machinery four Sulzer 8ZA40S ICE; bareboat charter to MoD(N).

2000

6 January: *Fort Grange* on Operation Grapple at Split since April 1997 departs for the UK.

11 March: Humanitarian relief – *Fort George* with embarked units of NAS 820, supported the international relief and rescue effort to flood victims in Mozambique; distributed around 530 tons of food, water and equipment; for her work she was later awarded the Wilkinson Sword of Peace.

24 March: *Fort George* left Mozambique area.

May: *Olna* (3) reactivated for fleet support in place of *Fort George* which was serving off Sierra Leone.

May–April 2003: *Sir Geraint*, *Sir Tristram* and *Sir Percivale* all provided support alongside to British forces in Sierra Leone in Operation Palliser; *Sir Percivale*, with a field surgical team deployed provided the base for a special hostage rescue operation – Operation Barras.

1 June: *Fort Grange* renamed RFA *Fort Rosalie* (2) to obviate confusion with *Fort George*, flight deck code FE, A385.

28 June: *Fort Rosalie* (2) arrived Gibraltar to act as support and accommodation ship for the crew of the nuclear submarine HMS *Tireless* during her lengthy repairs.

July: Aviation – *Olna* conducted extensive trials with the new Merlin

Protection of Military Remains Act

In 2001 the Ministry of Defence declared its intention to designate 16 Controlled Sites and five Protection Places under the Protection of Military Remains Act 1986, following a public consultation into the protection provided to military maritime wrecks and in particular military maritime graves. Eleven of the Controlled Sites are maritime graves within UK waters and the other five are within UK jurisdiction. Of these five one is an undisclosed U-boat to represent all others lost within UK jurisdiction. A Controlled Site is a restricted area and a licence must be obtained before any activities, including diving, can be carried out on the site.

There are five ships in international waters deemed to be at immediate and significant risk that are designed as Protected Places – the HM Ships *Gloucester*, *Hood*, *Prince of Wales* and *Repulse* and the RFA *Sir Galahad*. Protected Places allow diving, but on a 'look, do not touch' basis. No licence is needed.

helicopter when operating to the west of the Outer Hebrides.

31 July: Replenishment at sea – *Olna* conducted her last RAS with HMS *Coventry*.

3 August: First qualifying day for the RFA Long Service Medal.

3 September: First Merchant Navy Day.

19 September: *Olwen* (2) sold for scrap.

24 September: *Olna* (3) laid up at Portsmouth for disposal.

28 September: *Wave Knight* formally named, launching delayed due to high winds.

29 September: *Wave Knight* launched at Barrow.

2 November: Amphibious Ready Group (ARG) – *Argus* diverted to join the ARG for operations off Sierra Leone as a replacement for HMS *Fearless* which suffered an engine room fire; the rest of the ARG comprised RFAs *Brambleleaf*, *Fort Austin*, *Sir Bedivere*, *Sir Galahad* and HM Ships *Ocean* and *Northumberland*.

19 November: £140 million contract to design and built two Alternative Landing Ships to replace the 'Sir' class LSLs – RFAs *Largs Bay* and *Lyme Bay* – placed with Swan Hunter (Tyneside), Wallsend.

2001

2001: Exercise Argonaut 2001 maritime deployment included Exercise Saif Sareea II and was 'billed' as the largest RN deployment since the Falklands (1982) with HMS *Illustrious* and involved RFAs *Fort Victoria* (deploying 5 helicopters from 820 NAS), *Oakleaf*, *Bayleaf*, *Fort Austin*, *Fort Rosalie*, amphibious group included RFAs *Sir Tristram*, *Sir Galahad*, *Sir Bedivere* and *Sir Percivale*, RFA *Diligence* acted as command and support ship to four MCMVs and to accompanying SSNs; strategic lift was provided by RFA *Sea Centurion* and RFA *Sea Crusader*. *Argus* refitted at Cammell Laird, Birkenhead during which she was fitted with a 96-berth self-contained hospital. *Olna* (3) sold for scrap.

2 February: *Olwen* (2) sailed Portsmouth in tow for the breakers.

9 February: *Wave Ruler* launched at Govan.

9 March: *Olna* (3) sailed Portsmouth in tow for the breakers.

April: Operation Silkman – *Sir Percivale* temporarily relieved by RFA *Sir Tristram* as support ship at Freetown, Sierra Leone; *Sir Tristram* subsequently relieved by *Sir Geraint*.

11 April: A team from *Diligence*

The ro-ro strategic lift ship RFA *Sea Centurion* on Southampton Water. (ANRS)

assisted in painting a school in a deprived area of Rio Grande in Brazil.

28 May: Commemorative postage stamps from South Georgia and the South Sandwich Islands released – a set of four RFA *Tidespring* (37p), RFA *Sir Percivale* (37p), RFA *Diligence* (43p) and RFA *Gold Rover* (43p).

August: Project NavStar – the deployment of communication and information services in naval vessels announced.

October: The Royal Fleet Auxiliary Service Medal Royal Warrant: presented to Parliament by the Secretary of State for Defence by Command of Her Majesty.

1 October: *Largs Bay* and *Lyme Bay* laid down.

7 October: US-led Operation Enduring Freedom (Afghanistan) begins.

November: £120 million contract to built two Alternative Landing Ships – RFAs *Cardigan Bay* and *Mounts Bay* – placed with BAE Systems Naval Ships, Govan.

8 November: Humanitarian aid – RFA *Fort George* awarded the Wilkinson Sword of Peace for her services off Mozambique in March 2000. The following quote is from the citation: '*Fort George* provide a mix of personnel from three different services: the RFA, the RN and the STO(N). This group of people gelled into an exceedingly efficient team using their skills and expertise on a concerted effort to provide the maximum aid and support to the population of Mozambique. This combination played a unique role in the international response. A United Nations representative later stated that this had been the most efficient operation he had seen in 15 years of relief work.'

13 November: Humanitarian aid – *Gold Rover* rescued four crew from the yacht *Bon Socour* in the North Atlantic.

16 November: Announcement of the RFA Long Service Medal.

19 November *Cardigan Bay* and *Mounts Bay* ordered.

RFA Long Service Medal

The RFA Service Medal for Long and Meritorious service was introduced for service on or after 3 August 2000. All contracted RFA personnel having completed 20 years good conduct qualify for this new medal. Clasps are awarded for further periods of 10 years service. This 36.07mm circular medal, originally planned to be struck in cupro-nickel and now in 925 Silver, is marked with name rank/rate and date of qualification.

The obverse is the crowed 'Wynne' effigy of HM Queen Elizabeth II with the wording 'ELIZABETH II DEI GRATIA REGINA FTD. DEF.' and the reverse is based on the RFA badge – a roped anchor flanked on either side by a triton, with the inscription Royal Fleet Auxiliary for Long Service. The medal is suspended on a 1.25-inch ribbon – central broad stripe watermarked royal blue flanked on either side by narrow stripes of cypress green/yellow-gold and purple. Source DCI(Gen) 289/2001.

A view from Southampton Water of the Marchwood Sea Mounting Centre with RFAs *Sea Centurion* (left), *Sea Crusader* (middle) and *Sir Percivale* (right). (RFA Archive)

2002

2002: RFA Association created to provide social and welfare support for retired and serving RFA personnel. Introduction of the RFA Bureau and integration of the COMRFA into the CinC Fleet organisation based at Portsmouth. Operation Oracle – UK contribution to a large Coalition Task Group operating from the Northern Gulf to the Horn of Africa – HM Ships with supporting RFAs and supporting UN Security Council Resolution 661 – Maritime Interdiction Operations against illegal exports by Iraq.

1 February: The STCW 95 applies to every British Merchant Navy Master and officer.

March: Operation Veritas – UK contribution to Operation Enduring Freedom; 45 Commando Royal Marines with RN support including RFA LSLs.

4 June: RFA personnel represented as part of the Chamber of Shipping at the Grand Parade, The Queen's Golden Jubilee Celebrations in London.

12 June: Humanitarian aid – *Diligence* rescued 20 crew from the Tongan *Bella 1* (3,964/1978) off the coast of Somalia and was awarded the Lady Swathling Trophy for Skill and Gallantry.

27 June: Golden Jubilee visit to the Armed Forces by HM The Queen to

'Wave' (2) class

MOD(NAVY)-DESIGNED LARGE FLEET OILER

RFA *Wave Knight* **Pennant no:** A389

RFA *Wave Ruler* **Pennant no:** A390

Machinery: Diesel electric, one Alstom 14 MW electric main propulsion motor connected to four Alstom diesel generators driven by Wartsila V12 ICE; 27,200 hp; single shaft; 18 knots; bow and stern thrusters

Dimensions (loa/bp x beam): 596/–ft x 88ft

Tonnage measurements: 23,294 grt, 18,200 dwt

Displacement: 31,500 full load

Complement: 80 RFA + 20-man RN party

Remarks: +1001A double hull; +LMC class +UMS, ice class 1D. Officially known as 'auxiliary oilers' the 'Wave' class are built to replace *Olna* (3) and *Olwen* (2), they are double hulled and meet the latest SOLAS requirements. They are designed to support the cross section of Royal Navy forces operating in, for example, amphibious warfare and anti-submarine warfare environments. Cargo capacity 16,000 cubic metres including 3,000 cubic metres of aviation fuel, 380 cubic metres of fresh water and 500 cubic metres of dry cargo; can accommodate up to eight 'plug-in' ISO 20 refrigerated boxes. Fitted with a new design of dual-purpose RAS rig – two to port and one on starboard side, one large crane to starboard and one Hudson reel for astern fuelling. These tankers have extensive aviation facilities with a large one-spot flight deck, hangar and maintenance facilities capable of supporting the large Merlin helicopter. Defensive facilities include 30mm cannon and fittings for two Phalanx CIWS.

RFA *Wave Ruler* running sea trials. (BAE Systems)

Portsmouth, display included RFAs *Sir Bedivere* and *Black Rover*.

July: *Argus* placed at 25 days notice to support Operation Oracle.

19 July: *Sea Centurion* arrived Marchwood for the last time to destore for handover to owners.

25 July: *Sea Centurion* decommissioned as an RFA.

28 July: *Sir Geraint* sailed Freetown at the end of Operation Silkman.

6 August: *Sir Geraint* arrived Marchwood for the last time to commence destoring for disposal.

27 August: *Sea Centurion* returned to her owners, name unchanged, although the following year she was renamed *Mont Ventoux*.

5 September: Humanitarian aid – *Bayleaf* rescued five crew from the Guinean motor vessel *Falcon* which sank in the Indian Ocean and landed them in Dubai.

16 September: *Sir Geraint* arrived Portsmouth for lay up for disposal.

15 October: *Wave Knight* completed by BAE Systems Marine Ltd, Barrow for MoD(Navy).

30 October: *Wave Ruler* completed by BAE Systems Marine Ltd at Govan for MoD(Navy).

2003

2003: Captain R C Thornton RFA appointed Commodore (X) RFA and Assistant Chief of Staff (Sustainability). Second Officer RFA appointed Flag Lieutenant to First Sea Lord.

10 January: Aviation – RFA *Wave Ruler* in Plymouth Sound commences three weeks of trials with the RN's new Merlin helicopter to develop safe operating procedures with the new 'Wave' class.

15 January: Operation Telic – *Argus*, *Fort Victoria*, *Fort Rosalie*, *Fort Austin*, *Sir Galahad*, *Sir Tristram* and *Sir Percivale* sailed UK ports for Gulf – *Orangeleaf* diverted from the Mediterranean; *Bayleaf*, *Sir Bedivere* and *Diligence* already in the Gulf region.

1 February: RFA Medical Assistants reclassified as Medical Technicians.

28 March: Humanitarian relief – *Sir Galahad*, in the glare of international publicity and preceded by a Royal Navy *Sandown* class MCMV made a dangerous 7.5-hour passage down the Khwar Abd Allah waterway into the recently-captured south Iraqi port of Um Qasr with 650 tonnes of humanitarian aid.
April–May: Aviation – Operation Telic – RFA *Fort Victoria* deployed 814 NAS with four Merlin MH1 aircraft – first operational sea deployment.
7 April: Humanitarian relief – *Sir Percivale* at Um Qasr with 300 tonnes of relief aid that was also a gift from Kuwait.
8 April: *Wave Knight* (2) commissioned.
1 May: *Sir Geraint* officially withdrawn from service and laid up at Portsmouth for disposal.
23 June: Humanitarian aid – *Sir Tristram* rescued 27 crewmen from the Egyptian bulk carrier *Green Glory* (9,985/1979) that sank in the Indian Ocean and landed them in Djibouti.
18 July: *Largs Bay* floated out three months late at Wallsend.
23 July: Royal Navy Colour presented by HM the Queen aboard HMS *Ocean* in Plymouth sound – 20 other ships were present for review including RFAS *Argus*, *Sir Bedivere* and *Wave Knight* (2).
1 August: First of class RFA *Largs Bay* formally named at the Swan Hunter (Tyneside) Wallsend yard.
7 August: *Sea Crusader*, after at refit in Belfast, returned to her owners and reverted to original name *Celestine*.
24 October: *Brambleleaf* arrives Portland, last vessel home from Operation Telic.
30 October: Operational Honours List – Iraqi Supplement announces two OBEs (Military Division) and two Queen's Commendation for Valuable Service to the RFA.
November: First RFA officers' training course established at Britannia Royal Naval College, Dartmouth; this course comprised Supply Officers and System Engineers.

'Bay' class

MOD(NAVY)-DESIGNED LANDING SHIP DOCK (AUXILIARY)

RFA *Largs Bay*	Pennant no: L3006
RFA *Lyme Bay*	Pennant no: L3007
RFA *Mounts Bay*	Pennant no: L3008
RFA *Cardigan Bay*	Pennant no: L3009

Builders: Swan Hunter (Tyneside) Ltd (L3006 and L3007), Wallsend and BAE Systems Marine Ltd, Govan (L3008 and L3009)
Machinery: Diesel electric, two Wartsila BL26 ICE and two Wartsila 12V26 ICE; 18 knots; bow and stern thrusters
Dimensions (length oa/bp x beam): 176m/–ft x 26.5ft
Tonnage measurements: –
Displacement: 16,200 tons full load
Complement: 65 RFA + RN party and Mexeflot teams + 350 military lift
Remarks: +1001A; +LMC class +UMS. This is a new class and a very different type of ship for the RFA. Intended to replace the ageing 'Sir' class LSLs. Initially called the Alternative Landing Ship Logistics (ALSL), in 2002, to meet NATO designations reclassified as Landing Ship Dock (Auxiliary), this design is an adaptation of the Dutch *Rotterdam* class. These ships will be able to operate landing craft through a stern door; their large vehicle deck will support up to 24 main battle tanks accessible by a stern ramp and a side ramp. Two 30-ton decks cranes enable the handling of loads, such as, two Mexeflotes, two 25-ton LCVP Mk5s and ISO containers. The integral floodable dock can handle one 96ft long, 240-ton LCU Mk 10. Aviation facilities include a two-spot 'Chinook' capable flight deck but no hangar and maintenance facilities. Defensive facilities include four 30mm cannon and fittings for the Phalanx CIWS.

RFA *Largs Bay* being constructed at Swan Hunter, Newcastle. (Dr Ian Buxton)

The first of class should commence trials in 2005. This class will provide a major enhancement to the support for 3 Commando Brigade Royal Marines and to Britain's ability to provide humanitarian support worldwide.

Operation Telic

UK military contingency preparation in relation to Iraq underway with Naval Task Group 2003 which was augmented by a substantial maritime and amphibious capability. HMS *Ark Royal*, HMS *Ocean* with three Type 42 destroyers, one Type 23 frigate, two minehunters, fleet submarines with RFAS *Argus, Sir Tristram, Sir Galahad, Sir Percivale, Fort Victoria, Fort Rosalie, Fort Austin* and *Orangeleaf* – 4,000 RM Commandos with HQ 3 Commando Brigade and helicopter air groups + RFA *Sir Bedivere* as MCMV support vessel with Fleet Support Unit 02 aboard + RFA *Argus* role as Primary Casualty Receiving Ship + RFA *Bayleaf*, RFA *Grey Rover* and RFA *Diligence*; RFAs also carried Ship Protection Teams from the RN Fleet Protection Group – comprising RN, RM and RNR personnel.

RFA *Argus*	RFA *Bayleaf*	RFA *Diligence*
RFA *Fort Austin*	RFA *Fort Rosalie*	RFA *Fort Victoria*
RFA *Grey Rover*	RFA *Orangeleaf*	RFA *Sir Bedivere*
RFA *Sir Galahad*	RFA *Sir Percivale*	RFA *Sir Tristram*
RFA *Sea Crusader*		

2004

2004: Magallan Human Resources computer system is introduced into the RFA vessels; replacing the SOAP (Personnel Management) and Cashman (Cash Accounting) systems it enables automatic data exchange between ships and headquarters. RSS *Perseverance*, formerly RFA *Sir Lancelot*, sold by the Singapore Navy to a local defence company Glenn Defense Marine (Asia) for $1.65 million; renamed *Glenn Braveheart* and is being converted, at a cost of $3 million, for a counter-terrorism security role in the port of Singapore.

January–December: South Atlantic and Falkland Islands – RFA support to HM Ships in the protection of British interests, included RFA tanker.

January: The RFA Supply Department is renamed in line with RN practice as Logistics Supply Department and supply officers and ratings become Logistic Supply staff.

9 April: *Mounts Bay* launched at Govan.

May: Replenishment at sea – after training by staff from RFA *Wave Ruler* the Mexican Navy's frigate ARM *Victoria* conduced this navy's first ever RAS evolutions.

June: 60th anniversary of D-Day – RFA *Wave Knight* and RFA *Sir Percivale* present in support. Aurora Deployment was the British contribution to the large exercise Rapid Alliance conducted with the US; the UK Amphibious Group Four comprised RFAS *Fort Rosalie*, *Sir Galahad*, *Sir Tristram* and *Oakleaf* supporting HM Ships *Ocean*, *Albion* and *Marlborough. Sir Bedivere*, embarking the RN's Portsmouth based Forward Support Unit 01 was the Command and Support ship to the 2nd Mine Countermeasure Squadron comprising HM Ships *Pembroke*, *Walney*, *Sandown* and *Middleton* and the survey ship HMS *Roebuck* for participation in Exercise Rapid Alliance; during their trans-Atlantic passage they were accompanied by RFA *Brambleleaf*.

29 July: *Sir Percivale* in Portsmouth Naval Base conducts her Haul Down (lowering her RFA ensign – decommissions) and the 35-year-old ship prepares for Extended Readiness.

September: *Oakleaf*, support tanker on bareboat charter is purchased by the MoD(Navy) for continued RFA service. Humanitarian relief – Hurricane Frances threatened the

The Wilkinson Sword of Peace

This award was instituted in 1966 by Messrs Wilkinson Sword Ltd. Each year the company sponsors the award to the unit of each of the UK's armed services judged to have made the most valuable contribution towards establishing good and friendly relations with any community, at home or overseas. As part of the Naval Service, Royal Fleet Auxiliaries have received a number of these awards, sometimes individually, sometimes shared with other units.

The first award to an RFA was in 1970 when the recipient was RFA *Ennerdale* (2). The Admiralty nominated her for her part in the search and rescue of two meteorologists at Gough Island to the south-east of Tristan da Cunha in June 1969. This RFA tanker co-operated with the South African Navy when she was diverted to refuel SAS *Simon Van Der Stel* and then embarked a 12-man rescue team.

In 1995 RFA *Sir Galahad*, as an integral part of the British military's presence, Britlogbat, in Operation Chantress, shared the award for her UN-sponsored work in Angola following many years of internal strife there. RFA *Black Rover*, serving as WIGS tanker and RFA *Sir Tristram* shared in the October 1998 award when it went to Task Group 326.02 (including HM Ships *Ocean*, *Sheffield*, 40 Commando RM, 539 Assault Squadron RM, 845 NAS and 847 NAS) for their work in bringing aid to Nicaragua and Honduras following Hurricane Mitch. RFA *Fort George* (with 820 NAS embarked) was the recipient following her delivery of humanitarian aid in Mozambique after disastrous floods in March 2000.

RFA *Sir Galahad* received the award again, in 2004, after she took the first humanitarian supplies into Um Qasr following the Iraq War 2003.

The Defence of RFA Vessels

The defensive arming of RFAs has always been a difficult issue. With their status of merchant ships they could enter foreign ports for fuel and supplies without any formalities. As RFAs become more integrated it became increasing difficult to accept them as mere merchant ships and during the mid-1970s the diplomatic clearance procedures for warship to enter foreign ports became increasingly applied to RFAs. During both World Wars RFAs were treated as Defensively Equipped Merchant Ships (DEMS) and were fitted with, for example, deck stiffening, darkening-ship arrangements and officers and ratings attended Merchant Navy Defence Courses. The ship's crews were augmented with DEMS gunners and detachments from the Royal Maritime Artillery.

3-inch decoy launcher. (ANRS)

The early 'Tide' class tankers were the first large purpose built replenishment tankers and they were fitted to carry one 4-inch gun, eight 40mm Bofors and minesweeping paravanes. In 1963 the policy was that front-line RFAs should be fitted for but not with two single 40mm guns with the mountings and guns being held onboard in a preserved condition. The building plans for commercial ships built for chartering to the Admiralty, such as *Bacchus* and *Pearleaf* clearly indicate deck stiffening and gun mount areas. In the early 1970s the decision appears to have reversed with guns being removed.

The House of Commons Defence Committee's post-Falklands report endorsed the need for RFAs to contribute to their own defence with the provision of small calibre weapons and decoys. Since then RFAs have been fitted permanently with extensive defensive weapons, for example the 20mm and 30mm BMARC cannon, the deck mounted Plessey Shield decoy rocket launchers (outfit DLE) and the NATO Sea Gnat system (outfit DLA) (*aka* 'chaff launchers') and pintle mounts for machine guns. The 'Fort' (2) class AORs, originally intended to be fitted with vertical-launch Sea Wolf surface-to-air missiles are now carrying two Phalanx close-in weapon system (CIWS) and the new 'Wave' (2) class tankers and 'Bay' class landing ships are fitted for the same system. RFAs have moved from mere merchant ships to being very high-value fleet units and in the high risk operational area they carry enhanced systems, for example, in parts of the Gulf they have carried Royal Marines air defence detachments equipped with Javelin shoulder-launched SAMs and they frequently carry a permanent ship protection team assembled from the RN, RM and RNR.

RFA 30mm gun crew. (RFA Archive)

Turks & Caicos Islands – RFA *Wave Ruler* and HMS *Richmond* placed on standby; due to Hurricane Ivan redeployed from Curaçao to cover Barbados, Trinidad & Tobago and Grenada.

16 September: Humanitarian relief – Hurricane Ivan – RFA *Wave Ruler* with HMS *Richmond* deployed to the Grand Cayman Islands.

23 September: Humanitarian aid – *Sir Galahad* wins the Wilkinson Sword of Peace for its relief work in IRAQ; presented at Marchwood.

October: Aviation – RFA *Argus* – ship/helicopter operating limits (SHOL) with Apache AH1 aircraft.

5–9 October: Humanitarian assistance – following a fire aboard the Canadian submarine HMCS *Chicoutimi* when 140 miles off the west of Ireland – rescue ships included the RFAs *Wave Knight* and *Argus* with HM Ships *Montrose* and *Marlborough*, the US submarine support ship *Carolyn Chouest* and the HM Coast Guard duty tug *Anglian Prince*.

30 December: Humanitarian assistance – Operation Garron – RFA *Diligence* and HMS *Chatham* deployed to the Far East in support of the Asian tsunami relief work.

Commodores RFA 1951-2005

	From	*To*
S G Kent OBE	August 1951	May 1954
W Brunswick Brown OBE	June 1954	December 1955
T H Card OBE	December 1955	January 1957
T Elder CBE DSC	January 1957	March 1962
A E Curtain OBE RD	March 1962	August 1964
E Payne CBE	September 1964	June 1966
G O W Evans CBE DSC	June 1966	January 1968
J Dines CBE RD	January 1968	May 1971
H O L'Estrange DSC RD	June 1971	December 1972
G A Robson CBE	December 1972	May 1977
S C Dunlop DSO MBE	May 1977	March 1983
J G M Coull	March 1983	September 1985
B H Rutterford	September 1985	May 1989
R M Thorn CBE	May 1989	May 1994
N D Squire CBE	May 1994	March 1999
P J Lannin CBE	March 1999	September 2003
R C Thornton	October 2003	

Note: 1986 combined with post of Chief Marine Superintendent
April 1993 became COMRFA – Type Commander RFA

2005

2005: South Atlantic and Falkland Islands – RFA support to HM Ships in the protection of British interests, included RFA tanker. West Indies Guard Ship with support of an RFA tanker providing a presence in the region and conducting anti-drug smuggling operations with the US Coast Guard. Armilla Patrol – Gulf of Oman and Persian Gulf – RFA tanker support to HM Ships providing a British presence in the region to protect British shipping.

January: Humanitarian assistance – Operation Garron – Asian tsunami relief – RFA *Diligence* supporting Forward Support Unit and HMS *Chatham* arrived off Sri Lanka; *Bayleaf* in the Gulf on standby to join this operation; engineers from *Diligence* flew to the Maldives to assist in repair of electrical and water desalination plants. MARSTRIKE 05 – Royal Navy strike force departed Portsmouth for Middle Eastern exercises, led by HMS *Invincible* supported by RFA *Fort George* with four Merlin helicopters from 820 NAS embarked.

1 January: New insignia introduced for RFA cadets to reflect the three methods that an individual may use to obtain the appropriate Certificate of Competency: the traditional three-year Cadetship; the Degree officer under training route and the Rating to Officer-under-training route.

9 April: RFA *Cardigan Bay* launched.

During the course of 2005 the RFA is programmed to support a range of events around the UK:

May: VE/VJ day celebrations.

June/July: International Fleet Review in the Solent followed by an International Drumhead Ceremony. International Festival of the Sea, Portsmouth Naval Base

July and August: Centenary Tour – a series of UK port visits with RFA *Wave Ruler*, RFA *Argus* and RFA *Sir Galahad* covering London, Newcastle, Scarborough, Rosyth and Glasgow, Portmouth, Cardiff, Liverpool, Belfast, Dartmouth and Falmouth.

3 August: Royal Fleet Auxiliary centenary.

FLEET LIST

RFA	*Service*	*Admiralty role*	*Class or group*	*Type of ship*
Abadol see *Oakleaf* (1)	1915-1917	tanker		steam
Abbeydale	1937-1960	tanker	'Dale'	motor
Advice	1959-1963	tug, sea going	'Accord'	motor
Agile	1959-1985	tug		motor
Airsprite	1943-1965	spirit carrier	'Sprite'	steam
Aldersdale	1937-1942	tanker	'Dale'	motor
Allegiance	1950-1962	tug, rescue	*Assurance*	steam
Amherst	1951-1963	armament stores carrier		steam
Anchorite	14-18 War	mooring vessel		steam
Antic	1943-1969	tug		steam
Appleleaf (1)	1917-1946	tanker	'Fast Leaf'	steam
Appleleaf (2)	1959-1970	tanker, product	'Leaf'	motor
Appleleaf (3)	1979-1989	tanker, replenishment	'Leaf'	motor
Aquarius	1905-1906	stores ship/distilling ship		steam
Argo	1917-1921	coastal store carrier		steam
Argus	1988-cf	aviation training/casualty		motor
Arndale	1937-1960	tanker	'Dale'	motor
Aro	1915-1918	depot ship, submarine		steam
Ashleaf	1916	tanker		steam
Aspenleaf	1916-1919	tanker, freighting		steam
Attendant	1914-1935	tanker	*Attendant*	steam
Bacchus (1)	1915-1936	stores ship/water carrier		steam
Bacchus (2)	1936-1962	stores freighter		steam
Bacchus (3)	1962-1981	stores freighter	*Bacchus*	motor
Barkol	1916-1920	tanker		steam
Battersol	1916-1920	tanker		steam
Bayleaf (1)	1917-1919	tanker, freighting		steam
Bayleaf (2)	1959-1973	tanker, product	'Leaf'	steam
Bayleaf (3)	1982- cf	tanker, replenishment	'Leaf'	motor
Bayol see *Bayleaf*	1916	tanker		steam
Beechleaf	1917-1919	tanker, freighting		steam
Belgol	1917-1953	tanker	*Belgol*	steam
Berbice	1920-1921	hospital ship		steam
Bernol see *Cherryleaf* (1)				
Berta	1939-1945	tanker		steam
Birchleaf	1916-1919	tanker, freighter		steam
Birchol (1)	1917-1939	tanker	*Birchol*	steam
Birchol (2)	1946-1969	tanker, coastal	'Ol'	steam
Bishopdale	1937-1970	tanker	'Dale'	motor
Bison	1914-18 war	stores vessel		steam
Blackol	1916-1920	tanker		steam
Black Ranger	1941-1973	tanker, replenishment	'Ranger'	motor
Black Rover	1974- td	tanker, replenishment	'Rover'	motor
Blackstone	1915-1921	oil carrier		steam
Blue Ranger	1941-1972	tanker, replenishment	'Ranger'	motor
Blue Rover	1970-1993	tanker, replenishment	'Rover'	motor
Boardale	1937-1940	tanker	'Dale'	motor
Bornol see *Appleleaf* (1)		tanker	'Fast Leaf'	steam
Boxleaf	1916-1919	tanker, freighting		steam
Boxol	1917-1948	tanker	*Creosol*	steam
Back In Service	1951-1960			
Brambleleaf (1)	1917-1946	tanker, freighting		steam
Brambleleaf (2)	1959-1972	tanker, product	'Leaf'	motor
Brambleleaf (3)	1979 – cf	tanker, replenishment	'Leaf'	motor
Briarleaf	1916-1919	tanker, freighting		steam
British Beacon	1918-1937	tanker, freighting	'British'	steam
renamed *Olcades*				

RFA	Service	Admiralty role	Class or group	Type of ship
British Lantern renamed *Oligarch* (2)	1922-1937	tanker, freighting	'British'	steam
British Lady	1939-1945	tanker		steam
British Light renamed *Olwen* (1)	1922-1937	tanker, freighting	'British'	steam
British Star renamed *Olynthus* (2)	1922-1937	tanker, freighting	'British'	steam
Broomdale	1937-1959	tanker, freighting	'Dale'	motor
Brown Ranger	1941-1974	tanker, replenishment	'Ranger'	motor
Buffalo	1916	mooring vessel		steam
Bullfrog	1915-1923	salvage vessel		steam
Burma	1911-1935	tanker	*Burma*	steam
Bustler	1959-1973	tug, fleet	*Bustler*	motor
C8	1940-1959	lighter self propelled cargo		motor
C10 renamed *Destiny*	1938-1963	tug, fleet fuelling		motor
C11 renamed *Regard*	1938-1966	tug, fleet fuelling		steam
C65 renamed *Nora*				
C85	1940-1956	lighter, cargo		steam
C614	1943-1956	lighter, coaling		steam
C615	1943-1956	lighter, store		motor
C616	1943-1956	lighter, store		motor
C617	1943-1956	lighter, store		motor
C619	1943-1963	lighter, store		motor
C620	1944-1966	lighter, store		motor
C621	1944-1961	lighter, store		motor
C623	1944-–	lighter, fuel		steam
C624	1945-1969	lighter, fuel		steam
C625	1944-1963	lighter, fuel		steam
C633	1945-1956	lighter, coal		steam
C641	1946-1956	lighter, coal		steam
C642	1946-1956	lighter, coal		steam
C647	1947-1968	tanker		motor
C648	1949-1958	lighter		motor
C653	1948-1968	lighter, lubricating oil		motor
Cairndale	1939-1941	tanker	'Dale'	motor
Califol see *Roseleaf*	1916	tanker		steam
Canning	1916-1918	depot ship		steam
Cardigan Bay	building	landing ship dock	'Bay'	motor
Carol	1914-1935	tanker	*Attendant*	motor
Cautious	1940-1964	tug, rescue	*Assurance*	steam
Cedardale	1939-1961	tanker	'Dale'	motor
Cedarol see *Rowanol*	1946-1947	tanker		
Celerol	1917-1958	tanker	*Belgol*	steam
Cherryleaf (1)	1917-1946	tanker	'Fast Leaf'	steam
Cherryleaf (2)	1959-1966	tanker, product	'Leaf'	motor
Cherryleaf (3)	1973-1980	tanker, product	'Leaf'	motor
City of Oxford	1915-1919	depot ship/kit balloon ship		steam
Crenella	1916	stores ship/tanker		steam
Creosol	1916-1918	tanker	*Creosol*	steam
Cyclone see *Growler*	1947-1977	tug, fleet	*Bustler*	motor
Danmark	1942-1946	fuel hulk		steam
Dapper	1915-1923	salvage vessel		steam
Darkdale	1940-1941	tanker	'Dale'	steam
Delphinula	1915-1946	tanker		steam
Demeter	1942-1946	stores hulk		steam
Denbydale	1940-1955	tanker		motor
Derwentdale (1)	1941-1957	tanker/landing ship gantry	'Dale'	motor
Derwentdale (2)	1967-1974	tanker, mobile reserve	'Dale'	motor

RFA	Service	Admiralty role	Class or group	Type of ship
Dewdale (1)	1941-1959	tanker/landing ship gantry	'Dale'	motor
Dewdale (2)	1967-1977	tanker, mobile reserve	'Dale'	motor
Diligence	1984- cf	forward repair ship		motor
Dingledale	1942-1959	tanker	'Dale'	motor
Dinsdale	1942-1942	tanker	'Dale'	motor
Discovery II (RRS)	1950-1962	research ship		motor
Discovery (RRS)	1962-1968	research ship		DE
Dispenser	1950-1955	coastal salvage vessel	'Kin'	steam
Distol	1916-1947	tanker	*Creosol*	steam
Dockleaf	1917-1919	tanker, freighting	'Leaf'	steam
Dredgol	1918-1935	tanker		steam
Eaglesdale	1942-1959	tanker	'Dale'	steam
Earner	1943-1965	tug	*Assurance*	–
Easedale	1942-1959	tanker	'Dale'	steam
Ebonol (1)	1917-1942	tanker	*Creosol*	steam
Ebonol (2) see *Rowanol*				
Echoldale	1941-1961	tanker	'Dale'	motor
Eddybay	1952-1963	tanker	'Eddy'	steam
Eddybeach	1951-1964	tanker	'Eddy'	steam
Eddycliff	1953-1964	tanker	'Eddy'	steam
Eddycove	cancelled	tanker	'Eddy'	steam
Eddycreek	1953-1963	tanker	'Eddy'	steam
Eddyfirth	1954-1981	tanker, white oil	'Eddy'	steam
Eddymull	cancelled	tanker	'Eddy'	steam
Eddyness	1954-1970	tanker	'Eddy'	steam
Eddyreef	1953-1964	tanker	'Eddy'	steam
Eddyrock	1953-1967	tanker	'Eddy'	steam
Elderol	1917-1959	tanker	*Creosol*	steam
Elmleaf	1917-1919	tanker, freighting		steam
Elmol	1917-1959	tanker	*Creosol*	steam
Empire Ace	1961-1969	tug, berthing	*Hoedic*	steam
Empire Demon	1949-1965	tug	*Warrior*	steam
Empire Fred	1955-1973	tug, berthing	'Empire'	steam
Empire Gull	1970-1980	landing ship, ferry	LST3	steam
Empire Netta	1947-1967	tug, berthing	'Stella Imp'	steam
Empire Plane	1949-1957	tug	'Maple'	steam
Empire Rita	1949-1958	tug	'Stella Imp'	steam
Empire Rosa	1949-1977	tug, berthing	'Stella Imp'	steam
Empire Salvage	1941-1946	tanker, replenishment		motor
Empire Zona	1949-1957	tug	'Stella Imp'	steam
Encore	1958-1967	tug, fleet	*Envoy*	steam
Enforcer	1949-1963	tug, fleet	*Envoy*	steam
Engadine	1967-1989	helicopter training ship		motor
Ennerdale (1)	1941-1958	tanker/landing ship gantry	'Dale'	steam
Ennerdale (2)	1967-1970	tanker, mobile reserve	'Dale'	motor
Envoy	1949-1960	tug, fleet	*Envoy*	steam
Eppingdale	cancelled	tanker	'Dale'	motor
Fernleaf	1917-1920	tanker, freighting		steam
Ferol	1915-1920	tanker	*Attendant*	motor
Fidget	1915-1921	salvage vessel		steam
Fort Austin	1979-cf	fleet replenishment ship	'Fort' (2)	motor
Fort Beauharnois	1948-1962	stores ship	'Fort'	steam
Fort Charlotte	1947-1967	stores ship	'Fort'	steam
Fort Constantine	1949-1969	stores ship	'Fort'	steam
Fort Dunvegan	1951-1968	stores ship	'Fort'	steam
Fort Duquesne	1947-1967	stores ship	'Fort'	steam
Fort George	1993-cf	auxiliary oiler replenishment	'Fort' (3)	motor
Fort Grange renamed *Fort Rosalie* (2)	1993-2000	fleet replenishment ship	'Fort' (2)	motor

RFA	*Service*	*Admiralty role*	*Class or group*	*Type of ship*
Fort Langley	1954-1970	armament stores ship	'Fort'	steam
Fort Rosalie (1)	1947-1972	armament stores ship	'Fort'	steam
Fort Rosalie (2)				
ex *Fort Grange*	2000-cf	fleet replenishment ship	'Fort' (2)	motor
Fort Sandusky	1949-1972	stores ship	'Fort'	steam
Fort Victoria	1990-cf	auxiliary oiler replenishment	'Fort' (3)	steam
Fortol	1917-1958	tanker	*Belgol*	steam
Francol	1917-1942	tanker	*Belgol*	steam
Freshbrook	1941-1946	water tanker	'Fresh'	steam
Freshburn	1944-1946	water tanker	'Fresh'	steam
Freshener	1942-1946	water tanker	'Fresh'	steam
Freshet	1940-1946	water tanker	'Fresh'	steam
Freshford	1944-1946	water tanker	'Fresh'	steam
Freshlake	1942-1946	water tanker	'Fresh'	steam
Freshmere	1943-1946	water tanker	'Fresh'	steam
Freshpond	1945	water tanker	'Fresh'	steam
Freshpool	1943-1946	water tanker	'Fresh'	steam
Freshtarn	1944-1946	water tanker	'Fresh'	steam
Freshwater	1940-1946	water tanker	'Fresh'	steam
Freshwell	1943-1946	water tanker	'Fresh'	steam
Greenol	1916-1920	tanker		steam
Gold Ranger	1941-1973	tanker, RAS	'Ranger'	motor
Gold Rover	1974- cf	tanker, RAS	'Rover'	motor
Gray Ranger	1941-1942	tanker, RAS	'Ranger'	motor
Green Ranger	1941-1962	tanker, RAS	'Ranger'	motor
Green Rover	1969-1991	tanker, RAS	'Rover'	motor
Grey Rover	1970- cf	tanker, RAS	'Rover'	motor
Growler	1947-1977	tug, fleet	*Bustler*	motor
Gypol see *Pearleaf* (1)		tanker	'Fast Leaf'	steam
Hebe	1962-1978	stores freighter	*Bacchus*	motor
Hickorol	1918-1948	tanker	*Creosol*	steam
Holdfast	1915-1923	salvage vessel		steam
Hollyleaf	1917-1919	tanker, freighter		steam
Hughli	1915	salvage vessel		steam
Hungerford	1915-1917	store carrier/distilling ship		steam
Huntball	1916-1918	kite balloon ship/tanker		steam
Industry (1)	1914-1918	store carrier		steam
Industry (2)	1920-1924	store carrier		steam
Ingeborg	1940-1946	coastal tanker		steam
Innisfree	1915-1920	water carrier	'Innis'	motor
Innisinver	1915-1920	water carrier	'Innis'	motor
Innisjura	1915-1920	water carrier	'Innis'	motor
Innisshannon	1915-1920	water carrier	'Innis'	motor
Innissulva	1915-1920	water carrier	'Innis'	motor
Innistrahull	1916	water carrier	'Innis'	motor
Isla ex *Thistle*	1907-1921	tanker		steam
Jaunty	1949-1956	tug, rescue	*Assurance*	steam
Kharki	1907-1931	collier/tanker		steam
Kimmerol	1916-1947	tanker	*Creosol*	steam
Kinbrace	1950-1960	coastal salvage vessel	'Kin'	steam
Kingarth	1956-1954	coastal salvage vessel	'Kin'	steam
King Salvor	1942-1954	ocean salvage vessel	*King Salvor*	steam
Kurumba	1916-1919	tanker		steam
Larchol	1917-1958	tanker	*Creosol*	steam
Largs Bay	building	landing ship dock	'Bay'	motor
Laurelleaf	1916-1919	tanker, freighting		steam
Limeleaf	1916-1919	tanker, freighting		steam
Limol	1917-1959	tanker	*Creosol*	steam
Limpet	1915-1922	mooring vessel		

RFA	Service	Admiralty role	Class or group	Type of ship
Lucia	1915-1916	depot ship		steam
Lucigen	1939-1946	tanker		steam
Lyme Bay	building	landing ship dock	'Bay'	motor
Lyness	1966-1980	air stores support ship	'Ness'	motor
Maine (1)	1905-1914	hospital ship		steam
Maine (2)	cancelled	hospital ship		steam
Maine (3)	1921-1947	hospital ship		steam
Maine (4)	1948-1954	hospital ship		steam
Maine (5)	cancelled	hospital ship	-	
Mapleleaf	1916-1919	tanker		steam
Mariner	1915-1919	salvage vessel	*Mariner*	steam
Mediator see *Maine* (2)	1914	hospital ship		steam
Melita	1915	salvage vessel		steam
Mercedes	1908-1920	fleet collier		steam
Messenger	1916	mooring vessel		
Mixol	1916-1948	tanker	*Burma*	steam
Mollusc	1916	mooring vessel		steam
Montenol	1917-1942	tanker	*Belgol*	steam
Mounts Bay	building	landing ship dock	'Bay'	motor
Nasprite	1941-1963	spirit tanker	'Sprite'	steam
Nigeria	1916	store carrier		
Nimble	1944-1947	ferry		steam
Nora ex *C65*	1932-1939	coastal stores carrier/collier		steam
Nucula	1922-1924	tanker		steam
Oakleaf (1) ex *Abadol*	1916-1917	tanker, freighting		steam
Oakleaf (2)	1985- cf	tanker, replenishment		motor
Oakol (1)	1918-1920	tanker	*Creosol*	motor
Oakol (2)	1946-1969	tanker	'Ol'	steam
Ocean Salvor	1943-1960	ocean salvage vessel	*King Salvor*	steam
Olaf	cancelled	tanker	*Olympia*	motor
Olalla see *Laureleaf*	1916	tanker		steam
Olbury see *Birchleaf*	1916	tanker		steam
Olcades ex *British Beacon*	1919-1952	tanker		steam
Oleander see *Fernleaf*	1917	tanker		steam
Oleander (1)	1922-1940	tanker		steam
Oleander (2) renamed *Olmeda*	1965-1967	tanker, fleet replenishment	*Olynthus*	steam
Oleary see *Dockleaf*	1917	tanker		steam
Oleaster see *Hollyleaf*	1917	tanker		steam
Oletta see *Briarleaf*	1916	tanker		steam
Olga see *Ashleaf*	1916	tanker		steam
Oligarch see *Limeleaf*	1916	tanker		steam
Oligarch ex *British Lantern*	1919-1946	tanker		steam
Olinda see *Boxleaf*	1916	tanker		steam
Oliphant see *Palmleaf*	1916	tanker		steam
Olivet see *Elmleaf*	1917	tanker		steam
Oliver	cancelled	tanker	*Olympia*	motor
Olmos see *Beechleaf*	1917	tanker		steam
Olna	cancelled	tanker	*Olympia*	motor
Olna (1)	1921-1941	tanker		steam
Olna (2)	1945-1966	tanker		DE
Olna (3)	1966-2000	tanker, fleet replenishment	*Olwen*	steam
Olmeda ex *Oleander*	1967-1994	tanker, fleet replenishment	*Olwen*	steam
Olwen (1)	1919-1946	tanker		steam

RFA	Service	Admiralty role	Class or group	Type of ship
Olwen (2)				
see *Olynthus* (2)	1967-2000	tanker, fleet replenishment	*Olwen*	steam
Olympia				
see *Santa Margherita*		tanker, overseas		
Olynthus (1)	1919-1947	tanker		steam
Olynthus (2)				
renamed *Olwen* (2)	1965-1967	tanker, fleet replenishment	*Olynthus*	steam
Orangeleaf (1)	1917-1947	tanker	'Fast Leaf'	steam
Orangeleaf (2)	1959-1978	tanker, replenishment	'Leaf'	motor
Orangeleaf (3)	1984- cf	tanker, replenishment	'Leaf'	motor
Palmleaf	1916-1917	tanker		steam
Palmol	1918-1920	tanker	*Creosol*	motor
Pearleaf (1)	1917-1946	tanker	'Fast Leaf'	steam
Pearleaf (2)	1960-1986	tanker, replenishment	'Leaf'	motor
Persol				
see *Cherryleaf* (1)		tanker	'Fast Leaf'	steam
Perthshire	1915-1934	stores ship		steam
Petrella	1918-1946	spirit carrier	'Pet'	steam
Petrobus	1918-1959	spirit carrier	'Pet'	steam
Petroleum	1905-1937	tanker		steam
Petronel	1918-1945	spirit carrier	'Pet'	steam
Philol	1916-1949	tanker	*Creosol*	steam
Plumleaf (1)	1917-1942	tanker	'Fast Leaf'	steam
Plumleaf (2)	1960-1986	tanker, replenishment	'Leaf'	motor
Polavon	1915-1917	distilling ship/tanker		steam
Polgowan	1915-1916	fleet messenger/collier		steam
Polmont	1915-1916	water carrier		steam
Polshannon	1915-1919	tanker		steam
Prestol	1917-1958	tanker	*Belgol*	steam
Prince Salvor	1943-1966	ocean salvage vessel	*King Salvor*	steam
Princetown	1916-1917	repair ship		steam
Prosperous	1949-1961	tug, rescue	*Assurance*	steam
Purfol	1916-1920	tanker		steam
Racer	1920-1925	salvage vessel	*Mariner*	steam
Rangol see *Mapleleaf*	1915	tanker		steam
Rapidol	1917-1948	tanker	*Belgol*	steam
Red Dragon	1918-1946	fuel hulk		
Regent	1967-1993	fleet replenishment ship	'R'	steam
Reindeer	1915-1919	salvage vessel	*Mariner*	steam
Reliance	1915-1919	repair and store ship		steam
Reliant (1)	1933-1948	stores ship		steam
Reliant (2)				
ex *Somersby*	1958-1977	air stores support ship		motor
Reliant (3)	1983-1986	aviation ship (Arapaho)		motor
Resource	1967-1997	fleet replenishment ship	'R'	steam
Resurgent	1952-1981	armament stores ship		motor
Retainer	1952-1979	armament stores ship		motor
Reward	1963-1971	tug, fleet	*Bustler*	motor
Rippledyke	1951-1960	tanker		steam
Robert Dundas	1938-1972	coastal stores carrier	'Robert'	motor
Robert Middleton	1938-1972	coastal stores carrier	'Robert'	motor
Roseleaf	1916-1919	tanker, freighting		steam
Rowanol	1946-1971	tanker	'Ol'	steam
Rumol see *Brambleleaf* (1)		tanker	'Fast Leaf'	steam
Ruthenia	1914-1949	tanker/fuelling hulk		steam
Salvestor	1942-1970	ocean salvage vessel	*King Salvor*	steam
Salvictor	1944-1966	ocean salvage vessel	*King Salvor*	steam
Salviola	1945-1959	ocean salvage vessel	*King Salvor*	steam
Samsonia	1958-1974	tug, fleet	*Bustler*	motor

RFA	*Service*	*Admiralty role*	*Class or group*	*Type of ship*
Santa Margherita	1919-1918	tanker, freighting		motor
Saucy	1949-1965	tug	*Assurance*	steam
Saxol see *Aspenleaf*	1916	tanker		steam
Scotol	1916-1947	tanker	*Creosol*	steam
Scottish American	1939-1947	tanker		steam
Sea Centurion	1998-2002	ro-ro strategic lift ship		motor
Sea Chieftain	cancelled	ro-ro strategic lift ship		motor
Sea Crusader	1996-2003	ro-ro strategic lift ship		motor
Seafox	1952-1958	coastal stores carrier		motor
Sea Salvor	1944-1973	ocean salvage ship	*King Salvor*	steam
Serbol	1918-1958	tanker	*Belgol*	steam
Servitor	1915-1922	tanker	*Attendant*	steam
Silverol	1916-1920	tanker		steam
Sir Bedivere	1970- cf	landing ship logistics	'Sir'	motor
Sir Caradoc	1983-1988	ro-ro ferry		motor
Sir Galahad (1)	1970-1982	landing ship logistics	'Sir'	motor
Sir Galahad (2)	1987- cf	landing ship logistics	'Sir'	motor
Sir Geraint	1970-2003	landing ship logistics	'Sir'	motor
Sir Lamorak	1983-1986	ro-ro ferry		motor
Sir Lancelot	1970-1989	landing ship logistics	'Sir'	motor
Sir Percivale	1970-2004	landing ship logistics	'Sir'	motor
Sir Tristram	1970- cf	landing ship logistics	'Sir'	motor
Slavol	1917-1942	tanker	*Belgol*	steam
Sobo	1915-1920	depot ship	steam	
Sokoto	1915-1919	depot ship	steam	
Somersby see *Reliant* (2)	1957-1958	stores freighter		motor
Spa	1942-1946	water tanker	'Spa'	steam
Spabeck	1943-1966	water tanker/HTP carrier	'Spa'	steam
Spabrook	1942-1946	water tanker	'Spa'	steam
Spaburn	1942-1977	water tanker	'Spa'	steam
Spalake	1946-1947	water tanker	'Spa'	steam
Spapool	1946-1947	water tanker	'Spa'	steam
Sparkler	1949-1957	tug		steam
Sprucol	1918-1920	tanker	*Creosol*	motor
Steadfast	1917	mooring vessel		
Stromness	1967-1983	stores support ships	'Ness'	motor
Succour	1944-1973	coastal salvage vessel	'Kin'	steam
Sunhill	1915-1920	accommodation ship		steam
Surf Patrol	1951-1969	tanker	'Surf'	motor
Surf Pilot	1951	fuelling hulk		steam
Surf Pioneer	1951-1969	tanker	'Surf'	motor
Swin	1950-1960	coastal salvage vessel	'Kin'	steam
Tarakol see *Vineleaf*	1915-1915	tanker		steam
Tarbatness	1967-1991	stores support ship	'Ness'	motor
Teakol (1)	1918-1920	tanker	*Creosol*	motor
Teakol (2)	1946-1969	tanker	'Ol'	steam
Texol see *Pearleaf* (1)		tanker	'Fast Leaf'	steam
Thermol	1916-1947	tanker	Burma	steam
Thistle renamed *Isla*	1907	collier		steam
Thornol	1947-1948	tanker		steam
Thrush	1915	salvage vessel		steam
Tide Austral	1955-1962	tanker, fleet replenishment	'Tide'	steam
Tideflow ex *Tiderace*	1958-1976	tanker, fleet replenishment	'Tide'	steam
Tidepool	1963-1982	tanker, fleet replenishment	Later 'Tide'	steam
Tiderace renamed *Tideflow*	1956-1958	tanker, fleet replenishment	'Tide'	steam
Tiderange renamed *Tidesurge*	1955-1958	tanker, fleet replenishment	'Tide'	steam

RFA	*Service*	*Admiralty role*	*Class or group*	*Type of ship*
Tiderreach	1955-1979	tanker, fleet replenishment	'Tide'	steam
Tidespring	1963-1991	tanker, fleet replenishment	Later 'Tide'	steam
Tidesurge ex *Tiderange*	1958-1976	tanker, fleet replenishment	'Tide'	steam
Trefoil	1913-1935	tanker		steam
Trinol see *Plumleaf* (1)		tanker	'Fast Leaf'	steam
Turmoil (1)	1917-1935	tanker	*Burma*	steam
Turmoil (2)	1947-1963	tug, fleet	*Bustler*	motor
Typhoon	1960-1989	tug, ocean	*Typhoon*	motor
Uplifter	1955-1964	coastal salvage vessel	'Kin'	steam
Victorious	1916	accommodation		steam
Vineleaf	1916-1919	tanker, freighting		steam
Viscol	1916-1947	tanker	*Creosol*	steam
Vitol	1917-1918	tanker	*Belgol*	steam
Volunteer	1916	dockyard mooring vessel		steam
War Afridi	1921-1958	tanker, freighting	'War'	steam
War Bahadur	1921-1946	tanker, freighting	'War'	steam
War Bharata	1921-1947	tanker, freighting	'War'	steam
War Brahmin	1921-1959	tanker, freighting	'War'	steam
Warden	1951-1965	tug, fleet	*Bustler*	motor
War Diwan	1921-1944	tanker, freighting	'War'	steam
War Hindoo	1921-1958	tanker, freighting	'War'	steam
War Krishna	1921-1947	tanker, freighting	'War'	steam
War Mehtar	1938-1941	tanker, freighting	'War'	steam
War Nawab	1921-1946	tanker, freighting	'War'	steam
War Nizam	1921-1946	tanker, freighting	'War'	steam
War Pathan	1921-1947	tanker, freighting	'War'	steam
War Pindari	1921-1947	tanker, freighting	'War'	steam
War Sepoy	1937-1940	tanker, freighting	'War'	steam
War Sirdar	1937-1942	tanker, freighting	'War'	steam
War Sudra	1937-1948	tanker, freighting	'War'	steam
Waterwitch	1915	small despatch vessel		steam
Wave	1915	small despatch vessel		steam
Wave Baron	1948-1972	tanker, replenishment	'Wave'	steam
Wave Chief	1946-1974	tanker, replenishment	'Wave'	steam
Wave Commander	1946-1959	tanker, freighting	'Wave'	steam
Wave Conqueror	1946-1958	tanker, freighting	'Wave'	steam
Wave Duke	1946-1969	tanker, freighting	'Wave'	steam
Wave Emperor	1944-1960	tanker, freighting	'Wave'	steam
Wave Governor	1945-1960	tanker, freighting	'Wave'	steam
Wave King	1944-1960	tanker, freighting	'Wave'	steam
Wave Knight (1)	1947-1964	tanker, replenishment	'Wave'	steam
Wave Knight (2)	2002- cf	tanker, fleet replenishment	'Wave' (2)	DE
Wave Laird	1946-1970	tanker, freighting	'Wave'	steam
Wave Liberator	1946-1959	tanker, freighting	'Wave'	steam
Wave Master	1946-1963	tanker, replenishment	'Wave'	steam
Wave Monarch	1944-1960	tanker, freighting	'Wave'	steam
Wave Premier	1946-1960	tanker, freighting	'Wave'	steam
Wave Prince	1947-1971	tanker, replenishment	'Wave'	steam
Wave Protector	1946-1963	tanker, freighting	'Wave'	steam
Wave Regent	1945-1960	tanker, freighting	'Wave'	steam
Wave Ruler (1)	1947-1976	tanker, replenishment	'Wave'	steam
Wave Ruler (2)	2002- cf	tanker, fleet replenishment	'Wave' (2)	DE
Wave Sovereign	1946-1967	tanker, replenishment	'Wave'	steam
Wave Victor	1946-1971	tanker, replenishment	'Wave'	steam
William Scoresby (RRS)	1949-1953	research ship		steam

Appendices

APPENDIX A
Wrecks, losses and casualties

Shipping casualties generally fall into two categories – **War Risk** and **Marine Risk**. This appendix covers the Royal Fleet Auxiliary from its inception in 1905 and records the wrecks, losses and casualties. This list is arranged in alphabetical order – comprehensive details of each casualty are in the chronological chapters under the 'Date of Loss'.

RFA wrecks, losses and casualties (in alphabetical order)

Abbeydale tanker 27 June 1944
War risk – serious casualty
Aldersdale tanker 4 July 1942
War risk – constructive total loss
Birchol tanker 29 November 1939
Marine risk – constructive total loss
Boardale tanker 30 April 1940
Marine risk – constructive total loss
Brambleleaf tanker 10 June 1942
War risk – serious casualty
Cairndale tanker 30 May 1941
War risk – constructive total loss
Creosol tanker 7 February 1918
War risk – constructive total loss
Darkdale tanker 22 October 1941
War risk – constructive total loss
Denbydale tanker 20 September 1941
War risk – serious casualty
Dinsdale tanker 31 May 1942
War risk – constructive total loss
Ebonol tanker 12 December 1941
War risk – capture
Ennerdale (2) tanker 1 June 1970
Marine risk – constructive total loss
Francol tanker 4 March 1942
War risk – constructive total loss
Gray Ranger tanker 22 September 1942
War risk – constructive total loss
Green Ranger tanker 17 November 1962
Marine risk – constructive total loss
Hebe store freighter 30 November 1978
Marine risk – constructive total loss
Innistrahull water tanker 1916
War risk – constructive total loss
Maine (1) hospital ship 17 June 1914
Marine risk – constructive total loss
Montenol tanker 21 May 1942
War risk – constructive total loss
Oleander tanker 8 June 1940
War risk – constructive total loss
Oligarch tanker 1 July 1943
War risk – serious casualty
Olna tanker 22 April 1941
War risk – constructive total loss
Plumleaf tanker 26 March 1942
War risk – constructive total loss
Ruthenia fuel hulk 16 February 1942
War risk – capture
Sir Galahad (1) landing ship logistic 8 June 1982
War risk – constructive total loss
Sir Tristram landing ship logistic 8 June 1982
War risk – serious casualty
Slavol tanker 26 March 1942
War risk – constructive total loss
Vitol tanker 7 March 1918
War risk – constructive total loss
War Diwan tanker 16 December 1944
War risk – constructive total loss
War Mehtar tanker 19 November 1941
War risk – constructive total loss
War Sepoy tanker 19 July 1940
War risk – constructive total loss
War Sirdar tanker 28 February 1942
Marine risk – constructive total loss/capture

Additional Second World War casualties (chronological list)

Berta tanker May 1940
Bombed in Dover Straits; one officer injured
Broomdale tanker 16–18 May 1940
Bombed, one rating injured and transferred to HM Ship for medical treatment then to Hospital Ship *Atlantis* for passage to UK.
Scotol tanker 14 August 1940
Bombed at Portland; one officer injured
Denbydale tanker 4–5 May 1941
Bombed at Liverpool; no injuries reported
War Pindari tanker 14 July 1941
Bombed at Skaalefjord off Solmunde; no injuries
Maine hospital ship 6 September 1941
Bombed at Alexandria; three ratings killed, one officer injured; 10 RFA and two RN ratings injured
Petrella tanker 12 September 1941
Bombed in Mediterranean; chief engineer killed, one engineering rating injured
Pass of Balmaha sunk by enemy action 17 October 1941
Two officers (ex RFA *Reliant* and ex RFA *Slavol*) killed – had been transferred on C-in-C's instructions to complete complement. This ship was not serving as an RFA.
Lady Hawkins sunk by enemy action 19 January 1942
One officer killed ex RFA *Bishopdale*. This ship was not serving as an RFA.

Bishopdale tanker 4 August 1942
Struck a mine, no casualties, returned to port

Laconia torpedoed 12 September 1942
Chief Engineer ex RFA *Maine* killed; he was being repatriated to the UK. This ship was not serving as an RFA.

Mendoza torpedoed 1 October 1942
24 ratings ex RFA *Green Ranger*, 29 ratings ex RFA *Eaglesdale* and one officer ex RFA *Arndale* being repatriated to UK; nine ratings killed and eight injured. This ship was not serving as an RFA.

Abasso enemy action 30 October 1942
One rating ex RFA *Easedale* being repatriated to the UK was killed. This ship was not an RFA.

Ennerdale tanker /LSG 8 November 1942
Damaged by enemy action; no casualties

Dewdale tanker /LSG 20 November 1942
Bombed; one rating injured

Empress of Canada torpedoed 12–14 March 1943
The ex-captain of RFA *Arndale* being repatriated to the UK was killed. This ship was not serving as an RFA.

Belgol tanker 24 May 1943
Bombed; chief engineer injured, one rating and one gunner injured (burnt); letter of their Lordships appreciation of commendable services to the chief engineer

Derwentdale tanker /LSG 14 September 1943
Bombed in Mediterranean; engine room damaged, towed to Malta; one officer injured, three ratings injured

Eaglesdale
The Tower Hill War Memorial Registers record eight dead on the ship *Eaglesdale*. The only ship recorded during the Second World War to carry this name was the London registered RFA steam tanker. They were actually being repatriated to UK in the ss *Mendoza* when this ship was lost on 1 October 1942.

Ennderdale tanker /LSG 13 July 1943
Air attack at Sicily, shell exploded on No 8 port wing tank lid; one officer killed

War Nizam tanker 20 February 1944
Air raid near Southend-on-Sea; one seaman killed and one injured when returning from shore leave

Broomdale tanker 28 August 1944
Accidentally torpedoed by HMS *Severn*; holed in No 1 and No 2 port tanks; one Lascar rating injured

Abbeydale tanker 29 September 1944
The death of one rating is recorded in The Tower Hill War Memorial Registers

Bishopdale tanker 14 December 1944
San Pedro Bay, Leyte Gulf, Philippines when dive-bombed by Japanese aircraft that crashed into No 3 wing tank and exploded; she was just securing alongside to a US cruiser; two ratings killed, two ratings injured. One rating died on 16 December 1944 of injuries sustained.

Table of personnel war casualties
(Arranged in alphabetical order by ship name and including contract Radio Officers and DEMS personnel)

RFA	*Number lost*	*Numbered injured*
Abbeydale	1	
Belgol		3
Berta		1
Bishopdale	3	1
Brambleleaf	7	6
Broomdale		2
Cairndale	4	4
Darkdale	11	33
Derwentdale		4
Dewdale		1
Dinsdale	5	1
*Eaglesdale**	8	
Ebonol	1 (In PoW Camp)	
Ennerdale	1	
Francol	4	
Gray Ranger	6	1
Maine	3	13
Montenol	3	
Oleander		3
Olna	1	
Petrella	1	1
Scotol		1
Sir Galahad (1982)	5	11
Sir Tristram (1982)	2	
Slavol	36	1
War Diwan	5	1
War Mehtar		4
War Nizam	1	1
War Sepoy		1

Ship (non- RFA) lost	*Number injured*	*Numbered*
Abasso	1	
Empress of Canada	1	
Laconia	1	
Lady Hawkins	1	
*Mendoza**	9	8
Pass of Balmaha	2	
Atlantic Conveyor	1 (Falklands 1982)	

APPENDIX B
RFA MEDALS AND BATTLE HONOURS

DECORATIONS

Rewards for acts of gallantry and for service were first given in the mid-nineteenth century. Such decorations are divided into those awarded for individual acts of heroism and those conferred in recognition of distinguished service. The system for the Merchant Navy, and therefore the RFA, was administered by the Marine Department of the Board of Trade and its various successors, the Shipping Controller, the Ministry of War Transport. Rewards for acts of Naval gallantry and service were administered by the Admiralty and later the Ministry of Defence. Admiralty Fleet Order 560/1942 Honours and Awards extended the eligibility of the Merchant Navy (and hence RFA) for naval awards, *eg* VC (Victoria Cross), DSO (Distinguished Service Order), DSC (Distinguished Service Cross), CGM (Conspicuous Gallantry Medal), DSM (Distinguished Service Medal) and Mention-in-Despatches.

CAMPAIGN MEDALS

The evolution of medals struck to commemorate and later to reward participants in a battle or campaign (war medals) was a gradual process. The forerunner of the modern campaign medal being the commemorative Armada Medal of 1588. Cast in gold or silver and awarded to naval officers and distinguished persons after the defeat of the Spanish Armada. In the second half of the eighteenth century the East India Company took the lead in awarding medals to its troops, both officers and other ranks. Officers and other ranks that fought in the battle of the Nile (1798) and at Trafalgar (1805) were granted medals.

The two World Wars were recognised by groups of medals. First World War examples are the 1914–15 Star, the British War Medal 1914–20, the Mercantile Marine War Medal (issued by the Board of Trade for serving at least one voyage in a danger zone) with its distinctive ribbon of watered green and red with a thin white stripe down the centre – indicating port and starboard and steaming light of a ship and finally the Victory Medal.

Second World War examples are the 1939–45 Star (merchant seafarers qualified with six months service afloat with at least one voyage through specified 'dangerous waters') and the Atlantic Star (granted for six months service afloat in the Atlantic, home waters, convoys to Russia and certain parts of the South Atlantic) with its distinctive ribbon of shaded and watered blue, white and sea green. The Pacific Star (awarded for service in the Pacific theatre, including defence of Singapore, for operations between 8 December 1941 and September 1945). The Italy Star (for the period 11 June 1943 to 8 May 1945, it was awarded for active service afloat in or around Italy, Sicily, Greece, the Aegean and operations off the south of France) and the 1939–45 War Medal (awarded to all full time members of the armed forces who completed 28 days service and to merchant seafarers who had served 28 days at sea).

The Korean War (1950–3) was recognised by the British Korea Medal, awarded to members of the British Commonwealth Forces who fought on behalf of the United Nations on the side of South Korea. Qualifying requirements were one day's service in Korea or 28 days sea service in the operational areas of the Yellow Sea and Sea of Japan. The ribbon has five equal stripes of yellow, blue, yellow, and blue, yellow. Anyone who received the Korean Medal also received the United Nations Medal with the bar KOREA.

The Naval General Service Medal 1915–64 (NGSM 1915) with it crimson-coloured ribbon with three white stripes. The medal was not issued without a clasp. It appears to have been Admiralty practice to make this medal available to members of the RFA Service. The first reference being the Admiralty Fleet Order (AFO) 3733/1942 that listed ships that qualified for the NGSM 1915 with the clasp PALESTINE 36-39. This list included the hospital ship RFA *Maine*, hospital ship and the store ship RFA *Reliant*.

AFO405/1958 lists the qualifications for service and conditions for award for service in operations in the Near East between 31 October and 22 December 1956. This AFO lists the RFAs that served off the Egyptian coast (Mediterranean and Red Sea) and their personnel are listed as having qualified for the NGSM 1915 with the NEAR EAST clasp.

On 6 October 1964 the Ministry of Defence, to award personnel of all services, instituted the Campaign Service Medal (CSM) with a ribbon of purple with green edges. For the Navy this replaced Naval General Service Medal 1915 and like it the CSM is not issued without a clasp. RFA personnel standing by the construction of RFA *Argus* and RFA Fort Victoria at Harland and Wolff, Belfast have, *eg* been awarded clasps for NORTHERN IRELAND (14 August 1969 onwards). In 1989 HM the Queen approved award of the General Service Medal (GSM) to RFA personnel who met the eligibility requirements – GULF (minesweeping in the Persian Gulf and Gulf of Oman between 17 November 1986 and 31 October 1988 and 1 November 1988 to 28 February 1989). KUWAIT (30 days continuous in Kuwait and its territorial waters and the Northern Gulf between 8 March and 30 September 1991), and IRAQ & S TURKEY (30 days continuous service including Operation Haven).

There are also specific medals – South Atlantic Medal (1982) and the Gulf Medal (1992) and United Nations Medals awarded for supporting service in the former Yugoslavia and Bosnia. The first issue of a NATO Medal was for service in the former Yugoslavia, the Adriatic and Kosovo and Operational Service Medal for West Africa (Sierra Leone).

SOUTH ATLANTIC CAMPAIGN MEDAL

The South Atlantic medal was awarded to all personnel (British armed forces, RFA, Merchant Navy and civilians) who took part in operations in the South Atlantic for the liberation of South Georgia and the Falkland Islands following their invasion by the Argentine (Operations Paraquat and Corporate). To qualify, a recipient had to have at least one full day's service in the Falklands or South Georgia, or 30 days in the operational zone including Ascension Island. The ribbon has five vertical stripes of equal width, shaded and watered in blue, white, sea green, white and blue. A rosette denotes service within the combat zone. The South Atlantic Medal Association (SAMA82) show that 2,000 medals were issued to the Royal Fleet Auxiliary.

Gulf Medal (1992)

The Gulf Medal (1992) was awarded to all personnel (British armed forces, RFA, and civilians) who took part in the Kuwait and Saudi Arabia operations. To qualify, a recipient had to have 30 days continuous service in the Middle East (including Cyprus) between 2 August 1990 and 7 March 1991; or seven days service between 16 January 1991 and 28 February 1991 (Operation Granby). The ribbon has a sandy coloured centre flanked on either side equal width strips of light blue, red and dark blue.

Similar awards are being made for the Second Gulf War (Operation Telic)

RFA Service Medal

The RFA Service Medal for Long and Meritorious service was introduced for service on or after 3 August 2000. *See under the year 2000 for details; illustration in colour plates*

Queens' Golden Jubilee Medal

This commerative medal was awarded to all members of the armed forces, both regular and reserves, and to RFA personnel serving up to or on 6 February 2002 and with five or more years service.

NATO Medal

The NATO Medal was instituted on 20 December 1994 for personnel who took part in NATO operations in the theatre of operations in the former Yugoslavia. For service on NATO operations related to Kosovo it has been awarded to eligible RFA personnel – 30 days continuous or accumulated service in the area or 90 days in direct support. This bronze medal bears the NATO four-pointed star emblem enclosed in base by a wreath of olive. Reverse side has the inscription NORTH ATLANTIC TREATY ORGANIZATION/ORGANISATION DU TRAITE DE L'ATLANTIQUE NORD and IN SERVICE OF PEACE/AU SERVICE DE LA PAIX ET DE LA LIBERTE. The ribbon consists of blue and white strips. The NATO medal takes equal precedence to the General Service Medal in order of date of award.

United Nations medals

The UN Secretary-General established the UN medal for award, subject to the Regulations for the United Nations Medal, to military personnel and civilians who are or have been in the service of the UN. The UN medal is a bronze medallion issued with a specific ribbon indicating service with a particular peacekeeping mission, for example, UNPROFOR (United Nations Protection Force) established 1992 and the UNOMSIL/UNAMSIL (United Nations Observer Mission in Sierra Leone/United Nations Mission in Sierra Leone) announced in June 1998. RFA personnel who served on Operation Grapple deployments to the Adriatic Sea area have the UN Medal with the clasp 'FORMER YUGOSLAVIA'.

The Second World War (1939–45)

The author's have researched medals and awards and the following is a summary of those credited to the RFA.

Date announced *Rank/Rate (RFA)*	*Ship* *Honours/awards*	*Comment*
10 April 1940	RFA *Boardale*	
Chief Engineer	Reserve decoration	LtCdr(E), RNR
24 August 1940	RFA *Broomdale*	
Chief Engineer	OBE (civil) + Lloyd's Medal	Repeat air attacks holed the ship and
2nd Engineer	MBE (civil) + Lloyd's Medal	damaged machinery sinking and
2nd Engineer	MBE (civil) + Lloyd's Medal	abandoned three engineers remained aboard and saved ship.
January 1941	RFA *Cedardale*	
Master	MBE (civil)	
July 1941	RFA *Rapidol*	
Master	OBE	LtCdr, RNR
July 1941	RFA *Orangeleaf*	
Master	Mentions in Despatches	LtCdr, RN Retd
November 1941	RFA *Rapidol*	
2nd Engineer	Polar Medal (Bronze)	For service 1925 – 1939 in RRS *William*
4th Engineer	Polar Medal (Bronze)	*Scoresby* and RRS *Discovery II*
6 January 1942	RFA *Bishopdale*	
Master	Mentions in Despatches	
11 August 1942	RFA *Brown Ranger*	
Master	DSC	
25 August 1942	RFA *Easedale*	
Master	DSC	Diego Suarez
Boatswain	DSM	operation
Chief Engineer	Mentions in Despatches	
25 August 1942	RFA *Derwentdale*	Diego Suarez
Master	Mentions in Despatches	operation
10 November 1942	RFA *Dingledale*	
Master	Bar to DSC	Malta Convoys

Date announced *Rank/Rate (RFA)*	*Ship* *Honours/awards*	*Comment*
10 November 1942	RFA *Boxol*	
2nd Engineer	Commendation	Malta March-April 1942
1 December 1942	RFA *Gray Ranger*	
Master	DSO	Russian Convoys
1 December 1942	RFA *Black Ranger*	
Master	DSO	Russian Convoys
1 December 1942	RFA *Dingledale*	
Master	DSC	Malta Convoys
22 December 1942	RFA *Aldersdale*	
Chief Engineer	DSC	Russian Convoys
Master	DSC	
Chief Officer	DSC	
Boatswain	DSM	
Pump man	DSM	
12 February 1943	RFA *Gray Ranger*	
Chief Officer	DSC	Russian Convoys
Chief Engineer	DSC	
Petty Officer	DSM	
Boatswain	DSM	
12 February 1943	RFA *Black Ranger*	
Chief Officer	DSC	Russian Convoys
Chief Engineers	DSC	
Boatswain	DSM	
Carpenter	DSM	
Deck Greaser	DSM	
12 February 1943	RFA *Brown Ranger*	
Chief Officer	Mentions in Despatches	Malta Convoys
Chief Engineer	Mentions in Despatches	
12 February 1943	RFA *Dingledale*	
Chief Officer	Mentions in Despatches	Malta Convoys
Chief Engineer	Mentions in Despatches	
7 May 1943	RFA *Dewdale*	
Master	DSC	Enemy action and air attacks in Mediterranean
Chief Engineer	DSC	
2nd Officer	Mentions in Despatches	
DEMS Petty Officer	Mentions in Despatches	
Rating	Mentions in Despatches	
Cook	Mentions in Despatches	
DEMS gunner	Mentions in Despatches	
Sergeant RM DEMS	Mentions in Despatches	
Sergeant DEMS	Mentions in Despatches (posthumous)	
7 May 1943	RFA *Boxol*	
Master	DSC	Fuelling operations at Malta
Chief Officer	DSC	
Chief Engineer	DSC	
Donkeyman	DSM	
Signalman	DSM	
30 July 1943	RFA *Orangeleaf*	
Master	OBE (military)	
2nd Officer	MBE (civil)	
Junior Officer	MBE (civil)	
Able Seaman	BEM	
3 August 1943	RFA *Ennerdale*	
Master	OBE (civil)	North African Operations
1 January 1944	RFA *War Nawab*	
Master	OBE (military)	Cdr RNR
Chief Engineer	OBE (military)	
1 January 1944	RFA *War Hindoo*	
Chief Engineer	DSC	
1 January 1944	RFA *Oligarch*	
Master	DSC	
7 January 1944	RFA *Ennerdale*	
Master	DSC	Sicily landings
2nd Officer	DSC	
Chief Engineer	Mentions in Despatches (posthumous)	
Chief Officer	Mentions in Despatches	
5 ratings	Mentions in Despatches	
7 July 1944	RFA *Derwentdale*	
Master	DSC	Limiting damage to the ship during Salerno landings
Chief Engineer	Mentions in Despatches	
Boatswain	Mentions in Despatches	
11 September 1944	RFA *Derwentdale*	
Officer	Royal Humane Society Testimonial for lifesaving	
18 November 1944	RFA *Brown Ranger*	
Rating	Royal Humane Society Testimonial for lifesaving	
14 June 1945	RFA *Ennerdale*	
Chief Officer	Mentions in Despatches	
Boatswain	Mentions in Despatches	
11 December 1945	RFA *Maine*	
Master	Mentions in Despatches	Hospital Ship
14 December 1945	RFA *Bishopdale*	
Master	DSC	Aircraft damage to ship Leyte Gulf 14 Dec 1944 flooding, fire etc, and operational in 30 mins
Chief Officer	Mentions in Despatches	
2 ratings	Mentions in despatches	
1 January 1946	RFA *Wave King*	
Master	OBE	Pacific Fleet operations
1 January 1946	RFA *Echodale*	
Master	OBE	Pacific Fleet operations
11 June 1946	RFA *Dingledale*	
Master	OBE	Far East war service

Date announced Rank/Rate (RFA)	Ship Honours/awards	Comment
Chief Officer	OBE + Mentions in Despatches	
Rating	BEM	
11 June 1946	RFA *Arndale*	
Master	OBE	Far East war service
11 June 1946	RFA *Wave Monarch*	
Master	OBE	Far East war service
Chief Engineer	OBE	
Chief Officer	OBE	
Rating	BEM	
Rating	Mentions in Despatches	
11 June 1946	RFA *Cedardale*	
Master	OBE	Far East war service
Chief Officer	OBE + Mentions in Despatches	
2nd Officer	MBE	
2 Ratings	BEM	
2nd Engineer	Mentions in Despatches	
11 June 1946	RFA *Wave King*	
Chief Officer	OBE	Far East war service
Chief Engineer	OBE	
2nd Engineer	Mentions in Despatches	
11 June 1946	RFA *War Afridi*	
Master	OBE	Far East war service
11 June 1946	RFA *War Nizam*	
Chief Engineer	OBE	Far East war service
11 June 1946	RFA *Eaglesdale*	
Chief Engineer	OBE	Far East war service
5 July 1946	[no ship named]	
3rd Officer	Mentions in Despatches POW	For defence of Hong Kong and when a

THE KOREAN WAR (1950–3)

Date announced Rank/Rate (RFA)	Ship Honours/Awards	Comments
29 June 1951	RFA *Wave Laird*	
Master	OBE	Operations in Korean Waters
29 June 1951	RFA *Wave Premier*	
Master	Mentions in Despatches	Operations in Korean Waters
23 May 1952	RFA *Green Ranger*	
Master	Mentions in Despatches	Operations in Korean Waters
23 May 1952	RFA *Wave Premier*	
Chief Engineer	Mentions in Despatches	Operations in Korean Waters
3 October 1952	RFA *Fort Rosalie*	
Master	Mentions in Despatches	Operations in Korean Waters
3 October 1952	RFA *Wave Chief*	
Master	Mentions in Despatches	Operations in Korean Waters

Date announced Rank/Rate (RFA)	Ship Honours/awards	Comment
Chief Engineer	Mentions in Despatches	
1 January 1953	RFA *Wave Chief*	
Master	Mentions in Despatches	Operations in Korean Waters
1 January 1953	RFA *Wave Sovereign*	
Master	Mentions in Despatches	Operations in Korean Waters
10 November 1953	RFA *Wave Prince*	
Master	Mentions in Despatches	Operations in Korean Waters

SOUTH ATLANTIC CAMPAIGN
(Falklands Islands and South Georgia 1982)

Ship	Rank/Rate (RFA)	Honours/Awards
RFA *Fort Austin*	Commodore RFA	DSO + OBE
RFA *Sir Galahad*	Captain	DSO
	2nd Engineer	GM (Posthumous)
	Seaman (Chinese)	QM
	Chief Engineer	QGM
	3rd Officer	QGM
	2nd Officer	QC for Brave Conduct
RFA *Sir Tristram*	Captain	DSC
RFA *Sir Geraint*	Captain	DSC
RFA *Sir Percivale*	Captain	DSC
	Chief Officer	MID
RFA *Sir Bedivere*	Captain	OBE
RFA *Sir Lancelot*	Captain	OBE
	Chief Officer	Commander-in-Chief Fleet Commendation
	Chief Engineer	Commander-in-Chief Fleet Commendation
	1st Electrical Officer	Commander-in-Chief Fleet Commendation
	3rd Engineers	Commander-in-Chief Fleet Commendation
RFA *Olmeda*	Captain	OBE
RFA *Stromness*	Captain	OBE
RFA *Tidespring*	Captain	OBE
RFA *Resource*	Petty Officer (D)	Commander-in-Chief Fleet Commendation
	Seaman	Commander-in-Chief Fleet Commendation

Battle honours

Battle honours were first recorded to RFAs during the Second World War with North Africa, Salerno and Sicily. Nonetheless, the apparent omission of names from the published lists of battles and operations is quite surprising and reflects a degree of uncertainly on their accuracy. For example, RFAs worked hard and personnel won many awards on both the Malta and Arctic convoys but no RFA ship names appear in the respective battle honour lists.

The first major issue of battle honours to the RFA was after Operation Corporate – the 1982 South Atlantic Campaign, when the battle honour FALKLANDS 1982 was awarded to 22 RFAs:

RFA *Sir Bedivere* RFA *Sir Galahad* RFA *Sir Geraint*
RFA *Sir Lancelot* RFA *Sir Percivale* RFA *Sir Tristram*
RFA *Tidespring* RFA *Tidepool* RFA *Fort Austin*
RFA *Fort Grange* RFA *Regent* RFA *Resource*
RFA *Olmeda* RFA *Olna* RFA *Engadine*
RFA *Appleleaf* RFA *Bayleaf* RFA *Brambleleaf*
RFA *Pearleaf* RFA *Plumleaf* RFA *Stromness*
RFA *Blue Rover*

The earliest record of RFA battle honours is during the Second World War:

NORTH AFRICA 1942–43
RFA *Dingledale*

NORTH AFRICA 1942 (Operation Torch)
RFA *Abbeydale* RFA *Brown Ranger* RFA *Dertwendale*
RFA *Ennerdale* RFA *Nasprite*

SALERNO 1943 (9 September–6 October)
RFA *Derwentdale*

SICILY 1943 (10 July–17 August)
RFA *Cedardale* RFA *Derwentdale* RFA *Ennerdale*
RFA *Pearleaf*

The Korean War battle honour was made to the fleet tankers RFAs *Wave Premier* and *Wave Prince,* which were awarded the battle honour for KOREA 1950-53.

Many RFAs were operational in the Gulf War either actively engaged against Iraqi forces or engaged in logistic support duties in the central and northern Gulf to the west of 51E at any time between 17 January and 28 February 1991. The following were awarded the KUWAIT 1991 battle honour:

RFA *Argus* RFA *Bayleaf* RFA *Diligence*
RFA *Fort Grange* RFA *Olna* RFA *Orangeleaf*
RFA *Resource* RFA *Sir Bedivere* RFA *Sir Galahad*
RFA *Sir Percivale* RFA *Sir Tristram*

Where the RFA has inherited a previous ship name and that ship had a previously approved Battle Honour, *eg* RFA *Argus*, HMS *Argus* a name first carried by an RN ship in 1799. The battle honours continue to be recorded, *eg* ARCTIC 1941–45, NORTH AFRICA 1942 etc.

APPENDIX C
RFA Sea flags

See colour plates for illustrations.

Around 1687, Secretary of the British Admiralty, Samuel Pepys, when drawing up his *Sub-notes about Flags and Colours* made what is possibly the first observations that public service ships, used for duties other than fighting, *eg* non-commissioned victuallers, stores ships and transports, should wear some distinctive flag. On 12 July 1694, a Royal Proclamation finally provided that public service ships should fly their own flag. This is then described as a Red flag bearing the Union Flag and their Seal of Office.

It was 28 July 1707 when a Royal Proclamation by Queen Anne decreed that ensigns should bear the Union Flag in their 'upper-left canton'. One can assume that it was a practice of differing positioning of the Union Flag on ensigns that gave rise to the need for the Proclamation. The positioning of the Seal of Office did not become clear until 1806, when King's Regulations directed that the Seal of Office should be in the 'fly' of the ensign. Although matters were slightly confused in 1844 when Queen's Regulations stated that the Seal be placed in the centre of the ensign.

Ensigns identify a vessel's nationality and law – the Merchant Shipping Acts, Queens Regulations for the Royal Navy – and a complex set of unwritten customs and practices known as flag etiquette covers their use. This etiquette indicates that an ensign should be won on an ensign staff at the stern. Why? Because in the days of sailing warships, it was nearest the quarterdeck and the officers' cabins. Today most vessels move their ensign from the ensign staff to the mast as soon as they put to sea.

UK law requires that all vessels over 50 grt (other than fishing vessels) must wear their ensigns when entering or leaving a British port, when entering or leaving a foreign port or when instructed to do so by a vessel commanded by a serving naval officer. There is an indication here that you do not have to show an ensign while underway at sea or indeed when in harbour. Etiquette, however, decrees that naval traditions should be followed. These were originally intended to reduce wear and tear on flags, by hoisting the ensign at sunrise (known as colours) and taking it down at sunset (also known as evening colours). Etiquette also indicates such timings should be synchronised with those of the senior naval ship present.

The RFA Ensign

The RFA Ensign – a Blue Ensign defaced with a vertical gold anchor – was officially approved by HM Queen Elizabeth II in 1968 and was introduced from 16 June 1969. The flag proportion is 2:1.

Prior to this, RFA vessels wore a Blue Ensign defaced with a horizontal gold anchor and officially known as the Admiralty Blue Ensign.

Admiralty Blue Ensign.

This flag was frequently and incorrectly called the RFA Ensign. However, the flag was common to all non-commissioned Admiralty vessels. The flag proportion is 2:1.

The situation finally regarding flags worn by fleet auxiliaries began to take on a more stable practice when on 9 July 1864 an Admiralty Order-in-Council for the Regulation of the Naval Service was issued under the title *New Flags for Ships.*

This Order finally abolished the old Red, White and Blue squadron colours and issued directions that fundamentally are still in force. The Order directed that only commissioned Royal Navy vessels would wear the White Ensign; that the Blue Ensign represents the Royal Navy Reserve and non-commissioned Crown vessels and the Red Ensign become the flag of the British Mercantile Marine.

The Order changed the existing Public Service Ensign by directing that it becomes a Blue Ensign defaced in its fly by the Seal of Office. For the Navy's Transport and Civil Departments this meant a Blue Ensign defaced with the Admiralty Badge – which was the Seal of the old Transport Officer of 1694 – a plain horizontal gold anchor. In practice this meant that all the civilian manned auxiliary vessels, *eg* yard craft, storeships, tugs and transports, owned and even chartered by the Admiralty became legal wearers of this Ensign.

Of the mercantile vessels that were taken up on transport charter – Mercantile Fleet Auxiliaries or to given them their modern acronym STUFT – it would appear that what ensign they flew was more at the discretion of their individual Masters rather then the letter of the law as laid down by Order-in-Council.

In 1905, when the Admiralty first defined the term Royal Fleet Auxiliary (RFA) and a slightly separate shipping arm began to emerge, these Admiralty owned civilian craft had the right to wear the Admiralty Blue Ensign. Oddly, it would appear from Admiralty records that many of them did in fact fly the Red Ensign. Why they actually did this, we are unsure, but the practice, although often questioned, did continue until well after the First World War, indeed until the Head of Naval Law took steps to correct the situation in 1922.

The Head of Naval Law drew attention to the 1869 Order-in-Council and in January 1922 an Admiralty Fleet Order was issued directing that all Admiralty-owned RFA tankers, including those that were under commercial management, should wear the Admiralty Blue Ensign, except when on charter to commercial concerns, then they wear the Red Ensign.

In July 1922, a further directive stated that all Royal Fleet Auxiliaries, yard craft, and other non-commissioned vessels employed on Admiralty service were to fly the Admiralty Blue Ensign and on ceremonial occasions a Jack defaced by the Admiralty badge. This Jack was a square flag.

With the introduction of the specific RFA Ensign in 1969 this ensign because known as the Government Service Ensign.

Red Ensign

The plain Red Ensign (also known as the Red Duster) is worn by all British craft not entitled to display a White, Blue or defaced ensign, having replaced the St George's Cross as the national colour for ships *circa* 1700. The 1894 Merchant Shipping Act made it an offence for any British vessel to fly 'national colours' other than the Red Ensign or the Pilot Jack, without an Admiralty warrant.

During the 1920s, 1930s, late 1940s and 1950s many RFA tankers were chartered to commercial companies on time and voyage agreements. On these occasions and when on builder's trials they wore the Red Ensign. The flag proportion is 2:1.

RFA Jack

Initially the 1864 Order-in-Council directed that public service ships should in addition to the Public Service Ensign wear a Union Flag with a white all-round border – the flag commonly known as the Pilot Jack. However, in the Addenda of 1868 to Queen's Regulations and Admiralty Instructions, the use of the Pilot Jack was changed and a new square Public Service Jack introduced. It was stated that ships employed by any public office should fly this small blue flag with a Union Flag in the upper left-hand quarter, as a Jack. In the fly of this Jack should be the Seal of Office to which they belong. In the case of the Admiralty, the Admiralty Badge – the plain gold horizontal anchor – defaced the Jack.

In July 1922, a further directive stated that Royal Fleet Auxiliaries were to fly the Admiralty Blue Ensign and on ceremonial occasions a Jack defaced by the Admiralty badge. Two flags, one yard by one yard (92cm x 92cm square), for use as Jack would be allowed each RFA attached to the Fleet Fuelling Service and Store Carrying Service. No Jacks would be issued to vessels not accompanying the fleet.

The pre-1969 Jack was declared proper for ships employed by Government Offices, This small square flag, defaced with the horizontal Admiralty anchor was considered the correct Jack to be worn by RFAs. Post-1969, the RFA Jack was a square flag defaced with a vertical gold anchor. The flag proportion is 1:1 – 1 square yard (91cm x 91cm).

The RFA Jack is only worn on the Jackstaff when in harbour and when at anchor.

Commodore's Broad Pennant

On 5 October 1951 it was announced that in order to follow commercial practice the appointment of a Commodore was approved – the senior sea-going Master, and HM The King George VI approved the Commodore's Broad Pennant – a vertical gold anchor encircled by a gold rope on a navy blue field. First hoisted on Sunday 7 October 1951 on RFA *Fort Dunvegan* at Rosyth.

As is the practice with Commodore's RN, the Commodore RFA's Broad Pennant is worn on his flagship and/or at his headquarters on land.

According to the Defence Standard 83-77 there is also a Commodore's pennant with 'car fittings' so that it can be flow on a road vehicle.

APPENDIX D
RFA Colour Schemes

Colour scheme – 1937

A uniform colour scheme for freighting tankers, fleet attendant tankers, fleet supply ships, store carrying vessels at Home and in the Mediterranean plus RFA *Petronel* was introduced in 1937. With fleet attendant tankers stationed abroad –the colour scheme was left to Commander-in-Chief's (CinC's) discretion:

- bottom – Red
- hull/topsides – Black
- superstructure/upperworks – Mediterranean Grey
- funnel(s) – Grey + Black smoke band
- spars/boats – Grey

Colour scheme varied according to orders of local Commander-in-Chief. Early 1920s at Hong Kong and East Indies Station:

- hull – Light Grey
- upperworks – Dark Grey
- funnel(s) – Dark Grey

1937/39 RFA *Slavol* attached to 4th Cruiser Squadron, East Indies at Trincomalee:

- hull – White
- upperworks – Buff
- funnel(s) – Buff
- mast(s) – Buff

Wartime colour scheme (adopted 1940)

A colour scheme was adopted for the following:
Fleet attendant tankers (overseas), colour scheme left to local CinC, for example RFA *Cherryleaf*:

- hull – Black
- upperworks – Buff

Freighting Tankers, fleet attendant tankers, fleet supply ships, store carriers at home and in the Mediterranean:

- hull – Black bottom – Red
- upperworks – Grey
- funnel(s) – Grey with Black top band

Pacific Fleet colour coding

RFA tankers were an important element of the British Pacific Fleet Train in 1944/1945. For operational purposes an interesting funnel colour coding system of identification was introduced:
Wave Governor – yellow funnel, one black band
Wave King – red funnel, black top
Wave Monarch – yellow funnel, black top
Arndale – two white bands
Cedardale – one white band
Dingledale – three red bands
Eagledale – two red bands

Colour scheme – 1950

Painting of weather work on RFAs was detailed as:
Fleet attendant tankers – at discretion of respective CinC.
Freighting tankers

- bottom – Red
- topsides – Black
- superstructure – Light Grey
- funnel(s) – Light Grey + black smoke band
- spars/boats – Light Grey

Fleet attendant tankers, fleet supply ships, store carriers with Home Fleet – as above.

Fleet attendant tankers, fleet supply ships, store carriers with Mediterranean Fleet – Light Grey overall.

Fort Constantine *Fort Rosalie* *Fort Sandusky*
these were Light Grey overall, funnel with Black top band.
Fort Rosalie *Fort Sandusky* *Amherst*
these were Light Grey overall, funnel had additional Red band below the Black smoke top.

RFA *Somersby* renamed *Reliant* originally had the traditional broad Black funnel band, but it was clearly out of proportion and she was permitted to have just a narrow Black band only. Later she was, for appearance sake, permitted to have no Black smoke band. There is no positive record of her ever wearing the White function band.

Function bands – 1950s

For a period the practice of painting function bands on funnels was introduced in the early 1950s – painted below the Black smoke band:

- Red band – ammunition ships
- White band – victualling ship

The following RFAs are known to have carried RED bands:
Amherst *Retainer* *Resurgent*
Fort Langley *Fort Sandusky* *Fort Rosalie*

Resurgent and *Retainer* had thin White Bands either side of the broad Red bands; some of the 'Fort' class ammunition ships also had this arrangement. At times one or two tankers had the White Bands. RFA *Hebe* reportedly had her white band through 1970 and some of the 'Ness' class had a white band.

The practice of painting up Function Bands ceased from October 1969 when Circular Letter 116/69 decreed a common funnel-painting scheme.

Colour scheme – 1959

Painting of weather work on HM Ships and RFAs :

- topsides – Light Grey
- superstructure – Light Grey
- spars – Light Grey
- boats – Light Grey
- funnel(s) – Light Grey + Black smoke band
- boottopping – Black

Standard colour scheme – 1969

This scheme was approved for used throughout the Fleet:

- hull/upperworks – Light Grey
- boot topping – Black
- bottom – Red
- funnel(s) – Grey with Black smoke hand (excluding RFA *Reliant* (2))

- decks – Green
- flight deck – Black
- lifeboats – Grey or White
- ship name – Black (RFA *Reliant* name in Black with a 0.5-inch white edging)
- port of registry – Black
- exceptions were the LST3 RFA *Empire Gull* and the large mobile reserve tanker RFA *Dewdale* which retained their Black hulls

Reduced visibility scheme – 1982

During Operation Corporate (Falklands 1982) the RFA in common with the practice of HM Ships introduced and have retained a reduced visibility scheme which included the removal of the Black smoke band on all funnels and decks being painted Grey.

- topsides – Light Grey
- superstructure – Light Grey
- spars – Light Grey
- funnels – Light Grey
- boottopping – Black
- aluminium allow lifeboats – Light Grey
- GRP lifeboats – White
- internal surfaces of open boats – Day-Glo Orange (SOLAS requirement)
- lifeboats/survival aids – Day-Glo Orange
- GRP liferaft containers – White

The chartered Roll-on-Roll-off Strategic Sealift ships, *eg* RFA *Sea Crusader*, had a Grey hull with White upperworks. Their lifeboats are painted in Day-Glo Orange as required by SOLAS.

Hospital ship colour schemes

Hospital ships are protected from attack by the Geneva Convention and are, therefore, easily distinguished by a colour scheme prescribed by the Third Hague Convention 1907 and the later Tenth Hague Convention 1907. They are painted White overall, with a broad wide green band with a number of Red Crosses painted around the upper part of the hull. In 1940, identifying facilities from the air were improved with additional Red Crosses being painted horizontally from fore and aft on the top deck. At night the hulls are brilliantly illuminated and with a horizontal row of Green lights around the hull.

In 1947 the Geneva Convention modified the colour scheme by dropping the requirement of the broad Green hull hand.

Troopship colour scheme

When the SIR class landing ship logistics were operated under the commercial management of British India Steamship Navigation Co (BISN), they wore the traditional British troopship peacetime colour scheme, known affectionately as the 'Blue Band Margarine livery':

- hull – White with a broad Blue band around the hull
- superstructure – White
- funnel – Buff

Appendix E
RFA Ships' Badges and Funnel Badges

See colour plates for illustrations.

Ships' badges

Ships' Badges (or crests as they are incorrectly called) are official; the Board of Admiralty/Navy Board approves the individual design. The Ships Names and Badges Committee was formed in 1983 with the amalgamation of the Ships Badges Committee (founded in 1918) and the Ships Names Committee (founded in 1913). The Committee's role is to advise the Board on all matters concerned with Ship Badges, and also for submitting designs when these are required. The Naval Heraldry Adviser may be called upon to prepare designs.

In 1976, ships' badges were standardised. The shape of RFA badges was approved as pentagonal. Irrespective of shape, the badge has a rim of stylised rope and is surmounted by the Naval Crown. Below the Crown is a panel bearing the ship's name in capital letters.

Funnel badges

Over the years a number of unofficial and official badges have appeared on the funnels of RFAs. The most notable being the road safety traffic sign for 'Schools' that since *circa* 1976 was occasionally painted up on the funnel of the tanker attached to Flag Officer Sea Training at Portland. On one occasion when RFA *Gold Rover* was FOST tanker she had the red, white and black schools traffic sign pained on the starboard side of her funnel with a small red hippopotamus (called 'Humphrey') painted on the port side. During the withdrawal from Hong Kong, RFA *Sir Percivale* had a red dragon painted up.

NATO squadron badges have occasionally been placed on the funnel of individual tankers supporting, for example, standing forces in the Atlantic and Mediterranean.

The major official funnel badge displayed on RFA funnels is used by the 'Sir' class LSLs – the badge is a circular disc initially representing the Commodore Amphibious Warfare Group now Commander Amphibious Task Group. This first appeared on RFA funnels during the latter half of the 1990s. This badges is also worn by other amphibious warfare ships, such as HMS *Ocean*.

Appendix F
RFA pennant numbers

Pennant (or 'pendant') numbers have been used by British naval vessels for hundreds of years and are a combination of letters and figures. The prefix letter is known as the 'Flag Superior'. Pennant numbers are also allocated to ships and certain authorities of NATO countries where they are commonly known as *Visual Call Signs*.

The significant pennant numbers allocated to RFAs have been under the following Flag Superiors – X *circa* 1914–1947 system – the Flag Superior X was allocated to miscellaneous vessels including fleet auxiliaries from *circa* 1918 until replaced by the current 1947 system with Flag Superiors A, L and K applying to RFAs

Flag superior A – 1947 system

Pennant No	*RFA*
A 75	*Tidespring*
A 76	*Tidepool*
A 77	*Pearleaf* (2)
A 78	*Plumleaf* (2)
A 79	*Bayleaf* (2) /*Appleleaf* (3)
A 80	*Orangeleaf* (2)
A 81	*Brambleleaf* (2) / *Brambleleaf* (3)
A 82	*Cherryleaf* (2) / *Cherryleaf* (3)
A 83	*Appleleaf* (2)
A 84	*Reliant* (2)
A 88	*Agile* tug
A 89	*Advice* tug
A 90	*Accord* tug
A 95	*Typhoon* tug
A 96	*Tidereach* *Sea Crusader*
A 97	*Tiderace* *Tideflow*
A 98	*Tiderange* *Tidesurge* *Sea Centurion*
A 99	*Tide Austral*
A 100	*Wave Emperor*
A 101	
A 102	*C633*
A 103	*Bacchus* (2)
A 104	*Eaglesdale*
A 105	*Easedale*
A 106	*Belgol*
A 107	*Eddybay*/*Boxol*
A 108	*Wave Monarch*
A 109	*Abbeydale*/*Bayleaf* (3)
A 110	*Orangeleaf* (3)
A 111	*Growler* tug (*Cyclone*) *Oakleaf* (2)
A 112	
A 113	*C614*
A 114	*Derwentdale* (1)
A 115	*Airsprite*

Pennant No	*RFA*
A 116	*Celerol*
A 119	*Wave Laird*
A 120	*Limol*
A 121	HMS *Bulwayo* fleet tanker
A 122	*Olynthus* (2) *Olwen* (2)
A 123	*Olna* (3)
A 124	*Oleander* (3)/C85 *Olmeda*
A 126	*Fortol*
A 127	*Birchol* (2)
A 128	*Bishopdale*
A 129	*Wave Premier*
A 130	*Gold Ranger*
A 131	*Reliant* (3) Arapaho-equipped aviation ship
A 132	*Eddybeach* *Diligence* forward repair ship
A 133	*Arndale*
A 135	*Argus* aviation ship
A 137	*Larchol*
A 140	*Jaunty* tug
A 141	*Antic* tug
A 143	*Mixol*
A 144	*Dingledale*
A 150	*Allegiance* tug
A 151	*Dewdale* (1)
A 152	*Green Ranger*
A 153	
A 154	*Elmol* *Elderol*
A 155	*Prestol*
A 157	*Blue Ranger*
A 159	*Empire Salvage*
A 160	*Fort Dunvegan*
A 161	*Scotol*
A 162	*Serbol*
A 163	*Black Ranger*
A 165	*Envoy* tug
A 167	*Teakol* (3)

Pennant No	*RFA*
A 168	*Broomdale*
A 169	*Brown Ranger*
A 170	*Echoldale*
A 173	*Ennerdale* (1)
A 174	
A 175	
A 176	
A 177	*Enforcer* tug
A 178	
A 179	
A 180	
A 181	*Hickorol*
A 182	*Wave King*
A 186	*Fort Rosalie* (1)
A 190	*Eddycliff*
A 192	*Spa*
A 193	*Wave Master*
A 198	*Eddyrock*
A 200	
A 201	*C642*
A 202	*Eddyreef*
A 204	*Robert Dundas*
A 205	*Eddycove*
A 207	*Wave Prince*
A 208	*Scottish American* escort tanker MFA
A 209	*Earner* tug
A 210	*Wave Regent*
A 211	*Wave Sovereign*
A 212	*Wave Ruler* (1)
A 213	*Freshbrook*/*Ennerdale* (2)
A 214	*Seafox*
A 215	*Wave Protector*
A 216	*Olna* (2) ex HMS
A 218	*Samsonia* tug
A 219	*Dewdale* (2)
A 220	*Wave Victor*
A 221	*Derwentdale* (2)
A 222	*Spapool*
A 224	*Spabrook*
A 227	*Spabeck*

Pennant No	*RFA*
A 229	*Fort Duquesne*
A 230	*Fort Langley*
A 234	*Salvage Duke*
A 236	*Fort Charlotte*
A 237	*Fort Constantine*
A 238	*Amherst/Reliant* (1)
A 240	*Bustler* tug
A 241	*Robert Middleton*
A 242	*Wave Baron*
A 244	*Wave Commander*
A 245	*Wave Conqueror*
A 246	*Wave Duke*
A 247	*Wave Governor*
A 248	*Wave Liberator/Rapidol*
A 249	*Wave Knight* (1)
A 250	*Petrobus*
A 252	*Nasprite*
A 253	*Philol*
A 254	*Prosperous* tug
A 257	*Spaburn*
A 258	*Eddycreek*
A 260	*Spalake*
A 261	*Eddyfirth/Thornol* Admiralty tanker
A 264	*Reward* tug
A 265	*Wave Chief*
A 268	*Green Rover*
A 269	*Grey Rover*
A 270	*Blue Rover*
A 271	*Gold Rover*
A 273	*Black Rover*
A 275	*Viscol*
A 280	*Resurgent*
A 281	*Kinbrace* salvage vessel
A 284	*Rowanol*
A 285	*Fort Beauharnois*
A 287	*Eddymull/War Hindoo*
A 288	*War Brahmin*
A 289	*Confiance* tug/*War Bharata*
A 290	*Confident* tug
A 291	*King Salvor* salvage vessel
A 292	*Prince Salvor* salvage vessel
A 293	*Careful* tug
A 295	*Eddyness*
A 300	*Oakol* (2)
A 316	*Fort Sandusky/Warden* tug
A 329	*Retainer*
A 339	*Lyness*
A 344	*Stromness*
A 345	*Tarbatness*
A 349	*Freshwater*
A 356	*C668*
A 357	*Surf Patrol*

Pennant No	*RFA*
A 358	*C112*
A 262	*Dispenser* salvage vessel
A 365	*Surf Pioneer*
A 369	*Empire Demon* tug
A 370	*C618*
A 371	*C677*
A 372	*Empire Fred* tug
A 379	*Encore* tug
A 380	*Cedardale*
A 382	*Empire Netta* tug
A 384	*Salventure* salvage vessel
A 385	*Cautious* tug *Fort Grange* renamed *Fort Rosalie* (2)
A 386	*Saucy* tug *Fort Austin*
A 387	*Fort Victoria* AOR
A 388	*Fort George* AOR
A 389	*Wave Knight* (2)
A 390	*Samson* tug *Wave Ruler* (2)
A 393	*Empire Plane* tug
A 396	*Empire Rita* tug
A 399	*Empire Zona* tug
A 397	*Empire Rosa* tug
A 404	*Bacchus*
A 406	*Hebe*
A 480	*Resource*
A 486	*Regent*
A 492	*Ocean Salvor* salvage vessel
A 494	*Salvalour* salvage vessel
A 497	*Salveda* salvage vessel
A 499	*Salvestor* salvage vessel
A 500	*Salvictor*
A 501	*Salvigil*
A 502	*Salviola*
A 504	*Sparkler*
A 503	*Sea Salvor* salvage vessel
A 505	*Succour* salvage vessel
A 506	*Swin* salvage vessel
A 507	*Uplifter* salvage vessel
A 508	*Capable* tug

Flag superior L – 1947 system

Pennant No	*RFA amphibious warfare vessels*
L 3004	*Sir Bedivere* ('Sir' class LSL)
L 3005	*Sir Galahad* (1) *Sir Galahad* (2) (improved 'Sir' class LSLs)
L 3006	*Largs Bay* ('Bay' class LSD(A))
L 3007	*Lyme Bay* ('Bay' class LSD(A))
L 3008	*Mounts Bay* ('Bay' class LSD(A))
L 3009	*Cardigan Bay* ('Bay' class LSD(A))
L 3027	*Sir Geraint* ('Sir' class LSL)
L 3029	*Sir Lancelot* ('Sir' class LSL)
L 3036	*Sir Percivale* ('Sir' class LSL)
L 3505	*Sir Tristram* ('Sir' class LSL)
L 3522	*Sir Caradoc* (bareboat charter ro-ro)
L 3513	*Empire Gull* (LST3)
L 3532	*Sir Lamorak* (bareboat charter ro-ro)

Flag superior K – **1947 system**

Pennant No	*Miscellaneous fleet units*
K 08	RFA *Engadine* helicopter support ship

Index

(1), (2) indicates the first, second etc ship to carry the name.
Bold page reference indicates a photograph
* indicates war, marine loss or serious casualty

Abbreviations

+100A1	classed A1 by Lloyd's
+LMC	machinery built under Lloyd's rules
+UMC	unmanned machinery to Lloyd's rules
AB	able seaman
AFD	Admiralty Floating Dock
AEFS	auxiliary, explosives, food, stores ship
AOR	auxiliary oiler replenishment
ARG	amphibious ready group
ASW	anti-submarine warfare
AVSO	Aviation Support Officer
AWRE	Atomic Weapons Research Establishment
BEF	British Expeditionary Force
bhp	brake horse power
BISCO	British Iron & Steel Company
BISN Co	British India Steam Navigation Company
BoT	Board of Trade
BPFT	British Pacific Fleet Train
BTC	British Tanker Company
cf	in current fleet
CID	Committee of Imperial Defence
CinC	commander-in-chief
CIWS	close-in weapons system
COMRFA	Commodore Royal Fleet Auxiliary
COST	Continuation Operational Sea Training
CTS	Chief Technical Superintendent
cyl	cylinder
DEMS	defensively equipped merchant ship
DoS	Director of Stores
DST (FMV)	Directorate Supply and Transport (Fuel, Movements and Victualling)
dwt	deadweight tonnage
ELSA	Emergency Life Support Apparatus
FOST	Flag Officer Sea Training
GCBS	General Council of British Shipping
grt	gross registered tonnage
HIFR	helicopter in-flight refuelling
HMAS	His/Her Majesty's Australian Ship
HMCS	His/Her Majesty's Canadian Ship
HMHS	His/Her Majesty's Hospital Ship
HMS	His/Her Majesty's Ship
HMSV	His/Her Majesty's Salvage Vessel
HMZNS	His/Her Majesty's New Zealand Ship
HP	high pressure
HTP	high test peroxide
ICE	internal combustion engine
JRDF	Joint Rapid Deployment Force
LCM	landing craft mechanised
LSG	landing ship gantry
LSL	landing ship logistic
MMP	Marchwood Military Port (now Sea Mounting Centre)
MoD	Ministry of Defence
MoWT	Ministry of War Transport
MV/T	motor vessel/tanker
NAAFI	Navy, Army and Air Force Institutes
NAS	Naval Air Squadron
NATO	North Atlantic Treaty Organisation
NBCD	nuclear, bacteriological, chemical and damage control
NMB	National Maritime Board
PCRS	principal casualty receiving ship
PLA	Port of London Authority
PO	petty officer
PoW	prisoner of war
PTA	pilotless target aircraft
QARNNS	Queen Alexandra's Royal Naval Nursing Service
RAS	replenishment at sea
RFA	Royal Fleet Auxiliary
RFAASU	Royal Fleet Auxiliary Aviation Support Unit
RFAFLOT	Royal Fleet Auxiliary Flotilla
RFANSU	Royal Fleet Auxiliary Naval Support Unit
RFR	Royal Fleet Reserve
RLC	Royal Logistics Corps
RM	Royal Marines
RMAS	Royal Maritime Auxiliary Service
RN	Royal Navy
RNAS	Royal Naval Air Station
RNR	Royal Naval Reserve
RNSTS	Royal Naval Supply and Transport Service
RNVR	Royal Naval Volunteer Reserve
RRS	Royal Research Ship
SEATO	South East Asia Treaty Organisation
SLEP	Ship Life Extension Programme
SMAC	Short Miscellaneous Air Course
SOG	Stores Officer Grades
SOLAS	Safety of Life at Sea (International convention)
SS	steam ship
STUFT	ship taken up from trade
SWSA	Ship Weapon System Authority
TE	triple expansion (reciprocating machinery)
tpd	tons per day
TSS	triple screw ship
USNS	United States Naval Ship (US equivalent of RFA)
VERTREP	vertical replenishment
VLCC	Very Large Crude Carrier (*ie* a supertanker)
VSTOL	vertical/short take-off and landing
W/T	wireless telegraphy
WSA	Warship Support Agency

Sources and Acknowledgments

The research for this chronology is based on information from *Lloyd's Registers of Shipping*, *Jane's Fighting Ships*, *Combat Fleets of the World*, RFA Association's archive, augmented with a large quantity of additional technical and historical research gathered from unclassified official and private sources in the public domain. For example, Admiralty archives, Board of Trade and Ministry of Transport records in the National Archive at Kew, South West London; National Maritime Museum material; Imperial War Museum material; Lloyd's Marine Collection, Guildhall Library; RFA publications (*Force 4* and *Gunline*); recruitment information; material compiled from the English language defence, shipping and transport press, product leaflets and the World Ship Society Ltd's Warship Information Service (formerly the Central Record of Shipping Information) including the 'Tiny' Manuell RFA Collection, *List of Admiralty storeships – storecarriers – store transports and fuelling vessels 1600-1962* by E F S Fisher, *Royal Fleet Auxiliary* by Captain E E Sigwart, *The Royal Navy and the Falklands War* by David Brown and the unfaltering Naval Historical Branch and the Admiralty Library, with its wealth of material, such as, Pink Lists, Green Lists, Service Lists, the Admiralty War Diary, Ship Cards, Secret Military Branch Acquaints, Admiralty Fleet Orders, Confidential AFOs, Navy Lists and searches.

No record like this can be undertaken without being selective. No doubt our selection of information and supporting photographs may not please everyone and for that we apologise. Our thanks are given to the many sources ranging from colleagues and friends to the unique RFA Archive in the custody of the RFA Association and CinCFleet's Trafalgar 200 Team, the World Ship Society and many private sources.

Errors and omissions are ours. Now that this chronology has been established it is our intention to maintain it for the RFA's next century. If you have comments or suggestions they will be welcome – email auxiliary@tiscali.co.uk

Thomas A Adams
James R Smith